THIRD EDITION

GATEWAYS
TO DEMOCRACY
an Introduction to
American Government

THE ESSENTIALS

John G. **Geer**
Vanderbilt University

Wendy J. **Schiller**
Brown University

Jeffrey A. **Segal**
Stony Brook University

Richard **Herrera**
Arizona State University

Dana K. **Glencross**
Oklahoma City Community College

CENGAGE
Learning

Australia • Brazil • Mexico • Singapore • United Kingdom • United States

CENGAGE
Learning

Gateways to Democracy: An Introduction to American Government, The Essentials, **Third Edition**

John G. Geer, Wendy J. Schiller, Jeffrey A. Segal, Richard Herrera, Dana K. Glencross

Product Team Manager: Carolyn Merrill

Content Developer: Naomi Friedman

Managing Developer: Joanne Dauksewicz

Associate Content Developer: Amy Bither

Product Assistant: Abigail Hess

Senior Media Developer: Laura Hildebrand

Marketing Manager: Valerie Hartman

Content Project Manager: Cathy Brooks

Art Director: Linda May

Manufacturing Planner: Fola Orekoya

IP Analyst: Alexandra Ricciardi

IP Project Manager: Farah Fard

Production Service and Compositor: MPS Limited

Text Designer: Studio Montage

Cover Designer: Rokusek Design

Cover Image: Building: © Black Russian Studio/ Shutterstock.com; Man: © Joana Lopes/ Shutterstock.com

Library of Congress Control Number: 2014949551

Package ISBN: 978-1-285-85291-1

Text-only student edition ISBN: 978-1-285-85857-9

Loose-leaf edition ISBN: 978-1-305-63401-5

Cengage Learning
20 Channel Center Street
Boston, MA 02210
USA

Cengage Learning is a leading provider of customized learning solutions with office locations around the globe, including Singapore, the United Kingdom, Australia, Mexico, Brazil, and Japan. Locate your local office at **www.cengage.com/global**

Cengage Learning products are represented in Canada by Nelson Education, Ltd.

To learn more about Cengage Learning Solutions, visit **www.cengage.com**

Purchase any of our products at your local college store or at our preferred online store **www.cengagebrain.com**

Printed in the United States of America
Print Number: 01   Print Year: 2014

Brief Contents

Chapter 1   Gateways to American Democracy   3
Chapter 2   The Constitution   29
Chapter 3   Federalism   59
Chapter 4   Civil Liberties   87
Chapter 5   Civil Rights   119
Chapter 6   Public Opinion and the Media   155
Chapter 7   Interest Groups   199
Chapter 8   Political Parties   231
Chapter 9   Elections, Campaigns, and Voting   265
Chapter 10   Congress   309
Chapter 11   The Presidency   349
Chapter 12   The Bureaucracy   387
Chapter 13   The Judiciary   419
Chapter 14   Economic, Domestic, and Foreign Policy 455

Appendix

A. The Declaration of Independence   494
B. The Constitution of the United States   498
C. *Federalist Papers* 10 and 51   514

Contents

CHAPTER 1: Gateways to American Democracy 3

Gateways: Evaluating the American Political System 4

Democracy and the American Constitutional System 6

Liberty and Order 6

The Constitution as Gatekeeper 7

American Political Culture 11

Responsiveness and Equality: Does American Democracy Work? 13

The Demands of Democratic Government 16

Self-Interest and Civic Interest 18

Politics and the Public Sphere 18

Your Gateway to American Democracy 21

What you need to know about your text and online study tools to study efficiently and master the material 22

CHAPTER 2: The Constitution 29

Before the Constitution 30

The British Constitution 30

Toward Independence 31

The Declaration of Independence 33

The Articles of Confederation 33

The Constitutional Convention 35

Large versus Small States 35

Nation versus State 36

North versus South 36

Gates against Popular Influence 38

The Ratification Process 38

Government under the Constitution 40

The Structure of Government 40

The Amendment Process 41

The Partition of Power 42

The Ratification Debates 45

Federalists and Antifederalists 46

Consolidation of Federal Authority 46

The Scope of Executive Authority 46

The Scope of Legislative Authority 47

The Lack of a Bill of Rights 47

The Responsive Constitution 48

The Bill of Rights 48

The Civil War Amendments 50

Amendments That Expand Public Participation 50

Constitutional Interpretation 50

The Constitution and Democracy 54

CHAPTER 3: Federalism 59

Why Federalism? 60

Why Unify? 60

Confederal, Unitary, and Federal Systems 61

Constitutional Framework 64

Grants of Power 64

Limits on Power 65

Groundwork for Relationships 68

The Changing Nature of American Federalism 70

Nationalization in the Founding Generation (approximately 1789–1832) 71

The Revolt against National Authority: Nullification, Slavery, and the Civil War (approximately 1832–65) 71

Dual Federalism (approximately 1865–1932) 74

Cooperative Federalism: The New Deal and Civil Rights (approximately 1932–69) 74

The New Federalism (approximately 1969–93) 75

Summing Up: Were the Antifederalists Correct? 78

State and Local Governments 79

State Executive Branches 79

State Legislative Branches 79

State Judicial Branches 79

Local Governments 80

Direct Democracy 80

Federalism and Democracy 82

CHAPTER 4: Civil Liberties 87

What Are Civil Liberties? 88

Civil Liberties and Civil Rights 88

Balancing Liberty and Order 89

Constitutional Rights 90

The Bill of Rights and the States 90

Civil Liberties in Times of Crisis 92

The World Wars 92

The War on Terror 93

Civil Liberties and American Values 96

The First Amendment and Freedom of Expression 96

Freedom of Speech 96

Freedom of the Press 100

Religious Freedom 103

Free Exercise 103

The Establishment of Religion 104

The Right to Keep and Bear Arms 106

Criminal Procedure 106

Investigations 107

Trial Procedures 109

Verdict, Punishment, and Appeal 109

The Right to Privacy 111

Birth Control and Abortion 111

Homosexual Behavior 113

The Right to Die 114

Civil Liberties and Democracy 114

CHAPTER 5: Civil Rights 119

What Are Civil Rights? 120

Civil Rights and Civil Liberties 120

The Constitution and Civil Rights 120

Legal Restrictions on Civil Rights 121

Slavery 122

Restrictions on Citizenship 123

Racial Segregation and Discrimination 125

Ethnic Segregation and Discrimination 127

Women's Suffrage 127

Continued Gender Discrimination 129

The Expansion of Equal Protection 132

State Action 132

Judicial Review 133

The End of Legal Restrictions on Civil Rights 134

Dismantling Public Discrimination Based on Race 134

Dismantling Private Discrimination Based on Race 137

Dismantling Voting Barriers Based on Race 138

Dismantling Public Discrimination Based on Ethnicity 139

Dismantling Voting Barriers Based on Ethnicity 140

Dismantling Private Discrimination Based on Ethnicity 141

Dismantling Discrimination Based on Gender 142

Frontiers in Civil Rights 146

Sexual Orientation and Same-Sex Marriage 146

Disability Rights 149

Undocumented Immigrants 149

Civil Rights and Democracy 150

CHAPTER 6: Public Opinion and the Media 155

The Power of Public Opinion 156

What Is Public Opinion? 157

The Public's Support of Government 157

Public Opinion Polls 159

Scientific Polling and the Growth of Survey Research 159

Types of Polls 160

Error in Polls 162

The Shape of Public Opinion 163

Partisanship 164

Ideology 164

Is the Public Informed? 165

Is the Public Polarized? 167

Group Differences 170

Socioeconomic Status 170

Age 171

Religion 171

Gender 171

Race and Ethnicity 172

Education 174

The Political News 175

What Are the Mass Media? 175

The Functions of the News 175

The Law and the Free Press 176

The Mass Media in the Twenty-First Century 177

The Changing Media Environment 178

The Decline of Newspapers 179

The Durability of Radio 180

The Transformation of TV News 181

Infotainment 181

Blogs 182

Social Networking 183

The News Media and Latino Voters 184

The News and the Millennials 185

The Impact of the News Media on the Public 186

The Propaganda Model 186

The Minimal Effects Model 187

The Not-So-Minimal Effects Model 187

Evaluating the News Media 189

Are the Media Biased? 189

Quality of Information 190

Implications of the Internet 192

The Era of Media Choice 193

Public Opinion, the Media, and Democracy 193

CHAPTER 7: Interest Groups 199

Interest Groups and Politics 200

What Are Interest Groups? 200

The Right to Assemble and to Petition 201

The History of Interest Groups 202

Types of Interest Groups 204

Economic Interest Groups 204

Ideological and Issue-Oriented Groups 207

Foreign Policy and International Groups 208

What Interest Groups Do 210

Inform 210

Lobby 210

Campaign Activities 215

The Impact of Interest Groups on Democratic Processes 219

Natural Balance or Disproportionate Power 219

Self-Service or Public Service 220

Open or Closed Routes of Influence 222

Characteristics of Successful Interest Groups 224

Leadership Accountability 224

Membership Stability 224

Financial Stability 226

Influence in the Public Sphere 226

Interest Groups and Democracy 227

CHAPTER 8: Political Parties 231

The Role of Political Parties in American Democracy 232

What Are Political Parties? 232

What Political Parties Do 233

The Party Nomination Process 237

The Dynamics of Early Party Development 241

Political Factions: Federalist versus Antifederalist 241

Thomas Jefferson, Andrew Jackson, and the Emergence of the Democratic Party 242

The Antislavery Movement and the Formation of the Republican Party 243

Party Loyalty and Patronage 244

Reform and the Erosion of Party Control 245

The Effects of a Two-Party System 246

Limited Political Choice 246

The Structural Limits 247

The Role of Third Parties 247

The Tea Party 250

Obstacles to Third Parties and Independents 251

Challenges to Party Power from Interest Groups 254

Party Alignment and Ideology 254

The Parties after the Civil War 254

The New Deal and the Role of Ideology in Party Politics 255

Civil Rights, the Great Society, and Nixon's Southern Strategy 256

The Reagan Revolution and Conservative Party Politics 257

The Modern Partisan Landscape 258

Political Parties and Democracy 260

CHAPTER 9: Elections, Campaigns, and Voting 265

The Constitutional Requirements for Elections 266

Presidential Elections 266

Congressional Elections 271

The Presidential Campaign 273

Evolution of the Modern Campaign 273

The Caucuses and Primaries 274

The National Convention 274

Issues in Presidential Campaigns 275

Fundraising and Money 275

Swing States 277

Microtargeting 278

Campaign Issues 279

Negativity 279

Issues in Congressional Campaigns 280

Fundraising and Money 281

The Role of Political Parties 281

Incumbency Advantage 281

The Practice and Theory of Voting 283

The Constitution and Voting 283

Competing Views of Participation 283

The History of Voting in America 284

Who Votes? 287

Turnout 290

The Demographics of Turnout 291

Why Citizens Vote 293

An Economic Model of Voting 293

A Psychological Model of Voting 294

An Institutional Model of Voting 295

Is Voting in Your Genes? 296

Assessing Turnout 296

Is Turnout Low? 296

Do Turnout Rates Create Inequality? 299

Voting Laws and Regulations 300

   Reforms to Voting Laws in the 1890s 300

   The National Voter Registration Act 301

   New Forms of Voting 301

Elections, Campaigns, Voting, and Democracy 303

CHAPTER 10: Congress 309

Congress as the Legislative Branch 310

   Representation and Bicameralism 310

   Constitutional Differences between the House and Senate 311

The Powers of Congress 316

   Taxation and Appropriation 316

   War Powers 317

   Regulation of Commerce 317

   Appointments and Treaties 317

   Impeachment and Removal from Office 319

   Lawmaking 319

   Authorization of Courts 320

   Oversight 320

The Organization of Congress 322

   The Role of Political Parties 322

   The House of Representatives 323

   The Senate 325

   The Committee System 326

   Advocacy Caucuses 329

The Lawmaking Process 330

   The Procedural Rules of the House and Senate 330

   Legislative Proposals 333

   Committee Action 334

   Floor Action and the Vote 334

   Conference Committee 335

   The Budget Process and Reconciliation 335

   Presidential Signature or Veto, and the Veto Override 337

The Member of Congress at Work 337

   Offices and Staff 337

   Legislative Responsibilities 340

   Communication with Constituents 342

   The Next Election 342

Congress and Democracy 344

CHAPTER 11: The Presidency 349

Presidential Qualifications 350

   Constitutional Eligibility and Presidential Succession 350

   Background and Experience 352

   The Expansion of the Presidency 354

Presidential Power: Constitutional Grants and Limits 355

   Commander in Chief 355

   Power to Pardon 355

   Treaties and Recognition of Foreign Nations 356

   Executive and Judicial Nominations 357

   Veto and the Veto Override 359

   Other Powers 361

   Congress's Ultimate Check on the Executive: Impeachment 361

The Growth of Executive Influence 363

   Presidential Directives and Signing Statements 363

   Power to Persuade 365

   Agenda Setting 367

The President in Wartime 368

   Power Struggles between the President and Congress 369

   Power Struggles between the President and the Judiciary 374

The Organization of the Modern White House 375

   The Executive Office of the President 375

   The Office of the Vice President 376

Presidential Greatness 377

   Franklin Delano Roosevelt (1933–45): The New Deal and World War II 377

   Lyndon Baines Johnson (1963–69): The Great Society and Vietnam 379

   Ronald Reagan (1981–89): The Reagan Revolution and the End of the Cold War 380

The Presidency and Democracy 382

CHAPTER 12: The Bureaucracy 387

The American Bureaucracy 388

   What Is the Bureaucracy? 389

   Constitutional Foundations 390

   The Structure of the Bureaucracy 390

Core Components of the Bureaucracy 396

   Mission 396

   Hierarchical Decision-Making Process 396

   Expertise 397

   Bureaucratic Culture 397

The Historical Evolution of the Bureaucracy 399

   The Expansion of Executive Branch Departments 399

   The Growth of Regulatory Agencies and Other Organizations 400

   From Patronage to the Civil Service 401

   Career Civil Service 404

   Political Appointees 405

   Diversity in the Federal Bureaucracy 406

Private-Sector Contract Workers 407

Bureaucrats and Politics 408

**Accountability and Responsiveness
in the Bureaucracy 410**

The Roles of the Legislative and Judicial Branches 410

Efficiency and Transparency 411

Whistleblowing 414

Bureaucratic Failure 414

The Bureaucracy and Democracy 415

CHAPTER 13: The Judiciary 419

The Role and Powers of the Judiciary 420

English Legal Traditions 420

Constitutional Grants of Power 421

State and Lower Federal Courts 423

State Courts in the Federal Judicial System 423

The District Courts 426

The Courts of Appeals 428

The Supreme Court 430

Granting Review 430

Oral Arguments 431

The Decision 431

Judicial Decision Making 433

Judicial Restraint: The Legal Approach 434

Judicial Activism: The Extralegal Approach 435

Restraint and Activism in Judicial Decision Making 437

The Impact of Court Rulings 437

**The Appointment Process for Federal Judges
and Justices 438**

The District Courts 440

The Courts of Appeals 441

The Supreme Court 441

Demographic Diversity on the Court 443

Historical Trends in Supreme Court Rulings 444

Expansion of National Power under the Marshall Court 446

Limits on National Power, 1830s to 1930s 446

Strengthened National Power, 1930s to the Present 447

The Judiciary and Democracy 450

CHAPTER 14: Economic, Domestic, and Foreign Policy 455

Public Policy under a Constitutional System 456

The Process of Policy Making 457

The Regulatory Process 459

Blocking Implementation 460

State Governments and Public Policy 460

Domestic Policy 462

Entitlement Programs, Income Security, and Health Care
Overview 463

The Affordable Care Act (ACA) 465

Immigration Policy Overview 467

Energy, Environmental Policy, and Climate Change
Overview 469

Economic Policy 472

An Overview: Intervention in the Economy 472

Fiscal Policy 473

Monetary Policy 473

Trade Policy 477

Foreign Policy 482

An Overview: International Relations and U.S. Foreign Policy
Goals 482

Foreign Policy Tools 485

Public Policy and Democracy 490

Appendix

A. The Declaration of Independence 494
B. The Constitution of the United States 498
C. *Federalist Papers* 10 and 51 514

Glossary 522
Endnotes 532
Index 555

MindTap™ QUICK START GUIDE

1. To get started, navigate to: www.cengagebrain.com and select "Register a Product".

A new screen will appear prompting you to add a Course Key. A Course Key is a code given to you by your instructor - this is the first of two codes you will need to access MindTap. Every student in your course section should have the same Course Key.

2. Enter the Course Key and click "Register."

If you are accessing MindTap through your school's Learning Management System such as BlackBoard or Desire2Learn, you may be redirected to use your Course Key/Access Code there. Follow the prompts you are given and feel free to contact support if you need assistance.

3. Confirm your course information above, and proceed to the log in portion below.

If you have a CengageBrain username and password, enter it under "Returning Students" and click "Login." If this is your first time, register under "New Students" and click "Create a New Account."

4. Now that you are logged in, you can access the course for free by selecting "Start Free Trial" for 20 days, or enter in your Access Code.

Your Access Code is unique to you and acts as payment for MindTap. You may have received it with your book or purchased separately in the bookstore or at CengageBrain.com. Enter it and click "Register."

NEED HELP?

For CengageBrain Support: Login to **Support.Cengage.com**. Call **866-994-2427** or access our **24/7 Student Chat!** Or access the **First Day of School PowerPoint Presentation** found at cengagebrain.com.

Letter to Instructor...

Dear *Introduction to American Government* Instructor:

As teachers and scholars of American government, we have come together to write a textbook that would engage students in both the process and the policy outcomes of U.S. government. The book presents an updated lens through which we can examine the theoretical and structural foundations of American democracy and the resulting political process that demands an active and informed citizenry. To help students understand American democracy and see how they can be involved in their government, we peel back the layers of the political system to expose its inner workings and to examine how competing interests can both facilitate and block the people's will. In doing so, we use the conceptual framework of gateways. We contend that there are gates—formal and informal—that present obstacles to participation and empowerment. But there are also gateways that give students a chance to influence the process and to overcome the obstacles. The gateways framework helps students conceptualize participation and civic engagement—even democracy itself. Our book is both realistic and optimistic, contending that the American system can be open to the influence of students and responsive to their hopes and dreams—if they have information about how the system works. But we avoid cheerleading by also pointing out the many gates that undermine the workings of government. Although the size and complexity of the American constitutional system is daunting, it is imperative to prepare for the demands of democratic citizenship. This has never been truer than today, when we have a rapidly changing demographic balance within our population. Today groups that were formerly underrepresented in American politics and society, such as second- and third-generation Latinos, are a powerful force in our government. It is our hope that this textbook can awaken students and motivate them not only to learn about politics but to also participate actively throughout every stage of their lives.

In keeping with the theme of gates and gateways in American politics, we also open each chapter with a **vignette** that tells the story of people who have successfully navigated their own way in politics. The important role of the vignette for the instructor is to show the students how people like them have made a difference in American political and social life; our vignette subjects vary by historical era, career choice, gender, race, ethnicity, and party affiliation. We also include landmark **Supreme Court cases** related to every chapter's subject to show students the continuous and vital role it plays in both upholding and knocking down gates to policy implementation and political participation. We include **policy features** in each chapter to illustrate how the chapter's core content operates in a real-time, real-life basis. To round out our emphasis on how the core structure of a political system can encourage or discourage participation, we include a **Global Gateway feature** in each chapter, which informs students about politics around the globe and how it compares to what they see in the American context.

New to This Edition

- A new dedicated focus on Latino politics and participation reflects the changing demographic infrastructure in America today by providing new coverage of the politics and issues affecting Latinos in every chapter of the book:
  - New sections on the history of Latino civil rights, including a time line of significant events in Latino political history
  - New Supreme Court cases of significance to Latino constitutional and voting rights
  - New section on Latino political leaders and grassroots organizations
  - New chapter vignettes highlighting the gateways used by Latinos
  - Expanded discussion of the Latino vote and its implications for elections and governing
- New freestanding chapter on domestic, economic, and foreign policy making
- New freestanding chapter which combines the chapters on Public Opinion and the Media into one comprehensive chapter
- Revamped policy features embedded in each chapter that reflect the most current issues related to each chapter's subject

- Updated opening vignettes, Global Gateways, and new Supreme Court cases to incorporate the changes in American politics since the publication of the second edition
- Streamlined learning objectives and outcomes
- New coverage of the impact of the changes in campaign spending that arose from recent Supreme Court decisions
- Revamped discussion of microtargeting in light of the success of the Obama campaign in 2012
- New coverage of social media and its role in forging opportunities for participation
- Up-to-date coverage of the 2014 midterm elections examining the impact of the Tea Party, turnout trends, and the role of money in 2014 campaigns

Mindtap

As an instructor, MindTap is here to simplify your workload, organize and immediately grade your students' assignments, and allow you to customize your course as you see fit. Through deep-seated integration with your Learning Management System, grades are easily exported, and analytics are pulled with just the click of a button. MindTap provides you with a platform to easily add in current events videos and RSS feeds from national or local news sources. Looking to include more currency in the course? Add in our KnowNow American Government Blog link for weekly updated news coverage and pedagogy.

Teaching American government remains a vitally important but constantly challenging task for all of us. We know that there are many books to choose from to use in your course. We believe that *Gateways* is a book that has an innovative approach in reaching and engaging students across a range of backgrounds and enables instructors to more easily achieve their pedagogical goals in American government courses. We have seen it work for our students, and we know it will work for yours.

Sincerely,

John G. Geer, john.g.geer@vanderbilt.edu
Wendy J. Schiller, Wendy_Schiller@Brown.edu
Jeffrey A. Segal, jeffrey.segal@stonybrook.edu
Richard Herrera, Richard.Herrera@asu.edu
Dana K. Glencross, dglencross@occc.edu

Letter to Student...

Dear Student:

Our book begins with a simple question: How does anyone exert political influence in a country of more than 318 million people? Students in American government classrooms across the country are grappling with this question as they develop an appreciation of their role in American public life. In our own classrooms, students ask us, What is my responsibility? Can I make a difference? Does my participation matter? How can I get my opinions represented? These are gateway questions that probe the opportunities and limits on citizen involvement in a democracy. For that reason, we not only provide you with essential information about the American political system but also show you how to become a **more powerful advocate for yourself** within that system. It is not enough to know what you want your government and society to be—you must learn how to make it happen. This book shows you how people from all walks of life have opened gates to influence public policy, and it shows you the relevance of government in your life. It is our hope that this textbook motivates you not only to learn about politics but also to participate actively throughout every stage of your life.

In keeping with the theme of gates and gateways in American politics, we open each chapter with a vignette that tells the story of people who have successfully navigated their own way in politics. These are people like you who have different gender, ethnic, racial, and partisan backgrounds, and who have made a difference in American political and social life. We also include other features focusing on the Supreme Court, public policy, and global governance that show you how politics plays out in the United States and around the world. All of these special features are designed to relate specifically to you—the student—to give you a blueprint with which to navigate the political system. What makes our book different?

- Streamlined learning objectives and outcomes help you better understand the material and prepare for the graded assignments that go with the class. We have checkpoint questions at the end of each main section, as well as key terms study guide questions throughout each chapter.

- Latino politics and participation coverage reflect the changing demographic infrastructure in America, especially among young people by providing new coverage of the politics and issues affecting Latinos in every chapter of the book.

- Updated accounts are included of people who are changing American politics today.

- Current policy case studies are included on issues such as voting participation, environmental protection, military conflict, and personal privacy.

- A comprehensive chapter which discusses public opinion and the media.

- A comprehensive chapter on elections, campaigns, and voting.

As a student, the benefits of using MindTap with this book are endless. With automatically graded practice quizzes and activities, automatic detailed revision plans on your essay assignments offered through Write Experience, an easily navigated learning path, and an interactive eBook, you will be able to test yourself inside and outside the classroom with ease. The accessibility of current events coupled with interactive media makes the content fun and engaging. On your computer, phone, or tablet, MindTap is there when you need it, giving you easy access to flashcards, quizzes, readings, and assignments.

As teachers, our main goal both in this book and in the classroom is to empower you as active participants in American democracy. We know that you balance a lot of competing demands for your time, from other classes, to work, to family responsibilities. This book provides you with the core information you need to succeed in your American government classes, and just as important, to knock open the gates that may stand in your way to achieve your goals within the political system.

Sincerely,

John G. Geer, john.g.geer@vanderbilt.edu
Wendy J. Schiller, Wendy_Schiller@Brown.edu
Jeffrey A. Segal, jeffrey.segal@stonybrook.edu
Richard Herrera, Richard.Herrera@asu.edu
Dana K. Glencross, dglencross@occc.edu

Resources for Students and Instructors

Students

Access your Gateways to Democracy, Essentials, *3e, resources via*
www.cengagebrain.com/shop/isbn/9781285852911.

If you purchased MindTap or CourseReader access with your book, enter your access code, and click Register. You can also purchase the book's resources here separately through the Study Tools tab or access the free companion website through the Free Materials tab.

Instructors

Access your Gateways to Democracy, Essentials, *3e, resources via*
www.cengage.com/login.

Log in using your Cengage Learning single sign-on user name and password, or create a new instructor account by clicking on New Faculty User and following the instructions.

Gateways to Democracy, Essentials, 3e *– Text Only Edition*

ISBN: 978-1-285-85857-9

This copy of the book does not come bundled with MindTap.

MindTap for *Gateways to Democracy, Essentials,* 3e

Instant Access Code: 978-1-305-07863-5
Printed Access Code: 978-1-285-85859-3

MindTap for American Government is a fully online, personalized learning experience built upon Cengage Learning content. MindTap combines student learning tools—readings, multimedia, activities, and assessments—into a singular Learning Path that guides students through their course. Through a wealth of activities written to learning outcomes, it provides students with ample opportunities to check themselves for understanding, while also providing faculty and students alike with a clear way to measure and assess student progress.

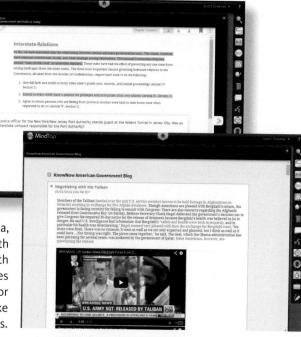

Faculty can use MindTap as a turnkey solution or customize it by adding YouTube videos, RSS feeds, or their own documents directly within the eBook or within each chapter's Learning Path. The product can be used fully online with its interactive eBook for *Gateways to Democracy* or in conjunction with the printed text.

Instructor Companion Website for *Gateways to Democracy, Essentials*, 3e

ISBN: 978-1-285-86567-6

This Instructor Companion website is an all-in-one multimedia online resource for class preparation, presentation, and testing. Accessible through Cengage.com/login with your faculty account, you will find available for download: book-specific Microsoft® PowerPoint® presentations, a test bank compatible with multiple Learning Management Systems, an Instructor's Manual, Microsoft® PowerPoint® Image Slides, and a JPEG Image Library.

The test bank, offered in Blackboard, Moodle, Desire2Learn, Canvas, and Angel formats, contains learning objective-specific multiple-choice, short answer, and essay questions for each chapter. Import the test bank into your Learning Management System to edit and manage questions, as well as to create tests.

The Instructor's Manual contains chapter-specific learning objectives, an outline, key terms with definitions, and a chapter summary. Additionally, the Instructor's Manual features a critical thinking question, lecture launching suggestion, and an in-class activity for each learning objective.

The Microsoft® PowerPoint® presentations are ready-to-use visual outlines of each chapter. These presentations are easily customized for your lectures and offered along with chapter-specific Microsoft® PowerPoint® Image Slides and JPEG Image Libraries. Access the Instructor Companion Website at www.cengage.com/login.

Student Companion Website for *Gateways to Democracy, Essentials*, 3e

ISBN: 978-1-285-86566-9

This free companion website for *Gateways to Democracy, 3e*, is accessible through cengagebrain.com and allows students access to chapter-specific interactive learning tools, including flashcards, glossaries, and more.

Cognero for *Gateways to Democracy, Essentials*, 3e

ISBN: 978-1-305-08130-7

Cengage Learning Testing Powered by Cognero is a flexible, online system that allows you to author, edit, and manage test bank content from multiple Cengage Learning solutions, create multiple test versions in an instant, and deliver tests from your Learning Management System, your classroom, or wherever you want. The test bank for *Gateways to Democracy* contains learning objective-specific multiple-choice, short answer, and essay questions for each chapter.

CourseReader

CourseReader for
American Government

CourseReader 0-30 Instant Access Code: 978-1-111-47997-8

CourseReader 0-30 Printed Access Code: 978-1-111-47995-4

CourseReader: American Government allows instructors to create your reader, your way, in just minutes. This affordable, fully customizable online reader provides access to thousands of permissions-cleared readings, articles, primary sources, and audio and video selections from the regularly updated Gale research library database. This easy-to-use solution allows you to search for and select just the material you want for your courses. Each selection opens with a descriptive introduction to provide context and concludes with critical-thinking and multiple-choice questions to reinforce key points. CourseReader is loaded with convenient tools such as highlighting, printing, note-taking, and downloadable PDFs and MP3 audio files for each reading. CourseReader is the perfect complement to any political science course. It can be bundled with your current textbook, sold alone, or integrated into your Learning Management System. CourseReader 0-30 allows access to up to 30 selections in the reader. Instructors can contact their Cengage Learning consultant for details. Students should only purchase CourseReader if assigned by their instructor.

Election 2014 Supplement

ISBN: 978-1-305-50018-1

Written by John Clark and Brian Schaffner, this booklet addresses the 2014 campaigns and elections, with real-time analysis and references.

Acknowledgments

Writing the third edition of an introductory textbook requires a dedicated and professional publishing team. We are thrilled that Richard Herrera, associate professor of political science at Arizona State University, has joined our team and brought with him his deep and rich understanding of Latino politics. We were also extremely fortunate to continue to work with a number of excellent people at Cengage Learning, including Carolyn Merrill. Carolyn has been a rock-steady foundation, and her choice of Naomi Friedman as our development editor was outstanding. Naomi has guided us through a comprehensive revision of the book to focus more on the vital role that traditionally underrepresented groups, such as Latinos, play in knocking down the gates that stand in the way of participation. Edward Dionne and Jill Traut have been vigilant managers of the copyedit process, and Reba Frederics has been terrific in updating our photo and images in the book. We also want to thank the entire sales force at Cengage Learning for their tireless efforts to promote the book.

Our gratitude goes to all of those who worked on the various supplements offered with this text, especially the test bank author, Nate Vanden Brook from Oklahoma City Community College, and the Instructor's Manual author, Adam Newmark from Appalachian State University.

By definition, an American government textbook is a sweeping endeavor, and it would not be possible to succeed without our reviewers. They provided truly constructive input throughout the review and revision process, especially on our new comprehensive policy chapter. We list their names on the following page, and we are grateful to them for their contributions to the development of this textbook.

Each of us would also like to thank the individuals who supported us throughout the project.

John G. Geer: I would like to thank Carrie Roush and Marc Trussler for their help with revising this textbook. Special mention goes to Drew Engelhardt for his amazing efforts in pulling together new material for this third edition. I owe many thanks to Jeff, Rick, and Wendy. They are fabulous collaborators and even better friends. I am lucky to know them and to have the chance to work with them on this project. My deepest and most heartfelt appreciation goes to Beth Prichard Geer. Beth has made possible a new edition of my life that I will be forever grateful for.

Wendy J. Schiller: I would also like to express my appreciation for the opportunity to work with John, Jeff, and Rick—each excellent scholars and colleagues. For her support on this edition, I would like to give a big thanks to Kaitlin Sidorsky for all her research assistance. I would also like to thank my husband, Robert Kalunian, who provides an endless supply of patience, support, and perspective.

Jeffrey A. Segal: I thank my previous co-authors, John and Wendy, for once again making the endeavor of the new edition a totally enjoyable experience; Naomi Friedman for her fresh look at the materials; Rick Herrera for joining the "Gater" team; and Carolyn Merrill for the foresight of asking him aboard. For the second straight edition, Justine D'Elia has provided invaluable research assistance. My professional colleagues, both at Stony Brook and beyond, have cheerfully answered innumerable queries from me. I appreciate their assistance.

Richard Herrera: I would like to thank John, Wendy, and Jeff for inviting me to join the author team. They are an exciting group of scholars with whom to work. The creative process that produced this edition has been a wonderful experience. Their support, along with Naomi Friedman's, has been most valuable as I navigated my way through the revision process. I would also like to thank Marian Norris for her support, patience, and encouragement throughout this new adventure.

Dana K. Glencross: My deepest appreciation and admiration goes to this tremendous team of authors for allowing me the opportunity to work with them yet again. My husband Carl deserves my thanks for his support and patience, as does Annalyn Gill who provides great insights and challenges to my questions. Reagan the basset hound earns recognition for providing companionship during many late hours spent working on this fantastic new edition.

Reviewers

We would also like to thank the instructors who have contributed their valuable feedback through reviews of the second edition in preparation for this third edition:

Martin Adamian, *California State University, Los Angeles*
Lynn Brink, *North Lake College*
Jeffrey Christiansen, *Seminole State College*
Monte Freidig, *Santa Rosa Junior College*

Lori Han, *Chapman University*
Sally Hansen, *Daytona State College*
Debra St. John, *Collin County Community College*

We also thank the reviewers of the previous editions:

Steve Anthony, *Georgia State University*
Wayne Ault, *Southwestern Illinois College*
Jane Bryant, *John A. Logan College*
Jared Burkholder, *Grace College*
David Dulio, *Oakland University*
Joshua Dyck, *University of Massachusetts, Lowell*
Matthew Eshbaugh-Soha, *University of North Texas*
Jeff Fine, *Clemson University*
Charles Finocchiaro, *University of South Carolina*
James Goss, *Tarrant County College, Trinity River*
Rhonda Gunter, *Maryland Community College*
Bill Horner, *University of Missouri, Columbia*
Amy Jasperson, *Rhodes College*
Mark Jendrysik, *University of North Dakota*
Aaron Knight, *Houston Community College, Northeast*
Lyn Maurer, *Southern Illinois University at Edwardsville*
Heather Myabe, *University of West Georgia*

James McCann, *Purdue University*
John Mercurio, *San Diego State University*
Michael Moore, *University of Texas at Arlington*
Jonathan Morris, *East Carolina University*
James Newman, *Idaho State University*
Mark Peplowski, *College of Southern Nevada*
Jamie Pimlott, *Niagara University*
Dave Price, *Santa Fe Community College*
Narges Rabii, *Saddleback College*
Tim Reynolds, *Alvin Community College*
David Ross, *Stark State College*
Margaret Scranton, *University of Arkansas at Little Rock*
John Shively, *Longview Community College*
Alec Thomson, *Schoolcraft College*
Nate Vander Brook, *Oklahoma City College*
Laura Wood, *Tarrant County College, Northwest Campus*
Davis Woodward, *Clemson University*

About the Authors

John G. Geer

(PhD, Princeton University) is the Gertrude Conaway Vanderbilt Professor of Political Science and co-directs the Vanderbilt Poll. Geer has published widely, including *In Defense of Negativity*, which won the Goldsmith Prize from the Shorenstein Center at Harvard University. Geer has been a visiting scholar at Harvard University and Princeton University. Geer teaches Introduction to American Politics, as well as specialty courses on elections and campaigns. His teaching has drawn much note, winning numerous teaching awards at both Arizona State University and Vanderbilt University. Geer is a frequent commentator in the press, with appearances on all the major networks (e.g., Fox News, CBS Evening News, CNN), and he has been quoted in newspapers ranging from *The New York Times* to *The Washington Post* to the *LA Times*. He has done interviews for major international outlets as well, such as BBC and Al Jazeera.

Wendy J. Schiller

(PhD, University of Rochester) is an Associate Professor of Political Science and Public Policy at Brown University (Twitter acct @profwschiller). She was legislative assistant for Senator Daniel P. Moynihan, a federal lobbyist for Governor Mario M. Cuomo, a Guest Scholar and PhD Fellow at the Brookings Institution, and a post-doctoral fellow at Princeton University. She has published *The Contemporary Congress* (2003, 2005) with Burdett Loomis, *Partners and Rivals: Representation in U.S. Senate Delegations* (2000), and *Electing the Senate: Indirect Democracy before the Seventeenth Amendment* (2014) with Charles Stewart III. She teaches courses on a wide range of American politics topics, including Introduction to the American Political Process, The American Presidency, Congress and Public Policy, Parties and Interest Groups, and The Philosophy of the American Founding. Professor Schiller is a political analyst for local and national media outlets, including CNN.com, Bloomberg Radio, NPR, and WJAR10, the local NBC affiliate in Providence.

Jeffrey A. Segal

(PhD, Michigan State University) is SUNY Distinguished Professor and Chair of the Political Science Department at Stony Brook University. He has served as Senior Visiting Research Scholar at Princeton University and held a Guggenheim Fellowship. Segal is best known, with Harold Spaeth, as the leading proponent of the attitudinal model of Supreme Court decision making. Segal has twice won the Wadsworth Award for a book (with Spaeth) or article 10 years or older with lasting influence on law and courts. He has also won the C. Herman Pritchett Award (again with Spaeth) for best book on law and courts. His work on the influence of strategic factors on Supreme Court decision making won the Franklin Burdette Award from APSA. With Lee Epstein, Kevin Quinn, and Andrew Martin, he won Green Bag's award for exemplary legal writing. He has also won a national award sponsored by the American Bar Association for innovative teaching and instructional methods and materials in law and courts.

Richard Herrera

(PhD, University of California Santa Barbara) is Associate Professor of Political Science and Associate Director for the School of Politics and Global Studies at Arizona State University. He directs the ASU Capital Scholars Washington, DC, Summer Internship program for ASU and coordinates the ASU-McCain Institute for International Leadership Internship Program. He has contributed articles to the *American Political Science Review*, *Journal of Politics*, *Legislative Studies Quarterly*, and *State Politics and Policy Quarterly*. His current research interests are focused on U.S. governors, their ideology, policy agendas, and representative functions. He teaches courses in American Politics, American Political Parties, and American Politics and Film.

Dana K. Glencross

(MA, Oklahoma State University) is a Professor of Political Science at Oklahoma City Community College, where she has served as Chair of the Department for History, Political Science, Geography, and Medical Terminology, and as Chair of the Faculty Association. Professor Glencross was a governor's appointee to the Oklahoma Commission for Teacher Preparation and a member of the the Faculty Advisory Council to the Oklahoma State Regents for Higher Education. She was elected as the national chairwoman of the Association of Chapter Advisors to the Phi Theta Kappa Honor Society. She co-authors a chapter on "Public Policy" in *Oklahoma Government and Politics: An Introduction* (2007, 2012, 2014). She teaches courses including American federal government, state and local government, comparative politics, and law. She is a regular guest on local television and radio broadcasts, discussing elections and current events. She received the OCCC President's Award for Excellence in Teaching and twice has been recognized as the Oklahoma Political Science Association's Teacher of the Year.

Career Opportunities: Political Science

Introduction

It is no secret that college graduates are facing one of the toughest job markets in the past fifty years. Despite this challenge, those with a college degree have done much better than those without since the 2008 recession. One of the most important decisions a student has to make is the choice of a major; many consider future job possibilities when making that call. A political science degree is incredibly useful for a successful career in many different fields, from lawyer to policy advocate, pollster to humanitarian worker. Employer surveys reveal that the skills that most employers value in successful employees—critical thinking, analytical reasoning, and clarity of verbal and written communication—are precisely the tools that political science courses should be helping you develop. This brief guide is intended to help spark ideas for what kinds of careers you might pursue with a political science degree and the types of activities you can engage in now to help you secure one of those positions after graduation.

Careers in Political Science

LAW AND CRIMINAL JUSTICE

Do you find that your favorite parts of your political science classes are those that deal with the Constitution, the legal system, and the courts? Then a career in law and criminal justice might be right for you. Traditional jobs in the field range from lawyer or judge to police or parole officer. Since 9/11, there has also been tremendous growth in the area of homeland security, which includes jobs in mission support, immigration, travel security, as well as prevention and response.

PUBLIC ADMINISTRATION

The many offices of the federal government combined represent one of the largest employers in the United States. Flip to the bureaucracy chapter of this textbook and consider that each federal department, agency, and bureau you see looks to political science majors for future employees. A partial list of such agencies would include the Department of Education, the Department of Health and Human Services, and the Federal Trade Commission. This does not even begin to account for the multitude of similar jobs in state and local governments that you might consider as well.

CAMPAIGNS, ELECTIONS, AND POLLING

Are campaigns and elections the most exciting part of political science for you? Then you might consider a career in the growing industry based around political campaigns. From volunteering and interning to consulting, marketing, and fundraising, there are many opportunities for those who enjoy the competitive and high-stakes electoral arena. For those looking for careers that combine political knowledge with statistical skills, there are careers in public opinion polling. Pollsters work for independent national organizations such as Gallup and YouGov, or as part of news operations and campaigns. For those who are interested in survey methodology there are also a wide variety of non-political career opportunities in marketing and survey design.

INTEREST GROUPS, INTERNATIONAL AND NONGOVERNMENTAL ORGANIZATIONS

Is there a cause that you are especially passionate about? If so, there is a good chance that there are interest groups out there that are working hard to see some progress made on similar issues. Many of the positions that one might find in for-profit companies also exist in their non-profit interest group and nongovernmental organization counterparts, including lobbying and high-level strategizing. Do not forget that there are also quite a few major international organizations—such as the United Nations, the World Health Organization, and the International Monetary Fund, where a degree in political science could be put to good use. While competition for those jobs tends to be fierce, your interest and knowledge about politics and policy will give you an advantage.

FOREIGN SERVICE

Does a career in diplomacy and foreign affairs, complete with the opportunity to live and work abroad, sound exciting for you? Tens of thousands of people work for the State Department, both in Washington D.C. and in consulates throughout the world. They represent the diplomatic interests of the United States abroad. Entrance into the Foreign Service follows a very specific process, starting with the Foreign Service Officers Test—an exam given three times a year that includes sections on American government, history, economics, and world affairs. Being a political science major is a significant help in taking the FSOT.

GRADUATE SCHOOL

While not a career, graduate school may be the appropriate next step for you after completing your undergraduate degree. Following the academic route, being awarded a Ph.D. or Master's degree in political science could open additional doors to a career in academia, as well as many of the professions mentioned earlier. If a career as a researcher in political science interests you, you should speak with your advisors about continuing your education.

Preparing While Still on Campus

INTERNSHIPS

One of the most useful steps you can take while still on campus is to visit your college's career center in regards to an internship in your field of interest. Not only does it give you a chance to experience life in the political science realm, it can lead to job opportunities later down the road and add experience to your resume.

SKILLS

In addition to your political science classes, there are a few skills any number of which will prove useful as a complement to your degree:

Writing: Like anything else, writing improves with practice. Writing is one of those skills that is applicable regardless of where your career might take you. Virtually every occupation relies on an ability to write cleanly, concisely, and persuasively.

Public Speaking: An oft-quoted 1977 survey showed that public speaking was the most commonly cited fear among respondents. And yet oral communication is a vital tool in the modern economy. You can practice this skill in a formal class setting or through extracurricular activities that get you in front of a group.

Quantitative Analysis: As the Internet aids in the collection of massive amounts of information, the nation is facing a drastic shortage of people with basic statistical skills to interpret and use this data. A political science degree can go hand-in-hand with courses in introductory statistics.

Foreign Language: One skill that often helps a student or future employee stand out in a crowded job market is the ability to communicate in a language other than English. Solidify or set the foundation for your verbal and written foreign language communication skills while in school.

STUDENT LEADERSHIP

One attribute that many employers look for is "leadership potential" which can be quite tricky to indicate on a resume or cover letter. What can help is a demonstrated record of involvement in clubs and organizations, preferably in a leadership role. While many people think immediately of student government, most student clubs allow you the opportunity to demonstrate your leadership skills.

Conclusion

Hopefully reading this has sparked some ideas on potential future careers. As a next step, visit your college's career placement office, which is a great place to further explore what you have read here. You might also visit your college's alumni office to connect with graduates who are working in your field of interest. Political science opens the door to a lot of exciting careers, have fun exploring the possibilities!

GATEWAYS

TO DEMOCRACY an Introduction to American Government

THE ESSENTIALS

"Educate and inform the whole mass of the people. . . . They are the only sure reliance for the preservation of our liberty."

THOMAS JEFFERSON
The College of William and Mary, Williamsburg, Virginia

1

Gateways to American Democracy

In 1760 Thomas Jefferson left his boyhood home in the hills of Piedmont, Virginia, to attend the College of William and Mary in the colonial capital of Williamsburg. There were only six colleges in the American colonies at that time, and Jefferson was fortunate to have the opportunity to pursue his education. At William and Mary, he studied mathematics, physics, ethics, and the law. He described himself as a "hard student," and, according to family tradition, he studied fifteen hours a day, rising at dawn and reading far past midnight. "Determine never to be idle," he later told his daughter. "It is wonderful how much may be done if we are always doing." His family's position in Virginia gave rise to expectations. Jefferson's father, Peter Jefferson, owned a considerable amount of land and, like his grandfather and great-grandfather, was involved in colonial politics.

Despite his family's wealth, however, Jefferson faced personal hardships. His father died unexpectedly in 1757, making him the head of the family at age 14. Once he turned 21, he would inherit most of his father's wealth and land, but until then, he had to pursue his education while assisting his seven siblings. He managed to fulfill his family responsibilities and complete his studies, staying in Williamsburg after graduating from William and Mary in 1762 to study law with one of the colony's leading lawyers. In 1769, at age 26, he won election to the House of Burgesses—the legislative assembly for the colony of Virginia.

Thomas Jefferson entered politics at a time of great upheaval in America. Discontent with British rule was rising, and Virginia was a hotbed of opposition. When the House of Burgesses began considering various measures in opposition to British rule, the colonial governor—a representative of the British Crown—dissolved it. This act closed an avenue—or what we call in this textbook a "gateway"—for participation. With no legitimate way to express grievances, the colonists began to talk of independence. Independence was a radical step; it meant revolution, and revolution would mean the end of colonial government and the creation of new institutions of government. Jefferson understood the connection between the people and their government as a social contract; if a government did not serve the people, the people should end it. In the Declaration of Independence, he speaks of revolution as a right of self-governing men:

"We hold these truths to be self-evident: That all men are created equal; that they are endowed by their Creator with

Need to Know

1.1 Identify the successes we have achieved and the obstacles we face in establishing a "more perfect union"

1.2 Analyze how the constitutional system balances liberty and order

1.3 Describe the political values and ideologies Americans share

1.4 Evaluate American democracy in terms of responsiveness and equality

1.5 List the responsibilities of individuals in a democracy

▶ **WATCH & LEARN** MindTap for American Government
Watch a brief "What Do You Know?" video summarizing The Democratic Republic.

certain unalienable rights; that among these are life, liberty, and the pursuit of happiness; that, to secure these rights, governments are instituted among men, deriving their just powers from the consent of the governed; that whenever any form of government becomes destructive of these ends, it is the right of the people to alter or to abolish it, and to institute new government, laying its foundation on such principles, and organizing its powers in such form, as to them shall seem most likely to effect their safety and happiness."

This passage from the Declaration of Independence is famous. Most Americans know the ringing statement on equality with which it begins. But it is also important to note Jefferson's statement that government not only derives its power "from the consent of the governed," but that if government is not responsive to the governed, the people have the right "to alter or to abolish it." In other words, it is the people's right—and responsibility—to ensure that the "gateways to democracy" are always open and available to them in their pursuit of life, liberty, and happiness. Jefferson and the other Founders in

effect sought to replace the British Crown and build effective and meaningful institutions (or gateways) whereby the people of the new nation could enjoy a responsive government while retaining their individual freedoms. These themes of the Declaration of Independence—equality and responsiveness—were present at the creation of the new government. They continue to shape the government as each generation of Americans has sought to make them a reality.

The questions we put before you are fundamental. How does American government work? Is our system of government really democratic? Does it foster equality and responsiveness?

These are not easy questions to answer, but they are important and enduring. The Founders wrestled with them more than 200 years ago. We hope this book helps you wrestle with them as well. Our goal is not to answer the questions for you. Rather, it is your responsibility to draw your own conclusions. The central aim of this book is to give you the information and the analytical tools you need to judge the Founders' democratic experiment for yourself.

1.1 Gateways: Evaluating the American Political System

> ❯ Identify the successes we have achieved and the obstacles we face in establishing a "more perfect union"

LISTEN & LEARN
MindTap for American Government

Access Read Speaker to listen to Chapter 1.

This textbook, *Gateways to Democracy*, explains how citizen involvement has expanded American democracy and how each of you can also influence the political system. We call the avenues of influence, as noted previously, "gateways." This book serves as a handbook for democratic citizenship by peeling back the layers of American government to reveal the ways you can get involved and to explain the reasons you should do so. The American political system is complicated, large, and sometimes frustrating. As the term *gateways* implies, there are also *gates*—obstacles to influence, institutional controls that limit access, and powerful interests that seem to block the people's will. We describe these as well because to be a productive and influential member of American society, you need to understand how American government and politics work.

Through citizen involvement, American democracy has achieved many successes:

- The nation and its institutions are amazingly stable. The United States has the oldest written constitution in the world.

- The government has weathered severe economic crises, a civil war, and two world wars; yet it still maintains peaceful transitions of power from one set of leaders to the next.

- Citizens are able to petition the government and to criticize it. They can assemble and protest the government's policies.

- The American economy has created an excellent standard of living, among the highest in the world.

- American society has attracted millions of immigrants, giving many of them a gateway to citizenship.
- Americans exhibit more commitment to civic duty than do citizens in nearly all other major democracies.[1]
- Americans show more tolerance of different political views than do citizens in other major democracies.[2]

These successes do not mean that there are not problems:

- Inequality persists, and government is sometimes slow to respond.
- Even with the election and reelection of President Barack Obama, racial tensions continue to haunt the country.
- The gap between the rich and the poor continues to grow, with increasing numbers of people living in poverty.[3]
- The public's trust in the institutions of government has never been so low.[4]
- The rate of turnout in elections is among the lowest of the major democracies.
- Despite a high level of religious tolerance, there is also persistent distrust of some religious minorities, such as Muslims and Mormons.[5]
- Despite being proud of our nation of immigrants, at times the country seeks to erect gates to certain groups as they seek to become citizens.
- Political polarization continues to increase, as reflected in staggering partisan differences in the public's judgment of President Obama.[6]
- The U.S. national debt is $17.7 trillion as of September 15, 2014, and growing every day.[7]

Social scientists have been measuring the gap between the rich and the poor since the 1930s, and that gap has grown in the past few decades. Reports in 2013 indicated that the incomes of the top 1 percent rose 20 percent, while the remaining 99 percent's income rose only 1 percent. The wealthiest 1 percent in 2012 earned 19 percent of all income in the United States. The wealthiest 10 percent earned nearly 50 percent of total earnings.[8]

To solve these and other problems and achieve the "more perfect Union" promised in the Constitution, the nation's citizens must be vigilant and engaged. We have framed our book with the goal of demonstrating the demands and rewards of democratic citizenship. As we explore the American political system, we place special emphasis on the multiple and varied connections among citizenship, participation, institutions, and public policy. Our focus is on the following gateway questions:

- How can you get yourself and your opinions represented in government?
- How can you make government more responsive, and responsible, to citizens?
- How can you make American democracy better?

The laws that regulate the American economy, social issues, and even political participation are examples of **public policy**—the intentional action by government to achieve a goal. In the arena of public policy, we determine who gets what, when, and how, and with what result. In each chapter of this book, we will examine a major public policy issue related to the chapter topic. You will find that the public policy process is often divided into stages: identification of the problem; placing the problem on the agenda of policy makers;

formulating a solution; enacting and implementing the solution; and finally evaluating the solution to make sure that it solves the problem and revising the solution to improve it. These stages combine to form an ideal model of the process; however, this process does not always unfold so neatly. You will also find that individuals, organizations, and political institutions all work together to determine public policies: Congress, the president, the executive branch agency that deals with the issue, the courts, political parties, interest groups, and interested citizens. In each chapter, you will learn about an important public policy, analyze who the stakeholders are and how the policy is formed, evaluate the policy, and, finally, construct your own solution (see Public Policy and Gateways to Democracy).

1.2 Democracy and the American Constitutional System

> Analyze how the constitutional system balances liberty and order

Democracy is the kind of government to which the people of many nations aspire, but it has not always been so. Only in the past two centuries—partly through the example of the United States—has democracy gained favor. Let us sketch some of the fundamental aspects of American democracy.

Liberty and Order

Literally and most simply, **democracy** is rule by the people, or **self-government**. In a democracy, the citizens hold political authority, and they develop the means to govern themselves. In practice, that means rule by the majority, and in the years before American independence, **majority rule** had little appeal. In 1644 John Cotton, a leading clergyman of the colonial period, declared democracy "the meanest and worst of all forms of government."[9] Even after American independence, Edmund Burke, a British political philosopher and politician, wrote that a "perfect democracy is . . . the most shameless thing in the world."[10] At the time democracy was associated with mob rule, and mobs were large, passionate, ignorant, and dangerous. If the mob ruled, the people would suffer. There would be no **liberty** or safety; there would be no **order**. Eighteenth-century mobs destroyed private property, burned effigies of leaders they detested, tarred and feathered their enemies, and threatened people who disagreed with them. In fact, such events occurred in the protests against British rule in the American colonies, and they were fresh in the minds of those who wrote the Declaration of Independence and the Constitution.

John Adams, a signer of the Declaration of Independence and later the nation's second president (1797–1801), was not a champion of this kind of democracy. "Democracy," he wrote, "is more bloody than either aristocracy or monarchy. Remember, democracy never lasts long. It soon wastes, exhausts, and murders itself. There is never a democracy that did not commit suicide."[11] Adams knew about mobs and their effects firsthand. As a young lawyer before the Revolution, he agreed to defend British soldiers who had been charged with murder for firing on protesters in the streets of Boston. The soldiers' cause was unpopular, for the people of Boston detested the British military presence. But Adams believed that, following British law, the soldiers had a right to counsel (a lawyer to defend them) and to a fair trial. In later years, he considered his defense of these British soldiers "one of the best pieces of service I ever rendered my country."[12]

Why? In defending the soldiers, Adams was standing up for the **rule of law**, the principle that could prevent mob rule and keep a political or popular majority under control so it could not trample on **minority rights**. An ancient British legal principle, the rule of law holds that all people are equal before the law, all are subject to the law, and no one is above it. Adams and the others who wrote America's founding documents believed in a **constitutional system** in which the people set up and agree on the basic rules and procedures that will govern them. A constitutional system is a government of laws, not of men. Without a constitution and rule of law, an unchecked majority could act to promote the welfare of some over the welfare of others, and society would be torn apart.

The American constitutional system, therefore, serves to protect both liberty and order. The Constitution sets up a governmental structure with built-in constraints on power (gates) and multiple points of access to power (gateways). It also has a built-in means for altering the basic rules and procedures of governance through amendments. As you might expect, the procedure for passing amendments comes with its own set of gates and gateways.

The Constitution as Gatekeeper

"If men were angels," wrote James Madison, a leading author of the Constitution and later the nation's fourth president (1809–17), "no government would be necessary. . . . In framing a government which is to be administered by men over men," he continued, "the great difficulty lies in this: You must first enable the government to control the governed; and in the next place oblige it to control itself" (see *Federalist* 51 in the Appendix). Madison and the other **Framers** of the Constitution recognized that the government they were designing had to be strong enough to rule but not strong enough to take away the people's rights. In other words, the Constitution had to serve as a gatekeeper, both allowing and limiting access to power at the same time.

James Madison, Thomas Jefferson, John Adams, and the other **Founders** had read many of the great political theorists. They drew, for example, on the ideas of the British political philosophers Thomas Hobbes and John Locke in perceiving the relationship between government and the governed as a **social contract**. If people lived in what these philosophers called a state of nature, without the rule of law, conflict would be unending, and the strong would destroy the weak. To secure order and safety, individuals come together to form a government and agree to live by its rules. In return, the government agrees to protect life, liberty, and property. The right to life, liberty, and property, said Locke, are **natural** or **unalienable rights**—rights so fundamental that government cannot take them away.

But these ideas about government as a social contract were untested theories when Madison and others began to write the Constitution. There were no working examples in other nations. The only model for self-government was ancient Athens, where the people had

Public Policy and Gateways to Democracy: Raising the Minimum Wage

The first federal minimum wage requirement was signed into law by President Franklin Delano Roosevelt in 1938 as part of the Fair Labor Standards Act; it set the minimum wage at 25 cents per hour and established a 44-hour workweek. States could mandate pay levels above the federal minimum wage, but they could not go below it. While he was lobbying Congress and the public on behalf of the bill, President Roosevelt said that the United States should give "all our able-bodied working men and women a fair day's pay for a fair day's work."[13] Others have also argued that individuals, families, and communities must be able to earn a living wage in order to rise above the poverty level, which would in turn give them more time and energy to participate in the democratic process.

Today the federal minimum wage is set at $7.25, although twenty-one states require employers to pay more than that wage (see Table 1.1). Still, even at that wage, working full time leaves workers 40 percent below the poverty level.[14] Some states, such as California and Connecticut, are considering proposals to raise the minimum wage to more than $10 an hour over a period of several years. However, there are also states that either have no state-mandated minimum wage or a minimum wage lower than the federal standard; in both cases, businesses earning more than $500,000 per year in revenues are required to meet the federal standards.[15]

Table 1.1 Minimum Wage (MW) by State

Greater Than Federal MW		Equals Federal MW of $7.25		Less Than Federal MW	No MW Required
AK–$7.75	MO–$7.50	DE	NH	AR–$6.25	AL
AZ–$7.90	MT–$7.90	HI	OK	GA–$5.15	LA
CA–$8.00	NJ–$8.25	IA	PA	WY–$5.15	MS
CO–$8.00	NM–$7.50	ID	SD		SC
CT–$8.70	NV–$8.25	IN	TX		TN
DC–$8.25	NY–$8.00	KS	UT		
FL–$7.93	OH–$7.95	KY	VA		
IL–$8.25	OR–$9.10	MD	WV		
MA–$8.00	RI–$8.00	NC	WI		
ME–$7.50	VT–$8.73	ND			
MI–$7.40	WA–$9.32	NE			
MN–$8.00*					

*scheduled to rise to $9.50 by 2016

Source: http://www.dol.gov/whd/minwage/america.htm#Washington

In February 2014, President Barack Obama echoed FDR's sentiment in his annual State of the Union address to Congress, when he announced that he would raise the minimum wage by executive order for all federally funded employees to $10.10 per hour. In his words, "if you cook our troops' meals or wash their dishes, you shouldn't have to live in poverty." [16] He went on to ask that Congress formally raise the federal minimum wage for all workers to that same level.[17]

The central argument against raising the minimum wage to $10.10 or even higher is that most of these types of jobs are located in small businesses that cannot afford to pay the higher wages. Opponents of higher minimum wages fear these employers will not hire more workers, and they may even fire existing workers, in order to keep their businesses profitable. Those who oppose raising the minimum wage also argue that open trade policies have given an unfair advantage to foreign manufacturers that can hire workers at very low wages and so produce and sell goods for less. However, it is difficult to assess the impact of raising the minimum wage on job growth or trade imbalances because there are so many other factors that affect the economy. For example, the last raise in the federal minimum wage occurred in 2009 in the midst of a major recession caused by a crash in the housing market. How many jobs were lost due to the recession, and how many resulted from the hike in minimum wage? It is possible that the increased minimum wage contributed to a decline in jobs, but it is also possible that the increase had no effect at all in the larger context of an economic downturn. Economists and other experts have not reached a consensus on this question.

In terms of policy choices then, society must judge what FDR called a "fair day's pay for a fair day's work." In the context of the American democracy, the minimum wage debate raises fundamental questions about the government's role in guaranteeing equality of economic opportunity.

CONNECT WITH YOUR CLASSMATES
MindTap for American Government

Access The Democratic Republic Forum: Discussion—Rule of Law and the Constitution.

Construct Your Own Policy

1. Using the table, figure out what the minimum wage is in your state. Do you think it is reasonable given the cost of living in your area? If you wanted to change the minimum wage laws in your area, what level of government would you have to lobby—local, state, federal, or a combination?

2. Construct a minimum wage policy that takes into account a worker's age, education, and family circumstance.

governed themselves in a **direct democracy**. In Athens, citizens met together to debate and to vote. That was possible because only property-owning males were citizens, and they were few in number and had similar interests and concerns.[18]

But the new United States was nothing like the old city-state of Athens. It was an alliance of thirteen states—former colonies—with nearly 4 million people spread across some 360,000 square miles. Direct democracy was impractical for such a large and diverse country, so those who wrote the Constitution created a **representative democracy** in which the people elect representatives who govern in their name. Some observers, including the Framers, call this arrangement a **republic**, a form of government in which power derives from the citizens, but their representatives make policy and govern according to existing law.

Could a republic work? No one knew, certainly not the Framers. The government they instituted was something of an experiment, and they developed their own theories about how it would work. Madison, for example, rejected the conventional view that a democracy had to be small and homogeneous so as to minimize conflict. He argued that size and diversity were assets because competing interests in a large country would balance and control—or check—one another and prevent abuse of power. Madison called these competing interests **factions**, and he believed that the most enduring source of faction was "the various and unequal distribution of property. Those who hold, and those who are without property, have ever formed distinct interests in society," he wrote. (See *Federalist 10* in the Appendix.)

In a pure democracy, where the people ruled directly, Madison expected that passions would outweigh judgments about the common good. Each individual would look out for himself, for his self-interest, and not necessarily for the interests of society as a whole, which is what we might call **civic interest**. In a republic, however, the people's representatives would of necessity have a broader view. Moreover, they would, Madison assumed, come from the better educated, a natural elite. The larger the republic, the larger the districts from which the representatives would be chosen, and thus the more likely that they would be civic-minded leaders of the highest quality. More important, in a large republic, it would be less likely that any one faction could form a majority. Interests would balance each other out, and selfish interests would actually be checked by majority rule.

Balance, control, order—these values were as important to the Framers as liberty. So while the Constitution vested political authority in the people, it also set up a governing system designed to prevent any set of individuals, any political majority, or even the government itself from becoming too powerful. The Framers purposely set up barriers and gates that blocked the excesses associated with mob rule.

Consequently, although the ultimate power lies with the people, the Constitution divides power both vertically and horizontally. Within the federal government, power is channeled into three different branches—the **legislature** (Congress), which makes the laws; the **executive** (the president and the government departments, or bureaucracy), which executes the laws; and the **judiciary** (the Supreme Court and the federal courts), which interprets the laws (see Figure 1.1). This vertical division of power is referred to as the **separation of powers**. To minimize the chance that one branch will become so strong that it can abuse its power and harm the citizenry, each branch has some power over the other two in a system known as

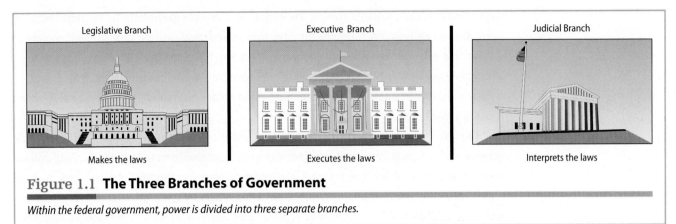

Legislative Branch	Executive Branch	Judicial Branch
Makes the laws	Executes the laws	Interprets the laws

Figure 1.1 The Three Branches of Government

Within the federal government, power is divided into three separate branches.

checks and balances. The Constitution also divides power horizontally, into layers, between the national government and the state governments. This arrangement is known as **federalism**. In a further division of powers, state governments create local governments.

The American constitutional system thus simultaneously provides gateways for access and gates that limit access. The people govern themselves, but they do so indirectly and through a system that disperses power among many competing interests. This textbook explores both the gateways and the gates that channel and block the influence of citizens.

Checkpoint

CAN YOU:

■ Make a connection between minority rights and democratic rule

■ Define social contract

■ Analyze how the Constitution divides power

1.3 American Political Culture

> Describe the political values and ideologies Americans share

As an experiment, the American republic has been open to change in the course of the nation's history. Despite their theorizing, the Framers could not have anticipated exactly how it would develop. Madison was right, however, about the enduring influence of factions. The people quickly divided themselves into competing interests and shortly into competing **political parties**, groups organized to win elections. The process by which competing interests determine who gets what, when, and how is what we call **politics**.[19]

Madison was right, too, about the sources of division, which are often centered in the unequal distribution of property and competing ideas about how far government should go to reduce inequality. Public opinion about such matters is sometimes described as falling on a scale that ranges from left to right, and when people have a fairly consistent set of views over a range of policy choices, they are said to have a **political ideology**, that is, a coherent way of thinking about government—a philosophy so to speak. In contrast, **party identification**, or partisanship, is a psychological attachment to a particular party. This attachment is related to political ideology, but it is more personal than philosophical.

A person's ideology can be a strong clue as to what he or she thinks about politics. On the left end of the scale are **liberals** who favor government efforts to increase equality, including higher rates of taxes on the wealthy than on the poor and greater provision of social benefits, such as health care, unemployment insurance, and welfare payments to support those in need. **Conservatives**, on the right, believe that lower taxes will prompt greater economic growth that will ultimately benefit everyone, including the poor. Thus, liberals support a large and active government that will regulate the economy, while conservatives fear that such a government will suppress individual liberty and create a dependency that actually harms those it aims to help.

The left–right division is not just about economics, however. For social issues, liberals generally favor less government interference, while conservatives favor rules that will uphold traditional moral values (see Figure 1.2). Conservatives are, therefore, more likely to support laws that ban abortion and same-sex marriage, while liberals are more likely to favor a woman's right to make decisions over reproductive matters as well as the right of same-sex couples to wed.

Although terms such as *conservative* and *liberal* are often used to label American political attitudes, most Americans are not very ideological in their orientation to politics. They are likely to take independent positions on various issues, leaning left on some and right on others. In fact, most Americans are **moderates**, not seeing themselves on one end of the

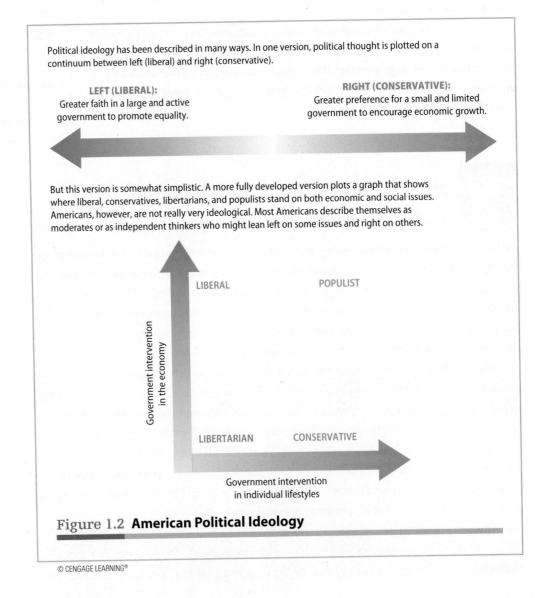

Political ideology has been described in many ways. In one version, political thought is plotted on a continuum between left (liberal) and right (conservative).

LEFT (LIBERAL):
Greater faith in a large and active government to promote equality.

RIGHT (CONSERVATIVE):
Greater preference for a small and limited government to encourage economic growth.

But this version is somewhat simplistic. A more fully developed version plots a graph that shows where liberal, conservatives, libertarians, and populists stand on both economic and social issues. Americans, however, are not really very ideological. Most Americans describe themselves as moderates or as independent thinkers who might lean left on some issues and right on others.

LIBERAL   POPULIST

Government intervention in the economy

LIBERTARIAN   CONSERVATIVE

Government intervention in individual lifestyles

Figure 1.2 **American Political Ideology**

scale or the other. A sizable number of Americans also describe themselves as **libertarians**, believing that government should not interfere in either economic matters or social matters. Others take a **populist** perspective, opposing concentrated wealth and adhering to traditional moral values.

Despite its many perspectives, American **political culture** as a whole generally favors **individualism** over communal approaches to property and poverty, especially in comparison to the industrialized democracies of Europe and elsewhere in the world (see Global Gateways: Social Welfare, Public Debt, and Free Enterprise). The United States spends less on government programs to help the less-well-off than many other countries, and it has historically refrained from assuming control of business enterprises, such as railroads and banks, except in times of crisis. The United States tends to favor **capitalism**, an economic system in which business enterprises and key industries are privately owned, as opposed to **socialism**, in which they are owned by government. Yet, to prevent the worst abuses of capitalism, which can arise as businesses pursue profit to the detriment of citizens, Congress has passed laws that regulate privately owned businesses and industries. For example, government monitors banks and financial markets, ensures airline safety, and protects workers from injury on the job.

In a republic, policy making should reflect the will of the people expressed through their elected representatives and interest groups. Madison envisioned that the people's representatives managing the policy-making process would be an elite—well-educated people of "merit." But if the people divide into different classes, as Madison also envisioned, there is a danger to democracy if the people's representatives are an elite who represent only their own interests and not civic-minded leaders who consider the common good. In the 1950s, the sociologist C. Wright Mills in fact wrote about a narrow **power elite** made up of leaders from corporations, government, and the military that controlled the gates and gateways to power. But in the 1960s, the political scientist Robert Dahl took issue with Mills and argued that policy making has a more **pluralist** basis, with authority held by different groups in different areas. In this view, coal companies, as stakeholders, have a large say in coal policy, and farmers, as stakeholders, have a large say in farm policy, rather than a single power elite controlling both policy areas.

Checkpoint

CAN YOU:

■ Explain the importance of political ideology

■ Distinguish between liberalism and conservatism

■ Identify the political values that most Americans share

1.4 Responsiveness and Equality: Does American Democracy Work?

> Evaluate American democracy in terms of responsiveness and equality

Does American democracy work? That is a question we will be asking in every chapter of this book, and we invite you to start working on an answer. As citizens, you have both a right and a responsibility to judge the government because it is *your* government.

globalgateways

Social Welfare, Public Debt, and Free Enterprise

Throughout this book, we look at American democracy from a global perspective, comparing aspects of the U.S. government and civic life to those similar aspects elsewhere in the world. We begin with three related items: the extent to which the United States and other countries provide social welfare benefits, the relative size of government debt, and the extent to which the economies of the United States and other countries are controlled by the government, shown as an economic freedom score.

The first column in the table shows that the United States allocates a smaller percentage of its budget to social welfare programs than do the industrial democracies of Western Europe. These democracies, however, have higher tax rates to pay for these benefits. France, for example, spends 13 percentage points more of its GDP (gross domestic product—the general measurement of the value of a nation's economy) on social welfare programs than does the United States. Democracies in Asia and Eastern Europe generally provide lower levels of benefits. The second column shows government debt as a percentage of its GDP. The debt ratio of the United States is higher than that of France or Germany but much lower than that of Japan or Greece. The third column presents the amount of control a nation exerts over its economy. Here the United States is fairly typical among the Western industrial democracies. In contrast, North Korea and Cuba, both nondemocratic, exercise much greater government control. There are no examples of nations that have exercised complete or nearly complete control over economic matters that have not simultaneously exercised complete or nearly complete control over political matters. Also note that nations with extensive social welfare systems can be both democratic and free market oriented. There is, in short, no easy formula for promoting both the economic health and social welfare of a country.

Table 1.2 Social Welfare Spending, Government Debt, and Economic Freedom: Fifteen Nations Compared

Nation	Social Welfare Spending (as a % of GDP), 2009	Debt (as a % of GDP), 2012	Economic Freedom Score, 2014 (lowest [0.0] to highest [100.0])
Cuba	NA	19	28.7
Denmark	30.2	45.4	76.1
Estonia	20	9.8	75.9
France	32.1	90.2	63.5
Germany	27.8	81	73.4
Greece	23.9	156.9	55.7
Ireland	23.6	117.4	76.2
Japan	22.192	211.7*	72.4
Mexico	8.2	42.85	66.8
New Zealand	21.2	35.9	81.2
North Korea	NA	NA	1
Portugal	25.6	55.6	63.5
Spain	26	86	67.2
Turkey	12.8	36	64.9
United States	19.2	101.6	75.5

* Data from 2011

NA = not available

Sources: Organization for Economic Co-Operation and Development, "Social Expenditure – Aggregated data, http://stats.oecd.org/Index.aspx?QueryId=4549; "Government Debt to GDP, List by Country," Trading Economics, 2012, http://www.tradingeconomics.com/government-debt-to-gdp-list-by-country; The Heritage Foundation, "2014 Index of Economic Freedom," http://www.heritage.org/index/ranking, all accessed January 17, 2014.

1. Why do countries that have free market economies also tend to be democratic?
2. On what dimension does the United States stand out in comparison to other countries?

To guide your thinking, we focus on two basic themes, **responsiveness** and **equality**. Is government responsive to the needs of its citizens? Do all citizens have an equal chance to make their voices heard? We ask you to keep these themes in mind as you learn about the U.S. political system. Throughout this textbook, we present the latest data that speak to these broad issues. It is important to remember that we are not offering our opinions about government; instead, we are putting forward the most important evidence and theories, from a variety of perspectives, over the past fifty or so years. It is up to you to consider them and form your own conclusions.

One way to begin to evaluate American democracy, and to appreciate it, is to look briefly at alternative models of government. In a **monarchy**, an **autocracy**, and an **oligarchy**, a single person or a small elite rules society. Such systems are by definition undemocratic. Rulers in these systems have little need to be responsive to the people. They hold most of the power and are not generally accountable to those they rule. They may try to satisfy the people with programs that meet basic needs for food and safety, but they do so to ensure submission. Rulers in such systems are overthrown when dissatisfaction rises to a level at which citizens are willing to risk their lives in open revolt, as they did in the Ukraine in 2014, or when the army or police conspire to replace one ruler with another.

In contrast, a democracy asks its citizens to be actively engaged in their own governance, for the benefit of all. As the preamble to the U.S. Constitution states, the people create government (agree to a social contract) to "establish Justice, insure domestic Tranquility, provide for the common defence, promote the general Welfare, and secure the Blessings of Liberty to ourselves and our Posterity." The American system of government fundamentally provides protection from foreign enemies and from internal disorder; it also strives to meet the common needs of all citizens.

To promote the general welfare, the government develops public policy, as we have seen. Through incentives, it can alter the actions of individuals that lead collectively to bad outcomes.

The government often has a stake in pursuing what economists call **public goods**: goods from which everyone benefits. The core idea is that no one can be excluded. We all get the benefits of clean air, even if we have been driving cars and not taking buses. The fact that people cannot, by definition, be denied access to public goods creates disincentives for people to contribute to their provision. Government can require people to contribute to public goods through taxation. This is a primary justification for government. **Private goods**, by contrast, can be extended to some individuals and denied to others. When a government awards a contract to build a new library, the firm that wins the contract gets private goods (that is, money) from the government. The firms that lost the bid are denied that chance.

Who determines what goods, whether private or public, the government should provide, at what levels, and how to pay for them? These are core public policy problems. There are competing interests at every point in determining who gets what, when, and how. Politics

EMMANUEL DUNAND/GETTY IMAGES

Citizens gathering to hear presidential candidate Rick Santorum in a classic town hall format. The candidate and these citizens get a chance to express their opinions.

is the process by which the people determine how government will respond. And it is in evaluating the basic fairness of government's response, and the basic equality of the people's general welfare that is thus secured, that we see whether American democracy is working.

Representative democracy succeeds when there is constant interaction between the people and the government. Government must be responsive to the needs and opinions of the people, and the public must find ways to hold government accountable.

For a government to respond fairly to citizens, all citizens must have an equal opportunity to participate in it. Each citizen must have a chance to have his or her voice heard, either by voting or by participating in the political process and public life. These ideas form the basis of **political equality**. If citizens are not treated equally, with the same degree of fairness, then the foundation of democratic government is weakened. Simply put, democracy requires political equality, and political equality requires democracy. One way to evaluate American democracy is to evaluate the degree to which political equality has been achieved.

There are other aspects of equality. **Equality of opportunity** is one aspect—the expectation that citizens will be treated equally before the law and have an equal opportunity to participate in government. Does equality of opportunity also mean that citizens have an equal opportunity to participate in the economy (to get a job, to get rich) and in social life (to join a club, to eat at a restaurant)? And what about **equality of outcome**, the expectation that incomes will level out or that standards of living will be roughly the same for all citizens? What can, or should, government do to ensure equality of opportunity, or equality of outcome? These questions are hotly contested (see Supreme Court Cases: *Plyler v. Doe*), especially efforts to forge equality of outcome. We return to these issues in the final section of this introductory chapter.

In President Obama's first inaugural address, he said, "I stand here today humbled by the task before us, grateful for the trust you have bestowed, mindful of the sacrifices borne by our ancestors."[20] Those ancestors include the millions of Americans who over more than two centuries have worked to make American democracy more responsive and to make America more equal. We challenge you to join them. This textbook will give you the information you need to understand the way American government works and to recognize the gates and the gateways. We also invite you to think critically about American democracy, to engage in a class-wide and nationwide conversation about how well it is working, to offer ideas for making it work better, to influence the decision makers who make public policy, and even to become one of them.

Checkpoint

CAN YOU:

- Identify the functions of government as defined by the Preamble
- Identify the roles individuals play in a democracy
- Explain the differences between equality of opportunity and equality of outcome

1.5 The Demands of Democratic Government

> List the responsibilities of individuals in a democracy

American democracy is not a spectator sport. It does not mean choosing sides and rooting for your team from the sidelines or from the comfort of your living room. It requires more than being a fan; you need to get into the game. But politics is more than a game. It shapes your life on a day-to-day basis. As a result, you have both rights and responsibilities. While the specific reasons to be involved in public life may vary, the need to participate does not.

2

The Constitution

Gus Garcia, high school valedictorian and star of the debate team at the University of Texas at Austin, grew up observing the social and legal discrimination against Latinos in Texas. It was the 1940s. Like Thurgood Marshall, the famed civil rights attorney and the first African American on the Supreme Court, Garcia wanted to fight for the rights of his people. Garcia followed his undergraduate years at the University of Texas with law school there. After serving in the Judge Advocate General Corps in the military, Garcia returned to Texas where he worked as legal counsel for the League of United Latin American Citizens (LULAC) and helped create the American GI Forum, a veterans group for Latinos, in 1948.

He also ran for the Board of Education in San Antonio, Texas, in 1948, joining forces with a local African American businessman. Their white opponents took out an ad in the local paper on the day before the election declaring, "It is your duty to keep racial and sectional strife out of your schools by electing experienced people who can work together in harmony.... Among the other candidates is a Negro undertaker [and] an active member of LULAC"[1] (i.e., Garcia). Garcia won the election, becoming the first Latino to serve on the San Antonio School Board.

In 1948, Garcia won a federal district (trial) court case on behalf of Minerva Delgado and others seeking to deny the state of Texas the authority to segregate Latino public school students as a violation of the Fourteenth Amendment, which guarantees equal protection of the law.[2] This decision, without recognition from higher courts, was largely ignored within the state of Texas. Thurgood Marshall, though, requested access to the *Delgado* case file from the attorneys in that case as part of his battle against racial

discrimination.[3] Yet Garcia continued the struggle for Latino civil rights.

In 1952 Garcia began work on the case of *Hernandez v. Texas*,[4] which would arguably become the most important constitutional decision by the Supreme Court regarding the Latino community in the United States.

The *Hernandez* case involved the murder conviction of Pedro Hernandez by an all-white jury in Texas. It was the first time that the Supreme Court dealt with a case involving issues related to Latinos as well as the first time a Latino attorney had argued before the Supreme Court. Texas argued that the equal protection clause only applied to African Americans, not other ethnic groups. Garcia, alternatively, argued that within

Need to Know

2.1 Assess what drove the colonists to seek independence

2.2 Identify the major compromises at the Constitutional Convention

2.3 Explain how the structure of the Constitution protects liberty

2.4 Analyze why the Antifederalists opposed the Constitution

2.5 Illustrate how the Constitution has stayed responsive to changing needs

▶ **WATCH & LEARN** MindTap‍ **for American Government**
Watch a brief "What Do You Know?" video summarizing The Constitution.

Texas, Mexican Americans were treated as "a class apart" from the white community and should receive the protections of the equal protection clause of the Fourteenth Amendment. The fact that Latinos still had separate schools and bathrooms, and did not sit on juries, convinced a unanimous Supreme Court that "the constitutional guarantee of equal protection of the laws is not directed solely against discrimination between whites and Negroes."[5] The justices were convinced that under the social and legal system in Texas, Mexican Americans were treated as "a separate class"[6] and as such deserved full constitutional protection from the equal protection clause, and that Texas denied Hernandez that protection by excluding Latinos from serving on juries. The Court, which had already heard, but not yet decided, the *Brown v. Board of Education* case, was interested enough in Garcia's argument that it gave him unscheduled extra time during oral argument, an extremely rare gesture. The Supreme Court reversed the conviction of Hernandez. That reversal allowed Texas to retry Hernandez by a jury that did not exclude Latinos. Hernandez was found guilty again.

Nevertheless, Gus Garcia's legal victory led to a fundamental change in how the U.S. Constitution is interpreted with regard to discrimination against Latinos, granting them legal security under the equal protection clause of the Fourteenth Amendment. Garcia used the constitutional system of the United States to create new rights for the Latino community. Moreover, just two weeks after the *Hernandez* decision, the Supreme Court struck down segregated schools in *Brown v. Board of Education*, a case in which Garcia had been a supporter.

In this chapter, we examine the governing documents prior to the Constitution, particularly the Articles of Confederation and its deficiencies. We also track the debates at the Constitutional Convention and afterward, as the people of the United States decided whether to ratify the new Constitution. They did ratify it, but almost immediately they amended it. After we examine the structure and philosophy behind the new Constitution, we consider its responsiveness, through both amendment and less formal procedures, to changing times.

The information from this vignette comes from the Salinas article cited in the first footnote as well as A Class Apart: A Mexican American Civil Rights Story, PBS Home Video, 2009, from which we pulled the opening quote.

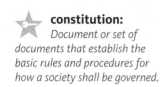
 ## 2.1 Before the Constitution

❯ Assess what drove the colonists to seek independence

From the beginning, Great Britain accorded the American colonists, as British subjects, a certain amount of self-rule. When the colonists perceived that Parliament and the king were blocking their participation in government, they moved toward independence from Britain. They established a new national government under documents that included state constitutions and a national Articles of Confederation. In this section, we trace that process.

The British Constitution

constitution:
Document or set of documents that establish the basic rules and procedures for how a society shall be governed.

A **constitution** is the fundamental law undergirding the structure of government. In a modern democracy, a constitution sets forth the basic rules and procedures for how the people shall be governed, including the powers and structure of the government, as well as the rights retained by the people.

Unlike many constitutions today, the British constitution is not a single document but rather a series of documents. Beginning with the Magna Carta in 1215, the British constitution defined the rights of the people and Parliament and limited the powers of the king. Following the so-called Glorious Revolution of 1688–89, Parliament asserted the power to suspend the law, to levy taxes, and to maintain a standing army. By the eighteenth century, British subjects believed that the British constitution guaranteed them certain rights, including the right not to be taxed without their consent and the right to be tried by a jury of their peers.

Toward Independence

The American colonists believed they had all the rights of British subjects. Thus they objected when, following the French and Indian War (1754–63), Great Britain tried to recoup some of the costs of defending the colonies by imposing regulations and taxes on them. The Sugar Act of 1764 set forth a long list of items that could be exported only to Great Britain, limiting competition for the colonists' goods. The Stamp Act of 1765 established a tax on virtually all forms of paper used by the colonists. Although Britain had previously levied import and export taxes on the colonies, this was the first direct tax by Britain on the colonists on products made and sold in America.

The colonists reacted angrily, forming trade associations to boycott, or refuse to buy, British goods. They also published pamphlets denouncing the loss of liberty. Led by Patrick Henry, they challenged not just the taxes themselves, but Parliament's authority to pass such measures. "Give me liberty," proclaimed Henry before the Virginia House of Burgesses, "or give me death." Soon enough, riots broke out against Stamp Act collectors, making enforcement impossible.

Britain repealed the Stamp Act in 1766 but replaced it with the Townshend Acts, which imposed new taxes on imports. The colonists mobilized against these new import taxes. Led by Samuel Adams, the Massachusetts legislature issued a letter declaring the Townshend Acts unconstitutional because they violated the principle of "no taxation without representation." The colonists thus began to insist that they had the right to participate in the political decisions that affected them.

The British justified their lack of representation by claiming that all English citizens were represented by all members of Parliament, who purportedly acted in the common good. As political thinker and politician Edmund Burke wrote, "Parliament is a *deliberative* assembly of *one* nation, with *one* interest, that of the whole."[7] The colonists, however, rejected this view.

→ KEY QUESTIONS:
What rights do you think you have as an American? When did you last think about those rights?

→ KEY QUESTIONS:
How does the American view of representation differ from the British view?

THE STAMP ACT RIOTS AT BOSTON.

NORTH WIND PICTURE ARCHIVES/ALAMY

American Colonists protest the British Stamp Act.

Table 2.1 Events Leading to the Revolution

Year	Event	Description
1764	Sugar Act	Required colonists to export certain items only to Britain
1765	Stamp Act	Imposed taxes on almost all paper products; boycotts and riots followed
1766	Townshend Act	Imposed new taxes on imports; led to rallying cry "no taxation without representation"
1770	Boston Massacre	Five colonists killed by British soldiers; led Parliament to repeal all Townshend Act taxes except for tea tax
1773	Boston Tea Party	Colonists dump taxed tea into Boston Harbor
1774	Coercive Act	Restricted political freedoms in Massachusetts
1774	Quartering Act	Required colonists to house British soldiers in their homes
1774	1st Continental Congress	Rejected Reconciliation with Britain and sent grievances to King George III
1775	2nd Continental Congress	Acted as the national government of states, 1775–1781; approved Declaration of Independence and appointed George Washington as commander of the army

© CENGAGE LEARNING®

→ KEY QUESTIONS:
What does today's Tea Party have in common with the Boston Tea Party?

Aggrieved by taxation without representation, the colonists continued to resist the Townshend Acts through boycotts of taxed goods. Britain responded by dissolving the Massachusetts legislature and seizing a ship belonging to John Hancock, one of the leaders of the resistance. Britain also sent troops to quell the resistance, but the presence of soldiers during peacetime aggravated tensions. British soldiers fired on a threatening crowd in 1770, killing five colonists and wounding six others in what became known as the Boston Massacre. With boycotts of British goods costing Britain far more than the taxes raised, Parliament rescinded all of the Townshend Act taxes except the one on tea. In 1773 Parliament granted the East India Company the exclusive right to sell tea to the colonies, and the company then granted local monopolies in the colonies. Angered by both the tax and the monopoly, colonists once again took action. Disguised as Indians, they dumped a shipload of tea in Boston Harbor.

In 1774 Britain responded to the Boston Tea Party with the Coercive Acts, which, among other things, gave the royal governor the right to select the upper house of the Massachusetts legislature. The Coercive Acts also denied Massachusetts the right to try British officials charged with capital offenses. Further legislation, the Quartering Act, required colonists to house British soldiers in their private homes, even during times of peace.[8] These acts convinced many colonists that their liberty was at stake and that rebellion and independence were the only alternatives to British tyranny.

In an attempt to present a more united front about colonial grievances, Benjamin Franklin proposed a congress, or assembly of representatives. The First Continental Congress, with delegates chosen by the colonial legislatures, met in Philadelphia in 1774. It rejected a reconciliation plan with England and instead sent King George III a list of grievances. It also adopted a very successful compact among the colonies not to import any English goods. Finally, it agreed to meet again as the Second Continental Congress in May 1775. This Second Continental Congress acted as the common government of the states between 1775 and 1781.

In April 1775, following skirmishes with British troops in Lexington and Concord, outside of Boston, the Second Continental Congress named George Washington commander of a new Continental Army. In 1776, with hostilities under way, Thomas Paine penned his influential pamphlet *Common Sense*, which called for independence from Britain. "There is something very absurd, in supposing a continent to be perpetually governed by an island," he argued.[9] *Common Sense* was the most widely distributed pamphlet of its time, and it helped convince many Americans that independence was the only way they could secure their right to self-government.

The Declaration of Independence

In June 1776, the Continental Congress debated an independence resolution but postponed a vote until July. Meanwhile, it instructed Thomas Jefferson and others to draft a **Declaration of Independence**. Congress approved the Declaration of Independence on July 4. Jefferson's Declaration relied in part on the writings of John Locke in asserting that people had certain natural (or unalienable) rights that government could not take away, including the right to life and liberty (see Chapter 1, Gateways to American Democracy). For Locke's reference to property, Jefferson substituted "the pursuit of happiness."

The Declaration listed grievances against King George III, including suspending popularly elected colonial legislatures, imposing taxes without representation, and conducting trials without juries. It then declared the united colonies to be thirteen "free and independent states." (The full text of the Declaration of Independence is in the Appendix.)

Even before the Declaration, the Continental Congress advised the colonies to adopt new constitutions "under the authority of the people." Reacting against the limitation on rights imposed by the British monarch and by royal governors in the colonies, these new state constitutions severely limited executive power but set few limits on legislative authority. At the same time, Americans made little effort to establish a national political authority, as most Americans considered themselves primarily citizens of the states in which they lived. Nevertheless, the Continental Congress needed legal authority for its actions, and, in 1777, its members proposed a governing document called the **Articles of Confederation**.

The Articles of Confederation

The Articles required unanimous consent of the states for adoption, which did not occur until 1781, just a few months before American victory in the Revolutionary War. They formally established "the United States of America," in contrast to the Declaration, which was a pronouncement of "Thirteen United States of America." According to the Declaration, each of the thirteen independent states had the authority to do all "acts and things which independent states may of right do," such as waging war, establishing alliances, and concluding peace. These were thirteen independent states united in a war of independence. With the Articles, the states became one nation with centralized control over making war and foreign affairs. But due to the belief that Great Britain had violated

→ KEY QUESTIONS:
Was the American Revolution really about taxation, or was it about something else?

Declaration of Independence: *The 1776 document declaring American independence from Great Britain and calling for equality, human rights, and citizen participation.*

Articles of Confederation: *Initial governing authority of the United States, 1781–88.*

fundamental liberties, the Articles emphasized freedom from national authority at the expense of order. Thus the states retained all powers not expressly granted to Congress under the Articles.

Moreover, those expressly granted powers were extremely limited. Congress had full authority over foreign, military, and Indian affairs. It could decide boundary and other disputes between the states, coin money, and establish post offices. But Congress did not have the authority to regulate commerce or, indeed, any authority to operate directly over citizens of the United States. For example, Congress could not tax citizens or products (such as imports) directly; it could only request (but not demand) revenues from the states.

In addition to limiting powers, the Articles made governing difficult. Each state had one vote in Congress, with the consent of nine of the thirteen required for most important matters, including borrowing and spending money. Amending the Articles required the unanimous consent of the states. In 1781 tiny Rhode Island, blocking an amendment that would have set a 5 percent tax on imports, denied the whole nation desperately needed revenue. Moreover, the Articles established no judicial branch, with the minor exception that Congress could establish judicial panels on an ad hoc basis to hear appeals involving disputes between states and to hear cases involving crimes on the high seas. There was no separate executive branch, but Congress had the authority to establish an executive committee along with a rotating president who would manage the general affairs of the United States when Congress was not in session.[10]

→ KEY QUESTIONS:
Why didn't the Articles of Confederation work as a governing document?

These deficiencies led to predictable problems. With insufficient funds, the nation's debts went unpaid, hampering its credit. Even obligations to pay salaries owed to the Revolutionary War troops went unfulfilled. Without a centralized authority to regulate commerce, states taxed imports from other states, stunting economic growth. Lack of military power allowed Spain to block commercial access to the Mississippi River. Barbary pirates off the shores of Tripoli captured American ships and held their crews for ransom.

While the government of the United States suffered from too little authority, James Madison, Thomas Jefferson, and others came to believe that the governments of the states possessed too much authority. Popularly elected legislatures with virtually no checks on their authority passed laws rescinding private debts and creating trade barriers against other states. They also began taking over both judicial and executive functions.

With the United States in desperate financial straits, James Madison proposed a convention of states to consider granting the national government the power to tax and to regulate trade. Only five states showed up at this 1786 Annapolis Convention, preventing it from accomplishing much.

As the Annapolis Convention took place, word spread of a revolt in western Massachusetts that made the weakness of the national government all too clear.

Daniel Shays led a protest movement of debt-ridden farmers facing foreclosures on their homes and farms. Demanding lower taxes and the issuance of paper money, they engaged in mob violence to force the Massachusetts courts to close.

Revolutionary War hero Daniel Shays and several thousand distressed farmers forced courts to close and threatened federal arsenals. Not until February 1787 did Massachusetts put down Shays's Rebellion. The revolt helped convince the states that, on top of the Articles' other problems, the document provided for too much freedom and not enough order. The Annapolis Convention thus issued an invitation to all thirteen states to meet in Philadelphia in May 1787 to consider revising the Articles of Confederation. This time only Rhode Island declined the invitation.

2.2 The Constitutional Convention

> Identify the major compromises at the Constitutional Convention

The delegates who met in Philadelphia were charged with amending the Articles of Confederation so that the national government could work more effectively. Almost immediately, however, they moved beyond that charge and began debating a brand new constitution. To complete that newly proposed constitution, the delegates needed to reach compromises between large and small states over representation, between northern and southern states over issues related to slavery, and between those who favored a strong national government and those who favored strong state governments. The Convention's rules granted each state one vote, regardless of the size of the state or the number of delegates it sent. The document they created, which was then sent to the states for ratification, is, with subsequent amendments, the same Constitution we live by today. (The full text of the Constitution of the United States is in the Appendix.)

Large versus Small States

Upon the opening of the Philadelphia Convention in May 1787, Edmund Randolph of Virginia presented the delegates with James Madison's radical proposal for a new government. Known as the Virginia Plan, Madison's proposal included a strong central government that could operate directly on the citizens of the United States without the states acting as intermediaries. The legislative branch would consist of two chambers: a lower chamber elected by the people and an upper chamber elected by the lower chamber. Each chamber would have representation proportional to the populations of the states: the larger the population, the more representatives a state would have. The legislature would have general authority to pass laws that would "promote the harmony" of the United States and could veto laws passed by the states. The Virginia Plan proposed a national executive and a national judiciary, both chosen by the legislature. A council of revision, composed of the executive and judicial members, would have final approval over all legislative acts.

Madison's proposals astonished many of the delegates from the smaller states and some from the larger states as well. To counter the Virginia Plan, on June 15 William Patterson of New Jersey presented the Convention with the New Jersey Plan, which strengthened the

Articles by providing Congress with the authority to regulate commerce and to directly tax imports and paper items. It also proposed a national executive chosen by the legislature and a national judiciary chosen by the executive.[11] Each state would retain equal representation in Congress.

The question of proportional or equal representation generated enormous controversy. Madison insisted that proportional representation for both chambers was the only fair system, and the small states insisted that they would walk out if they lost their equal vote. Roger Sherman of Connecticut proposed what became known as the **Connecticut Compromise**. The makeup of the lower chamber, the House of Representatives, would be proportional to population, but the upper chamber, the Senate, would represent each state equally.

Nation versus State

While the question of representation threatened the Convention, there was substantial agreement over the role of the national government. The delegates rejected the New Jersey Plan, which would have continued government under the Articles.

The delegates also did not approve the Virginia Plan in full, but the plan substantially influenced the proposed Constitution. Under the new Constitution, the government had the authority to operate directly on the citizens of the United States. Congress was not granted general legislative power, but rather **enumerated powers**, that is, a list of powers it could employ. Among its enumerated powers were the authority to tax to provide for the general welfare; to regulate commerce among the states and with foreign nations; to borrow money; to declare war, raise armies, and maintain a navy; and to make all laws "necessary and proper for carrying into Execution the foregoing Powers." The tax and commerce powers were among those missing from the Articles.

Congress did not receive the authority to veto state laws, but the Constitution declared that national law would be supreme over state law, bound state judges to that decision, and created a national judiciary that would help ensure such rulings. Moreover, the Convention set explicit limits on state authority, prohibiting the states from carrying on foreign relations, coining money, and infringing on certain rights. Finally, the Convention approved a national executive (that is, the president) who could serve as a unifying force throughout the land. Table 2.2 presents the components of the Virginia Plan, the New Jersey Plan, and the proposed Constitution.

North versus South

Resolving the question of nation versus state proved less difficult than resolving the question of representation. More difficult still were questions related to slavery. Although slavery existed in every state except Massachusetts, the overwhelming majority of slaves, nearly 95 percent, were in the southern states, from Maryland to Georgia.[12] As Madison put it, "The States were divided into different interests not by their difference of size, but principally from their having or not having slaves."[13] Not all northern delegates at the Convention opposed slavery, but those who were abolitionists wanted an immediate ban on importing slaves from Africa, prohibitions against the expansion of slavery into the western territories, and the adoption of a plan for the gradual freeing of

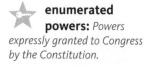

Connecticut Compromise: *Compromise on legislative representation whereby the lower chamber is based on population, and the upper chamber provides equal representation to the states.*

enumerated powers: *Powers expressly granted to Congress by the Constitution.*

Table 2.2 The Virginia and New Jersey Plans Compared to the Constitution

Issue	Virginia Plan	New Jersey Plan	Constitution
Operation	Directly on people	Through the states	Directly on people
Legislative structure	Bicameral and proportional	Unicameral and equal	Bicameral, with lower chamber proportional and upper chamber equal
Legislative authority	General: power to promote the harmony of the United States	Strict enumerated powers of the Articles of Confederation, plus power to regulate commerce and limited power to tax	Broad enumerated powers
Check on legislative authority	Council of revision	None	Presidential veto, with possibility of a two-thirds override
Executive	Unitary national executive chosen by legislature	Plural national executive chosen by legislature	Unitary national executive chosen by Electoral College
Judiciary	National judiciary chosen by legislature	National judiciary chosen by executive	National judiciary chosen by president with advice and consent of Senate

© CENGAGE LEARNING®

slaves. Delegates from Georgia and South Carolina, whose states would never accept the Constitution on these terms, wanted guaranteed protections for slavery and the slave trade and no restrictions on slavery in the territories. To secure a Constitution, compromises were necessary.

Many supporters of slavery recognized the horrors of the foreign slave trade, and by 1779 all states except North Carolina, South Carolina, and Georgia had banned it. Leaving the authority to regulate the foreign slave trade to Congress would inevitably have resulted in its being banned everywhere and probably would have kept those three states from joining the union. Thus, a slave trade compromise prohibited Congress from stopping the slave trade until 1808.

A second compromise involved how slaves should be counted when calculating population for purposes of representation. Madison's Virginia Plan based representation on the number of free inhabitants of each state, whereas the southernmost slave states wanted slaves to be fully counted for purposes of representation. Delegates from the northern states, on the other hand, argued that slave states, which by definition denied the humanity of slaves, should not benefit by receiving extra representation based on the number of slaves that they had. Under the Articles, taxes requested of the states were based on the population of each state, with five slaves counting as three people. The Convention agreed to use this **three-fifths** formula not just for representation but also for whatever direct or population taxes the national government might choose to levy. This compromise had a significant impact on representation in the House of Representatives.[14]

A third compromise involved slavery in the western territories, and it came not from the Convention but from the government under the Articles, which passed the Northwest

> → KEY QUESTIONS:
> Were the delegates right or wrong to compromise on slavery?

⭐ **three-fifths compromise:**
Compromise over slavery at the Constitutional Convention that granted states extra representation in the House of Representatives based on their number of slaves at the ratio of three-fifths.

Ordinance in July 1787. This ordinance, which established the means for governing the western lands north of the Ohio River (eventually the states of Ohio, Indiana, Illinois, Michigan, and Wisconsin, and parts of Minnesota), prohibited slavery in this territory but also provided that fugitive slaves who escaped to the territory would be returned to their owners. The Constitution incorporated these provisions.

With the precedent of prohibiting slavery in the Northwest Territory established in the Northwest Ordinance, the Convention gave Congress the right to regulate the territories of the United States without mentioning whether slavery could be allowed or prohibited.

Gates against Popular Influence

Compared to the British constitutional system, the 1787 Constitution provided direct and indirect gateways for popular involvement (see Figure 2.1). Nevertheless, the Framers did not trust the people to have complete control over choosing the government. In two important ways—the election of the president and the election of the Senate—the Constitution limited popular control.

Originally, state legislatures selected U.S. senators. The Framers feared that a Congress elected directly by the people would be too responsive to the popular will. The indirect election of senators was thus intended to serve as a check on the popular will. In 1913, the Seventeenth Amendment granted the people the right to elect senators directly.

Another gate against the people's participation was the election of the president through the **Electoral College**. Rather than directly electing the president through a popular vote, the Constitution established an Electoral College, in which electors actually choose the president. Each state receives a number of electors equal to its number of representatives plus senators, and each state legislature chooses the manner for selecting the electors from its state—by popular vote, legislative selection, or some other mechanism. State legislatures used to select electors. Today, each state legislature allows the people of the state to choose that state's electors, but in the early days of the **republic**, many state legislatures kept that right for themselves. Yet, the Electoral College remains in effect as a gate against direct popular control.

The Ratification Process

With agreements reached on representation in Congress, federal or national power, and slavery, the delegates made a few final decisions. First, despite the urging of George Mason of Virginia, the delegates chose not to include a **Bill of Rights**—a listing of rights retained by the

→ KEY QUESTIONS:
What compromises made the Constitution possible? Is compromise, as a political strategy, good or bad for democracy? Why is it out of favor today?

→ KEY QUESTIONS:
Why did the delegates set up gates against citizen participation? Whose participation did they not consider at all?

Electoral College: *The presidential electors, selected to represent the votes of their respective states, who meet every four years to cast the electoral votes for president and vice president.*

republic: *Form of government in which power derives from citizens, but public officials make policy and govern according to existing law.*

→ KEY QUESTIONS:
Did the delegates trust the people?

Bill of Rights: *First ten amendments to the Constitution, which provide basic political rights.*

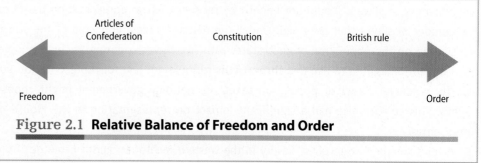

Figure 2.1 Relative Balance of Freedom and Order

Articles of Confederation — Constitution — British rule

Freedom ←——————————————————→ Order

© CENGAGE LEARNING®

people that Congress did not have the authority to take away, such as freedom of speech and freedom of religion. Because Congress had enumerated powers only, and because the authority to regulate speech, religion, and other freedoms was not among the powers granted to Congress, delegates believed there was no need to prohibit Congress from abridging such rights.

Second, the delegates needed a method for ratifying, or granting final approval of, the Constitution. Fortunately, the states had already established a precedent for ratifying constitutions in state conventions, rather than through state legislatures.

Similarly, the delegates at the Constitutional Convention chose to send the proposed Constitution to the states for approval via special ratifying conventions to be chosen by the people. The Constitution would take effect among those states approving it when nine of the thirteen states ratified it. The Articles had required that all state legislatures approve a proposed amendment for it to pass, but the Constitutional Convention sought approval from a higher authority: the people of the United States. This process for ratification followed the statement in the Declaration of Independence that "it is the right of the people…to institute new government." Hence, the Constitution's preamble establishes the Constitution in the name of "We the People of the United States."

In September 1787, with these final steps taken, delegates to the Constitutional Convention believed they had produced a constitution that remedied the deficiencies of the Articles (see Table 2.3), and they voted on the final document. Some of the delegates had left by September, but thirty-nine signed the document, with only three refusing to do so. Crucially, given Convention rules, a majority of the delegates from each of the states voted yes.

→ KEY QUESTIONS:
Do the people today retain the right to institute new government?

Checkpoint

CAN YOU:

- Characterize the delegates to the Constitutional Convention
- Explain how the interests of large and small states differed
- State why the Convention rejected the Virginia Plan
- Explain how the interests of the northern states and the southern states differed
- Describe how the 1787 Constitution protected against too much popular influence
- Recall who would ratify the new constitution

Table 2.3 Deficiencies of the Articles of Confederation and Constitutional Remedies

Deficiency in the Articles of Confederation	Remedy in the Constitution
Legislative branch could not regulate commerce	Congress can regulate commerce "among the states"
Legislative branch could only request taxes from states	Congress can directly raise taxes from individuals
Approval of nine of thirteen states needed for passage of major legislation	Approval of a majority of both legislative chambers needed for passage of all legislation; a two-thirds majority needed to override presidential vetoes
No permanent executive branch	A "President of the United States"
No permanent judicial branch	A Supreme Court plus other inferior courts that Congress can establish
Unanimity for constitutional amendments	Approval of two-thirds of each chamber plus three-fourths of the states
Few limits on state authority, mostly over foreign affairs	States limited in foreign affairs, plus could not suppress certain rights through bills of attainder, *ex post facto* laws, and so on

© CENGAGE LEARNING®

2.3 Government under the Constitution

> › Explain how the structure of the Constitution protects liberty

The final document sent to the states for ratification laid out a structure of democratic government and proposed mechanisms whereby the Constitution could be amended. It also reflected the Framers' attempt to establish a government powerful enough to ensure public order yet containing enough gateways to guarantee individual liberty.

The Structure of Government

The Constitution established three branches of government: the legislative, the executive, and the judicial.

The Legislative Branch. The legislative branch, as explained in Chapter 1, makes the laws. The Constitution established a bicameral Congress, consisting of two chambers. The lower chamber, the House of Representatives, is proportioned by population (until the Thirteenth Amendment, the slave population was added to the free population according to the three-fifths formula described previously). Members of the House are elected for two-year terms directly by the people, with voting eligibility determined by each state. Representatives have to be at least 25 years old, residents of the state they serve, and U.S. citizens for at least the previous seven years.

The upper chamber, the Senate, consists of two senators from each state, regardless of size. Designed to serve as a check on the popular will, which would be expressed in the House of Representatives, state legislatures chose senators until 1913 when the Seventeenth Amendment granted the people of each state the exclusive right to do so.[15] A six-year term also serves to limit responsiveness to popular whims, and an age minimum of 30 presumably provides more mature and levelheaded thinking. Senators also have to be residents of the state in which they serve and U.S. citizens for nine years or more.

Bills to levy taxes have to originate in the House, but other bills may originate in either chamber. To become law, a bill has to pass each chamber in identical form and is then presented to the president for his signature. If the president signs the bill, it becomes law, but if he disapproves, he can **veto** the bill. Congress can then override the veto by a two-thirds majority in each chamber.

Article I, Section 8, of the Constitution limits Congress's authority to an eighteen-paragraph list, or enumeration, of certain powers. The first paragraph grants Congress the authority "to Collect Taxes…to pay the Debts and provide for the common Defence and general Welfare of the United States." Paragraphs 2 through 17 grant additional powers such as borrowing and coining money, regulating commerce, and raising an army. Then paragraph 18 grants Congress the authority to pass all laws "necessary and proper for carrying into Execution the foregoing Powers."

Additionally, the Constitution gives the House the authority to impeach—to bring charges against—the president and other federal officials. The Senate has the sole authority to try cases of impeachment, with a two-thirds vote required for removal from

CONNECT WITH YOUR CLASSMATES
MindTap for American Government

Access The Constitution Forum: Discussion—The Constitution and Law Making.

veto: *Authority of the president to block legislation passed by Congress. Congress can override a veto by a two-thirds majority in each chamber.*

office. The Senate also has the sole authority to ratify treaties, which also require a two-thirds vote, and to confirm executive and judicial branch appointments by majority vote.

The Executive Branch.   The executive branch of government consists of a unitary president, chosen for a four-year term by an Electoral College. The Electoral College itself is chosen in a manner set by the legislature of each state. Eventually, every state gave the people the power to vote for its electors (as discussed earlier).

A president must be at least 35 years of age, a resident of the United States for the previous fourteen years, and either a natural-born citizen of the United States or a citizen of the United States at the time of the adoption of the Constitution.

Because the Framers believed that the legislative branch would naturally be stronger than the executive branch, they did not feel the need to enumerate the executive powers as they did the legislative powers. Recall that Congress does not have a general legislative authority, but only those legislative powers granted under the Constitution. In contrast, the Constitution provides the president with a general grant of "the executive Power" and certain specific powers, including the right to veto legislation and grant pardons. The president also is commander in chief of the armed forces. With the advice and consent of the Senate, the president makes treaties and appoints ambassadors, judges, and other public officials. The president leads the executive branch of government, being charged with taking care that the laws are faithfully executed.

The Judicial Branch.   The Constitution vests the judicial authority of the United States in one Supreme Court and other inferior courts that Congress might choose to establish. The president appoints judges with the advice and consent of the Senate. They serve "during good Behaviour," which, short of impeachment, means a life term.

→ KEY QUESTIONS:
Why did the delegates establish three branches of government?

The Constitution extends the authority of the federal courts to hear cases involving certain classes of parties to a suit—cases involving the United States, ambassadors, and other public ministers; suits between two or more states or citizens from different states—and certain classes of cases, most notably cases arising under the Constitution, laws, and treaties of the United States. In the historic case *Marbury v. Madison* (1803), the Supreme Court took this authority to hear cases arising under the Constitution of the United States to establish the power of **judicial review**, the authority of the Court to strike down any law passed by Congress when the Court believes the law violates the Constitution (see Supreme Court Cases: *Marbury v. Madison*).[16]

judicial review: *Authority of courts to declare laws passed by Congress and acts of the executive branch to be unconstitutional.*

The Amendment Process

The Constitution provides two paths for changing the Constitution via **amendment**. The first path requires a two-thirds vote in each chamber of Congress, followed by the approval of three-fourths of the states. That statewide approval can be attained either through the state legislatures or through state ratifying conventions, as directed by Congress. The second path allows two-thirds of the states to request a national constitutional convention that could propose amendments that would go into effect when approved by three-fourths of the states (see Figure 2.2). Again, this approval could be obtained through state legislatures or through state ratifying conventions. Additionally, the Constitution prohibits amendments that would

amendment: *Formal process of changing the Constitution.*

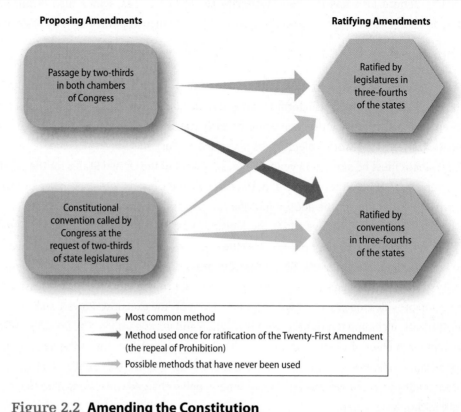

Proposing Amendments

Passage by two-thirds in both chambers of Congress

Constitutional convention called by Congress at the request of two-thirds of state legislatures

Ratifying Amendments

Ratified by legislatures in three-fourths of the states

Ratified by conventions in three-fourths of the states

→ Most common method

→ Method used once for ratification of the Twenty-First Amendment (the repeal of Prohibition)

→ Possible methods that have never been used

Figure 2.2 Amending the Constitution

An amendment can be proposed by two-thirds of each chamber of Congress or by a constitutional convention called by two-thirds of state legislatures. Either way, ratification requires three-quarters of the states to approve the amendment. Why do you think the methods indicated by the blue arrows have never been used?

deny any state an equal vote in the Senate or any amendment that would have allowed a banning of the foreign slave trade before 1808. Both paths for amending the Constitution are complex and difficult, which has kept the Constitution from being modified over popular but short-lived issues.

The Partition of Power

In attempting to explain and justify the constitutional structure, James Madison wrote of "the necessary partition of power among the several departments as laid down in the constitution" (see *Federalist* 51 in the Appendix). He acknowledged that elections serve as the primary means of ensuring that the government is responsive to the wishes of the people. If it is not, the people can vote for a new government. Under the Constitution, the people have direct authority to elect the House of Representatives. But to prevent the majority from imposing oppressive laws on the minority, the rest of the government was chosen indirectly, as we have seen.

Lest the people not be sufficient to keep government under control, however, the Constitution had built in "auxiliary precautions," as Madison called them, to make sure government could not concentrate power. Thus, **federalism** splits power between nation and state, **separation of powers** divides the powers that remained with the national government among the three branches of government, and **checks and balances** give each branch some

federalism: *System of government in which sovereignty is constitutionally divided between national and state governments.*

separation of powers: *Government structure in which authority is divided among branches (executive, legislative, and judicial), with each holding separate and independent powers and areas of responsibility.*

checks and balances: *Government structure that authorizes each branch of government (executive, legislative, and judicial) to share powers with the other branches, thereby holding some scrutiny of and control over the other branches.*

supreme court cases

Marbury v. Madison (1803)

QUESTION: Does Congress have the authority to expand the Supreme Court's original jurisdiction beyond that granted by the Constitution?

ORAL ARGUMENT: February 10, 1803

DECISION: February 23, 1803 (read at http://www.law.cornell.edu/supremecourt/text/5/137)

OUTCOME: No, thus establishing the power of judicial review (4–0)

It is hard to imagine a more momentous decision resulting from what the historian John A. Garraty called, this "trivial squabble over a few petty political plums."* In the closing days of President John Adams's administration, the Federalist Adams nominated William Marbury to the position of justice of the peace for the District of Columbia, and the Federalist Senate confirmed the nomination. But in the hectic final hours of Adams's administration, Secretary of State John Marshall neglected to deliver the commission. When Democratic-Republican Thomas Jefferson became president, his new secretary of state, James Madison, refused to deliver the commission, thus keeping Marbury from assuming his office.

Marbury filed suit at the Supreme Court, believing that the Judiciary Act of 1789 expanded the Court's original jurisdiction to give the Court the authority to hear cases involving writs of *mandamus* (orders to government officials to undertake specific acts) as an original matter, that is, as a trial, and not just as an appeal.

The Supreme Court declared that because the Constitution precisely specified which types of cases the Supreme Court could hear as an original matter, the section of the Judiciary Act that expanded the Court's original jurisdiction conflicted with the Constitution. Moreover, if a law conflicts with the Constitution, either the law is supreme over the

Constitution, or the Constitution is supreme over the law. The Court ruled that it must be the case that the Constitution is supreme over the law. Finally, the Court declared that the judiciary would decide such issues. "It is emphatically the province and duty of the judicial department to say what the law is," wrote Marshall, who in the closing days of the Adams administration had been nominated and confirmed as chief justice of the United States. The Supreme Court would not order Madison to deliver the commission to Marbury. Marbury presumably had the right to get the commission from a different court but never sought to do so. Instead, he returned to his highly successful banking career.

The Court in *Marbury* granted itself the momentous authority of judicial review, the power to strike down laws passed by Congress and state legislatures on the grounds that those laws violate the Constitution. Although the Court did not frequently use this power in the early days of the republic, citizens filing lawsuits would later use it to get the Court to strike down, among other things, segregated schools (*Brown v. Board of Education*, 1954), anti-abortion statutes (*Roe v. Wade*, 1973), and federal refusal to recognize same sex marriages (*U.S. v. Windsor*, 2013).

1. How does judicial review provide a gateway to participation in the political system?
2. Why is it the judiciary's job to determine whether a law is unconstitutional?

*"The Case of the Missing Commissions," in John A. Garraty, ed., *Quarrels That Have Shaped the Constitution* (New York: Harper and Row, 1964, p. 13.

Public Policy and the Constitution:
The Death Penalty

The Constitution contains some degree of ambiguity about the death penalty. In several places, it seems to allow capital punishment. The Fourteenth Amendment's due process clause says that states may not deprive people of life, liberty, or property without due process of law, thus suggesting that life, liberty, and property may be taken so long as the states follow due process. Similarly, the Fifth Amendment declares that no person shall be held for a capital crime without indictment by a grand jury. In contrast, the Eighth Amendment prohibits "cruel and unusual" punishments.

Before 1972, most states allowed capital punishment and did so by declaring crimes for which capital punishment could be imposed (usually murder, but sometimes also rape) and then leaving it up to the jury to decide whether capital punishment should be inflicted in a specific case. In 1972, the Supreme Court put a temporary halt to capital punishment, declaring that the process of complete jury discretion was cruel and unusual in that it led to an arbitrary and unequal imposition of the death penalty.[21] According to one justice in this sharply divided case, who received the death penalty and who did not was as arbitrary as who gets hit by lightning. (Figure 2.5 shows the fluctuations in the number of executions per year.)

Various states responded to this decision by requiring juries to follow certain guidelines before imposing the death penalty. In 1976, the Supreme Court ruled 7–2 that the death penalty with such guidelines did not constitute cruel and unusual punishment under the

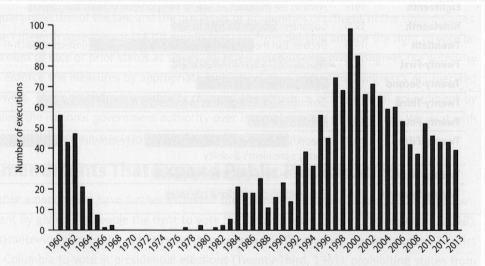

Figure 2.5   Annual executions in the United States, 1960–2013

Annual executions dropped significantly in the years before the Supreme Court's temporary halt of capital punishment in 1972, but public support for capital punishment remained high. After the Court reinstituted capital punishment in 1976, the number of executions rose. The number later dipped, as DNA evidence revealing that some death row inmates had been wrongly convicted made the public wary about the death penalty.

Source: Annual Executions, 1960–2013. Death Penalty Information Center, 2013.

Constitution.[22] Currently, thirty-two states permit capital punishment.[23] Given strong public approval for the death penalty—nearly 2-1 in an October 2013 Gallup poll[24]—Congress allows it for certain federal crimes, including terrorist acts that result in death, murder for hire, kidnappings that result in murder, and murder related to the smuggling of aliens.[25] The United States is seeking the death penalty in the case of Dzhokhar Tsarnaev, the accused Boston Marathon bomber, even though Massachusetts does not allow capital punishment.[26]

Although the Supreme Court has attempted to limit the unequal application of the death penalty, one clear finding from studies is the effect of the race of the victim: Juries are far more likely to impose the death penalty when the victim is white than when the victim is black.[27] The Supreme Court has ruled that, even if this were the case overall, someone challenging a death sentence based on such statistics would have to prove that the jury intentionally discriminated in the particular case.[28]

The Supreme Court has put limits on who can be sentenced to death. Offenders who were under the age of 18 when their crimes were committed and those convicted of rape, even the rape of a child, cannot receive the death penalty.[29]

Some states have begun to limit their own use of this punishment. The Innocence Project, a group dedicated to reversing convictions of people who were innocent, reports 312 death penalty cases in which DNA testing demonstrated that the wrong person was convicted of the crime.[30] This finding has led many states to reduce the number of death penalty sentences. It has also led many, but not all, states to allow convicted criminals access to DNA evidence, though the Supreme Court does not require them to do so.[31] Illinois was the first state to suspend the use of the death penalty because the evidence in several death penalty cases was shown to be insufficient in establishing guilt, and the newest scientific methods using DNA exonerated several death row inmates.

In considering how well policy making works in the constitutional system, it is worth noting the inconsistent use of the death penalty across states. If two individuals commit the same crime in different states, one criminal might be put to death, and the other might be allowed to live. Should states have their own policies on capital punishment, or should the federal government impose a uniform policy on them? The inconsistent use of the death penalty raises questions about equality under the constitutional system and serves as one of the most important examples of the unintended consequences of constitutional design.

▶ Construct Your Own Policy

1. Draft a constitutional amendment that would eliminate the death penalty in all fifty states, and include an alternative sentence for crimes that might otherwise qualify for the death penalty.

2. Draft a set of five requirements for the imposition of the death penalty that would apply in all fifty states.

Checkpoint

CAN YOU:

■ List the major rights protected by the Bill of Rights

■ List the major rights protected by the Civil War amendments

■ Explain how amendments have expanded the gateways to public participation

■ Describe how the meaning of the Constitution can change without formal amendments

→ KEY QUESTIONS:
What is the significance of judicial review?

Additionally, Congress's authority to regulate commerce between the states is now so grand that it covers virtually all commercial activity, including wheat grown by a farmer for consumption by livestock on that farmer's land because of the effect that all similarly situated wheat could have on national grain markets.[32] But in 2012, the Supreme Court held that the commerce clause did not give Congress the right to mandate that individuals purchase health insurance, upholding that requirement under the taxing part of the general welfare clause.[33]

The Constitution and Democracy

Government under the 1787 Constitution would today be considered severely lacking in both democracy and equality. The government allowed some of the people, mostly white males with property, to choose one chamber of the legislative branch of their government but did not grant the people a direct vote for the other chamber of the legislature or for the chief executive. And a government that allowed slavery would today be a pariah, an outcast, among the nations of the world.

Moreover, in 1787, states regulated the right to vote. Slaves were not allowed to vote, but states differed as to whether women, free blacks, and men without property could vote. Yet, compared to the despots and monarchs who had long ruled other countries, the government of 1787 allowed for a remarkable degree of participation by the common person. By giving voters a direct say in their state legislatures and at least indirect influence in all branches of the national government, the 1787 Constitution was a striking break with the past, even if it did not live up to the Declaration's statement that "all men are created equal."

Today participation is much more widespread than in 1787. Although the Electoral College continues to play its role every four years, each state allows the people to choose their electors. In addition, amendments to the Constitution have widened the gateways to democracy. Due to the Seventeenth Amendment, the people today directly choose their senators, making that body directly responsive to public wishes. Moreover, voting equality is guaranteed in various ways: Poll taxes are illegal (Twenty-Fourth Amendment), and voting rights, which are now guaranteed to those 18 years old and older (Twenty-Sixth Amendment), may not be abridged due to race (Fifteenth Amendment) or sex (Nineteenth Amendment).

Although the 1787 Constitution allowed the national government to exercise direct control over the citizenry, the tiny size of the national government left the people with far more control over their daily lives than they have today. But it is also the case that today the people have more control over the government. In addition to new constitutional gateways, opportunities for participation are greater than ever, with the Internet relaying information virtually instantly. It is much easier for representatives to be responsive to their constituents' desires when they can easily learn what their constituents believe, and constituents can readily learn what their representatives have done.

Master the Concept
of The Constitution with MindTap™ for American Government

 REVIEW MindTap™ **for American Government**
Access Key Term Flashcards for Chapter 2.

 STAY CURRENT MindTap™ **for American Government**
Access the KnowNow blog and customized RSS for updates on current events.

 TEST YOURSELF MindTap™ **for American Government**
Take the Wrap It Up Quiz for Chapter 2.

 STAY FOCUSED MindTap™ **for American Government**
Complete the Focus Activities for The Constitution.

⭐ Key Concepts

amendment (p. 41). Why did the Framers make amending the Constitution so difficult?

Antifederalists (p. 46). What were the Antifederalist arguments against the proposed Constitution?

Articles of Confederation (p. 33). What were the deficiencies of the Articles of Confederation?

Bill of Rights (p. 38). What are the basic protections in the Bill of Rights?

checks and balances (p. 42). Why does government need checks and balances?

Connecticut Compromise (p. 36). What did the Connecticut Compromise accomplish?

constitution (p. 30). Why is a constitution needed instead of ordinary laws that can say the same things?

Declaration of Independence (p. 33). What are the basic principles of the Declaration of Independence?

Electoral College (p. 38). Why does the Constitution provide for an Electoral College?

enumerated powers (p. 36). Why are Congress's powers enumerated?

federalism (p. 42). What does a federal system try to do?

Federalists (p. 46). Who were the Federalists?

general welfare clause (p. 47). What does the general welfare clause do?

implied powers (p. 47). Does the Constitution grant implied powers?

judicial review (p. 41). What is judicial review?

necessary and proper clause (p. 47). What does the necessary and proper clause do?

republic (p. 38). What distinguishes a republic from other forms of government?

separation of powers (p. 42). Why do governments chosen by the people still need a separation of powers?

three-fifths compromise (p. 37). What were the problems of the three-fifths compromise?

veto (p. 40). Why is the president given veto power?

Learning Outcomes: What You Need . . .

To Know	To Test Yourself	To Participate
▶ Assess what drove the colonists to seek independence		
The colonists declared independence from Britain because they believed that the British Parliament and king were denying their rights as British subjects. Congress's powers under the Articles of Confederation were limited, and the structure the Articles established made governing difficult.	• Define a constitution. • State the colonists' grievances against Great Britain. • Explain the key concepts in the Declaration of Independence. • Describe the problems with the Articles of Confederation.	• Appreciate American political culture. • Formulate grievances you might have about the government today. • Evaluate the impact of governing documents.
▶ Identify the major compromises at the Constitutional Convention		
In 1787, delegates from twelve states met in Philadelphia to amend the Articles; instead, they wrote a new Constitution. To secure the assent of all states represented at the Constitutional Convention, the delegates reached compromises between large and small states over representation, between northern and southern states over issues related to slavery, and between those who favored a strong national government and those who favored strong state governments in the balance of power between the two. This newly proposed Constitution was then sent to the states for ratification, and it is, with subsequent amendments, the same Constitution Americans live by today.	• Explain how the interests of the large and small states differed. • State why the convention rejected the Virginia Plan. • Explain how the interests of the northern states and the southern states differed. • Describe how the 1787 Constitution protected against too much popular influence. • Recall who would ratify the new Constitution.	• Characterize the people who hold power today. • Justify (or critique) equal representation in the Senate. • Evaluate compromise as a tool for governing.

To Know	To Test Yourself	To Participate

▶ **Explain how the structure of the Constitution protects liberty**

The Constitution lays out the structure of democratic government and the means by which the Constitution can be amended. It reflects the Framers' attempt to establish a government powerful enough to ensure public order yet restrained enough to guarantee individual liberty.	• Describe the basic structure of the U.S. Constitution. • Explain how amendments get proposed and ratified. • Evaluate why power is partitioned.	• Evaluate whether the Constitution provides gateways for, or gates against, public participation. • Determine whether the amendment process is too difficult. • Evaluate the dangers of unified power.

▶ **Analyze why the Antifederalists opposed the Constitution**

Debates over the ratification of the Constitution centered on a fear of consolidated federal authority over the states, the scope of executive and legislative power, and the lack of a bill of rights. To achieve ratification, the Federalists gave in to Antifederalist demands for a bill of rights, passing one as the first ten amendments to the Constitution.	• Characterize the Federalists and Antifederalists. • Compare competing arguments over who was sovereign under the Constitution. • Explain why the Antifederalists believed the president had too much power. • Explain why the Antifederalists believed Congress had too much power. • Recall which problem in the proposed Constitution the Federalists agreed to correct.	• Identify these positions in politics today. • Argue whether the national government or the people are sovereign today. • Evaluate the extent of presidential power. • Evaluate the extent of congressional power.

▶ **Illustrate how the Constitution has stayed responsive to changing needs**

Subsequent amendments ended slavery, protected the rights of African Americans, and generally extended public participation in government while also expanding federal authority over the states. The constitutional system established in 1787 has also been changed by constitutional interpretation and its operation altered by the development of political parties.	• List the major rights protected by the Bill of Rights. • List the major rights protected by the Civil War amendments. • Explain how amendments have expanded the gateways to public participation. • Describe how the meaning of the Constitution can change without formal amendments. • Identify the informal practices that have changed how the Constitution operates.	• Propose new rights that you would like to see constitutionally protected. • Contrast the gateways to public participation that exist today and those that existed in 1787. • Examine the evolution of constitutional meaning, and judge whether it is valid.

AP IMAGES/THE OKLAHOMAN, BRYAN TERRY

"Whenever you feel something could be better, you should step up and do it or help someone who can. Many of the greatest achievements came as a result of people volunteering their time towards making a positive impact."

BRIAN MAUGHAN
Oklahoma City
Community College

COURTESY OKLAHOMA CITY COMMUNITY COLLEGE

3

Federalism

The impacts of federal, state, and local government decisions are not just theory to Brian Maughan. They first got his attention when he was a student at Oklahoma City Community College (OCCC), and now, in his job as county commissioner, they are daily fare.

Maughan grew up in the community he now serves. His commitment to his community developed in high school, when his principal used community service to instill self-worth in at-risk students. For college, Maughan remained close by, where he could stay in touch with Ben, his best friend, who was a quadriplegic as the result of a car accident and who faced a difficult situation. The state program that supplemented federal funding for his in-home health care was being defunded, and it looked like he would be removed from his home and placed in a state care facility. The federal program—Social Security Disability Insurance (SSDI)—would not pay for a family member to provide in-home health care at the advanced level Ben's condition required. If state funding could be restored, however, Ben could remain at home, and the family member who cared for him would receive compensation. Obviously, this arrangement was preferred. Maughan took on Ben's cause as his own. While keeping up with his classes and holding down a job to pay his tuition, Maughan researched funding options and learned that the Oklahoma Developmental Disability Council could provide the aid Ben needed. For two years, he actively sought the governor's support. Because of his commitment, the governor appointed Maughan to the council, and shortly after Maughan's graduation, funding for Ben's situation was restored. Ben was able to remain at home where his family cared for him until his death, a short time later. Maughan's success on behalf of his friend demonstrates the gateways for influence at the state and local levels that are often easier to access than the federal level.

Recognizing that active citizenship can change policies that have negative effects, Maughan decided to make government and community service his career. Today, as a county commissioner, he navigates the multiple layers of government. An accidental fire, propelled by raging winds and severe drought conditions, consumed many homes in his district. Then a tornado caused more property loss and raised public safety concerns. Maughan's job was to oversee federal disaster assistance in the removal of debris so that homeowners could begin to clean up and rebuild. But federal and county disaster aid funded only the removal of trees and natural materials; the removal of other debris was the responsibility of the homeowner and the insurance company.

Need to Know

3.1 Explain why the Framers chose a federal system

3.2 Summarize how the Constitution institutes the federal system

3.3 Outline how U.S. federalism has changed over time

3.4 Compare and contrast national and state governments

▶ **WATCH & LEARN** MindTap for American Government
Watch a brief "What Do You Know?" video summarizing Federalism.

Frustrated homeowners leveled criticism at Maughan. He found an innovative solution: He mobilized more than a thousand volunteers, who donated more than ten thousand hours assisting homeowners.

Maughan does not ask more of others than he asks of himself. In a snowstorm, when snow removal resources were limited, he helped plow, sand, and salt the 177 lane miles in his district. To clean up blight, he enlists college students and offenders sentenced to community service in a program he founded called SHINE (Start Helping Impacted Neighborhoods Everywhere). The National Association of Counties recognized the program with its "2014 Achievement Award." SHINE's success also led to the passage of a state law, the "Safari McDoulett Community Service Act" (SB 1875), authorizing similar community service programs to be adopted by all counties in the state (McDoulett was the staff person responsible for administering the program but was killed in an automobile accident). The program has been modeled by the capital city of Rwanda in Africa and presents yearly awards to students who complete 100 hours of community service. Maughan likes to tell volunteers the "broken window" story that political scientist James Q. Wilson made famous—how one unattended broken window can invite trash, graffiti, and an opportunity for more serious crimes. Volunteer labor helps Maughan stretch tight budgets and inspires civic engagement that improves the community as a whole.[1]

In federal political systems where national, state, and local governments wield power, the interplay of responsibilities is often complex and overlapping or may leave areas unfunded, as Maughan's experiences reveal. But they also offer multiple gateways to participation, policy change, and government office. In this chapter, we examine the federal system of government, including the authority of national, state, and local governments; how that authority has shifted over time; and how federalism can both enhance and impede American democracy.

3.1 Why Federalism?

> Explain why the Framers chose a federal system

The delegates to the 1787 Constitutional Convention in Philadelphia recognized that the system of government established by the Articles of Confederation was failing. Congress did not have the authority to regulate commerce or to raise money by taxing citizens or imports; it could only request revenues from the states. Thus, the nation's debts went unpaid, and its credit was sinking. Moreover, trade barriers erected by states against other states impeded commerce. Something had to be done. If the delegates were not able to fix the problems caused by the Articles, James Madison and others feared that the union could disintegrate.[2]

Why Unify?

Federalism presupposes some form of union, so the answer to the question "why federalism?" first requires an answer to the question "why unify?"

The primary answer to the unification question is that some form of union allows smaller political entities to pool their resources to fight a common enemy. The colonists could not have won the Revolutionary War if they had not banded together to fight the British. Benjamin Franklin

THE GRANGER COLLECTION, NYC

Benjamin Franklin published this political cartoon in his *Pennsylvania Gazette* on May 9, 1754, shortly after hostilities began in the French and Indian War. The earliest depiction of the need for union among Britain's American colonies, it shows New England as one segment and leaves out Delaware and Georgia altogether. Later, during the Revolution, it was a powerful symbol of American unity.

published his famous "Join or Die" cartoon to represent the need for the colonists to stick together in military battles in the French and Indian War (1754–63).[3] By the late 1760s, though, the cartoon had come to symbolize the need for united action against British rule. After the Revolution, common threats remained not only from England but also from France and various Native American tribes.

Beyond military necessity, the colonists considered themselves to be part of a common nation with Americans in the other states. A nation is said to exist when people in a country have a sense of common identity due to a common origin, history, or ancestry, all of which the colonists shared. This sense of common identity made some form of union not only a military necessity but also a political advantage. The American people, however, also had strong loyalties to their states, an attachment that would have made eliminating states politically impossible. How strong the national government would be was the subject of heated debate at the Constitutional Convention.

→ KEY QUESTIONS:
Today the people of the United States no longer share a common origin, history, or ancestry. Does it matter?

Confederal, Unitary, and Federal Systems

A **confederal system** had existed under the Articles of Confederation. In a confederal system, independent states grant powers to a national government to rule for the common good in certain limited areas such as defense. The independent states that make up the confederation usually have an equal vote, and the confederation might require unanimous consent or other supermajorities (for example, two-thirds or three-quarters) to pass legislation. The confederal organization usually acts through the states that constitute it rather than acting directly on the citizens of those states.

But the Framers who met in Philadelphia in 1787 were not inclined to continue the confederal system. A majority of the delegates believed that the New Jersey Plan, which would have strengthened the national government but still granted each state one vote and still required a supermajority to pass most important issues, did not go far enough. They knew that the United States needed a stronger national government.

If a confederal system gives hardly any power to the national government, a **unitary system** of government gives it virtually every power. State or regional governments might still exist under a unitary system, but their powers and, in fact, their very existence, are entirely up to the national government. The authority of a state or regional government in a pure unitary system is similar to the relationship between a state government today and the cities and counties that exist under the state's jurisdiction. Counties can make local decisions, but they exist only because their state established them, and a county has only the authority the state grants to it.

A confederal system was too weak for the United States, and an overly strong central government would pose its own set of problems. The Framers particularly feared that too much power in any government could lead to tyranny. Freedom would be better guaranteed by dividing governmental powers, rather than by concentrating them in a central government.

The Framers thus established a new system of government, **federalism**. A federal system, like that of the United States, mixes features of confederal and unitary governments. The Constitution created one legislative chamber chosen by the people and based on population, and another chosen by the states and based on equal representation. Within the states' areas of authority—those areas not granted to the national government—their

confederal system: *System of government in which ultimate authority rests with the regional (for example, state) governments.*

unitary system: *System of government in which ultimate authority rests with the national government.*

federalism: *System of government in which sovereignty is constitutionally divided between national and state governments.*

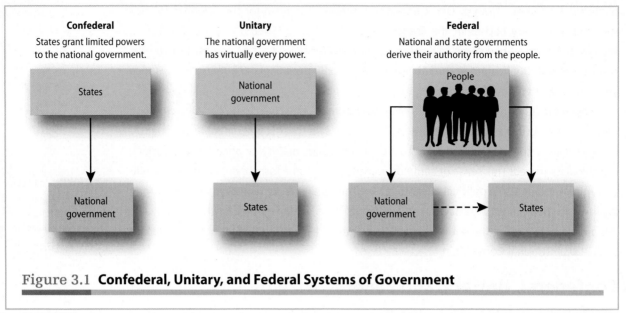

Figure 3.1 Confederal, Unitary, and Federal Systems of Government

decisions are final and cannot be overturned by the national government. Moreover, the existence of states in a federal system does not depend on the national government; rather, the states derive their authority directly from the people. Nevertheless, within areas of authority granted to the national government, or areas of authority shared by the states and the national government, the national government reigns supreme. Political scientist William Riker defines federalism as a system of government in which there exists "a government of the federation [that is, a national government] and a set of governments of the member units [that is, the states] in which both kinds of governments rule over the same territory and people, and each kind has the authority to make some decisions independently of the other" (see Figure 3.1).[4]

A federal system not only reduces the risks of tyranny; it promotes self-government. While any representative democracy involves **self-government**, or government by the people, self-government is enhanced when the decisions that affect the citizens' lives are made by representatives who are local, closer to them, and more similar to them, rather than by representatives who live far away and are dissimilar. Thus self-government is enhanced when people in Massachusetts, to the extent possible, make rules for the people who live in Massachusetts, while people in Texas make rules for the people who live in Texas.

The Framers' choice of a federal system of government was innovative because virtually all of the world's governments at the time were either unitary or confederal. Madison's original Virginia Plan did not propose a pure unitary system—Congress could not eliminate the states. However, by giving Congress a complete veto over laws passed by the states and by granting Congress the general authority to pass laws that would promote "the harmony" of the United States,[5] it would have moved the United States in that direction. The American system was an experiment, and its evolution has been shaped by the tensions, even conflicts, inherent in a system in which power is both divided and shared. Since 1787, about two dozen other nations have ordered themselves as federal systems (see Global Gateways: Federal Political Systems).

→ KEY QUESTIONS:
Which government has the biggest impact on you—the federal government or your state government?

 self-government: *Rule by the people.*

→ KEY QUESTIONS:
In addition to federalism, in what other ways was the Constitution of 1787 innovative, even experimental?

Checkpoint

CAN YOU:

- Explain why the Founders chose to unify
- Compare the alternatives to federalism
- Consider how we might know if the Framers' experiment with federalism was successful

Only a small percentage of the world's nations are federalist systems, but the tendency of larger nations to rely on federalism means that federal systems cover a vast majority of the world's landmass. Of the world's largest countries—Russia, Canada, the United States, China, Australia, and Brazil—all but China are federalist. Note that federalism does not necessarily mean democratic (as in Russia), and democratic does not necessarily mean federalist (as in the United Kingdom).

Within federal political systems, there are many variations. With the recent devolution of power to Scotland, Wales, and Northern Ireland, however, the United Kingdom is not quite as unitary as it once was. Scotland held a vote for independence in September 2014. The UK promised Scotland and other member states greater local authority if Scotland voted to stay in the UK, which it did. India, a multilingual nation, has a federal system with twenty-eight states and seven territories. Its federal system has a stronger national government as compared with the government of the United States, with reserve powers belonging to the national government and the states' powers enumerated. South Africa is another multilingual nation with a federal system.

The constitution divides the country into nine provinces and delegates certain powers to the national government and others to the provincial governments. Unlike the United States, the provinces do not retain reserve powers. Mexico is a federal system with thirty-one states plus a federal district. The Mexican constitution limits the form of those state governments in ways that the U.S. Constitution does not.

Those governing multilingual and multiethnic nations around the globe perceive a greater need to provide the local autonomy that comes with federalism. Sudan, which has seen its southern region secede and become South Sudan, is, along with Iraq, in the process of transitioning toward federalism. These countries hope that providing greater autonomy to different regions will keep the nation from falling apart.

1. Why have certain nations chosen a federal system?
2. Why have most nations not chosen a federal system?

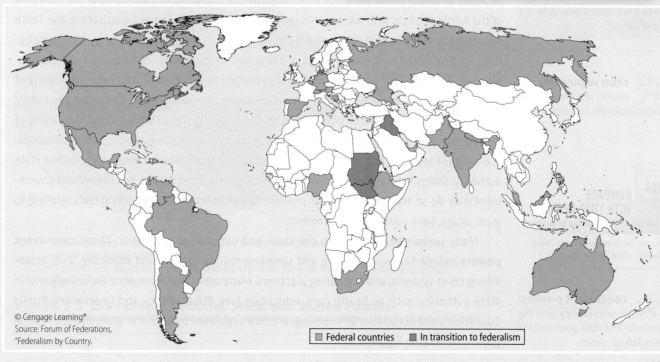

© Cengage Learning®
Source: Forum of Federations, "Federalism by Country.

□ Federal countries   ■ In transition to federalism

Public Policy and Federalism:
Public Education

Despite the fact that federally elected politicians talk frequently about the importance of education, the federal government itself funds about 12 percent of all elementary and secondary education spending.[6] The primary reason for this minimal funding is the federal structure. With education among the reserved powers left to the states, state and local governments developed the responsibility for educating the populace. Originally, states set education policy that local communities then implemented through locally elected school boards.[7] Depending on the state, local school boards had differing amounts of power to establish the curriculum, support extracurricular activities, hire and fire teachers, negotiate salaries for school district employees, and set standards for graduation. Over time, funding for elementary and secondary education became based on local property taxes, with some additional assistance from state governments. Just as the overall wealth of local communities and states varies, so does the amount of funding available for education.

The federal government has intervened in public education for two main reasons: to overcome the denial of equality of educational opportunity by the states and to improve the quality of education. The Supreme Court has struck down segregated schools for black students in *Brown v. The Board of Education*[8] and for Mexican Americans in *Cisneros v. Corpus Christi*[9]; however, despite these legal restrictions on segregation, many African American and Latino students continue to attend schools that are predominantly minority as shown by Figure 3.4.

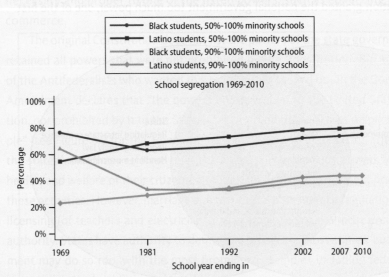

Figure 3.4 **Percent of African American and Latino Students Attending Highly Segregated Schools 1969–2010**

The percent of African American students attending highly segregated schools (greater than 90 percent minority) dropped sharply between 1969 and 1981 but has slowly risen since then. The percent of Latino students attending highly segregated schools has been increasing as well. That number is now greater for Latino students than for African American students.

Source: Adapted from Gary Orfield, John Kucsera, and Genevieve Siegel-Hawley, "E Pluribus Separation," 2012, The Civil Rights Project. Available at http://civilrightsproject.ucla.edu/research /k-12-education/integration-and-diversity/mlk-national/e-pluribus...separation-deepening-double-segregation-for-more-students/orfield_epluribus_revised_omplete_2012.pdf.

England states threatened to ignore the Embargo Act of 1807, and, in 1828, Vice President John C. Calhoun insisted on South Carolina's right to nullify a federal tariff. As the union was merely a compact among the states, Calhoun argued, dissenting states even had the right to **secede**. Against such claims, Senator Daniel Webster insisted that the union was not a compact of states, but a compact among the people of the United States.

★ **secede:** *To formally withdraw from a nation-state.*

Because nothing in the Constitution suggested that Congress had the power to limit slavery in the states, the most heated contests over congressional authority to regulate slavery involved the territories. This debate split abolitionists who wanted to ban slavery in the territories, states' rights supporters such as John C. Calhoun who thought that slave owners had the right to take their slaves into any territory, and those who favored compromises that would allow slavery in some territories but not in others. In 1857, the Supreme Court sided with the states' rights supporters, declaring in *Dred Scott v. Sandford* that Congress had no authority to regulate slavery in the territories (see Chapter 5).[22]

When Abraham Lincoln (1861–65), who favored federal efforts to prohibit slavery in the territories, won the presidential election of 1860, South Carolina seceded. Virtually every grievance listed by South Carolina involved slavery.[23] Other southern states followed, with most noting the question of slavery,[24] and they soon established their own constitution.

During the Civil War, Lincoln used his power as commander in chief to issue the Emancipation Proclamation, which prohibited slavery in states under rebellion, as slave labor was an asset to the Confederate army. Slaves in some of these states were not emancipated until ratification of the Thirteenth Amendment, which prohibited slavery throughout the nation as of December 18, 1865.

The Congresses that followed the Civil War tried to exert federal power over the states to promote equality between freedmen and whites, but President Andrew Johnson (1865–69) vetoed a civil rights bill, claiming it represented a trend toward "centralization and the concentration of all legislative power in the National Government."[25] The bill granted former slaves the rights to make contracts; sue; give evidence; and inherit, purchase, lease, and convey real and personal property. In 1866, Congress passed it over Johnson's veto. But as part of the effort to ensure that all such laws would be constitutional, Congress proposed and the states ratified the Fourteenth Amendment (1868) and the Fifteenth Amendment (1870). These greatly expanded the authority of the national government over the states. The Fourteenth Amendment requires states to provide each person due process of law (see Chapter 4) and the equal protection of the laws (see Chapter 5). The Fifteenth Amendment prevents states from abridging the right to vote on account of race. Like the Thirteenth Amendment, the Fourteenth and Fifteenth Amendments granted Congress the authority to enforce their provisions by appropriate legislation, thus adding to Congress's enumerated powers.

In 1883, however, the Supreme Court decided in the *Civil Rights Cases* to keep Congress's powers within the words of the amendments: Congress could prevent states from denying people equality, but it could not prevent private businesses or individuals from doing so, for example, by refusing to hire former slaves or to serve them at inns or restaurants. The Court thus invalidated Congress's Civil Rights Act of 1875, which had prohibited this type of private discrimination. This era, covering the period before and after the Civil War, saw the defeat of the most strident (secessionist) state-centered views, but with the Supreme Court's interpretation of the Civil War amendments, state authority remained strong.

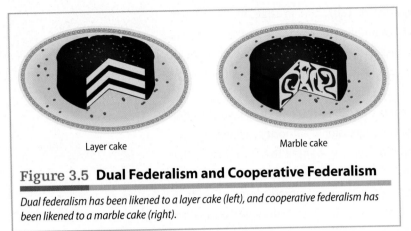

Layer cake   Marble cake

Figure 3.5 Dual Federalism and Cooperative Federalism

Dual federalism has been likened to a layer cake (left), and cooperative federalism has been likened to a marble cake (right).

Source: LAITS, University of Texas College of Liberal Arts, © CENGAGE LEARNING®

Dual Federalism (approximately 1865–1932)

Although the supporters of state-centered federalism lost the Civil War, the viewpoint of a national government with limited powers did not disappear. A new viewpoint, **dual federalism**, recognized that while the national government was supreme in some spheres, the state governments remained supreme in others, with layers of authority separate from one another; political scientists later compared this arrangement to a "layer cake"[26] (see Figure 3.5). Thus the national government would be supreme over issues such as foreign affairs and interstate commerce, and the states would be supreme in matters concerning intrastate commerce and police powers.

⭐ **dual federalism:**
Doctrine holding that state governments and the federal government have almost completely separate functions.

In 1913, Congress passed and the states ratified the Sixteenth Amendment, which granted Congress the power to tax income from whatever source derived, giving the national government access to millions (and later billions and even trillions) of dollars in revenue. The increase in federal authority over areas once left to the states was aided that same year by the ratification of the Seventeenth Amendment, which took the selection of U.S. senators out of the hands of state legislatures and required that they be directly elected by the people of each state. Before 1914, state legislatures hoped senators would be responsive to the needs of the states, but with direct elections, senators had to be responsive to the needs of the people.[27]

Cooperative Federalism: The New Deal and Civil Rights (approximately 1932–69)

With the onset of the Great Depression following the stock market crash of 1929, the people wanted national action to aid the economy, and the nation-centered federalism signaled by the Sixteenth and Seventeenth Amendments strengthened considerably the ability to be responsive to those wishes. In 1932, voters elected Franklin Roosevelt as president. During his campaign, Roosevelt had promised a "New Deal" to Americans who had lost their jobs, their homes, and their savings. Following Roosevelt's inauguration, Congress passed a series of laws designed to lift the ailing economy. As before, Congress asserted its authority under the commerce clause to regulate American industry. As before, the Supreme Court rejected such legislation, claiming in one case that the mining of coal by a company with operations in several states was production and not interstate commerce.[28]

⭐ **Court-packing plan:**
President Franklin Roosevelt's proposal to add new justices to the Supreme Court so that the Court would uphold his policies.

Despite vast support from Congress and the American people for his New Deal policies, Roosevelt saw the Supreme Court strike down one law after another, often by 5–4 or 6–3 votes. In response, Roosevelt proposed in 1937 to increase the number of justices on the Supreme Court. He would then be able to pack the Court with his own appointees. This controversial **Court-packing plan** met with fierce opposition in Congress. The Supreme Court, however, made passage of the plan unnecessary, for shortly after Roosevelt's proposal, the Court reversed itself and started accepting the broad authority of Congress to regulate the economy.

On taxing and spending, the Court accepted the view that virtually any taxing or spending plan that Congress believed supported the general welfare would be acceptable.

On commerce, the Court began by accepting the regulation of a giant steel company with operations throughout the United States as an appropriate regulation of interstate commerce.[29] Congress could also use the commerce clause to regulate employment conditions, said the Court, rejecting the Tenth Amendment as a limit on federal power.[30] The Court's definition of what constituted interstate commerce grew to include anything that affected interstate commerce, whether over several states or confined to one state. Roosevelt's nation-centered federalism was said by political scientists to more closely resemble a "marble cake," with specific powers under both national and state authority, than the layer-cake structure of dual federalism.[31]

Nation-centered federalism continued to dominate dual federalism through World War II and beyond. President Lyndon Baines Johnson's (1963–69) Great Society program expanded national authority even further, with federal aid to public schools—traditionally a state duty—and health care coverage to the poor (Medicaid) and elderly (Medicare). The Johnson administration gave money to the states for its programs through categorical grants—money for the states to use on what the national government wanted.

The Johnson administration also expanded national power to ensure greater equality, pushing for passage of the Civil Rights Act (1964), which prohibited job discrimination and segregation in public accommodations, and the Voting Rights Act (1965), which regulated voting rules that had largely been left to the states since the adoption of the Constitution (see Chapter 5).

State-centered federalism gained some traction, though, in opposition to the push toward equality and civil rights. In 1954 in *Brown v. Board of Education*, the Supreme Court struck down school segregation, which had been legally mandated or permitted in twenty states plus the District of Columbia. This Supreme Court decision helped put the federal government at the forefront of the fight for equality.

The New Federalism (approximately 1969–93)

In one of the last challenges to integration, segregationist Governor George Wallace of Alabama ran for president in 1968. His party, the American Independent Party, condemned what it considered to be the unconstitutional use of federal power to desegregate schools and enforce voting rights.[32] Wallace received more than 9 million votes and won the electoral votes of five states. Although Wallace ultimately lost the race, the strength of his campaign signaled a degree of wariness among voters about the powers of the national government. Other politicians, starting with Richard Nixon, the winner of the 1968 election, responded to these concerns.[33]

Presidents, Congress, and the New Federalism.
The Nixon administration began the trend, labeled New Federalism, of shifting powers back to the states.[34] The Nixon administration began a general revenue-sharing program that gave the states greater leeway about how the funds could be spent. The main idea behind Nixon's federalism was that states could more efficiently spend governmental resources than the enormous federal bureaucracy could.

Republican President Ronald Reagan (1981–89) sought to reduce the power of government in general and, as an avid supporter of the New Federalism, of the federal government

→ KEY QUESTIONS:
Why do citizens look to the federal government in times of crisis?

→ KEY QUESTIONS:
Was the Johnson administration right to use federal power to ensure equality?

→ KEY QUESTIONS:
Was Reagan right in stating that "government is the problem"?

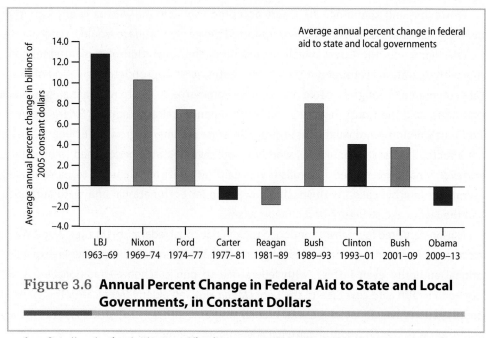

Figure 3.6 **Annual Percent Change in Federal Aid to State and Local Governments, in Constant Dollars**

Source: Derived by authors from the White House, Office of Management and Budget, Historical Tables, Table 12.1, accessed April 5, 2014, http://www.whitehouse.gov/omb/budget/historicals. The data for Obama appear low due to the stimulus spending by George W. Bush in the 2008 fiscal year.

in particular. In his first inaugural address, he declared, "Government is not the solution to our problem; government is the problem."[35] He thus cut back on categorical grants, replacing them with fewer, more flexible block grants, which set fewer restrictions on how the money could be spent. He also eliminated federal aid to state and local governments (see Figure 3.6). Nevertheless, Reagan did sign the National Minimum Drinking Age Act, which withheld a percentage of federal highway funds from states that did not increase their drinking age to 21.

The Modern Era (1993–present). During President Bill Clinton's administration, Congress moved to shift the balance of power toward the states in several ways. First, it limited unfunded mandates—legal requirements Congress imposes on the states (for example, to provide clean air, disability access, or health benefits to poor people under Medicaid) without supplying the resources to accomplish those activities. Congress did not eliminate such mandates, but it did make them harder to impose. Second, Clinton and Congress overhauled the federal welfare system, ending the federal guarantee of welfare to poor families with children, leaving final say on welfare spending with the states. Third, Congress abandoned national speed limits that had been established at the time of the 1973 Arab oil embargo and allowed states to set whatever speed limits they desired.

Although Republicans have typically supported state authority over that of the national government since the New Deal, President George W. Bush (2001–09) oversaw an administration that strengthened national authority, sometimes at the expense of the states.[36] His most prominent actions in this regard included the No Child Left Behind Act (2002), which increased federal involvement in public education, and his prescription drug plan for Medicare, which increased federal involvement in health care.[37]

Following the terrorist attacks of September 11, 2001, Congress and the Bush administration expanded national power in various ways, including the establishment of national standards for driver's licenses and new powers to monitor electronic communications.

On the other hand, the Obama administration has endorsed state-centered federalism, at least where the policies support Democratic Party positions: support for permitting states to set higher standards than the federal government on fuel economy and tailpipe emissions and a reversal of the Bush administration's crackdown on state medical marijuana programs.[38] The Obama Administration is choosing not to use federal authority to prosecute people in Colorado and Washington who legally, under the state laws thereof, use marijuana for recreational or medical purposes. In supporting national policies, President Obama has reminded Americans of the historic relationship between federalism and the oppression of minority rights in the United States.

The Supreme Court and the New Federalism.

By nominating William Rehnquist to be chief justice in 1986, Reagan hoped to move the Court toward state-centered federalism. He was not disappointed. As an associate justice (1972–86), Rehnquist had pressed, often alone on the Court, for what the Supreme Court once labeled "Our Federalism."[39] As chief justice (1986–2005), he further advanced New Federalism, now aided by a Republican bloc that grew to include seven justices. The Rehnquist Court put together pro-state majorities in decisions involving interstate commerce and sovereign immunity.

Concerning interstate commerce, for the first time since 1937, the Court rejected national laws as beyond Congress's authority to regulate under the commerce clause. In one case, the Court struck down congressional legislation banning the possession of guns near schools, declaring that the possession of a gun near a school is not an economic activity.[40] Similarly, the Court rejected a central provision of the Violence Against Women Act, which gave victims of gender-based violence the right to sue their attackers in federal court. A Virginia Tech student who had allegedly been raped by members of the football team sued her attacker and Virginia Tech, a state university, in federal court after the state chose not to bring criminal charges. The Court rejected congressional findings on the effect of such violence on commerce, and it ruled that the section of the act that allowed the lawsuits was beyond Congress's authority either under the commerce clause or under its authority to enforce the equal protection of the laws under the Fourteenth Amendment.

Although these decisions stand in contrast to the decidedly pro-national decisions of the Court since the New Deal, most questions of federal authority still are decided in favor of the national government. The Court allowed Congress to condition highway funds on states having a drinking age of 21, as the small amount of funds at risk (5 percent) made the condition a "pressure" to comply and not a "compulsion."[41] And while it did not allow Congress to take away all federal Medicaid dollars for states rejecting the growth in Medicaid under the Affordable Care Act, it did allow Congress to keep states that rejected the expansion from receiving any new Medicaid money under the Act.[42] The Court also affirmed that Congress

When terrorists hijacked planes and crashed them into the World Trade Center Towers in New York City on September 11, 2001, most Americans said their lives changed forever. As with all national crises, following the terrorist attacks, the national government took a greater share of power because only the national government can protect against foreign adversaries. On October 26, 2001, President George W. Bush signed the USA PATRIOT Act, which granted the federal government increased powers over financial transactions, immigration, and domestic criminal activity.

> **→ KEY QUESTIONS:**
> Do you tend to support nation-centered federalism or state-centered federalism? Which is more responsive? Which ensures citizen equality?

> **→ KEY QUESTIONS:**
> Should guns be allowed in or near schools and college campuses? Who should decide?

CONNECT WITH YOUR CLASSMATES
MindTap™ for American Government

Access the Federalism Forum: Discussion—Patient Protection and Affordable Care Act.

can criminalize home-grown marijuana production and use even if state law allows it for medical purposes.[43] (Nevertheless, the Obama administration used its discretion not to prosecute such cases when state laws allow such use for medicinal purposes.) Indeed, the Supreme Court continues to uphold Congress's authority to regulate commercial activity.

→ KEY QUESTIONS:
Were the Antifederalists right to fear the power of the national government?

And while the Roberts Court (2005–present) did not uphold the health care law on commerce grounds, it did uphold the law through the taxing clause, thus allowing the further nationalization of health care policy in the United States.[44]

Summing Up: Were the Antifederalists Correct?

The people of the United States ratified the Constitution over the protests of Antifederalists, who claimed that the Constitution gave virtually unlimited powers to the national government. Nevertheless, until the New Deal, either because of congressional inaction or Supreme Court reaction when Congress did act, the powers exercised by the national government were clearly limited. Today, however, due to the popular belief in the need to regulate a complex economy, the historical role that states' rights advocates have played in supporting slavery and segregation, and the Supreme Court's interpretation of the Constitution, Congress has vast powers. The fact that Congress can spend money on virtually anything as long as it is not specifically prohibited by the Constitution, and that the "necessary and proper clause means "ordinary and appropriate" leads to the conclusion that as far as the powers of the national government are concerned, the Antifederalists were correct: The federal government's powers have few limits. However, in 2013, a majority of Americans reported that they thought the federal government had too much power (see Figure 3.7). In the 2014 midterm congressional elections, voters were again asked to choose between candidates of two parties with very different views about the balance of the nation-state relationship. Thus in the U.S. federal system, the voters get to decide on that balance.

Checkpoint

CAN YOU:

- Describe the role that federalism played in the run-up to the Civil War
- Explain the "layer-cake" analogy in dual federalism
- Compare dual federalism with cooperative federalism
- Explain what led to the New Federalism
- Find Antifederalist arguments in today's political debates

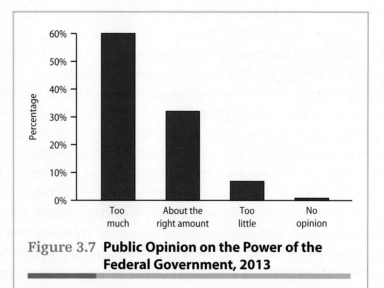

Figure 3.7 Public Opinion on the Power of the Federal Government, 2013

Source: Gallup Poll, September 2013, retrieved April 5, 2014, from the iPOLL Databank, The Roper Center for Public Opinion Research, University of Connecticut.

3.4 State and Local Governments

> Compare and contrast national and state governments

The Constitution requires that the states maintain a republican form of government, and all have done so by patterning their structure after the national government, with separate legislative, judicial, and executive branches. With the exception of procedures that allow citizens to place proposed laws directly on the ballot, state governments look remarkably similar to the federal government. Local governments, however, use a greater range of organizational options.

State Executive Branches

All fifty states choose the head of the executive branch by direct election. Most states have four-year gubernatorial terms, limit their governors to two consecutive terms, and provide for succession by the lieutenant governor.

The governors of all fifty states have the authority to veto laws subject to override by the state legislatures. Most states further grant their governors a line-item veto, the ability to veto certain parts of a spending bill without vetoing the entire bill. The president does not have this power, so when Congress passes spending bills, it usually does so by combining tens of thousands of separate spending items in an omnibus bill. The president's choice is to sign the entire bill or to veto it; he cannot veto only the appropriations he disfavors. Governors in forty-four states do have that authority, however, giving them a much stronger tool to control spending than the president has. Every state except Vermont requires a balanced budget. Unlike the federal government, which can borrow money to pay for spending programs, typically popular spending increases in the states have to be matched by typically unpopular tax increases.

The Twenty-Second Amendment (ratified in 1947) limits the president of the United States to two terms in office. Similarly, thirty-five states limit governors to two terms, Virginia limits governors to one consecutive term, and fourteen states allow unlimited terms.

→ KEY QUESTIONS:
What would happen if the president had a line-item veto?

State Legislative Branches

On the legislative side, forty-nine of the fifty states have bicameral (two-chamber) legislative branches; Nebraska has only a single chamber. Nebraska also has nonpartisan elections, meaning that candidates for election are not listed under a party banner. Most states have four-year terms for their upper chambers and two-year terms for their lower chambers.

State Judicial Branches

The greatest differences between the national and the state governments appear at the judicial level. Federal judges are nominated by the president and confirmed by the Senate. States have various procedures for selecting judges: Nearly half use an appointment process for judges on their highest court, while the rest use elections. For states that use appointments, most grant the governor the right to make appointments (usually with the consent of the state senate).

→ KEY QUESTIONS:
What effects do judicial elections have on judges' decisions? What effects should they have?

The New England town meeting, like this one in Strong, Maine, is an example of direct democracy at the local level. New England town meetings allow residents to vote directly on budgets and taxes without the election of representatives as intermediaries.

Local Governments

→ KEY QUESTIONS:
What impact does your local government have on you?

Local governments are far more diverse in function and design than state governments. First, there can be several different layers of local governments, with residents regulated by villages, cities, and towns or townships at the most local level and by counties above that. Some local governments run all local services, including police, schools, and sanitation. Many states, however, delegate specialized activities to special jurisdiction governments, such as school boards, water districts, fire districts, library districts, and sewer districts. The United States contains more than 38,000 special jurisdiction governments plus another 13,000 school boards. Overall, there are nearly 90,000 governmental units in the United States[45] providing hundreds of thousands of citizens a ready gateway for citizen involvement in public affairs, as Brian Maughan's story illustrates at the beginning of this chapter.

Second, local governments, unlike state governments, do not necessarily consist of three separate branches. One reason is that criminal and civil trials are usually handled in state courts, leaving little need for a local community to have its own judicial branch. Many local governments have elected leaders of the executive branch—mayors for villages and cities, county executives for counties, and supervisors for townships—but many use a city-manager system in which the legislative branch appoints a professional administrator to run the executive branch.

Direct Democracy

People also possess the ability to govern. Direct gateways to democracy in American federalism include the use of recall, initiatives, and referendums (see Figure 3.8). Recall allows citizens who gather enough petition signatures to force a special vote to remove state or

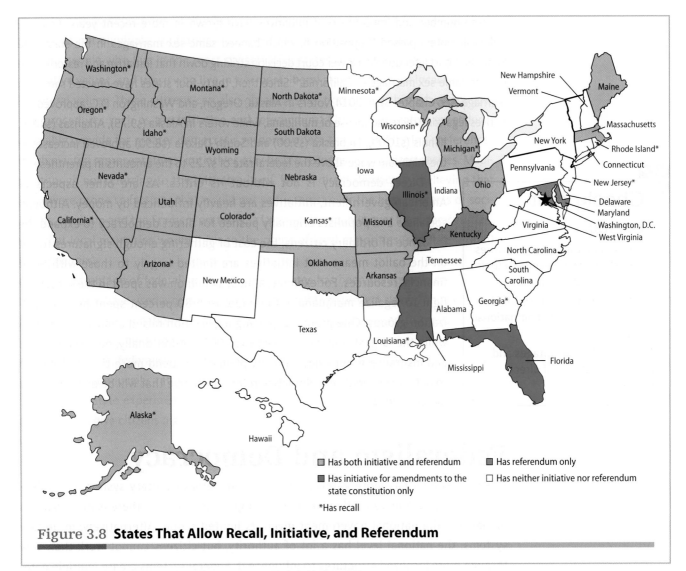

Figure 3.8 States That Allow Recall, Initiative, and Referendum

☐ Has both initiative and referendum   ☐ Has referendum only

☐ Has initiative for amendments to the   ☐ Has neither initiative nor referendum
   state constitution only

*Has recall

Source: © Cengage Learning®; data from Council of State Governments, *The Book of the States,* 2013.

local elected officials before their terms expire. Permitted in eighteen states, recall allowed a recall in Arizona of State Senator Russell Peirce, notably the author of SB 1070, the anti-immigration legislation.[46] Wisconsin voters in 2012 reconsidered the tenure of Governor Scott Walker, who had supported legislation that severely curtailed the collective bargaining rights of public employees. Walker won.

Initiative is a process that allows citizens who collect the required number of petition signatures to place proposed laws directly on the ballot for the state's citizens to vote on. Referendum allows legislatures to put certain issues on the ballot for citizen approval and requires legislatures to seek citizen approval for certain actions. Depending on the state, these actions could be proposals to borrow money, increase taxes, or approve constitutional amendments. All fifty states require referenda on some issues. Only twenty-four states allow initiatives.[47] Both procedures enable well-organized citizens to bypass the elected representatives in their state. The U.S. Constitution, in setting specific terms for senators, representatives, and presidents, prohibits recall of federal officials, and in granting all legislative powers to Congress, similarly prohibits initiative and referendum at the national level.

→ KEY QUESTIONS:
The last time you voted, were there any initiatives or referenda on the ballot? Did you know enough about them to make an informed choice?

Master the Concept
of Federalism with MindTap™ for American Government

 REVIEW MindTap™ **for American Government**
Access Key Term Flashcards for Chapter 3.

 TEST YOURSELF MindTap™ **for American Government**
Take the Wrap It Up Quiz for Chapter 3.

 STAY CURRENT MindTap™ **for American Government**
Access the KnowNow blog and customized RSS for updates on current events.

 STAY FOCUSED MindTap™ **for American Government**
Complete the Focus Activities for Federalism.

★ Key Concepts

commerce clause (p. 69). How has the Supreme Court's interpretation of the commerce clause changed over time?

concurrent powers (p. 64). Why do concurrent powers exist?

confederal system (p. 61). What are the likely problems of confederal systems?

Court-packing plan (p. 74). How would this plan have impacted the independence of the judiciary?

direct democracy (p. 68). What forms of direct democracy exist in the United States?

dual federalism (p. 74). Can dual federalism work in a modern nation?

enumerated powers (p. 64). Why are Congress's powers enumerated?

federalism (p. 61). What type of nation is more likely to adopt a federal system?

implied powers (p. 69). What are some examples of implied powers?

McCulloch v. Maryland (p. 71). Does Congress need to establish a national bank?

necessary and proper clause (p. 64). How has the Supreme Court interpreted "necessary and proper"?

reserve powers (p. 64). What does it mean that states have reserve powers?

secession (p. 73). Should there ever be a right to secede from a national government?

self-government (p. 62). If you were to rank personal liberties, where would you rank self-government?

supremacy clause (p. 68). What would happen to the U.S. constitutional system without the supremacy clause?

unitary system (p. 61). What is the effect of unitary systems on gateways to participation?

Learning Outcomes: What You Need . . .

To Know	To Test Yourself	To Participate
▶ Explain why the Framers chose a federal system		
In writing a new Constitution in 1787, the Framers established a new system of government—federalism—in which state and national governments share power.	• Explain why the Founders chose to unify. • Compare the alternatives to federalism.	• Appreciate why you are a citizen of the nation and of a state.
▶ Summarize how the Constitution institutes the federal system		
The Constitution grants specified powers to the national government, reserving all remaining powers to the states and to the people. It also limits both federal and state powers and lays out the relationships among the states and between the states and the federal government.	• Describe the different types of powers in the Constitution. • State the limits on powers established in the Constitution. • Explain how the Constitution helps set the relationship between the national and federal governments.	• Propose additional limits that you would like to see on governmental power.
▶ Outline how U.S. federalism has changed over time		
The American system was an experiment, and its evolution has been shaped by the tensions, even conflicts, inherent in a system in which power is both divided and shared. From the beginning, nation- and state-centered interests have been pitted against each other. One recurring substantive theme in the federalism debate has involved slavery, race, and equality, with nation-centered federalism used generally to advance equality for minorities subject to discrimination. Over the years, nation-centered federalism has generally expanded through legislation and court interpretation, although there have been eras in which the Court held Congress back, and elections in which the people indicated that they thought the national government had too much power.	• Describe the role that federalism played in the run-up to the Civil War. • Explain the "layer cake" analogy in dual federalism. • Compare dual federalism with cooperative federalism. • Explain what led to the New Federalism. • Find Antifederalist arguments in today's political debates.	• Evaluate whether the federal government is too powerful. • Detect friction in your community between state and federal powers. • Decide whether the Antifederalists were correct.
▶ Compare and contrast national and state governments		
All fifty states have separate legislative, executive, and judicial branches that look remarkably similar to those of the federal government, while local governments use a greater range of organizational options. The structure of the federal system has a profound effect on public policy, allowing states to learn from each other but sometimes forcing them into competition with each other. The federal system also allows for vast disparities among the states, particularly in the quality of elementary and secondary education. Benefits of federalism include multiple gateways to influence, including methods of direct democracy such as the initiative and referendum. Federalism also enhances democracy by enabling more people to live under laws that are made locally, rather than forcing nationwide conformity.	• Compare the general features of state governments to their national counterparts. • Compare the features of local governments to their national counterparts. • Weigh the advantages and disadvantages of direct democracy.	• Lobby a state representative on a state issue that is important to you. • Lobby a local official on a local issue that is important to you. • Draft a referendum you would like to see your state vote on.

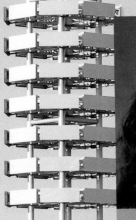

"My greatest regret is that rather than believing in myself, I allowed someone else's opinion to postpone my dreams."

R. STEPHANIE GOOD
Stony Brook University,
Stony Brook, New York

4

Civil Liberties

R. Stephanie Good started her college career later in life than many people, waiting until she was in her mid-thirties before enrolling first at Nassau Community College on Long Island in New York and then at nearby Stony Brook University. She graduated from both schools with highest honors, but she was as well known for her political activism as she was for her academic excellence. During her college years, she campaigned for public officials, demonstrated on behalf of environmental issues, and got arrested at Stony Brook as part of a "tent-city" protest over housing for graduate students. Committed to the idea that justice is served only when citizens take action on their own behalf, she went on to law school, earning a law degree at Hofstra University and, ten years later, a master's degree in law.

While practicing law, Good started writing. Her first book, *Law School 101,* presents survival techniques for law school and life as an attorney. Her next two books (both coauthored) uncovered corruption in notorious criminal proceedings. *Aruba: The Tragic Untold Story of Natalee Holloway and Corruption in Paradise*, a *New York Times* best seller, recounts the disappearance and presumed murder of a high school student on a school graduation trip. *A Rush to Injustice* tells the story of the Duke University lacrosse case, in which a reelection-seeking prosecutor maliciously filed felony sexual assault charges against college students whom he knew were innocent.

Good's commitment to protection of the innocent was also personal. When she was in law school, she learned that one of her sons had been subjected to inappropriate solicitations by an instructor at their local church. After she went public about this violation, other families revealed inappropriate touching by the instructor. Yet the judicial system did not consider the matter to be serious, and the instructor received only a fifteen-day sentence. Years later, when Good thought the instructor might be seeking out her son again, she decided to go online to try to find boys who also received unwarranted attention from the instructor, creating a fictitious 13-year-old girl with the AOL handle "teen2hot4u." That handle attracted interest from adult men interested in sex with an underage girl. Good then contacted the Federal

Need to Know

4.1 Identify what civil liberties are

4.2 Explain why civil liberties are limited in times of crisis

4.3 Distinguish what rights of expression the First Amendment protects

4.4 Determine what religious freedoms the First Amendment protects

4.5 Outline how the "right to bear arms" has been interpreted

4.6 Describe what protections the Bill of Rights provides to those accused of crimes

4.7 Assess what constitutes the right to privacy

▶ **WATCH & LEARN** MindTap™ for American Government
Watch a brief "What Do You Know?" video summarizing Civil Liberties.

Bureau of Investigation (FBI), which asked her to continue to play out her undercover role. Agents schooled Good on how to avoid violating the rights of the people with whom she communicated because although they may have been intent on breaking laws regarding the molestation of children, their rights as citizens also had to be protected, including their right to fair legal proceedings and their right to be considered legally innocent until proven guilty. First, she could not initiate conversations with anyone. Second, she could not be the first person to mention sex. And third, she could not be the first person to suggest a meeting. Despite these restrictions, teen-2hot4u attracted the attention of hundreds of men, more than twenty of whom tried to arrange a sexual meeting, got arrested, and then, with Good's testimony, were convicted and sentenced to prison. Good's efforts literally saved hundreds of young children from having their lives ruined. She recounted the story in her fourth book, *Exposed: The Harrowing Story of a Mother's Undercover Work with the FBI to Save Children from Internet Sex Predators.* Congressman Tim Bishop (D-N.Y.) awarded Good a certificate of commendation for her work.

In a democracy, criminal investigations must be conducted in a way that protects both the victims and society and those who are accused of crimes. Reprehensible crimes, such as sexual abuse of children, test people's willingness to recognize the rights of the accused. Yet without standard and fair criminal proceedings, citizens would be subjected to arbitrary arrest and possibly punishment, as the Duke lacrosse case shows. The tensions surrounding freedom and fair treatment in a democracy extend beyond criminal procedure. Disagreements about politics, particularly during wartime, also test people's willingness to tolerate differences in opinion. Even in peacetime, the tension between liberty, the desire to say or do what one wants, and order, the need for rules necessary for society to function, divide society. Americans want their homes to be secure against police intrusions, but they also want the police to be able to find evidence of crimes committed by others. They want freedom to follow their personal religious beliefs, but they do not want illegal practices to be allowed just because one religion might endorse them. In this chapter, we examine the balance and tension between liberty and order, with particular attention to the liberties guaranteed in the U.S. Constitution.

4.1 What Are Civil Liberties?

› Identify what civil liberties are

civil liberties: *Those rights, such as freedom of speech and religion, that are so fundamental that they are outside the authority of government to regulate.*

Bill of Rights: *First ten amendments to the Constitution, which provide basic political rights.*

natural (unalienable) rights: *Rights that every individual has and that government cannot legitimately take away.*

LISTEN & LEARN

MindTap™ for American Government

Access Read Speaker to listen to Chapter 4.

In 1787, the most powerful argument of the Antifederalists against the proposed constitution was that it did not protect fundamental liberties. The Antifederalist declared that these liberties, including the rights of conscience and the right of accused criminals to hear the charges against them, needed to be explicitly stated.[1] As we saw in Chapter 2, The Constitution, the Federalists eventually agreed and, to secure ratification of the Constitution, promised to amend it immediately.

Civil Liberties and Civil Rights

The **civil liberties** that were then written into the Constitution as the first ten amendments, or **Bill of Rights**, were freedoms that Americans held to be so fundamental that government may not legitimately take them away. This placed into law some of the **natural** or **unalienable rights** that Thomas Jefferson spoke about in the Declaration of Independence. These include, among others, freedom of speech and religious belief. As Supreme Court justice, Robert Jackson wrote in a 1943 case striking down a mandatory flag salute for school children that the government has no authority whatsoever over what we say or think. "If there is any fixed star in our constitutional constellation, it is that no official, high or petty, can prescribe what shall be orthodox in politics, nationalism, religion, or other

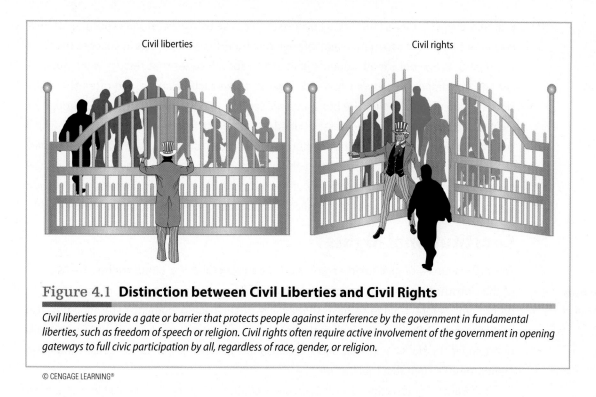

Civil liberties   Civil rights

Figure 4.1 Distinction between Civil Liberties and Civil Rights

Civil liberties provide a gate or barrier that protects people against interference by the government in fundamental liberties, such as freedom of speech or religion. Civil rights often require active involvement of the government in opening gateways to full civic participation by all, regardless of race, gender, or religion.

© CENGAGE LEARNING®

matters of opinion or force citizens to confess by word or act their faith therein."[2] Civil *liberties* are outside government's authority to regulate, whereas civil *rights* are rights that government is obliged to protect (see Figure 4.1). These are based on the expectation of equality under the law and relate to the duties of citizenship and to opportunities for full participation in civic life. Civil rights are the subject of the next chapter.

Balancing Liberty and Order

The protection of civil liberties requires a governmental system designed to do so. James Madison argued in *Federalist* 10 (see the Appendix) that a representative democracy will be able to keep a minority from violating the rights of others but may not be able to hold back a majority. Thus if a majority wishes to infringe on rights, it often falls to the judiciary, which is not designed to be responsive to public desires, to protect those rights.[3] In this way, the system of separation of powers and of checks and balances would help ensure the rights of all.

→ KEY QUESTIONS:
Why aren't civil liberties subject to majority rule?

While maximizing individual liberty might seem like a great idea, complete liberty could lead to a breakdown of order. As Supreme Court Justice Oliver Wendell Holmes wrote in a World War I speech case, freedom of speech does not mean that an individual has the right to falsely shout "Fire!" in a crowded theater and cause a panic.[4] Nor can liberty completely protect people from police investigations when criminal activity is suspected. Too much freedom can lead to anarchy, a state in which everyone does as he or she chooses without regard to others. Alternatively, too much order can lead to tyranny, a state in which the people are not free to make decisions about the private aspects of their lives. Protecting civil liberties thus requires a balance between individual liberty and public order.

→ KEY QUESTIONS:
Which is more important to you, liberty or order?

The freedom obtained through civil liberties can conflict not only with order but also with equality. In fact, civil liberties and civil rights sometimes conflict with each other. For example, civil rights laws that forbid businesses to refuse to serve customers because of their race limit freedom of association and infringe on property rights. Efforts at colleges to create an equal environment for all students have led to speech codes that restrict what students can say on campus. Society must decide how to strike such balances, and often that decision is a difficult one. In the case of businesses serving all customers, the nation, through its elected representatives in Congress, decided that the restriction on liberty was well worth the gain in equality. In the case of campus speech codes, students have successfully pressured many universities to rescind speech codes, and where the universities have kept the codes, students have used the gateway of the judicial system to bring lawsuits against their schools. The courts have consistently ruled that speech codes violate the First Amendment.

Constitutional Rights

writ of *habeas corpus*: *Right of individuals who have been arrested and jailed to go before a judge, who determines whether their detention is legal.*

The main sources of civil liberties are the Constitution and the Bill of Rights. The articles of the Constitution protect the right to a **writ of *habeas corpus*,** the right of individuals to be brought before a judge to have the legality of their imprisonment determined. It also prohibits *ex post facto* laws, which make an act a crime after the act is committed, and bills of attainder, legislative acts that declare individuals guilty of a crime. The Constitution also guarantees the right to a trial by jury.

The Bill of Rights, ratified in 1791, protects additional rights, such as freedom of expression, the right to keep and bear arms, and criminal procedure (see Figure 4.2). We will examine each in detail later in the chapter.

The Bill of Rights and the States

incorporate: *Process of applying provisions of the Bill of Rights to the states.*

As originally written, the Bill of Rights limited the activities of the national government, not the state governments. Only at the end of the nineteenth century did the Supreme Court slowly begin to apply, or **incorporate**, the provisions of the Bill of Rights to the states.

Figure 4.2 Constitutional Amendments That Pertain to Civil Liberties

Color Code: Criminal procedure | Participation | Equality | Structure | Miscellaneous

First	1791	Prohibits abridging freedoms of religion, speech, press, assembly, and petition
Second	1791	Prohibits abridging the right to bear arms
Third	1791	Prohibits the involuntary quartering of soldiers in a person's home during peacetime
Fourth	1791	Prohibits unreasonable searches and seizures
Fifth	1791	Affirms the right to indictment by a grand jury and right to due process; protects against double jeopardy, self-incrimination, and taking of property without just compensation
Sixth	1791	Affirms rights to speedy and public trial, to confront witnesses, and to counsel
Seventh	1791	Affirms right to jury trials in civil suits over $20
Eighth	1791	Prohibits excessive bail, excessive fines, and cruel and unusual punishments
Ninth	1791	Declares that the enumeration of certain rights does not limit other rights retained by the people
Tenth	1791	Reserves the powers not granted to the national government to the states or to the people
Fourteenth	1868	Makes all persons born in the United States citizens of the United States and prohibits states from denying persons within its jurisdiction the privileges or immunities of citizens, the due process of law, and equal protection of the laws; apportionment by whole persons

© CENGAGE LEARNING®

The First Amendment is explicit about its application to the national government as it forbids certain actions by Congress. But other amendments are not explicitly tied to the national government. Thus the Fifth Amendment prohibits taking private property without just compensation. Was this a protection of citizens only against actions by the federal government or against their state governments as well?

The original answer, given by the Supreme Court in *Barron v. Baltimore* (1833), was that the Bill of Rights applied to the national government only. Under the *Barron* decision, state governments could abridge freedom of speech, the press, and religion; could conduct unreasonable searches and seizures; and more without violating the Constitution. State constitutions might protect such rights, but often they did not.

The Fourteenth Amendment (1868), which adds several restrictions on what the states can do, became a vehicle for the applications of the Bill of Rights to the states. One section declares, "No State shall make or enforce any law which shall abridge the privileges or immunities of citizens of the United States; nor shall any State deprive any person of life, liberty, or property, without due process of law." Some of those who wrote this amendment stated that one of its purposes was to overturn the *Barron v. Baltimore* decision and make the entire Bill of Rights applicable to the states.[5]

The Supreme Court never agreed with this position, known as total incorporation. But beginning in 1897, it slowly began to use the protection of "life, liberty, or property" in the Fourteenth Amendment's due process clause to incorporate some of the provisions of the Bill of Rights as binding on the states. In the 1897 case, the Court used this clause to hold that states could not deprive a railroad of its property without just compensation, a right similarly protected by the Fifth Amendment.[6] In 1925, the Court assumed that the protection of liberty in the due process clause prevented states from restricting freedom of speech, a right similarly protected by the First Amendment.[7] By 1937, the Court had settled on a process of **selective incorporation**, using the due process clause to bind the states to those provisions of the Bill of Rights that it deems to be fundamental rights.[8] This process helps equalize the protection of rights across the United States.

Today, almost all of the provisions of the First, Second, Fourth, Fifth, Sixth, and Eighth Amendments have been incorporated, with the exception of grand jury indictment and excessive fines (see Table 4.1). Thus, states can indict people, or bring them up on charges, through

→ KEY QUESTIONS:
Which government are citizens more likely to need a gate against—national or state?

selective incorporation:
Doctrine used by the Supreme Court to make those provisions of the Bill of Rights that are fundamental rights binding on the states.

Table 4.1 Incorporated and Not Incorporated Provisions of the First through Eighth Amendments

Amendment	Provisions Incorporated	Provisions Not Incorporated
First	Religion, speech, press, assembly, petition	
Second	Keep and bear arms	
Third		Quarter soldiers
Fourth	No unreasonable searches and seizures	
Fifth	Double jeopardy, self-incrimination, due process, taking of property without just compensation	Grand jury indictment
Sixth	Speedy and public trial, right to confront witnesses, right to counsel	
Seventh		Jury trials in civil suits over $20
Eighth	Cruel and unusual punishments, excessive bail	Excessive fines

Source: © Cengage Learning®

compelling interest test: *Standard frequently used by the Supreme Court in civil liberties cases to determine whether a state has a compelling interest for infringing on a right and whether the law is narrowly drawn to meet that interest.*

Checkpoint

CAN YOU:

■ Compare civil liberties to civil rights

■ Contrast the problems of too much freedom to those of too much order

■ Compare the importance of the rights in the 1787 Constitution with those in the Bill of Rights

■ State the extent and the limits of the original Bill of Rights

the decision of judges, though charges in federal courts need the approval of a grand jury, a special jury whose sole duty is to determine whether an individual should be put on trial. The Third Amendment's protection against the quartering of soldiers in one's home during peacetime, a practice that angered the colonists, has not been incorporated but is not likely to be used today. Nor are states required, as the Seventh Amendment commands, to provide jury trials in civil suits over $20.

Once incorporated, the Court needs to determine whether that right has been violated. Generally speaking, rather than rule on each case purely on its own, the Court adopts a test to guide its decision and applies the test to the case at hand to determine whether a particular limitation of rights is acceptable. For the political rights in the Bill of Rights, such as freedom of speech, the Court most commonly uses variations of the **compelling interest test**. Under the compelling interest test, the federal government or a state can limit rights only if the Supreme Court decides that (1) the government has a compelling interest in passing the law (for example, the law is necessary for the functioning of government), and (2) the law is narrowly drawn to meet that interest. For example, the government might have a compelling interest in banning speech that might incite religious wars, but such a law would have to be narrowly drawn so as not to prevent religious speech that merely calls for struggle against oppression. However, even with such a precise definition, individuals have fought over what constitutes a compelling interest throughout American history.

→ KEY QUESTIONS:
What civil liberties are you willing to give up to ensure more protection against terrorist attacks?

→ KEY QUESTIONS:
How free should you be to criticize the government? Should you be less free in wartime? Following 9/11?

→ KEY QUESTIONS:
Should enemy combatants have the same procedural safeguards as American citizens? What if the enemy combatant is an American citizen?

4.2 Civil Liberties in Times of Crisis

> Explain why civil liberties are limited in times of crisis

Attempts to limit civil liberties are more frequent in wartime or when other threats arise as a result of the government's increased concern for order and citizens' increased concerns about security. This pattern has existed from the earliest days of the republic; it continued during the Civil War, the two world wars, and the Cold War, and following the terrorist attacks of September 11, 2001. Popular support for civil liberties usually rebounds after the crisis ends.

The World Wars

During World War I, Congress passed the Espionage Act of 1917, which made it a crime to obstruct military recruiting, and amendments known as the Sedition Act of 1918, which banned "disloyal, profane, scurrilous or abusive language" about the Constitution or the government of the United States, as well as speech that interfered with the war effort. Subsequently, juries convicted antiwar activist Charles Schenck for circulating a flyer to draftees that compared the draft to the involuntary servitude prohibited by the Thirteenth Amendment, and Socialist Party presidential candidate Eugene V. Debs for giving a speech criticizing the war. The Supreme Court upheld both convictions, noting that greater restrictions on speech could be allowed in wartime.[9] After the war, Congress repealed the Sedition

Act, and President Warren G. Harding (1921–23) pardoned Debs. In no subsequent wars has the government restricted speech as it did with the Sedition Acts of 1798 and 1918.

The War on Terror

After 9/11, Congress passed the USA PATRIOT Act. The act allowed greater sharing of intelligence information and enhancement of law enforcement's ability to tap telephone and e-mail communications. It also regulated financial transactions with overseas entities and eased the process of deporting immigrants suspected of terrorist activities. Beyond the act, President George W. Bush (2001–2009) claimed the right, as commander in chief, to detain alleged enemy combatants indefinitely, whether U.S. citizens or foreign nationals. Thus Bush declared Jose Padilla, an American allegedly involved in a plan to detonate a radioactive bomb in the United States, an "enemy combatant" and transferred him from civilian to military authority, where he would have few, if any, procedural rights. The government kept Padilla in complete isolation for more than three and a half years. Unique among those declared enemy combatants, Padilla had not been captured on the field of battle but on American soil, and, having been born in Brooklyn, he was an American citizen.

When the Supreme Court ruled that noncitizens could not be held indefinitely as enemy combatants, it became clear that the government could not hold Padilla either. So, the Justice Department removed Padilla from military custody and charged him under federal criminal law with providing material support to terrorist organizations. The government did not charge him with attempting to detonate a radioactive bomb in the United States or with conspiring to commit terrorist acts in the United States, suggesting that the original claims against him might not have held up in a court of law. His trial in Miami, with the full set of constitutional rights, required that Padilla be represented by counsel, that he be allowed to cross-examine witnesses, and that the government prove its case beyond a reasonable doubt. The government proved its case, and a jury quickly determined that Padilla was guilty. The judge then sentenced him to seventeen years in prison.

Although fewer rights exist for enemy combatants who are not U.S. citizens,[10] the Supreme Court has ruled that Congress must authorize hearings to determine the legality of the detention of even foreign enemy combatants. Such hearings must be consistent with the 1949 Geneva Conventions, an international treaty that protects the rights of prisoners of war.[11]

Beyond the enemy combatant cases, President Bush and President Obama have ordered warrantless wiretapping of conversations and interception of e-mail between American citizens and suspected foreign terrorists; normally, wiretapping requires a warrant signed by a judge or magistrate backed by probable cause that a crime is being committed. (See Public Policy and Civil Liberties: National Security Surveillance.)

Speaking in Canton, Ohio, on June 16, 1918, Eugene V. Debs, labor organizer and three-time Socialist Party candidate for president, criticized the government for restricting free speech during wartime and declared, "If war is right let it be declared by the people." Charged with sedition, he was convicted and sentenced to prison. While in jail, he ran for president once again and received more than 900,000 votes, about 3.4 percent of all votes cast.

→ KEY QUESTIONS: Should government have access to your phone calls and e-mail messages?

→ KEY QUESTIONS: Should the United States obey the Geneva Conventions?

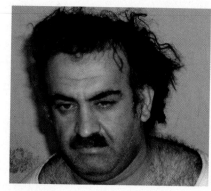

This widely circulated photograph of Khalid Sheikh Mohammed was taken on March 1, 2003, shortly after his capture during a raid in Pakistan. He is accused of masterminding the September 11, 2001, terrorist attacks on the United States and is being held at Guantanamo Bay, Cuba, awaiting trial. Local opposition prevented the Obama administration from trying him in an open criminal trial, with full legal rights, just blocks from the site of the World Trade Center attacks.

Public Policy and Civil Liberties:
National Security Surveillance

As President Obama has noted, protection against terrorist threats requires some restrictions on liberty and privacy. Though many people think of the CIA as the main intelligence agency in the United States, it is the National Security Agency (NSA) that conducts virtually all of the security-related electronic surveillance for the government, such as listening to phone calls and reading e-mails. In 1978, Congress passed the Foreign Intelligence Surveillance Act (FISA). The Act established secret FISA Courts to determine whether the United States could authorize the NSA to conduct national security wiretaps within the United States. The judges on that court are all appointed by the chief justice of the United States from among the U.S. District Courts without confirmation by the Senate. Prior to the 9/11 attacks in 2001, the FISA courts had never denied a government request for electronic surveillance.[12]

Just six weeks after the 9/11 attacks on the United States, Congress overwhelmingly passed the USA PATRIOT Act. The Act expanded the surveillance capabilities of the United States in several ways: It granted the NSA new authority to monitor e-mail, and it allowed a single warrant to cover all phones that a suspect might use.[13] President Bush ordered warrantless wiretapping (by the NSA) of conversations and interception of e-mail between American citizens and suspected foreign terrorists. Congress did endorse aspects of the president's plan after the *New York Times* published stories about the then-secret program. The program expired, but the Obama administration moved—on national security grounds—to block a lawsuit over the wiretapping brought by an Islamic charity alleged to be involved in terrorist activities.[14] In 2012, a 9th Circuit Court of Appeals panel overturned a district court ruling that the program was illegal and blocked damages claimed by the Al-Haramain Islamic Foundation.[15]

Then in 2013, Edward Snowden, a former employee of the NSA, stole and leaked tens of thousands of documents that he had access to. Those documents revealed that the NSA kept track of every phone call made in the United States, regardless of whether there was any evidence of suspicious activity. These records tracked who called whom and when, but they did not record conversations. The NSA believed that such records could help it uncover information to aid in preventing terrorist attacks.

Many Americans were outraged at what they felt to be a violation of their right to privacy. Yet the 1979 Supreme Court case *Smith v. Maryland* seemed to uphold the constitutionality of the government's warrantless use of "pen registers," devices that kept track of who called whom when without recording the conversations. Smith had robbed a woman and then began calling her. With a lead from a license plate, the police placed the pen register on Smith's phone to prove that he had been calling the robbery victim. The fact that the Court upheld the use of pen registers suggests that the NSA program is constitutional.[16] President Obama additionally defended the program by stating, "You can't have 100% security and then have 100% privacy and zero inconvenience. You know, we're going to have to make some choices as a society."[17]

Nevertheless, a lower court judge ruled that the ability of the government to obtain these records *en masse* made the violation far more serious than the individual record keeping from

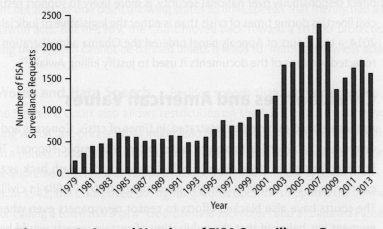

Figure 4.3 **Annual Number of FISA Surveillance Requests**

Note: The number of rejected surveillance applications are as follows: 2003 (4), 2006 (1), 2007 (4), 2008 (1), 2009 (1). In all other years, the number of rejected surveillance applications was 0.

Source: Adapted from the source material here: http://epic.org/privacy/wiretap/stats/fisa_stats.html

the 1979 case. The case against the NSA may become moot, however, because President Obama called for an end to the NSA's bulk collection of data in March 2014.[18] Yet, the issue may reemerge in the future until it is resolved in court.

The NSA has also filed individualized surveillance requests as shown in Figure 4.3. Between 2002 and 2012, the court rejected only eleven of nearly twenty thousand surveillance applications, about 0.05 percent.[19] Part of the reason for this is that the objects of the surveillance obviously do not get to provide evidence to counter the government's position. The director of the Administrative Office of the U.S. Courts has proposed a special advocate to promote the public's privacy interests in any particular case.[20] The ACLU filed suit against the NSA, but federal courts ruled that without evidence proving they were wiretapped, they didn't have standing to sue.

Following the 9/11 attacks, public opinion shifted strongly toward governmental efforts to increase security, even at the expense of liberty and privacy. If these programs keep future attacks from occurring, they may be very effective at keeping the freedom–order equation in balance.

Construct Your Own Policy

1. Design a policy that allows an advocate for privacy rights to rebut the government's case for surveillance.
2. Design a policy to investigate foreign and internal threats to the United States that distinguishes among postal mail, cell phone conversations, and e-mail activity.

supreme court cases

Snyder v. Phelps (2011)

QUESTION: May antimilitary and antigay protesters be sued for the distress they caused to the father of a marine killed in action in Iraq when they picketed at the marine's funeral?

ORAL ARGUMENT: October 6, 2010 (listen at http://www.oyez.org/cases/2010-2019/2010/2010_09_751)

DECISION: March 2, 2011 (read at http://www.law.cornell.edu/supct/html/09-751.ZS.html)

OUTCOME: The protesters are protected by the First Amendment because they are speaking out on a question of public concern.

For more than twenty years, the congregation of the Westboro Baptist Church in Topeka, Kansas, has picketed the funerals of members of the U.S. military. The church does so to show its opposition to homosexuality and the army's toleration thereof since the establishment of the "Don't Ask, Don't Tell" policy during the Clinton administration. Their pickets infamously declare that "God hates f* [pejorative for homosexuals]" and "Thank God for Dead Soldiers." These pickets at the funeral of Matthew Snyder aggravated his father, who sued the church, the minister (Fred Phelps, now deceased), and several of Phelps's daughters for intentional infliction of emotional distress. A jury awarded Snyder nearly $11 million in damages. When the U.S. Court of Appeals overturned the verdict, Snyder appealed to the Supreme Court.

The Supreme Court ruled 8–1 in favor of the protesters, declaring that the church's views on homosexuality in the military were a matter of public concern, and as such, it did not matter how crudely those concerns were expressed. They compared this intentional infliction of emotional distress to an earlier case upholding a suit dealing with an individual's credit report, which was purely a private matter. Nor did the Court find that the Westboro protests involved "fighting words," which the Court has ruled to be beyond the protections of the First Amendment. Justice Samuel Alito, in dissent, argued that the First Amendment does not give the church the right to brutalize Matthew's father while he is burying his only son. In an earlier speech case, the Court ruled that the function of the First Amendment is to "invite dispute." The boundary between "inviting dispute," which is protected, and "fighting words," which are not, is not always clear.

1. Do you believe that the Westboro Church's position on homosexuals and the military is a question of public concern? Explain.

2. Do you believe that the Westboro Church's protests at the funeral constituted "fighting words"? Explain.

to be a form of hate speech that could be banned.[29] On the other hand, the Court did not consider picketers at the funerals of U.S. soldiers to be engaged in hate speech, despite their inflammatory signs against homosexuals (see Supreme Court Cases: *Snyder v. Phelps*).

→ KEY QUESTIONS:
Should Americans be required to salute the flag? Should they be prevented from burning the flag?

Symbolic Speech.   In the 1960s, the Des Moines school district suspended students Mary Beth Tinker, her brother John, and a third student when they wore black armbands to protest the Vietnam War. The students voiced no opinions while wearing these armbands, and no disruptions in their schools occurred. The Iowa Civil Liberties Union, an interest group that supports civil rights and liberties, brought suit against the school board, claiming that students are equal to other Americans and retain the freedom of speech rights granted by the First Amendment. The Supreme Court agreed.[30] In this instance, the armbands were considered **symbolic speech**, like other nonverbal activities that convey a political message, such as saluting the flag, burning the flag, or burning draft cards—the latter two actions also undertaken by anti–Vietnam War protesters. Alternatively, in another case, employees of a local sheriff's office "liked" the Facebook page of the person running for office against the sheriff. The sheriff fired the employees, who argued that their First Amendment rights had been violated. The court has ruled that "liking" a Facebook page is too shallow an expressive act to count as constitutionally protected speech.[31]

symbolic speech:
Actions, such as burning the flag, that convey a political message without spoken words.

The Court has allowed prohibitions on the burning of draft cards because Congress has a **content-neutral** justification for requiring draft-eligible citizens to be in possession of their draft cards. That is, draft cards are essential to the smooth running of the draft,[32] and prohibiting their destruction is not intended to suppress the views of those who burn them. The Court once ruled that states also have a neutral justification for limiting protests near health care facilities, even if most of the protesters are advocating pro-life positions.[33] But in 2014 the Court reached a unanimous decision striking down a Massachusetts law limiting protests at facilities where abortions are performed. The Court has also overturned laws that require saluting the flag, as such laws do intend to instill a political viewpoint.[34] Similarly, the Court has overturned laws prohibiting flag burning, as such laws are not content neutral: They are based almost entirely on opposition to the idea being delivered by flag burning.[35] Of course, flag burners can be arrested on charges that would apply to anyone who starts a fire in public.

content-neutral:
Free speech doctrine that allows certain types of regulation of speech, as long as the restriction does not favor one side or another of a controversy.

On the other hand, the content-neutral rule, like most constitutional rules, is not absolute. Some messages can be regulated solely because of opposition to the message, as when the Supreme Court upheld a student's suspension for unfurling a banner at a parade that declared "Bong Hits 4 Jesus" because of the banner's promotion of drug use.[36] It is easy for the Court to formulate simple rules, such as a prohibition on content-based regulations, but harder for the Court to apply those rules consistently in the unusual cases that come before it.

BETTMANN/CORBIS

Mary Beth and John Tinker were teenagers in 1965 when they wore black armbands to school to protest the Vietnam War, and they were suspended. Arguing that students have free speech rights, the Iowa Civil Liberties Union sued the school district on their behalf and appealed the suspension in a series of cases that were finally appealed to the Supreme Court. In 1969, the Court ruled in the Tinkers' favor, stating: "It can hardly be argued that either students or teachers shed their constitutional rights to freedom of speech or expression at the schoolhouse gate."

Time, Place, and Manner Regulations.   The fact that the First Amendment protects freedom of speech does not mean there is a right to speak wherever one wants, whenever one wants.

In 2002, high school student Joseph Frederick unfurled this banner while his class watched the Olympic Torch relay pass through Juneau, Alaska. When the principal suspended Frederick for the banner's message about drugs, Frederick sued, saying that his free speech rights had been violated. The court of appeals, relying on the *Tinker* case, reversed the suspension, but in 2007, the Supreme Court upheld it, saying a student's free speech rights did not extend to the promotion of illegal drugs.

Regulations of the time, place, and manner of speech, such as when or where protests may take place, are generally valid as long as they are neutral or equal, that is, they do not favor one side or another of a controversy. Thus states can prohibit protests near school grounds that interfere with school activities as there is no indication that such bans favor one side of any controversy over any other side.[37]

Freedom of the Press

Thomas Jefferson, among other Founders, thought freedom of the press crucial to a free society because the press keeps the public informed about the government's activities. When the Bill of Rights was written, "the press" meant newspapers; today the term covers not only the large companies that own television and radio stations but also individually run blogs and Internet sites that anyone can create. While freedom of the press once belonged to those who owned one, today it belongs to everyone.

Like freedom of speech, however, freedom of the press is not absolute. In extraordinarily extreme cases, the government can censor items before they are published. This practice is known as **prior restraint**. In other situations, the government can punish people after the fact for what they publish.

prior restraint: *Government restrictions on freedom of the press that prevent material from being published.*

Prior Restraint.   Following English law, freedom of the press in the colonies and in the early years of the United States meant freedom from prior censorship;[38] today, an extraordinary burden of proof of imminent harm is needed before the courts will shut down a newspaper before a story is printed. Even when the *New York Times* began publishing excerpts from a top-secret Pentagon analysis of U.S. involvement in the Vietnam War, the courts refused to stop the presses. The story of this case, *New York Times v. United States* (1971),[39] is told in more detail in Chapter 6, Public Opinion and the Media. One case in which the courts said that the government had met the extraordinary burden standard involved the publication of instructions on how to build a hydrogen bomb,[40] but generally, court approval of censorship by prior restraint has been so difficult to achieve that the federal government has not sought it since the 1970s. Thus even as many major newspapers published information leaked by Edward Snowden that the United States considered to be highly classified, the government did not attempt to prevent the news media from publishing it, although they did indict Edward Snowden.

First Amendment law protects the Internet and blogs from government censorship in much the same way that it protects newspapers, but the technology of the Internet makes censorship far more difficult. This was the lesson learned by a federal judge who tried to censor Julian Assange's Wikileaks website,[41] which publishes confidential documents from government, business, and religious organizations. Though the judge ordered the Wikileaks. org domain name disabled, Wikileaks already had mirror sites set up all over the world. Facing a barrage of criticism from bloggers and mainstream media groups, and given the ineffectiveness of his original decision, the judge reversed himself. But while many people may support the right of Wikileaks to publish allegations of money laundering by a Swiss bank, as in this case, what happens when Wikileaks publishes, as it has, a diagram of the first atomic bomb or secret documents about the war in Afghanistan?[42] Such cases show the difficulty of balancing freedom of the press versus censorship in a dangerous world.

→ KEY QUESTIONS:
What information on the web should the government censor?

Subsequent Punishment.   In certain instances, the government can engage in subsequent punishment, fining, and/or imprisoning writers and publishers after the fact for what they publish. Examples here include penalties for libel and for publishing obscenity, incitement to acts of violence, and secret military information.

The standards for convicting in a case of libel—the publishing of false and damaging statements about another person—vary according to whether that person is a public figure. The Supreme Court has made it harder for public figures than for ordinary individuals to sue for libel because public figures have access to the media and can more readily defend themselves without lawsuits. For public figures to sue, the materials must be false and damaging, and the writer or publisher must have acted with actual malice, that is, with knowledge that the material was false or with reckless disregard of whether it was true or false. Further, satire is largely exempt from libel laws. Such was in the case in *Hustler Magazine's* spoof on the "first time" for the Reverend Jerry Falwell, the founder of the conservative Christian group, Moral Majority.[43] For private figures to sue for libel, the material must be false and damaging, and there must be some degree of negligence, but the actual malice test does not apply. In democratic countries, courts can protect satire against public figures. That is less true in authoritarian countries, as the girls behind the Russian rock band Pussy Riot discovered (see Global Gateways).

→ KEY QUESTIONS:
How can you protect yourself from what others may say about you on the web?

Before development of the World Wide Web, only those who published printed materials could libel someone, but even then, the damage would largely be limited to those who subscribed to the publication. With the Internet, anyone can libel anyone else, and the whole world can see it. At Yale University, for example, anonymous contributors to a popular law school message board wrote derogatory comments about several female law students, including fabricated statements about their mental capacity and sexual activities. Because anyone, including potential employers, can see such statements, the potential for harm is enormous.[44] Given the anonymous nature of the posts, identifying and prosecuting the source of the statements can be difficult, if not impossible. Because freedom of speech is a fundamental right, there is no easy solution to protecting privacy in the Internet age.

Today, the government can seek subsequent punishment against individuals who publish military secrets or obscene materials. Pornographic material is not necessarily obscene, and pornography that falls short of the legal definition of obscenity receives First Amendment protection. Specifically, for materials to be obscene, they must pass all three parts of what has become known as the *Miller* test: (1) to the average person, applying contemporary community standards as established by the relevant state, the work, taken as a whole (not just isolated passages), appeals to the prurient (sexual) interest; (2) the work depicts in an offensive way sexual conduct specifically defined by the state law; and (3) the work lacks serious literary, artistic, political, or scientific value.[45]

Miller **test:** *Supreme Court test for determining whether material is obscene.*

→ KEY QUESTIONS:
Should pornography be submitted to the marketplace of ideas? Or should it be censored? On what legal grounds?

globalgateways

Pussy Riot

When the Communist Soviet Union disbanded in 1991, Boris Yeltsin became the first president of the Russian Federation, which made up the bulk of the territory, population, and military might of the former Soviet Union. Twice elected president of a burgeoning Russian democracy, Yeltsin suddenly resigned in 1999, leaving Vladimir Putin, the former director of the Soviet Secret Service (KGB) as president. Putin proved not to be a supporter of democracy and began to crack down on powerful oligarchs and powerless individuals who opposed him.

Among the powerless who opposed him was the female punk rock group Pussy Riot. In February 2012, the group, wearing masks, satirized Putin in a song they played at the main Russian Orthodox Church in Moscow. Russian authorities arrested three of the group's members, and two of them were sentenced to two years in prison. After an early release that preceded the 2014 Winter Olympics in Sochi, Russia, Amnesty International (a group that promotes freedom worldwide) brought the formerly imprisoned members, Nadezhda Tolokonnikova and Maria Alyokhina, to the United States to publicize their fight for freedom in Russia. When asked by late night talk show host Stephen Colbert why they were arrested, Alyokhina replied "We sang a fun song in a church."[46]

Before they formed Pussy Riot, Tolokonnikova and Alyokhina protested Russia's laws against homosexual behavior by kissing "forty police women."[47] When the *New York Times* asked them whether they were afraid they would be imprisoned again, Alyokhina responded, "In the two years since we were imprisoned, the situation in Russia has gotten so much worse. And if we couldn't keep quiet about it then, we certainly won't keep quiet about it now."[48] At great personal risk, the members of Pussy Riot used punk rock music as their gateway to influence their fellow citizens in a country where most of the gateways to civic influence are closed off.

1. Why would a leader such as Putin be afraid of satire?
2. Do you know musical groups that have used satire to make political points?

Under the *Miller* test, only "hard-core" materials could be banned.[49] The government has much greater leeway to prohibit "kiddie porn" that uses actual children[50] but not "virtual child pornography," which uses computer-simulated children.[51] Nor can the government's desire to protect children from indecent materials be used as a justification for prohibiting pornography that does not reach the level of obscenity from the Internet.[52] Similarly, the state may not ban the purchase of violent video games by minors.[53] According to a 2010 decision, under the *Miller* test, states may not ban fetish videos that, in the case at hand, showed women in high heels crushing the skulls of puppies.[54]

Checkpoint

CAN YOU:

- State the limits on the First Amendment's right to freedom of speech
- Compare prior restraint on the press to subsequent punishment

4.4 Religious Freedom

> Determine what religious freedoms the First Amendment protects

The First Amendment sets forth two distinct protections about religion. Congress, and now the states, generally may not prevent people from practicing their religious beliefs. They also cannot pass laws that establish an official religion or even favor one religion over another.

Free Exercise

Many of the first settlers in the American colonies came because of restrictions on their religious beliefs in England, where the Anglican Church was established as the official religion. When these settlers first arrived, they did not establish general freedom of religion but, rather, freedom for their religion.

> **KEY QUESTIONS:**
> Should all religions get equal treatment?

Victories for religious freedom, though significant, were rare in the colonial period. In 1786, however, the Virginia General Assembly passed Thomas Jefferson's Statute for Religious Freedom, which declared freedom of religious conscience to be a natural right of mankind that governments could not restrict. Five years later, this right was affirmed in the **free exercise clause** of the Bill of Rights. Like all the provisions of the Bill of Rights, however, it originally protected individuals only against the national government, and at the time only two states—Virginia and Rhode Island—had unqualified religious freedom. So ingrained was state authority to regulate religion that when James Madison proposed an amendment that would have limited such authority, Congress rejected it.[55] Today, however, with the incorporation of the Bill of Rights, the right of individuals to the free exercise of religion is also outside of state authority to regulate.

free exercise clause: *First Amendment clause protecting the free exercise of religion.*

Under the First Amendment, the government cannot criminalize an individual's private religious beliefs. Nor can the government ban specific religious activities, including student-run publications,[56] just because they are based on religious beliefs. For example, the Supreme Court struck down a ban on religious-based animal sacrifices because killing animals for other reasons was not prohibited.[57] But not all religious-based activities are protected, and states are generally free to pass laws that restrict religious practices as long as such laws have a **valid secular (nonreligious) purpose**. For example, states can ban polygamy, even though marriage with multiple wives is a central belief in some religions.[58] The state court of Utah, however, in response to a case brought by the family featured on the television show *Sister Wives*, has recently ruled that the ban on cohabitation is an unconstitutional violation

valid secular purpose: *Supreme Court test that allows states to ban activities that infringe on religious practices as long as the state has a nonreligious rationale for prohibiting the behavior.*

In 2014, the Court decided that the Hobby Lobby Corporation, which is owned by a devout Christian, did not have to abide by the requirement in the Affordable Care Act that its employee health care plan provide free access to birth control pills when the corporate owner believes that such pills can result, not just in the prevention of, but in the termination of pregnancy.

of religious freedom. Thus while the state may continue to prevent a man from having multiple marriage licenses, it cannot prevent a man from living with multiple women.[59]

In the 1960s, the Court ruled that states must have a compelling interest before they can abridge people's religious practices, even if the law restricting the practice has a valid secular purpose. Thus even though the government has a valid secular purpose in conducting a military draft, members of religious groups that oppose warfare, such as Quakers, may be exempt. In the case of former boxing champion Muhammad Ali, a Muslim, who argued that he could only fight wars declared by Allah or the Prophet, the Court overturned a conviction for draft evasion.[60]

One case that demonstrates the contest between the branches of government over what constitutes free exercise concerns the use of the hallucinogenic drug peyote in religious rituals. In 1990, when two Native American drug counselors who used peyote were fired from their jobs and denied unemployment compensation, the Supreme Court used the valid secular purpose test to uphold Oregon's decision to deny this compensation.[61] Members of Congress overwhelmingly disapproved, however, and passed legislation stating that the Supreme Court must use the compelling interest test in deciding free exercise cases. The Supreme Court responded by declaring part of the Religious Freedom Restoration Act unconstitutional repeating the statement from *Marbury v. Madison* that the province of the judicial branch is "to say what the law is."[62] Congress does have the authority, however, to declare the religious use of peyote to be legal, and it has done so. Moreover, Congress has decided that its own laws must have a compelling interest before they can limit religious freedom.

Generally, states need only have a valid secular purpose to pass laws that also happen to restrict religious practices. On the other hand, the Supreme Court has established a "ministerial exception" that frees religious organizations from having to abide by federal anti-discrimination laws—in this case, the Americans with Disabilities Act—when choosing their ministers. The Court here used the free exercise clause to limit the scope of an otherwise valid act of Congress.[63]

The Establishment of Religion

establishment clause: *First Amendment clause prohibiting governmental establishment of religion.*

The **establishment clause** of the First Amendment prevents Congress from recognizing one church as the nation's official church, as Britain had done with the Anglican (Episcopal) Church. Originally, states were free to establish state religions if they chose to, and when the Constitution was adopted, nearly half the states had done so.[64] The antiestablishment movement began in Virginia, where between 1784 and 1785, James Madison fought tax assessments used to support Christian religious teachers, and Thomas Jefferson secured passage of the Disestablishment Bill in 1786, which ended Virginia's official establishment of the Anglican Church. In an 1802 letter to the Baptists of Danbury, Connecticut, Jefferson called for a "wall of separation" between church and state. The Supreme Court adopted that phrase in 1947 but declared that using taxpayer funds to provide public transportation to parochial schools did not breach the wall.[65]

The establishment clause literally prohibits not just the establishment of religion but also any law "respecting an establishment of religion." The Supreme Court has taken this phrase to mean that steps by the government favoring one religion over another, or even religion over no religion, cannot be taken, even if those steps fall far short of an official establishment of religion.

Chaplain leads American Air Force crew serving in Afghanistan in prayer.

The Supreme Court's test for determining whether laws violate the establishment clause is known as the **Lemon test**, named after a litigant in a 1971 case.[66] Under this test, a challenged law must be shown to have a secular (nonreligious) legislative purpose and a primary effect that neither advances nor inhibits religion. The law must also avoid an excessive entanglement between church and state, such as a strict monitoring of church activities. Using these standards, the Supreme Court has banned organized school prayers and devotional Bible readings.[67] The Bible can be read as part of a comparative religion course, however, and students can pray silently. The Supreme Court has also used this test to strike down laws that prohibited the teaching of evolution[68] as well as laws granting equal time for creation science—the position that scientific evidence supports the biblical view of creation—if evolution is taught.[69] Whether doctrines are called creation science or intelligent design, courts have ruled that they are religious doctrines that cannot constitutionally be taught as part of the science curricula in public schools. Nevertheless, state legislatures, presumably in an attempt to be responsive to their constituents, continue to approve creation science curricula.

It is often difficult to understand why some activities violate the establishment clause and others do not. Separationists believe, with Jefferson, that there should be a strict wall between church and state. Accommodationists, on the other hand, believe that as long as the state does not favor one religion over another, it can generally pass laws that support religion. The Supreme Court's decisions on these grounds have been mixed, with conservative justices typically supporting the accommodationist position, and liberal justices typically supporting the separationist view (see Chapter 13, The Judiciary, on ideology and the Supreme Court). The end result has been confusion: The Court allows short religious prayers by clergy at high school graduation ceremonies as long as students are not compelled to participate[70] but not by students at high school football games.[71] States may provide textbooks for secular subjects in parochial schools[72] but not instructional aids such as charts and maps.[73]

Lemon test: *Test for determining whether aid to religion violates the establishment clause.*

→ KEY QUESTIONS:
Should prayers be allowed in school? Under what circumstances? What types of prayers? Is saying a silent prayer the same as wearing an armband?

Checkpoint

CAN YOU:

■ Explain the difference between free exercise of religion and the establishment of religion

■ State the difference between separationists and accommodationists

⭐ Key Concepts

Bill of Rights (p. 88). Why is the Bill of Rights so important?

civil liberties (p. 88). What is the difference between civil liberties and civil rights?

clear and present danger test (p. 97). How much leeway does the clear and present danger test provide to dangerous speech?

compelling interest test (p. 92). What does the compelling interest test require?

content-neutral (p. 99). Why must time, place, and manner regulations be content-neutral?

establishment clause (p. 104). What were the Framers trying to prohibit with the establishment clause?

exclusionary rule (p. 108). Is the exclusionary rule fair?

expectation of privacy test (p. 107). What problems can you foresee with the expectation of privacy test?

free exercise clause (p. 103). Can the free exercise clause protect behavior, or does it just protect beliefs?

incorporate (p. 90). Why has incorporation been so important to our liberties?

Lawrence v. Texas (p. 113). Are laws that discriminate against gays or lesbians likely to continue to survive?

Lemon test (p. 105). Which prong(s) of the *Lemon* test might be violated if a state prohibits the teaching of evolution?

Miller test (p. 101). Does the *Miller* test go too far in regulating pornography, or does it not go far enough?

natural (unalienable) rights (p. 88). Which rights do you believe are unalienable?

political tolerance (p. 114). Why is political tolerance so essential for democracy?

prior restraint (p. 100). How does prior restraint harm the marketplace of ideas?

right to privacy (p. 111). What rights are protected under the right to privacy?

Roe v. Wade (p. 113). What would happen if the Constitution did not protect abortion rights?

selective incorporation (p. 91). How does selective incorporation differ from total incorporation?

symbolic speech (p. 99). How might one protest inequality without speaking any words?

valid secular purpose (p. 103). Why is the valid secular purpose test necessary?

writ of *habeas corpus* (p. 90). Why was this one of the few rights originally enshrined in the Constitution?

Learning Outcomes: What You Need . . .

To Know	To Test Yourself	To Participate
▶ **Identify what civil liberties are**		
Civil liberties are freedoms so fundamental that they are outside the authority of government to regulate. It often falls to the judiciary to protect them. They include, among others, rights surrounding freedom of expression and criminal procedure, and they were written into the Constitution in 1791 as the first ten amendments, or the Bill of Rights. Although these protections of individual freedoms at first applied only to the federal government, Supreme Court decisions have gradually applied many of them to the states as well.	• Compare civil liberties to civil rights. • Contrast the problems of too much freedom to those of too much order. • Compare the importance of the rights in the 1787 Constitution with those in the Bill of Rights. • State the extent and the limits of the original Bill of Rights.	• Know your constitutional rights. • Decide if any constitutional rights provide too much freedom. • Consider what would happen if civil liberties were subject to majority rule.
▶ **Explain why civil liberties are limited in times of crisis**		
Attempts to limit civil liberties are more frequent in wartime and during other threats, given increased government need for order and increased citizen concern about security. But support for the protection of civil liberties usually rebounds after the crisis ends. The scope of First Amendment freedoms of expression has generally expanded, although during wartime they are likely to be curtailed. Even in wartime, the courts have almost always protected the press from government censorship, but the government can prosecute newspapers for publishing obscenity, secret military information, and articles that incite violence.	• Identify the major targets of civil liberty restrictions during the world wars. • Describe the change and continuity in security regulations from President George W. Bush to President Obama. • Explain why wartime deprivation of rights ratchet back after the crisis ends.	• Consider whether dissent in wartime is unpatriotic. • Evaluate the role of the media in times of crisis. • Evaluate the threats to freedom from responses to terrorism.

To Know	To Test Yourself	To Participate
▶ **Distinguish what rights of expression the First Amendment protects**		
The First Amendment protects rights of speech, press, and assembly.	• State the limits on the First Amendment's right to freedom of speech. • Compare prior restraint on the press to subsequent punishment.	• Discuss whether First Amendment rights can be absolute.
▶ **Determine what religious freedoms the First Amendment protects**		
The First Amendment also protects freedom of religious practice and prevents the government from establishing one religion over all the others.	• Explain the difference between the free exercise of religion and the establishment of religion. • State the difference between separationists and accommodationists.	• Consider what would happen if the First Amendment granted a complete exemption from secular laws that violated one's religious beliefs. • Debate the "wall of separation" between church and state.
▶ **Outline how the "right to bear arms" has been interpreted**		
The Supreme Court has declared that the Second Amendment protects an individual right to bear arms for self-defense in one's home.	• Explain why the Second Amendment is ambiguous about an individual's right to keep and bear arms.	• Debate what limits should exist on gun rights and on what grounds.
▶ **Describe what protections the Bill of Rights provides to those accused of crimes**		
Provisions in the Fourth, Fifth, Sixth, and Eighth Amendments protect individuals accused of crimes in police investigations and regulate trial procedures and types of punishments.	• Describe the limits on police investigations of crimes. • Explain the trial rights protected by the Constitution. • State the protections for those convicted of crimes.	• List any additional limits you might like to see on police investigations or trial rights. • Debate the death penalty.
▶ **Assess what constitutes the right to privacy**		
Although the Constitution and its amendments do not explicitly grant a general right to privacy, the Supreme Court has used various constitutional provisions to establish this right, creating one of the most contentious areas of constitutional law and interpretation.	• Compare privacy rights in birth control and abortion. • Evaluate the role of public opinion on public laws toward homosexuality.	• Debate whether health insurance laws should require coverage for birth control. • Consider whether judicial protection of homosexual rights are necessary. • Write your own "living will" stating your preferences for medical treatment if at the time you were unable to make them known.

"I need everyone to stop pretending that nothing is wrong."

ERIKA ANDIOLA,
on YouTube, following the arrest of her mother and brother by immigration police, Arizona State University*

5

Civil Rights

Escaping domestic violence, Erika Andiola's mother, came to the United States from Mexico without documentation with Erika and two of Erika's siblings when Erika was only eleven. Erika originally received a scholarship to attend Arizona State University, but a new Arizona law prohibited undocumented students from receiving scholarships, so the scholarship was rescinded. Even though her undocumented status made it difficult to find employment, Erika worked to pay for tuition, studied, and graduated from Arizona State in 2009 with a B.A. in psychology. Erika then went to work for Congresswoman Kyrsten Sinema (see the opening vignette in Chapter 9, Elections, Campaigns, and Voting). She also began lobbying to support President Obama's proposed DREAM Act, which would have granted permanent residency to undocumented immigrants if they arrived in the United States before they turned 16, received an honorable discharge from the military, or completed at least two years toward a college degree. While the bill passed the House in 2010, it never received the supermajority necessary to end the filibuster against it in the Senate. In 2012, however, President Obama directed Immigration and Customs Enforcement (ICE) to stop deporting undocumented students who met DREAM Act standards.

Despite the president's order, in 2013, agents from ICE broke into the Andiola family house, arresting Erika's mother and brother. Erika organized a huge protest against the arrests, and they were released the following day. As Marielena Hincapié, executive director of the National Immigration Law Center, put it, "Not all immigrant families have the benefit of Erika to mobilize the whole country

overnight." Erika used the gateway of grassroots activism to get the government to use its discretion to not deport her family. Due to the massive support she received from around the country, her efforts succeeded.

In 2014, Andiola began a hunger strike at Immigration and Customs Enforcement (ICE) headquarters in Phoenix Arizona. One week later, Phoenix police arrested her, a move that could have led to her deportation but, perhaps due to her status as an activist for undocumented Americans, did not. She launched #not1more in an attempt to get President Obama, who has deported more undocumented residents than any other president, to end deportations. She also launched a hunger strike at the White House.

Andiola remains optimistic about the future. When asked by the *New York Times* where her activism is leading,

Need to Know

5.1 Define civil rights

5.2 Explain how the federal and state governments suppressed civil rights

5.3 Assess how equal protection has expanded

5.4 Identify the groups at the forefront of the civil rights movement

5.5 Describe the new battles for civil rights

▶ **WATCH & LEARN** MindTap for American Government
Watch a brief "What Do You Know?" video summarizing Civil Rights.

the woman who originally went to college to become a psychologist replied, "I haven't been able to think that far. At this point, I just want to be able to pass immigration reform. I want to be able to keep my mom here, and we'll see where life takes me from there."[1]

In this chapter, we look at the idea of equality, how it has changed, and how the federal government's enforcement of it has changed as well. We examine how grassroots racial, ethnic, and gender-based movements pressured the courts to protect civil rights and how Congress enforced court rulings with legislation. As with civil liberties (see Chapter 4, Civil Liberties), however, finding the right balance of rights for minority groups frequently divides members of society from one another, and divides democratically responsive legislatures from lifetime-appointed judges.

LISTEN & LEARN
MindTap for American Government

Access Read Speaker to listen to Chapter 5.

5.1 What Are Civil Rights?

› Define civil rights

Although the Declaration of Independence declared that "All men are created equal," the Constitution originally had little to say about equality, at least as the concept is understood today. Even the debate over the ratification of the Constitution had little to do with equality. It was much more about how much power to invest in the federal government. Today, however, equality is a hallowed principle of American political culture, but the notion and the reality evolved slowly over two centuries.

Civil Rights and Civil Liberties

civil rights: *Set of rights centered around the concept of equal treatment that government is obliged to protect.*

Civil rights are rights related to the duties of citizenship and the opportunities for participation in civic life that the government is obliged to protect. These rights are based on the expectation of equality under the law. The most important is the right to vote. In contrast to civil liberties (see Chapter 4), Americans have struggled hard to gain civil rights.

Civil rights also differ from civil liberties in that while government is the only authority that can suppress liberties—for example, by suppressing freedom of speech or forbidding a certain religious belief—both government and private entities, such as individuals or businesses, have the capacity to engage in discrimination by treating people unequally.

→ KEY QUESTIONS:
Why would a government discriminate?

The government can therefore take three different roles when it comes to civil rights. It can engage in state-sponsored or **public discrimination** by actively discriminating against people. It can treat people equally but permit **private discrimination** by allowing individuals or businesses to discriminate. Finally, it can try, as the U.S. government has since the 1960s, to treat people equally and to prevent individuals or businesses from discriminating. Thus it falls to government to protect individuals against unequal treatment and to citizens to ensure that the government itself is not discriminating against individuals or groups. In a democracy, the majority rules, but the gateways for minorities must also be kept open.

public discrimination:
Discrimination by national, state, or local governments.

private discrimination:
Discrimination by private individuals or businesses.

The Constitution and Civil Rights

Despite the statement on equality in the Declaration of Independence, the role of the government with regard to ensuring equality was not written into the Constitution, and the United States has a bleak history on civil rights. The Founders were not much concerned with equality as it is understood today. Many of them owned slaves, and they did not see a contradiction between doing so and the Declaration's statement on equality. The Constitution gave the states authority over voting, and most states restricted the right to vote to free males with a certain amount of property. Slaves could not vote, and in a few states, even free African Americans could not vote—neither could women (except in New Jersey) or Native Americans.[2] During the nation's first century and even thereafter, state laws and the national government actively discriminated against people on the basis of race, gender, and ethnic background.

Following the Civil War, the Thirteenth Amendment ended slavery, and the Fourteenth Amendment forbade states to deny any person "the equal protection of the laws." Nevertheless, the equality of African Americans was not thereby guaranteed. Some of the members of Congress who wrote the Fourteenth Amendment believed that equality was limited to "the right to go and come; the right to enforce contracts; the right to convey his property; the right to buy property" and little more.[3] The courts agreed, and the federal government made little effort to ensure equal treatment during the nation's second century.

Meanwhile, women won the right to vote (1920) but not the right to full participation in public life. Native Americans born on reservations became citizens (1924), but not until the civil rights and women's movements of the 1950s and 1960s did legal discrimination against African Americans, women, and ethnic minorities end. Today, the government actively aims to treat individuals and groups as equals before the law and to use its authority to prevent state and local governments, and individuals and businesses, from discriminating.

In the past half-century, the meaning of "all men are created equal" has been expanded to include women and all people subject to the jurisdiction of the United States. Yet Americans still debate the meaning of *equality*. Should, or can, the government ensure **equality of opportunity** for all people? Should, or can, it engineer **equality of outcome**? That is, is it enough for society to provide equality of opportunity by prohibiting discrimination? What if that still leaves members of groups that have historically been discriminated against, such as women and minorities, with fewer advanced degrees and lower incomes? As it has throughout the course of the nation's history, the meaning of equality continues to evolve.

In the next sections, we see how, as the idea of equality expanded, the federal government moved from actively treating different groups unequally under the law, to asserting equality under the law but doing little to protect it, to actively enforcing it.

→ KEY QUESTIONS:
What did equality mean to the Founders?

→ KEY QUESTIONS:
What is your idea of equality—equality of opportunity or equality of outcome?

equality of opportunity: *Expectation that citizens may not be discriminated against on account of race, gender, or national background and that every citizen should have an equal chance to succeed in life.*

equality of outcome: *Expectation that equality is achieved if results are comparable for all citizens regardless of race, gender, or national background or that such groups are proportionally represented in measures of success in life.*

Checkpoint

CAN YOU:

- Compare civil rights to civil liberties
- Track changes in civil rights from the Constitution as originally ratified to today

5.2 Legal Restrictions on Civil Rights

> Explain how the federal and state governments suppressed civil rights

Slavery split the United States from the founding of the nation through the Civil War. After the Civil War, the Constitution prohibited slavery. It also prohibited the states from denying equality, but many states continued to discriminate. Both Congress and the Supreme Court had the authority to enforce equality, but neither took action. Women, African Americans, and ethnic minorities suffered under unequal laws, with denial of the right to vote and laws that limited their full participation in labor markets, professions, and public life. Discriminatory laws also affected Asians, prohibiting those who were not born in the United States from becoming citizens and later preventing them from immigrating to the United States altogether.

Slavery

→ **KEY QUESTIONS:**
Describe the role of compromise in American politics. Is it wise or foolish for politicians to compromise?

Slavery came to the colonies in 1619 when a Virginian purchased Africans from a Dutch shipper. Colonial Africans originally were servants, largely indistinct from indentured servants of other races who bound themselves to service for a limited number of years in return for free passage to Britain's American colonies. But African slavery soon became established in colonial law. In 1664, Maryland passed legislation declaring that all "Negroes or other slaves hereafter imported . . . shall serve for life."[4] The law also made slaves of the children of slaves.

The compromises made at the Constitutional Convention allowed the United States to form, but they also allowed slavery to grow and spread. By 1808, when Congress banned the further importation of slaves from Africa, the slave population had reached 1 million, and it continued growing through natural increase thereafter. With neither slave nor free forces dominant politically, Congress continued to compromise. The Missouri Compromise (1820) banned slavery in the territories north of the southern border of Missouri, thus keeping most of the vast lands of the Louisiana Purchase free. The Compromise of 1850 allowed territories captured in the Mexican War to decide for themselves whether to be free or slave. The Kansas-Nebraska Act (1854) undid the Missouri Compromise by allowing each territory to vote on whether to allow slavery. The Supreme Court further extended the reach of slavery in **Dred Scott v. Sandford** (1857).[5]

Dred Scott v. Sandford: *The 1857 Supreme Court decision declaring that blacks could not be citizens and Congress could not ban slavery in the territories.*

Dred Scott, a slave who had moved with his master from the slave state of Missouri to the free Wisconsin Territory and then back to Missouri, sued in federal court for his freedom based on his extended stay in free territory. The Supreme Court's decision in the case, written by Chief Justice Roger Taney, a former slave owner, declared (1) that no black—slave or free—could be an American citizen, and thus that no black could sue in a federal court; (2) that blacks were "beings of an inferior order" who had "no rights which the white man was bound to respect"; (3) that the Declaration of Independence's statement that "all men are created equal" did not include men of African heritage; (4) that Congress's authority to "make all needful Rules and Regulations respecting the Territory . . . [of] the United States" did not include the right to prohibit slavery in those territories; and (5) that slaves were the property of their owners, so freeing Scott would violate his owner's Fifth Amendment right not to be deprived of his property without due process of law. With this decision, the regulation of slavery in the territories was removed from the national authority of Congress and placed in the hands of local authorities in the territories.

The 1860 election of Abraham Lincoln (1861–65), who opposed the extension of slavery, prompted southern states to secede from the union. During the ensuing Civil War, Lincoln issued the Emancipation Proclamation, which made slavery illegal in those states in rebellion as of January 1, 1863. The Proclamation did not pertain to border states that retained slavery but remained in the Union. Slavery was finally ended in the United States following Union victory and ratification of the Thirteenth Amendment in 1865 (see Figure 5.1).

Figure 5.1 Constitutional Amendments That Pertain to Civil Rights

Color Code:	Criminal procedure	Participation	Equality

Thirteenth	1865	Prohibits slavery in the United States
Fourteenth	1868	Makes all persons born in the United States citizens of the United States and prohibits states from denying persons within its jurisdiction the privileges or immunities of citizens, the due process of law, and equal protection of the laws; apportionment by whole persons
Fifteenth	1870	Prohibits states from denying the right to vote on account of race
Nineteenth	1920	Guarantees women the right to vote
Twenty-Fourth	1964	Prohibits poll taxes

© CENGAGE LEARNING®

Restrictions on Citizenship

The Constitution was not explicit on birthright citizenship, but the clause requiring that presidents be natural-born citizens seemingly implies that people born in the United States are citizens.[6] Yet on the basis of ethnic background, some groups were denied the status of **citizenship** and the privileges it entailed, such as property rights and the protection of civil liberties.

citizenship:
Full-fledged membership in a nation.

The Constitution explicitly allows people not born in the United States to become citizens through naturalization by granting Congress the authority "to establish a uniform rule of naturalization." Congress's first such law, the Naturalization Act of 1790, restricted citizenship to "free white persons" who had lived in the United States for two years, swore allegiance to the United States, and had "good character." Though restrictive on race, the act allowed Catholics, Jews, and other "free white persons" to become naturalized citizens, rights that most European nations did not allow. The act also declared people born overseas to parents who were U.S. citizens to be natural-born citizens. Congress first allowed nonwhites to become naturalized citizens in 1870, when it extended naturalization to "persons of African descent."

Native Americans. In 1823, the Supreme Court declared that Native Americans were merely inhabitants, "an inferior race of people, without the privileges of citizens."[7] The legislative policy of the United States toward Native Americans included forcible removal from various territories under the Indian Removal Act of 1830 and the creation of land reserved for them (Reservations) starting with the Indian Appropriations Act in 1851. The Fourteenth Amendment's citizenship clause did not remedy this situation: The Court ruled in 1884 that the clause did not provide citizenship to Native Americans born on reservations because reservations are not fully under the jurisdiction of the United States.[8] Not until the Indian Citizenship Act of 1924 did Congress provide natural-born citizenship to Native Americans born on reservations.

Latinos. Latinos in the Southwestern United States arrived prior to American settlers. They lived in areas from Texas to California, and Tejanos, the term for people of Mexican descent living in Texas, fought alongside other Texans in battles against the Mexican Army. Perhaps due to the close affiliation with Mexico, many Tejanos, Californios, and other Latinos lost their properties after the Treaty of Guadalupe Hidalgo, which ended the Mexican-American War and resulted in Mexico ceding what is now California, Nevada, New Mexico, Arizona, Utah, Texas, Wyoming, and Colorado. After the United States annexed Texas, Anglos forcibly expelled many Tejanos. Those who remained, though formally granted citizenship, were often faced with "second-class" status with few recognized rights.[9]

The history of the treatment of Latinos by the U.S. government is a mixed one. In the late 1920s and early 1930s, approximately 2 million people of Mexican descent were deported to Mexico due to economic and political pressures stemming from the Great Depression. Roughly 60 percent of those expelled during what became known as the Mexican Repatriation were U.S. citizens. "Federal, state, and local governments working together involuntarily removed many U.S. citizens of Mexican ancestry, many of whom were born in the United States. These citizens cannot be said to have been 'repatriated' to their native land."[10] As a result of the Mexican Repatriation, ". . . the nation lost roughly one-third of its Mexican population. A similar program took place in the 1950s under the offensive name "Operation Wetback,"[11] and similar "roundups" have occurred as recently as 1997.[12] In 2005, the California Assembly passed the "Apology Act for the 1930s Mexican Repatriation Program" in recognition of the coerced removal of legal residents of Mexican descent.

→ KEY QUESTIONS:
Who should be a citizen?

The Mexican Repatriation delayed for decades the full emergence of the Latino community as a political, economic, and social force in the United States."[13] Civil rights enjoyed by Latinos today were not always recognized as such nor are they guaranteed to be so in the future. As Latinos continue to be the fastest growing ethnic group in the United States, it is clear there have been many gates to political participation placed before them, which are discussed more in depth in Chapter 9, Elections, Campaigns, and Voting.

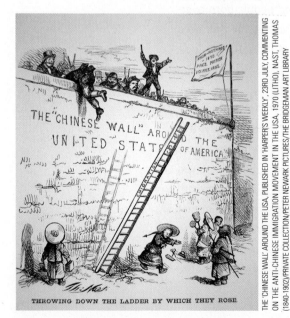

THE "CHINESE WALL" AROUND THE USA, PUBLISHED IN 'HARPER'S WEEKLY', 23RD JULY, COMMENTING ON THE ANTI-CHINESE IMMIGRATION MOVEMENT IN THE USA, 1970 (LITHO), NAST, THOMAS (1840-1902)/PRIVATE COLLECTION/PETER NEWARK PICTURES/THE BRIDGEMAN ART LIBRARY

Drawing of a wall depicting the exclusion of Chinese immigrants from the United States.

Asian Americans. Even after Congress allowed "persons of African descent" to become naturalized citizens in 1870, Asians still could not become naturalized citizens. Often states enacted discriminatory legislation to bar Asians from benefiting from opportunities granted to other residents. California's 1879 constitution prohibited Chinese from voting and from employment in state and local government. In 1913, California prohibited Japanese immigrants from purchasing farmland.[14]

Indeed, fear of Chinese immigrants led to an 1882 prohibition on the immigration of Chinese to America. That ban was the first significant restriction on immigration to the United States. Congress extended this ban to all Asians in 1921. The ban stayed in effect until 1943, when Congress allowed an annual quota of 105 immigrants from China, a World War II ally. The 1943 act also allowed Chinese to become naturalized citizens but did not allow other Asians to do so. Congress ended this restriction on Asian naturalization in 1952 but kept strict limits on the number of Asian immigrants until 1965.

Beyond the setbacks of the anti-Asian immigration policies, President Franklin Delano Roosevelt (1933–45) issued an executive order for the evacuation of all 110,000 people of Japanese ancestry who resided west of the Rocky Mountains—whether citizen (most of them) or not—and their placement in relocation camps following the Japanese attack on Pearl Harbor. Congress ratified the president's order, and in 1944, the Supreme Court endorsed it in *Korematsu v. United States (1944)* ruling that the authority for relocation was within the war power of the United States.[15]

→ KEY QUESTIONS: Does military necessity overrule civil rights? If so, under what circumstances?

Although the government justified the program on the grounds of military necessity rather than racial animosity, it did not attempt wholesale roundups of German Americans despite the existence of the German American Bund, a pro-Nazi association with about twenty thousand members before the war. That the government even rounded up Japanese American children from orphanages suggests that racial animosity was more important than security concerns.[16] The program remained in effect through the war years, although the government filed no charges of disloyalty or subversion against any person of Japanese ancestry. Many Japanese Americans valiantly served the United States in segregated military units during the war.

Immigration Limits.   Congress used immigration laws to keep out ethnic groups as well as anyone considered undesirable, including "idiots," insane people, paupers, felons, polygamists, anarchists, and people coming for "immoral purposes."[17] Immigration officials used the morality clauses to keep homosexuals from entering the country until 1979.[18]

→ KEY QUESTIONS: What restrictions, if any, should there be on immigration?

In the early twentieth century, immigration soared, only to drop back during World War I. After the war, the Ku Klux Klan resurfaced, now targeting immigrants, Catholics, and Jews as well as blacks. With nearly 5 million members and chapters throughout the country, the Klan joined others with less violent supremacist beliefs to pressure Congress to limit immigration.[19] The Immigration Act of 1924 established quotas for ethnic groups based on the proportion of Americans from each nationality resident in 1890, thereby severely limiting the number of whites considered to be of "lower race," that is, those from southern and eastern Europe,[20] who constituted a huge proportion of immigrants from the 1890s on. Under the act, the quota for Italy, for example, dropped more than 90 percent[21] from the percentage allowed in the Immigration Act of 1921, which also established quotas but based them on the proportion of each nationality resident in 1910.

In 1952, President Harry S. Truman (1945–53), claiming that such quotas were un-American, vetoed a bill that continued the national quota system, but Congress overrode his veto. With the Immigration and Nationality Act of 1965, Congress rescinded the quota system and the especially severe restrictions on Asian immigration. Today, to apply for citizenship, one must have had legal permanent residence for five years, or three years if married to a U.S. citizen. Applicants also must be of good moral character and must be able to pass a test on questions such as "who elects the president?".

Racial Segregation and Discrimination

The end of slavery did not make former slaves equal citizens. Immediately after the war, southern states wrote new constitutions that severely limited the civil and political rights of the freedmen. These so-called black codes prevented them from voting, owning land, and

★ **Reconstruction:** *The period from 1865 to 1877 in which the former Confederate states gained readmission to the Union and the federal government passed laws to help the emancipated slaves.*

★ **equal protection clause:** *Prevents states from denying any person the equal protection of the laws (Fourteenth Amendment).*

leaving their plantations. Congress responded with the Civil Rights Act of 1866, which guaranteed the right of freedmen to make contracts, sue in court if those contracts were violated, and own property. Congress also established military rule over the former Confederate states, which would end in a state when it passed a new state constitution that guaranteed black suffrage and when it ratified the Fourteenth Amendment. With former Confederates barred from voting, blacks constituted a majority of the electorate in several states, and more than six hundred freedmen served in state legislatures during **Reconstruction,** as this era was called.

The Fourteenth Amendment (1868), in addition to guaranteeing that no state shall deny any person due process of law (see Chapter 4), prohibits states from denying any person the **equal protection** of the law. It also makes all people born in the United States citizens of the United States, overturning the Supreme Court's ruling in the *Dred Scott* case that blacks could not be U.S. citizens. In an attempt to prevent states from rescinding the right of black suffrage, the Fifteenth Amendment (1870) declared that the right to vote could not be abridged on account of race.

SOUTH CAROLINA DEPT. OF ARCHIVES AND HISTORY

SOUTH CAROLINA DEPT. OF ARCHIVES AND HISTORY

In segregated school systems, the schools for black children and the schools for white children were almost never equal. These insurance photographs show Liberty Hill Colored School and Summerton Graded School in Clarendon County, South Carolina, in 1948. They were used as evidence in *Briggs v. Elliott,* one of the school segregation cases decided with *Brown v. Board of Education* (1954).

Opponents of freedmen rights turned to violence. In 1866, Confederate veterans formed the Ku Klux Klan (KKK), a terrorist organization aimed at restoring white supremacy. In 1873, white supremacists massacred more than a hundred blacks in Colfax, Louisiana, as part of an ongoing election dispute. The federal government brought charges against three of the perpetrators, but the Supreme Court reversed their conviction, arguing that the Fourteenth Amendment gave Congress the authority to act only against states that violated civil rights (public discrimination), not against individuals who did so (private discrimination).[22]

Reconstruction ended with a deal over the 1876 election. A close and contested race between Republican Rutherford B. Hayes and Democrat Samuel Tilden was resolved when southern Democrats in Congress agreed to allow Hayes to become president in return for the withdrawal of federal troops from the South. Freed from military rule, white supremacist groups such as the Klan embarked on a campaign of lynching and other forms of terrorism against blacks.

State governments were not responsive to the victims because, despite the Fifteenth Amendment, southern politicians established a set of rules that kept blacks from voting. **Poll taxes** limited the voting of poor blacks (as well as of poor whites). The white primary took advantage of the fact that, with the Republican Party negatively associated with Lincoln and the Civil War, the Democratic Party completely dominated southern politics. Therefore, whoever won the local Democratic primary for an office was sure to win in the general election. Excluding blacks from voting in Democratic primaries meant that blacks had no effective vote at all. Even so, states used literacy tests to disqualify voters. These involved reading and interpreting difficult passages. To avoid disqualifying white voters as well, grandfather clauses gave exemptions to men whose grandfathers had been eligible to vote. The men who received these exemptions were, of course, always white (see Chapter 9 for further discussion of these techniques and an example of a literacy test).

These legal strategies effectively disenfranchised black men. In addition, state and local **Jim Crow laws** enforced segregation of whites and blacks in all public places. When a New Orleans civil rights organization challenged a Louisiana law requiring segregated railway cars by having Homer Plessy, who was one-eighth black, sit in the whites-only car, the Supreme Court upheld the segregation.[23] _Plessy v. Ferguson_ (1896) established the **separate-but-equal doctrine,** which held that states could segregate the races without violating the equal protection clause of the Fourteenth Amendment as long as the separate facilities were equal.[24] Southern states segregated schools, libraries, and other public institutions and required the segregation of restaurants, inns, and other places of public accommodation. The facilities were almost never equal. African Americans in northern states often experienced discrimination in hiring, housing, hotels, and restaurants, though segregation was not enforced by law. African Americans could serve in the military but generally in segregated units under white officers. During the late nineteenth and early twentieth centuries, discrimination was state-sponsored in the South; elsewhere in the nation, people engaged in private discrimination without challenge.

Ethnic Segregation and Discrimination

Latinos and other ethnic groups experienced many of the same discriminatory practices as did African Americans. The separate but equal doctrine of _Plessy v. Ferguson_ (1896) applied to Hispanics and other minorities. White voters instituted segregation in the South and the West. Phoenix, Arizona, ran separate schools for blacks, Indians, and Mexicans.[25] California ran separate schools for Asians as well as Mexicans,[26] while Texas kept Mexican Americans in separate classrooms.[27] In areas of the Southwestern United States, Latinos were required to sit in the back of buses, sit in movie theater balconies, and attend separate public schools. The end of segregation practices aimed at African Americans did not necessarily end them for Latinos (see Table 5.1).

Women's Suffrage

By law and by custom, women were also excluded from public life from the earliest days of the nation. In 1776, Abigail Adams had urged her husband, John Adams, to "remember the ladies" in drafting the nation's founding documents. In language similar to that later used by Jefferson in the Declaration, she warned, "if particular care and attention is not

poll taxes: _Tax on voting; prohibited by the Twenty-Fourth Amendment (1964)._

Jim Crow laws: _Southern laws that established strict segregation of the races and gave their name to the segregation era._

separate-but-equal doctrine: _Supreme Court doctrine that upheld segregation as long as there were equivalent facilities for blacks._

→ KEY QUESTIONS:
If some people are blocked from voting, what is the effect on government?

→ KEY QUESTIONS:
Should all citizens have the right to vote? Are there any citizens who should not have this right?

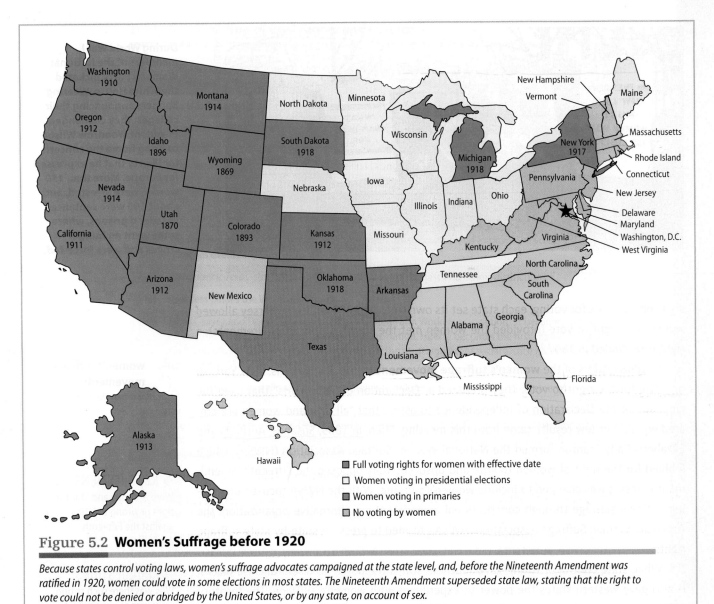

Figure 5.2 Women's Suffrage before 1920

Because states control voting laws, women's suffrage advocates campaigned at the state level, and, before the Nineteenth Amendment was ratified in 1920, women could vote in some elections in most states. The Nineteenth Amendment superseded state law, stating that the right to vote could not be denied or abridged by the United States, or by any state, on account of sex.

Source: © Cengage Learning; data from Mary Beth Norton et al., *A People and a Nation: A History of the United States,* 8th ed. (Boston: Houghton Mifflin, 2008), 608.

would have overturned protective legislation and other laws that treated men and women differently. Although introduced in Congress in 1923 and every year thereafter, it was not taken seriously. Even in 1945, only a minority of white males thought that women should be able to take jobs outside the home.[31]

Not surprisingly, the federal and state governments were responsive to these sorts of views. As late as 1972, eleven states continued to enforce coverture laws.[32] Louisiana, for example, gave a husband "as 'head and master' of property jointly owned with his wife," the complete right to dispose of such property without his wife's consent.[33] Teachers were commonly forced to retire if they got married.[34] Outside of coverture laws, Social Security provided survivors' benefits for children if their working fathers died but not if their working mothers died. It similarly provided unemployment benefits to children of unemployed fathers but not to children of unemployed mothers. Males in the military received benefits for their

globalgateways

Equal Treatment of Women

Virtually all nations formally protect equality under the law, but the degree to which women actually obtain equal treatment varies enormously, as does the degree to which women are elected or appointed to positions of authority.

India. Females suffer from legal and societal discrimination, including forced prostitution, prisoner rape, and the murder of female babies. The murder of women for bringing dishonor to their families, or their husbands' families, continues. *Sati*, the custom in which a widow kills herself on the funeral pyre of her husband, also continues. Dowry, the exchange of money or goods from the bride's family to the groom's, is also illegal, yet the press regularly reports on dowry disputes that have led to the murder of the bride. Nevertheless, a woman, Indira Gandhi, served as India's prime minister (1966–77 and 1980–84). Additionally, as of 2012, women in India also have positions as the head of several states and as the speaker of the Lok Sabha, the lower house in India's parliament.

Israel. Israel guarantees equality on account of sex, and equality is largely the case in secular society. Military service is compulsory for men and women. The nation's fourth prime minister was a woman—Golda Meir (1969–74). Today, women hold over 20 percent of the seats in the Knesset. Religious authorities, on the other hand, still have control over some civil matters, such as marriage, burial, and control of holy sites. Consequently, Jewish and Muslim women can have difficulty obtaining divorces without the consent of their husbands. However, Israeli law allows courts to fine and imprison unwilling husbands. Moreover, heterosexual and same-sex couples who do not marry in religious courts are granted legal privileges through the common law marriage.

South Africa. South Africa's constitution prohibits discrimination on account of sex, but there is pervasive violence and discrimination against women in South Africa, including violence by the military. Rape, sexual abuse, and forced marriages are very serious problems. Women have achieved some representation in South Africa's government and in fact hold a large share of seats in the National Assembly.

1. Why have other democracies elected female heads of government (prime ministers) while the United States has not had a female president?

2. Why do constitutional guarantees of equal rights for women not always translate into actual equality for women?

Source: Freedom House; U.S. Department of State.

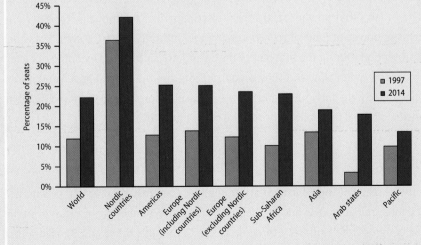

Note: The Nordic countries are Denmark, Finland, Iceland, Norway, Sweden, the Faroe Islands, Greenland, and the Åland Islands.

WORLD AND REGIONAL AVERAGES OF WOMEN IN PARLIAMENT, 1997 AND 2014

One measure of progress for women is the percent of women in national legislatures. As can be seen from this figure, women are an increasing percentage of national legislatures in every region of the world. See the Global Gateways box in Chapter 13, The Judiciary, for the percentage of national high court judges held by women.

Source: Adapted from Inter-Parliamentary Union, 2011, "Women in Parliament in 2010: The Year in Perspective," Table 2.

Checkpoint

CAN YOU:

- Describe the role of the Supreme Court in the expansion of slavery
- Enumerate ways that racial discrimination persisted after emancipation
- Track the steps in the achievement of women's suffrage
- Survey the laws that discriminated against women
- Identify the groups that have been denied rights to U.S. citizenship
- Discuss restraints on civil rights during wartime

dependents that females in the military did not receive. Idaho gave preferences to men over women in determining who would administer a dead relative's estate. Utah required parents to support sons until age 21 but daughters only until age 18. A woman could not work as a bartender in Michigan unless she was the wife or daughter of the bar's owner.[35]

Because women were treated differently than men under the law, many laws also discriminated against men. Colorado allowed females to drink beer at age 18; males had to wait until they turned 21. California, like many states, made it a crime for males of any age to have sexual relations with females under the age of 18 but had no corresponding penalty for females having sexual relations with underage males. Alabama, like many states, imposed alimony obligations on men only. New York allowed unwed mothers, but not unwed fathers, to block the adoption of their children. Florida provided property tax relief to widows but not to widowers. Even today, only males have to register for the military draft.[36] Many of these laws were based on an implicit assumption that women, viewed as the weaker sex, needed special protection by the government.[37] As late as 1961, the Supreme Court exempted women from jury duty because they were "the center of home and family life."[38]

5.3 The Expansion of Equal Protection

> Assess how equal protection has expanded

Today, Congress, constitutional amendments, and court decisions have largely put an end to public discrimination, and no clause has been as powerful in this effort as the equal protection clause of the Fourteenth Amendment, which prohibits states from denying any person the equal protection of the law. The amendment gives Congress the authority to enforce its provisions by appropriate legislation, adding to Congress's enumerated powers by allowing the passage of laws that prevent states from discriminating. Additionally, the Supreme Court, through the power of judicial review, retains the authority to strike state laws that violate equal protection. During the first half of the twentieth century, the meaning of equality changed for many Americans, and they organized to press the federal government into playing a crucial role to fight both public and private discrimination. This section examines the gradual expansion of equal protection prior to the civil rights movement.

→ **KEY QUESTIONS:**
If equality was not explicitly protected in the Constitution as originally ratified, how did it get to be so important today?

State Action

CONNECT WITH YOUR CLASSMATES
MindTap for American Government

Access the Civil Rights Forum: Discussion—Minority Rights Protection.

Shortly after the passage of the Fourteenth Amendment, Congress tried to ban private discrimination at inns, public conveyances, theaters, and other public places. The Supreme Court rejected congressional authority to do so in the *Civil Rights Cases* (1883), ruling that the Fourteenth Amendment prohibited public discrimination by the states only, not private discrimination by businesses or individuals. From the 1880s until the 1940s, the federal government remained passive with regard to discrimination, allowing states and locales to require segregation of the races and permitting public and private institutions to make their own rules regarding it.

In 1948, however, the Court ruled that private discrimination can be prohibited if it involves significant **state action**. The case involved housing. A group of homeowners signed a contract pledging never to sell their homes to blacks, but one of the homeowners did so. The neighbors sued to prevent the new owners from taking possession of the house, and the state supreme court ruled in favor of the neighbors. The U.S. Supreme Court reversed the state supreme court, ruling that judicial enforcement of the discriminatory private contract constitutes state action and thus is prohibited by the Fourteenth Amendment.[39] *equal protection violation*

→ **KEY QUESTIONS:**
Why is majority rule not always congruent with civil rights?

⭐ **state action:** *Action by a state, as opposed to a private person, that constitutes discrimination and therefore is an equal protection violation.*

Judicial Review

While the state-action doctrine allowed the Supreme Court to prohibit limited types of private discrimination, the equal protection clause of the Fourteenth Amendment is better suited to fighting public discrimination. In the next two decades, the Supreme Court actively applied the equal protection clause of the Fourteenth Amendment to do so. Congress also has the authority to enforce the equal protection clause, but democratically elected legislatures and executives are not necessarily designed to be responsive to minority groups, for they are chosen by a majority of voters. Thus civil rights organizations such as the National Association for the Advancement of Colored People (NAACP) and the League of United Latin American Citizens (LULAC) turned to the judiciary, whose members are not elected and so do not directly depend on majority support, for assistance in establishing legal equality.

As with civil liberties issues, for which the Court uses the standard of compelling interest (see Chapter 4), in civil rights cases, the Court has constructed tests to determine whether laws violate the equal protection clause. Depending upon the group whose right has been violated, the Court sets different standards of how closely it will scrutinize the law alleged to violate equal protection. There are at least three levels. The Court reserves the toughest standard of review, strict scrutiny, for laws alleged to discriminate on account of race, ethnicity, religion, or status as a legally admitted alien. It uses mid-level, or heightened scrutiny, for laws that discriminate on account of sex and the lowest level of scrutiny, rational basis, for general claims of discrimination (see Table 5.2).

→ **KEY QUESTIONS:**
Who should ensure citizen equality? State governments? The federal government? The president? Congress? The courts? Citizens?

Checkpoint

CAN YOU:

■ Track the changing meaning of equality

■ Explain why "state action" is so important to the equal protection clause

■ Demonstrate that the judicial branch might be a better protector of civil rights than the legislative branch

Table 5.2 Supreme Court Scrutiny in Equal Protection Cases

Claim of Discrimination	Standard of Review	Test
Unprotected category	Lowest	Rational basis to achieve a legitimate governmental objective
Sex	Heightened	Exceedingly persuasive justification; use of sex as a governmental category must be substantially related to important governmental objectives
Race, ethnicity, religion, and legally admitted aliens	Strict	Most rigid scrutiny; use of race as a governmental category must be precisely tailored to meet a compelling governmental interest

© CENGAGE LEARNING®

→ KEY QUESTIONS:
What gateways did citizens
use to end segregation?

5.4 The End of Legal Restrictions on Civil Rights

> Identify the groups at the forefront of the civil rights movement

The events that brought about the government's shift from enforcing discrimination to protecting against it did not begin with the government. It began with pressure from groups that were discriminated against that mobilized on their own behalf. This gateway of public pressure generally involves the use of civil liberties such as freedom of speech and of assembly to engage in protests and other activities aside from voting because minority groups, by definition, do not have the numbers to change policies through the ballot box alone.

Dismantling Public Discrimination Based on Race

Brown v. Board of Education: *The 1954 Supreme Court decision striking down segregated schools.*

In 1950, when Linda Brown was entering third grade, her father Oliver Brown tried to enroll her in the Sumner School. The 10-year-old had been going to Monroe School, walking between train tracks and along streets without sidewalks to get there. Although it was closer, Sumner was for white students, and when Oliver Brown was told Linda could not attend, he took his case to the NAACP. Here the family stands in front of their home; Linda is on the left.

Among the most consequential forms of segregation from the Jim Crow era was the mandatory separation of schools for whites and blacks. Beginning in 1935, the NAACP's Legal Defense Fund embarked on a legal campaign—led by Thurgood Marshall, who would later become the first African American to serve on the Supreme Court—to dismantle the system of separate-but-equal schools in southern and border states that were always separate but rarely equal. After a series of cases in which the Supreme Court struck down specific segregated schools because they were not equal,[40] the Court ruled more generally in **Brown v. Board of Education** (1954) that separate schools were inherently unequal, even should facilities be essentially similar (see Supreme Court Cases: *Brown v. Board of Education*). Segregation in schools violated the equal protection clause of the Fourteenth Amendment. The Fourteenth Amendment only requires that states provide equal protection of the laws, but on the same day as the *Brown* decision, the Supreme Court used the due process clause of the Fifth Amendment to prohibit the national government from denying equal protection.[41]

As historic as the *Brown* decision was, the case by itself did little to desegregate southern schools. Part of the problem was that the Court allowed local circumstances to influence the rate of integration, ambiguously requiring that local districts desegregate "with all deliberate speed."[42] Further, southern segregationists launched a massive resistance to the *Brown* decision. This campaign included "The Southern Manifesto," a document signed by 101 southern members of Congress deploring the *Brown* decision; the denial of state funds to any integrated school; and tuition grants for white students to attend segregated private schools. In addition, unruly segregationist mobs threatened black students seeking to integrate previously white schools. While neither the Supreme Court nor the Dwight D. Eisenhower administration (1953–61) could prevent every school disruption by segregationist mobs, both intervened in Little Rock, Arkansas. Eisenhower

CARL IWASAKI/TIME LIFE PICTURES/GETTY IMAGES

supreme court cases

Hernandez v. Texas (1954)
Brown v. Board of Education (1954)

QUESTIONS: *Hernandez:* Does the equal protection clause allow Texas to exclude Mexican Americans from juries? *Brown:* Can states provide segregated schools for black and white schoolchildren?

ORAL ARGUMENT

Hernandez: January 11, 1954

Brown: December 7–9, 1953

DECISION:

Hernandez: May 3, 1954 (read at http://laws.findlaw .com/us/347/475.html)

Brown: May 17, 1954 (read at http://laws.findlaw.com /us/347/483.html)

OUTCOME:

Hernandez: No. The equal protection clause protects Mexican Americans (9–0).

Brown: No. Separate educational facilities are inherently unequal (9–0).

As noted in Chapter 2, The Constitution, Texas systematically excluded Mexican Americans from the murder trial of Pete Hernandez. Famed attorney and activist Gus Garcia told the Supreme Court that while the intent of the equal protection clause was to prevent racial discrimination against former slaves and their descendants, Texas treated Mexican Americans as a "class apart," and they therefore should be shielded against discriminatory laws by the equal protection clause. The Court agreed.

Two weeks later, the Supreme Court decided the *Brown* case. When Linda Brown was in third grade, her father, with the help of the NAACP, brought a suit against the Topeka school board for refusing to allow her to attend the local school that white children in their neighborhood attended.

In *Plessy v. Ferguson* (1896), the Supreme Court had ruled that the equal protection clause of the Fourteenth Amendment did not prohibit the states from establishing separate-but-equal facilities for whites

and blacks. The Court did not really begin to look at whether the facilities were equal or not until 1938, when it held that Missouri's paying for blacks to go to law school out of state was not the same as providing facilities within the state that were equal to its white law school.* A pair of 1950 cases declared, first, that admitting a black to an all-white school but forcing him to sit in a separate row and dine at a separate table was unconstitutional,† and second, that the equality of separate schools had to be compared on both objective factors that could be measured, such as the number of faculty members, and subjective factors that could not be measured, such as the reputation of the faculty.‡

The *Brown* case came to the Supreme Court with similar desegregation cases from South Carolina, Virginia, Delaware, and Washington, D.C. Thurgood Marshall, who was in charge of legal strategy for the NAACP and would later become the first African American to serve on the Supreme Court, argued the *Brown* case. He readily admitted that the schools in Linda Brown's case were roughly equal in objective characteristics but argued that segregation in and of itself denied black students the equal protection of the laws by creating a feeling of inferiority among them.

The Supreme Court's preliminary vote following the arguments showed a majority favoring striking segregation, with two or three dissenters. Chief Justice Earl Warren, however, thought that a decision that was bound to be met with resistance in the South should be unanimous if at all possible. Following several months of bargaining and persuasion, he eventually got every member of the Court to agree that the Court should strike down school segregation.

1. Can separate schools ever be equal?
2. Why were the courts more likely to be responsive to the problems of segregation than the legislature would be?

---

* *Missouri ex rel. Gaines v. Canada,* 305 U.S. 337 (1938).

† *McLaurin v. Oklahoma,* 339 U.S. 637 (1950).

‡ *Sweatt v. Painter,* 339 U.S. 629 (1950).

federalized the Arkansas National Guard and sent in the 101st Airborne to protect the black students seeking to integrate Central High School, while the Supreme Court, declaring that it had the final say on what the Constitution means, rejected the threat of violence as a justification for delaying integration (see Chapter 11, The Presidency, and Chapter 13, The Judiciary, for more on the Little Rock case).[43]

To desegregate universities, President John F. Kennedy (1961–63) sent twenty-five thousand federal troops to ensure the enrollment of one black man, James Meredith, at the University of Mississippi in 1962. The following year, segregationist Governor George Wallace of Alabama famously "stood at the schoolhouse door" to prevent two black students from registering at the University of Alabama. He stepped aside only when Kennedy again sent troops to enforce integration.

Nevertheless, with few blacks able to vote, there was little need for southern politicians or school board officials to be responsive to their concerns, especially given massive opposition to desegregation by those who could vote. Only when the federal government took action did states respond. After Congress cut off federal aid to segregated schools in 1964, many districts began to integrate.[44] The rate of integration increased further in the late 1960s when the Supreme Court ended the "all deliberate speed" era and required an immediate end to segregated schools, thus pushing open the gateways to greater equality.[45]

→ KEY QUESTIONS:
What are terrorists? Were the people who bombed King's house terrorists?

Outside of schools, civil rights activists fought segregation in public facilities. The first grassroots action to receive nationwide attention was a bus boycott in Montgomery, Alabama. On December 1, 1955, police arrested Rosa Parks, a 42-year-old black seamstress and an active member of the NAACP, for refusing to give her seat to a white person. In response, the black community, led by a 26-year-old Baptist minister, Martin Luther King Jr., launched a boycott of city buses. Blacks walked, bicycled, and shared rides to avoid using the Montgomery bus system. Although the city arrested boycotters, and violent segregationist terrorists firebombed King's home, the boycotters held firm for more than a year. The Supreme Court then declared Montgomery's segregated bus system unconstitutional.[46] A new ordinance allowing blacks to sit anywhere on any bus ended the boycott. King became one of the national leaders of the emerging civil rights movement and Rosa Parks its first heroine.

→ KEY QUESTIONS:
What is more important, equality or freedom of association?

Childhood sweethearts Mildred and Richard Loving married in Washington, D.C., because they could not marry in Virginia, where they lived. One month later, police burst into their bedroom and arrested them for violating Virginia's Racial Integrity Act. The couple eventually sued Virginia with legal assistance from the American Civil Liberties Union. In 1967, the Supreme Court struck down Virginia's law.

BETTMANN/CORBIS

With the *Brown* precedent in hand, the Supreme Court struck down state-mandated segregation not only in public transportation but also in other public facilities, such as beaches and city auditoriums. Given the massive opposition to the *Brown* decision, however, the Court refused to hear the appeal by a black woman sentenced to prison for the crime of marrying a white man.[47] As one justice reportedly said when the Court rejected another interracial marriage case, "One bombshell at a time is enough."[48] Not until 1967 in *Loving v. Virginia* did the Court strike down miscegenation, finding no compelling interest in a law that prohibited interracial marriage.[49]

Dismantling Private Discrimination Based on Race

The decisions of businesses about whether to serve customers or hire workers on account of their race (or sex) were largely beyond judicial authority because the Fourteenth Amendment's equal protection clause only prevents states from discriminating; it does not bar private discrimination. Thus, if a restaurant chose not to serve blacks or an employer chose not to hire them, there was little a court could do unless Congress passed legislation forbidding such actions. The effort to dismantle private discrimination thus took two tracks: protests to pressure businesses into serving blacks, and lobbying to pressure Congress into passing legislation that would make private discrimination in commercial matters illegal.

The grassroots protests began when four African American freshmen at North Carolina Agricultural and Technical College in Greensboro sat down at the whites-only counter at Woolworth's, asked for coffee, and refused to leave when not served. Within weeks, the sit-ins spread to dozens of other cities. One protest leader, Diane Nash, along with other young participants in the sit-ins, formed the Student Nonviolent Coordinating Committee (SNCC), which along with the Congress of Racial Equality (CORE) served as the more activist "younger brothers" of the NAACP.

In 1961, CORE organized freedom rides, trips on interstate buses into the segregated South, where the integrated buses were legal under federal law even though they violated local segregation rules. Mobs attacked the buses—firebombing one of them—and beat the riders. Under pressure from the federal government, including protection of the riders by federal marshals, the states eventually agreed not to interfere with interstate travelers.[50]

In the spring of 1963, Martin Luther King Jr.'s Southern Christian Leadership Conference (SCLC) led demonstrations in Birmingham, Alabama, to bring about the integration of downtown businesses. The police met demonstrators with fire hoses, police dogs, and cattle prods. Police arrested hundreds of protesters, including King. When white clergymen questioned why King, an outsider, had come to Birmingham, King answered in his famous "Letter from Birmingham Jail": "I am in Birmingham because injustice is here."[51] Rejecting violence, King insisted that peaceful civil disobedience was the only gateway to negotiation. The negotiations took place and ended with Birmingham businesses agreeing to integrate lunch counters and hire more blacks. Nevertheless, or perhaps because of this, members of the KKK exploded a bomb at a local black church on a Sunday morning, murdering four young girls.

> **→ KEY QUESTIONS:**
> If a law is immoral, are you right or wrong to disobey it? What is the remedy?

Earlier that summer, King had led two hundred thousand protesters at the March on Washington. It was there that King delivered his historic "I Have a Dream" speech, in which he declared:

> **→ KEY QUESTIONS:**
> Which branch of government has been most powerful in ensuring equality? Why?

I have a dream that one day this nation will rise up and live out the true meaning of its creed: "We hold these truths to be self-evident: that all men are created equal." I have a dream that one day on the red hills of Georgia the sons of former slaves and the sons of former slave owners will be able to sit down together at the table of brotherhood. I have a dream that one day even the state of Mississippi, a state sweltering with the heat of injustice, sweltering with the heat of oppression, will be transformed into an oasis of freedom and justice. I have a dream that my four little children will one day live in a nation where they will not be judged by the color of their skin but by the content of their character.[52]

President Kennedy proposed a civil rights bill that would have banned discrimination in public accommodations, such as restaurants and hotels. Five days after Kennedy's assassination in November 1963, President Lyndon Baines Johnson (1963–69) told Congress that nothing could better honor Kennedy than passage of this bill. The next year, Congress passed the **Civil Rights Act**, which significantly strengthened Kennedy's original bill by also prohibiting employment discrimination on account of "race, color, religion, sex, or national origin."

Because the Fourteenth Amendment's equal protection clause applies only to state-sponsored discrimination, the Supreme Court upheld Congress's authority to ban private discrimination under the interstate commerce clause. Given the Court's broad interpretation of interstate commerce (see Chapter 3, Federalism), the Court ruled that even small inns and restaurants had to abide by the act.[53]

Civil Rights Act: *Prohibits discrimination in employment, education, and places of public accommodation (1964).*

Dismantling Voting Barriers Based on Race

As noted previously, the end of Reconstruction left black men in the South with a constitutional right to vote but a hostile social and legal environment that made it extremely difficult for them to do so. The Supreme Court pushed things along, striking down grandfather clauses (1915) and white primaries (1944), the latter in a suit filed by the NAACP.[54] Congress and the states pushed things along further, outlawing poll taxes with the Twenty-Fourth Amendment (1964). Martin Luther King Jr. identified four gates that kept blacks from voting: white terrorist control of local governments and sheriffs' departments; arrests on trumped-up charges of those seeking to vote; the discretion given to registrars, where "the latitude for discrimination is almost endless"; and the arbitrary nature of literacy tests.[55]

During the summer of 1964, voting rights supporters from around the country, many of them college students, moved south to help with voter registration drives. Klansmen murdered three of the volunteers in Philadelphia, Mississippi, that June. In March 1965, King organized a voting rights march from Selma to Montgomery, Alabama. With national news media on hand, Alabama police, under the authority of Governor George Wallace, beat the marchers with whips, nightsticks, and cattle prods. Selma natives murdered two more voting rights activists.

A week later, President Johnson addressed a joint session of Congress, calling for passage of the strictest possible voting rights legislation. Congress responded by passing the **Voting Rights Act (VRA)** in August 1965. The act limited literacy, interpretation, and other such tests for voting. It required states with low voter registration levels, essentially seven southern states plus Alaska, to receive preclearance from the Justice Department for any changes to its voting laws. It also established new criminal penalties for those who sought to keep people from voting on account of race. The law was an enormous success. By 2008, blacks and whites voted at essentially the same rate nationwide[56] and at slightly higher rates in some southern states.[57] In 2012, blacks had a higher turnout rate than whites.[58] In 2013, however, the Supreme Court voted 5-4 in *Shelby County v. Holder* to strike down the 1965 formula that established which jurisdictions needed to obtain preclearance.[59] Until Congress passes a new formula, no jurisdictions need to obtain preclearance.

Voting Rights Act: *Gives the federal government the power to prevent discrimination in voting rights (1965).*

→ KEY QUESTIONS:
How has expansion of the right to vote affected citizen participation? How has it affected public policy?

This decision may depress future black turnout as states like Texas move to pass Voter ID laws that were previously blocked under the VRA by the Justice Department[60] (see Figure 5.3).

Dismantling Public Discrimination Based on Ethnicity

Similar to African Americans, Latinos began the struggle for civil rights in the court system through interest groups such as the American G.I. Forum, LULAC, and later the Mexican American Legal Defense and Education Fund (MALDEF). One of the first steps Latinos took toward securing civil rights was to be recognized as a protected class of people under the Fourteenth Amendment. As we have seen, the attorneys in *Hernandez v. Texas* argued that Hispanics were a class of individuals entitled to the same due process guarantees as were African Americans and other racial groups.[61] The court agreed and also ruled that Mexican Americans could not be systematically excluded from juries, a key form of citizenship.

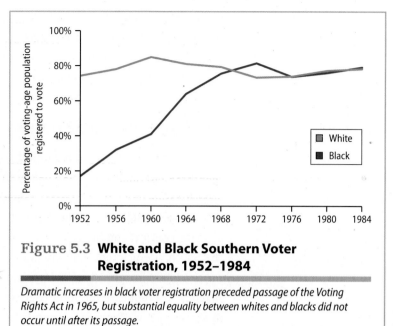

Figure 5.3 White and Black Southern Voter Registration, 1952–1984

Dramatic increases in black voter registration preceded passage of the Voting Rights Act in 1965, but substantial equality between whites and blacks did not occur until after its passage.

Source: Data from Harold W. Stanley, *Voter Mobilization and the Politics of Race* (New York: Praeger, 1987), Appendix A.

In 1970, the Supreme Court extended the *Brown* ruling to apply to Latinos and other minority groups in *Cisneros v. Corpus Christi Independent School District*.[62] Because Mexican Americans were considered white, the Corpus Christi Independent School District created two sets of schools: one set for African American and Latino children and the other for "All-White" (non-Latino) children. In that way, they circumvented the desegregation ruling of *Brown*. Attorney James de Anda, supported by the MALDEF, argued that the separate schools system was unconstitutional because Mexican Americans were a separate and distinct group from whites. The Supreme Court recognized Latinos as a distinct ethnic minority group that had been subject to discriminatory practices.[63] Latino American school children were no longer subject to separate but equal educational facilities. In *Plyler v. Doe* (1982), described in Chapter 1, Gateways to American Democracy, the court expanded protections further, deciding that the children of undocumented workers were entitled to free public education in Texas.[64]

Public education is a major gateway to participation in civic life. Its denial constitutes a gate that prevents equality. Yet other gates in lesser, yet important areas, also existed. The use of public swimming pools, buses, and water fountains, for example, were segregated. In the early 1950s, sometimes there was no "equal" facility available to Latinos. Latino elected officials helped lead the effort to break down these and other types of barriers to citizenship. Prominent among them is Henry B. Gonzalez, the first Mexican American to be elected to the San Antonio City Council. One of his first victories was opening public facilities such as swimming pools to all residents. When he served in the Texas Senate, he filibustered a series of bills aimed at circumventing the *Brown* case. He held the floor for a record twenty-two hours and defeated all but two of the bills. He later served as Congressman from the 20th District in Texas, now occupied by Joaquín Castro (see the opening vignette in Chapter 10, Congress).[65]

Dismantling Voting Barriers Based on Ethnicity

Just as segregation was not limited to African Americans, voting laws created gates blocking Latinos' ability to exercise the right to vote. Poll taxes influenced Mexican Americans in the Southwest, for whom the cost to vote was a greater burden than for white voters. And while the Jim Crow version of literacy tests often involved tests of obscure political and historical facts for first-time voters, such as African Americans in the South, literacy requirements influenced Latinos differently. New York, for example, required "new" voters (i.e., Puerto Ricans) to provide evidence of English language proficiency as a requisite for voter registration. In 1966, however, the Supreme Court ruled in *Katzenbach v. Morgan* (see Supreme Court Cases, Chapter 11) and *Cardona v. Power* that provisions of the 1966 VRA prevented New York from imposing English language requirements for voting.[66] In 1970, the VRA was amended to eliminate all literacy tests, and, in 1975, Congress further amended the VRA to protect language minorities. As a result of those and subsequent amendments to the VRA, states and other political units such as counties or cities, must provide voting information, assistance, and ballots in the minority language if more than 5 percent of the citizens of voting age in the jurisdiction are of a language minority or their number exceeds ten thousand.[67]

DOUGLAS GRAHAM/CQ-ROLL CALL GROUP/CONGRESSIONAL QUARTERLY/GETTY IMAGES

Former Congressman Henry B. Gonzalez, the first Latino elected to Congress from Texas, rose to become the Chair of the House Committee on Banking, Finance, and Urban Affairs.

Language requirements were only one type of gate. Other, less obvious gates to participation blocked Latino voters. The manner by which elections are structured may also create gates to meaningful participation. In Dallas County and Bexar County in Texas, for example, elections had been conducted on an at-large basis, meaning that candidates ran in multi-member districts. Ethnic minorities could not corral a high enough percent of the vote to elect Latino or other representatives who embodied their interests. This form of election is still common in many jurisdictions and is not necessarily a violation of voting rights.

In 1973, however, the Supreme Court ruled in *White v. Regester* that the VRA prohibited electoral plans that may effectively dilute the voting strength of minorities, in this case, Latinos.[68] The multi-member district elections in those jurisdictions were being used a means to minimize the voting strength of Hispanic (in San Antonio) and African American (in Dallas) citizens. Such plans limited the effective participation of those groups to elect candidates of their choice. The Supreme Court mandated that single-member districts be used. As a result of this decision, groups such as MALDEF, Communities Organized for Public Service (COPS) and Southwest Voter Registration and Education Project (SWVREP) and their leaders organized to change the way many local elections were structured (see below). Evidence shows the impact of election practices was dramatic. After the switch to single-member districts in 1977, the San Antonio city elected five Mexican Americans to the city council as well as one African American candidate. For the first time in the city's history, a majority of the city council was composed of minorities.[69]

It was MALDEF that brought *White v. Regester* and many other cases forward. In the 1970s, MALDEF undertook ninety-three federal and state cases in Texas alone: 76 percent of the cases involved desegregation, and 14 percent were cases about voting and other political rights.[70] That is one reason why MALDEF has come to be known as the "law firm of the Latino community." See Chapter 9 for a discussion of the impact of the VRA and Supreme Court decisions on Latino voter turnout.

Dismantling Private Discrimination Based on Ethnicity

Like women, Latinos have faced an uphill battle in the workplace. Deprived of their lands following Texas' break with Mexico, deported during the Great Depression and other periods, Latinos have long filled the demand for the need for unskilled labor, particularly in the field of agriculture. As a result, perhaps the most well known of civil rights efforts among Latinos is in the agriculture industry. Cesar Chavez and Dolores Huerta organized the United Farm Workers (UFW) union to secure safe working conditions and increased wages for laborers. Formed in 1962, the UFW continues to work to improve conditions for agriculture workers. When the UFW began, farm workers earned less than one dollar per hour. The first task of Chavez and Huerta was to organize the workers so that they could bargain collectively with growers. Once formed, they called for boycotts of fruit and vegetables as well as strikes against growers in order to gain the right to bargain collectively. The UFW counts among its successes bargaining agreements that required growers to provide rest periods for workers, toilets in fields, clean drinking water, and protections against dangerous pesticides.[71] The UFW increased the collective voice of Latinos in the agriculture industry and fought for basic human and civil rights.

The UFW also registered Latinos to vote and encouraged them to become active politically. The success of the UFW and other Latino organizations to end segregation and discrimination continues as it does for other groups. For Latinos, efforts continue to expand educational opportunities to DREAMers, and prevent the efforts by some to limit political participation (see the discussion of Voter ID laws in Chapter 9).[72] As with any social movement, leadership and organization

Young undocumented immigrants protesting outside the Federal Building in Detroit, Michigan.

is vital to the success of groups seeking equal protection and due process. As noted at the beginning of this section, much of the impetus for change begins with pressure from groups. As Cesar Chavez said, "Those who attack our union often say, 'It's not really a union. It's something else: A social movement. A civil rights movement. It's something dangerous. . . .' [T]he UFW has always been something more than a union—although it's never been dangerous if you believe in the Bill of Rights."[73] As Latinos continue to be the fastest growing ethnic group in the United States, it is clear that many gates to political participation have been placed before them. Latinos are slowly becoming a political force in the United States (see Chapter 9). Emerging generations of Latinos such as Erika Andiola, leader of the Arizona DREAM Coalition, are poised to continue working to secure those rights.

★ **Equal Pay Act:**
Prohibits different pay for males and females for the same work (1963).

Dismantling Discrimination Based on Gender

The success of the civil rights movement inspired other groups, most notably women, to put pressure on the political system to obtain equal rights under the law. Women active in the civil rights movement easily shifted the movement's strategies to promoting rights for women, particularly after the publication of Betty Friedan's *The Feminine Mystique* (1963), a book considered by many to have launched the modern American feminist movement. Based on a survey Friedan sent to her Smith College classmates in advance of their fifteenth reunion, the book broadcast the dissatisfaction that many American women felt in their roles as wives and mothers. About the same time, the Kennedy administration's President's Commission on the Status of Women, charged with making recommendations for overcoming sex discrimination, urged passage of the **Equal Pay Act**. Passed by Congress in 1963, the act prohibits employers from paying different wages for the same job on account of sex. Although the act did not prohibit discrimination in the hiring of male and female workers, that prohibition came with the Civil Rights Act of 1964. See Public Policy and Civil Rights: Workplace Equality.

Following passage of the Civil Rights Act, Friedan helped found the National Organization for Women (NOW), which advocated for women's rights through education and litigation. NOW protested airline policies that forced stewardesses to retire at marriage or age 32 and help-wanted ads that listed jobs by gender, as well as protective legislation. NOW also supported abortion rights and a proposed Equal Rights Amendment (ERA), which would have prohibited the federal government and the states from discriminating on account of sex.

In 1972, the American Civil Liberties Union (ACLU) established the Women's Rights Project, which worked to eliminate discriminatory laws. The first project director, future Supreme Court Justice Ruth Bader Ginsburg, developed a litigation strategy for ending gender-based discrimination. Prior to Ginsburg's work, the Court had rejected equal protection claims for women. Ginsburg first persuaded the Court to strike laws based on the rational-basis

BETTMANN/CORBIS

In 1960, when Columbia law student Ruth Bader Ginsburg applied for a Supreme Court clerkship, Justice Felix Frankfurter chose not to interview her. Ginsburg went on to a distinguished career as a professor of law and chief litigator for the American Civil Liberties Union, eventually arguing cases before the Court, which she joined in 1993 as the second female associate justice. She is pictured here in 1977.

standard and then got the Court to approve a heightened-scrutiny standard. This is a step below the strict scrutiny used in cases discriminating on account of race, but the standard is tough enough that the Court usually strikes laws that discriminate according to sex.

Meanwhile, the Equal Rights Amendment (ERA), passed by Congress and sent to the states for ratification in 1972, began to falter. An anti-ERA movement led by political activist Phyllis Schlafly reversed the momentum by arguing that the amendment would remove special privileges women enjoyed with regard to protective legislation, Society Security benefits, and exemption from the draft. Ironically, another argument against the ERA was that it was unnecessary because the Supreme Court was striking down most laws that discriminated on account of sex. Despite an extension of the deadline to 1982, the ERA ultimately fell three states short of the three-quarters majority needed to pass an amendment (see Figure 5.4).

Checkpoint

CAN YOU:

- Explain why the *Brown* decision by itself had only a minimal effect on school desegregation
- Identify the grassroots protests that opened the gateways to ending private discrimination
- Describe how Congress and the courts have pushed along voting rights
- Draw parallels between the civil rights movement for African Americans and the women's rights movement

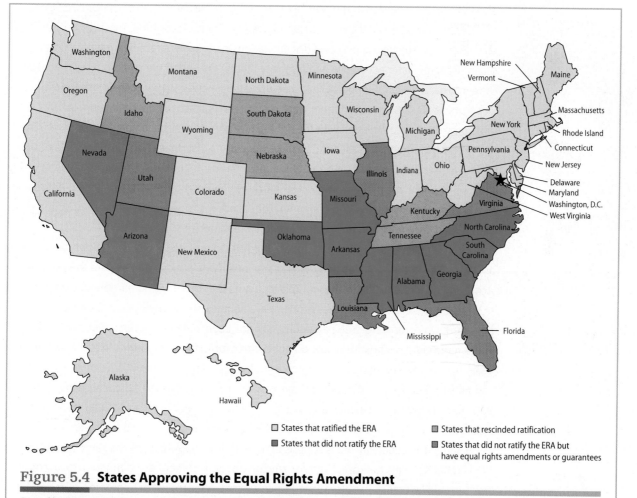

☐ States that ratified the ERA   ☐ States that rescinded ratification

■ States that did not ratify the ERA   ■ States that did not ratify the ERA but have equal rights amendments or guarantees

Figure 5.4   States Approving the Equal Rights Amendment

Passed by Congress in 1972 and sent to the states for ratification, the Equal Rights Amendment got a quick start and then faltered as opposition materialized and grew. In 1979, Congress extended the deadline for ratification to 1982, but in 1982, the amendment expired. Thirty-five states (of the thirty-eight needed) had voted to ratify it, and five states had voted to rescind ratification.

Source: © Cengage Learning®; data from http://www.equalrightsamendment.org.

Public Policy and Civil Rights:
Workplace Equality

Although national legislation and constitutional amendments define civil rights policy, and the Supreme Court interprets such laws—deciding whether they are constitutional and, if so, what they mean—the day-to-day protection of civil rights now falls to two separate executive branch agencies. One is the Civil Rights Division of the Department of Justice, with sections on educational opportunity, employment, housing, voting, and disability rights. The other is the Equal Employment Opportunity Commission (EEOC), which protects against sexual harassment in the workplace and promotes gender equity.

The EEOC is an independent agency with commissioners selected for five-year fixed terms. Unlike the heads of government departments, EEOC commissioners cannot be removed by the president. They are thus thought to be shielded from political pressures, but fixed terms also limit responsiveness to the president, who is the chief executive of the United States.

Congress established the EEOC as part of the Civil Rights Act of 1964. The original EEOC could receive and investigate complaints of discrimination on the basis of race, sex, religion, and national origin (Congress later added age and disability status). As one of the compromises that allowed the act to pass, the EEOC originally had no enforcement power. Rather, it could refer to the Justice Department any case in which there were patterns or practices of discrimination. In 1972, Congress provided the commission with the right to file lawsuits against companies that discriminate.

Although Congress passed the basic law declaring discrimination based on race or sex to be illegal, the EEOC established the guidelines that prohibited discrimination against hiring married women, pregnant women, and mothers. The commission also allowed companies that had previously engaged in discriminatory practices to establish affirmative action plans with quotas for hiring and promoting women and minorities.

From a policy standpoint, the underlying principle of equal pay is that two people who are employed in the same job and do the same quality of work should be paid the same wage. Achieving gender equality in the workplace means that there are no barriers to advancement or hiring based on gender and that gender plays no role in how employees are treated and compensated. Unfortunately, true pay equity has not been achieved in the American workplace. Though the census statistics below do not control for the type of job worked, data from 2012 show that women earned only 80.8 percent of what men earned in 2012. For African American and Latino women, this percentage was a bit higher: African American women earned 90.1 percent and Latinas earned 88.0 percent of what African American and Latino men made.[74] Additionally, the gap falls to slightly above 90.2 percent for women under the age of 35.[75]

Though the Equal Pay Act is supposed to guarantee equal pay for the same work, and the Civil Rights Act aims to protect against any form of employment discrimination on account of sex, the judicial branch has also played a pivotal role. A recent set of Supreme Court decisions has prompted changes in the laws governing discrimination, harassment, and pay equity in the workplace. In one case, the Supreme Court ruled in favor of a woman who was suspended without pay for more than a month and was reassigned to a less desirable position after she claimed sex discrimination in the workplace. The Court decided that an indefinite suspension without pay is retaliation that would reasonably deter any employee from making a discrimination complaint, and, therefore, it was illegal.[76]

But the Court's 2007 ruling in *Ledbetter v. Goodyear Tire and Rubber Co.* had the greatest impact on public policy.[77] In 1998, Lilly Ledbetter filed a complaint with the EEOC that she had consistently received poor job performance evaluations because of her gender and that over the nineteen years she had worked at the Goodyear Tire plant, she had fallen well below her male colleagues who did the same type of job. Her employer countered that, even if that had been true in the past, she did not file her complaint within the 180 days required by the Civil Rights Act. The Court ruled in favor of Goodyear, stating that Ledbetter's claims alleging sex discrimination were time-barred because the discriminatory decisions relating to pay had been made more than 180 days prior to the day she filed the charge with the EEOC. In her dissent, Justice Ruth Bader Ginsburg wrote that the effect of this ruling would allow "any annual pay decision not contested immediately (within 180 days) . . . [to become] grandfathered, a fait accompli beyond the province of Title VII ever to repair."[78] Basically, a company could pay a woman less on the basis of gender, and as long as she did not contest the discriminatory wage within 180 days, the discriminatory wage could not be challenged in federal court.

In 2009, Congress reversed the Court's ruling by passing the Lilly Ledbetter Fair Pay Act, which was the first Act that President Obama signed into law. The act restarts the clock each time an employee receives a paycheck that has been compromised by discriminatory practices.[79] Many equal pay advocates think that this new law will be helpful but not nearly helpful enough to close the salary gap between men and women. Indeed, early reports suggest that some individual women have been able to sue who would not have been able to do so before the act but that these individual suits have done little to close the gender pay gap.[80]

In 2014, President Obama moved to increase equality through the Paycheck Fairness Act, which would revise remedies for paycheck inequality, increase enforcement activity against unequal pay, and limit exceptions to rules against sex discrimination in wages.[81] With every Republican voting against it, the Senate failed to obtain the sixty votes needed to cut off debate.[82] With this legislative stalemate, President Obama issued two executive orders to accomplish what he could on his own. First, federal contractors could not punish workers for discussing their wages among one another. He also required federal contractors to file data with the federal government showing how they pay employees by race and by sex.[83]

Construct Your Own Policy

1. Design a system of evaluation in the private sector workplace to ensure that decisions on pay raises and promotions are not made on the basis of race, sex, or sexual orientation.

2. Develop a plan for state and local government enforcement of workplace equality, replacing federal government oversight.

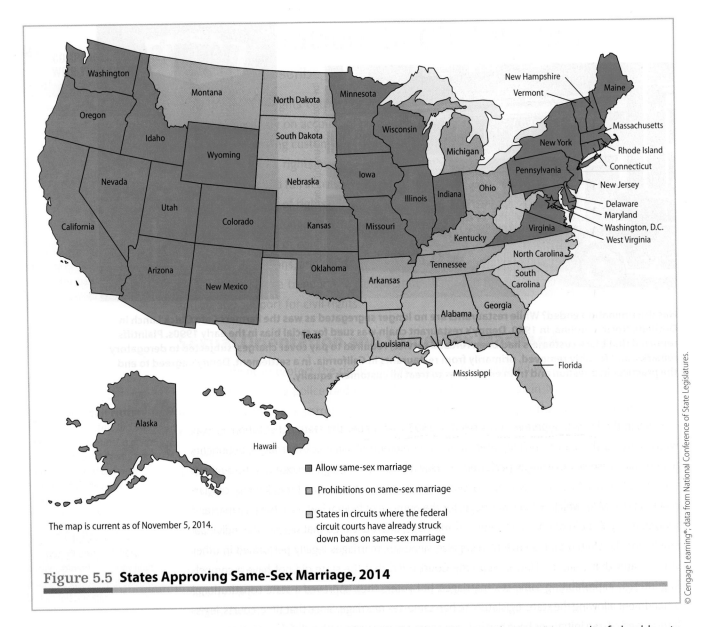

Figure 5.5 **States Approving Same-Sex Marriage, 2014**

Washington
Montana
North Dakota
Minnesota
New Hampshire
Vermont
Maine
Oregon
Idaho
South Dakota
Wisconsin
Michigan
Massachusetts
New York
Rhode Island
Connecticut
Wyoming
Nebraska
Iowa
Pennsylvania
Nevada
Utah
Colorado
Nebraska
Illinois
Indiana
Ohio
New Jersey
Delaware
Maryland
Washington, D.C.
West Virginia
California
Kansas
Missouri
Kentucky
Virginia
Arizona
Oklahoma
Tennessee
North Carolina
New Mexico
Arkansas
South Carolina
Texas
Alabama
Georgia
Louisiana
Mississippi
Florida
Alaska
Hawaii

- Allow same-sex marriage
- Prohibitions on same-sex marriage
- States in circuits where the federal circuit courts have already struck down bans on same-sex marriage

The map is current as of November 5, 2014.

© Cengage Learning®, data from National Conference of State Legislatures.

v. *Windsor* that the section of DOMA that limited spousal recognition under federal law to a man and a woman was unconstitutional.[88] By November 5, 2014, the Supreme Court let stand Court of Appeals decisions from various lower court circuits upholding the right to same sex marriages in Wisconsin, Indiana, Virginia, Oklahoma, Utah, Idaho, Nevada, Colorado, Wyoming, Kansas, and Missouri. Those circuits also cover North Carolina, South Carolina, and West Virginia, so it is likely that those states will soon have legal same-sex marriages too.

National public opinion remains mixed on the matter of same-sex marriage (see Figure 5.6). While a substantial majority of Americans favor allowing same-sex marriage,[89] only thirty-four states and the District of Columbia have legally recognized same-sex marriage. The major political parties are divided on the issue: Democrats are typically more supportive of same-sex marriage than Republicans are. Because support for same-sex marriage is much greater among younger Americans than among older Americans, legal recognition of same-sex marriage will almost certainly increase over time. In November 2014, the Sixth Circuit upheld Michigan's ban on same-sex marriage, creating a conflict between circuits that will likely lead to review by the Supreme Court.

Disability Rights

Advocates for the rights of the disabled, encouraged by the civil rights, women's rights, and other movements, successfully lobbied for the Rehabilitation Act of 1973, which prohibits discrimination against disabled individuals by any federal agency or by any private program or activity that receives federal funds. The landmark Americans with Disabilities Act (ADA) passed in 1990 goes further, requiring public and private employers to make "reasonable accommodations" to known physical and mental limitations of employees with disabilities and, if possible, to modify performance standards to accommodate an employee's disability.

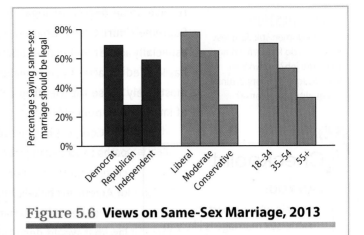

Figure 5.6 Views on Same-Sex Marriage, 2013

Source: Jeffrey M. Jones, "Same-Sex Marriage Support Solidifies above 50% in the U.S.: Support Has been 50% or Above in Three Separate Readings in Last Year," *Gallup*, May 13, 2013, accessed April 14, 2014, http://www.gallup.com/poll/162398/sex-marriage-support-solidifies-above.aspx.

To comply with the act, public transportation authorities have made buses and trains accessible to people in wheelchairs. Public accommodations, such as restaurants, hotels, movie theaters, and doctors' offices, must also meet ADA accessibility standards, within reason, removing barriers from existing structures. Related legislation, the Individuals with Disabilities Education Act (IDEA; 1990, updated 2004) requires states to provide free public education to all children with disabilities in the least-restrictive environment appropriate to their particular needs.

Congress does not provide a full list of disabilities covered under the ADA, but rather covers any disability that "substantially limits a major life activity." Thus, a trucking company need not make accommodations for a driver who can see clearly out of only one eye because the disability does not substantially limit a major life activity. On the other hand, the ADA does protect people who have HIV or AIDS. It even protects people with severe drug and alcohol problems, provided the drug use in question is not illegal.[90]

Many organized interests support the rights of the disabled. While prejudice against people of different races, religions, sexual orientation, and country of origin might lead responsive representatives to oppose the rights of minorities, there are few if any votes to be had by lobbying against the rights of the disabled. Nevertheless, when at the end of 2011 the Department of Labor proposed new rules that would push employers toward a goal of having 7 percent of their employees be people with disabilities, business groups opposed the rules, claiming they would be costly to implement.[91]

Undocumented Immigrants

The Fourteenth Amendment's equal protection clause prohibits states from denying to any person—in other words, not just citizens—equal protection under the law. Thus even undocumented immigrants

Beverly Jones, a plaintiff in a Tennessee case challenging the lack of access for people in wheelchairs to the upper floors of Tennessee courthouses. The U.S. Supreme Court upheld her challenge under the Americans with Disabilities Act.

⭐ Key Concepts

Brown v. Board of Education (p. 134). What was the reasoning behind the *Brown* decision?

citizenship (p. 123). What are the different paths to citizenship?

civil rights (p. 120). What is the government's role with regards to civil rights?

Civil Rights Act (p. 138). What did the Civil Rights Act prohibit?

Dred Scott v. Sandford (p. 122). What seems wrong about the *Dred Scott* decision?

equality of opportunity (p. 121). How would you measure equality of opportunity?

equality of outcome (p. 121). How would you measure equality of outcome?

Equal Pay Act (p. 142). How effective has the Equal Pay Act been?

equal protection clause (p. 126). What does the equal protection clause command?

Jim Crow laws (p. 127). What were Jim Crow laws?

poll taxes (p. 127). What were the various types of poll taxes?

private discrimination (p. 120). What constitutes private discrimination?

public discrimination (p. 120). What constitutes public discrimination?

Reconstruction (p. 126). What happened when Reconstruction ended?

separate-but-equal doctrine (p. 127). Can separate schools ever be equal?

state action (p. 133). What makes state action so important to government efforts to protect civil rights?

Stonewall riots (p. 146). What movement did the Stonewall riots spark?

Voting Rights Act (p. 138). What did the Voting Rights Act prohibit?

women's suffrage movement (p. 129). What gateways did the women's suffrage movement use to gain the right to vote?

Learning Outcomes: What You Need . . .

To Know	To Test Yourself	To Participate
▶ **Define civil rights**		
Civil rights relate to the duties of citizenship and opportunities for civic participation that the government is obliged to protect. They are based on the expectation of equality under the law. The most important is the right to vote.	• Compare civil rights to civil liberties. • Track changes in civil rights from the Constitution as originally ratified to today.	• Know your civil rights. • Understand the debt you owe to the actions of citizens for the civil rights you enjoy today.
▶ **Explain how the federal and state governments suppressed civil rights**		
With regard to civil rights, the government can engage in state-sponsored or public discrimination; treat people equally but permit private discrimination; or try, as it has since the 1960s, both to treat people equally and to prevent individuals or businesses from discriminating. It falls to government to protect individuals against unequal treatment and to citizens to ensure that government does not discriminate against individuals or groups. During the nation's first century, and even thereafter, state laws and the national government actively discriminated against people on the basis of race, gender, and ethnic background.	• Describe the role of the Supreme Court in the expansion of slavery. • Enumerate ways that racial discrimination persisted after emancipation. • Track the steps in the achievement of women's suffrage. • Survey the laws that discriminated against women. • Identify the groups that have been denied rights to U.S. citizenship. • Discuss restraints on civil rights during wartime.	• Read excerpts from the *Dred Scott* decision (http://web.utk.edu/~scheb/decisions/dredscott.htm) and from the Mississippi black code established after the Civil War (https://chnm.gmu.edu/courses/122/recon/code.html) and comment on them. • Consider how disenfranchisement of women affected U.S. politics before 1920. • Speculate on why the United States limited citizenship. • Evaluate what these mean for living in a time of prolonged terrorism.

To Know	To Test Yourself	To Participate

▶ **Assess how equal protection has expanded**

To Know	To Test Yourself	To Participate
During the nation's second century, discrimination was state-sponsored in the South; elsewhere private discrimination was practiced without challenge.	• Track the changing meaning of equality. • Explain why "state action" is so important to the equal protection clause. • Demonstrate that the judicial branch might be a better protector of civil rights than the legislative branch.	• Decide whether we are all equal now. • Weigh your respect for the legislative branch versus the judicial branch.

▶ **Identify the groups at the forefront of the civil rights movement**

To Know	To Test Yourself	To Participate
Today public discrimination has been ended by constitutional amendments and the courts, largely through the Fourteenth Amendment's equal protection clause. Beginning in the 1950s, litigation and grassroots protests led the federal government to end segregation and secure voting rights for African Americans and to end limits to women's full participation in public life.	• Explain why the *Brown* decision by itself had only a minimal effect on school desegregation. • Identify the grassroots protests that opened the gateways to ending private discrimination. • Describe how Congress and the courts have pushed along voting rights. • Draw parallels between the civil rights movement for African Americans, Latinos, and women.	• Weigh the impact on social policy of the legislative branch against that of the judicial branch. • Appreciate the impact active citizens can have on government. • Appreciate the impact law can have on politics and society.

▶ **Describe the new battles for civil rights**

To Know	To Test Yourself	To Participate
The expanded notion of equality promoted by the civil rights and women's rights movements inspired other groups, such as homosexuals and the disabled, to demand full access to equality. The extension of rights for some may involve a loss of privileges for others, and sometimes rights clash. Congress and the courts seek to define the meaning and limits of rights in new areas of contention. The trend has always been for a broader meaning of equality and greater support for civil rights.	• Explain why support for same-sex marriage is likely to increase over time. • Recall why legislatures have been so responsive to people with disabilities. • State why the U.S.-born children of illegal immigrants are automatically U.S. citizens.	• Determine whether you think all of the civil rights battles have been won. • Find disability rights organizations in your community. • Find instances of profiling in the news or in your community. • Analyze the racial and ethnic composition of the prison population, and determine if prohibiting voting rights for felons is discriminatory. • Debate whether the Constitution should be amended with regard to citizenship.

RICHARD ELLIS/ALAMY

"… you have one thing that may save you, and that is your youth. This is your great strength. It is also why I hate and fear you."

STEPHEN COLBERT
Northwestern University

BRIAN KERSEY/PIKIMEDS.COM

6

Public Opinion and the Media

Stephen Colbert has literally laughed his way to influence in our political system. *The Colbert Report* is a popular satirical news show that seeks to use humor to discuss pressing issues of the day. Colbert's gateway to influence underscores the many changes in public opinion and the media over the past twenty-five years. It used to be that "the media" were dominated by a handful of outlets (e.g., *The New York Times*, *CBS News*) that sought to lay out descriptively the day's events. The media have multiplied and decentralized, seeking often to interpret the news, aid citizens in the formation of their political ideas, and entertain us along the way.

The expression of the public will is the bedrock of democracy. For politicians, knowing which way the public leans or what citizens think is one of their gateways to power. For citizens, being able to express an opinion and know it is being heard is a gateway for their influence. But reading public opinion correctly is not easy. Polls are a great help, but they can be flawed. Even if well measured, public opinion does not always point toward the best path for the country. Making the right choices requires an informed citizenry. However, the days of striving for serious, unbiased media coverage are long gone.

It is a new game in many ways. Just consider Colbert's influence. In 2011, he drew attention to the rise of so called "Super PACs" by forming his own Colbert Super PAC. His goal was to raise awareness about the new election laws that allowed these PACs to form. He was worried that these PACs would inject too much money into the political process. In an e-mail to supporters in October of 2011, he wrote, "As you know, when we began Colbert Super PAC, we had a simple dream: to use the Supreme Court's *Citizens United* ruling to fashion a massive money cannon that would make all those who seek the

White House quake with fear and beg our allegiance... in strict accordance with federal election law."[1] By poking fun at *Citizens' United*, Colbert helped inform the public about these new PACs and their possible role in the 2012 campaign.

More recently, during a March 2014 show, Colbert discussed Vladimir Putin and Russia's controversial annexation of the Crimea. He did so through sarcastic commentary about Putin's motives. Colbert has talked about global warming with Al Gore and discussed Jeb Bush's statement

Need to Know

6.1 Decide why public opinion is powerful

6.2 Describe how well polls measure public opinion

6.3 Discover how ideology and partisanship shape public opinion

6.4 Describe how demographic characteristics influence public opinion

6.5 Determine why the media are important in a democracy

6.6 Analyze how the law protects the press

6.7 Explain how changes in the mass media have changed the information environment

6.8 Assess how the news media affect public opinion

6.9 Evaluate the news media

▶ **WATCH & LEARN** MindTap™ for American Government
Watch a brief "What Do You Know?" video summarizing Public Opinion and Political Socialization.

in 2014 that crossing the U.S. border is not a felony, but "an act of love" for those individuals who cross as they seek to support their families. Colbert's goal was to poke fun at those who were adamantly opposed to undocumented immigration. Some may not like his politics, but Colbert shines a bright light on the workings of American politics.

This show carries a good deal of weight with younger Americans. According to a survey by the Pew Research Center, about 5 percent of Americans watch the show regularly. But the audience tends to be young, liberal, and educated. So, for example, 10 percent of Millennials claim to watch the show regularly and just 2 percent of those over 65 years old—a five-fold difference. Liberals are also five times more likely to watch the show than conservatives. Those with a high school degree are three times less likely to watch the show than those who have advanced graduate degrees.[2] But Colbert's influence extends beyond those who tune in on particular nights. His skits are picked up by other outlets and become part of the broader national conversation, increasing his gateway to influence.

Few would have thought that Stephen Colbert was on a path that would lead to such political influence. He grew up in South Carolina, the youngest of eleven children. His father was a physician and died when Colbert was just 10 years old.[3] Colbert first attended Hampden-Sydney College in Virginia—a small private liberal arts college for men. This college has a deep history, striving to instill in its students a desire to "behave as gentleman at all times and in all places."[4] In retrospect, that may not have been a good fit for Colbert, and he did in fact end up transferring to Northwestern University. In 1986, he graduated with a degree in theatre.[5]

His time at Northwestern was transformative. He began doing improv on campus and around Chicago. He had a knack for being good on stage and for being funny. *Second City* gave him a big break, where he served as understudy to Steve Carell. In 1995, he began his career at Comedy Central, joining *The Daily Show* two years later as a correspondent where he developed his now-famous Colbert persona.[6] *The Colbert Report* started as a spin-off from *The Daily Show* in 2005. Early

on, he introduced "Truthiness"[7] to the political discourse. He basically used the concept to lob satirical bombs at the personalities and issues of the day. The term caught on so much that it became the "Word of the Year" in 2006.[8] Even if Colbert gave a guest a hard time on a show, they relished the chance to be on the show. Why? The Colbert Bump. There is evidence that guests got a boost in popularity from being on the show.[9] So what celebrity or politician could resist?

While Colbert is first and foremost an entertainer, he does care about issues and takes his gateway to influence seriously. So, for example, he testified before the House Judiciary Committee's Subcommittee on Immigration, Citizenship, and Border Security in 2010.[10] He did so because he likes "talking about people who don't have any power." He goes on to say that migrant workers "come and do our work, but don't have any rights . . . yet we still invite them to come here and at the same time ask them to leave . . . that's an interesting contradiction."[11]

Colbert's influence speaks volumes about the many changes in the media in just the past decade. In 2015, he took over David Letterman's late night show on CBS. The announcement drew strong reactions from some. Conservative talk show host Rush Limbaugh contended that "CBS has just declared war on the heartland of America."[12] Such partisan reactions are part and parcel of the media today. We can continue to expect such partisan reactions.

The popularity of Stephen Colbert's humor-infused partisanship is a near perfect symbol of the many changes in public opinion and the media, and we will use this chapter to map out and to assess these changes. We do so with a keen understanding of the critical role that the expression of public opinion and the media play in a democracy. In this chapter, we investigate how public opinion is formed, expressed, and measured, and its impact in our democracy. To discuss "the media," we analyze the functions and impact of the press, survey its history, and describe and evaluate these new forms of communication in the twenty-first century. By so doing, we can better understand whether and how the media and a freely expressed public opinion promote democracy.

6.1 The Power of Public Opinion

> Decide why public opinion is powerful

LISTEN & LEARN

MindTap™ for American Government

Access Read Speaker to listen to Chapter 6.

"Our government rests on public opinion," claimed Abraham Lincoln. "Public sentiment is everything. With public sentiment, nothing can fail. Without it, nothing can succeed."[13] The nation's sixteenth president (1861–65) was, of course, the great champion of "government of the people, by the people, and for the people," as he expressed it in his Gettysburg Address. He understood that democratic government must be responsive to the will of the people. The hope in a democracy is that each citizen has an equal voice and that those voices, collectively, will be heard by government officials and will guide their actions. Knowing what the public is thinking and having public support are a powerful combination. Writing more than 100 years ago, James Bryce, a famous observer of U.S. politics, contended that public opinion is "the greatest source of power" in the United States, more important than the power of presidents, Congress, and political parties.[14]

What Is Public Opinion?

Public opinion is recognized for its power, but it is ever changing, hard to measure, harder to predict, and nearly impossible to control. **Public opinion** is the aggregate of individual attitudes or beliefs about certain issues or officials, and it is the foundation of any democracy.

public opinion: *Aggregate of individual attitudes or beliefs about certain issues or officials.*

Of course, the electorate expresses its opinion primarily through voting, and elections are the most visible means by which citizens hold elected officials accountable. But a democratic system should not rely just on elections to ensure that politicians are doing the people's will. Elections are not held very often, and they give signals but not directions. For example, the electoral success of the Republicans in the 2014 midterm elections was hailed as a sign that the public was unhappy with the Obama administration's handling of the economy, heath care, the Ebola scare, and conflicts in the Middle East. But what does "unhappiness" say about specific policies? Did the people want big spending cuts? Or did they want additional government efforts to stimulate the economy? Did they want Obamacare reformed or just want it to work better? Election results do not send clear signals on such specific questions. Voters can indicate only whether they like one candidate more than the other; they cannot convey the reasons for their vote. So legislators and elected executives who want to stay in power expend considerable energy trying to find out what the public wants and to respond accordingly. Because public opinion plays such an important role in forging responsiveness, it is central to understanding U.S. politics.

Today, public opinion polls are the most reliable indicators of what Americans are thinking, and a whole industry and science have grown up around measuring opinion on everything from presidents to toothpaste. Polls are not the only sources of public opinion. Other sources of public opinion are the size of rallies and protests, the tone of letters sent to elected officials or newspapers, the amount of money given to particular causes or candidates, the content of newspaper editorials, information gleaned from day-to-day conversations with average Americans, and shifts in public opinion can also be detected in Supreme Court decisions (see Supreme Court Cases: *Bowers v. Hardwick* and *United States v. Windsor in this chapter*).

The Public's Support of Government

The health and stability of a democracy rest with the public. Just as government must respond to what the people want, so citizens must view the system as legitimate and want to be part of it. If the public withdraws its support, the government collapses. For these reasons, political scientists have sought to measure the public's faith in the political system. Two of the most common efforts involve assessing whether the people trust their government and whether they believe their participation in government matters. Political scientists call the latter **efficacy**—the extent to which people believe their actions affect the course of government. **Political trust** is the extent to which people believe the government acts in their best

efficacy: *Extent to which people believe their actions can affect public affairs and the actions of government.*

political trust: *Extent to which people believe the government acts in their best interests.*

supreme court cases

Bowers v. Hardwick (1986)
United States v. Windsor (2013)

QUESTION: *Bowers:* May states prosecute consensual sexual activity by members of the same sex?

WINDSOR: May the United States discriminate against legal same-sex marriages?

ORAL ARGUMENT: *Bowers:* March 31, 1986 (listen at http://www.oyez.org/cases/1980-1989/1985/1985_85_140)

WINDSOR: March 27, 2013 (listen at **http://www.oyez.org/cases/2010-2019/2012/2012_12_307**)

DECISION: *Bowers:* June 30, 1986 (read at http://caselaw.lp.findlaw.com/scripts/getcase.pl?court=US&vol=478&invol=186).

WINDSOR: March 27, 2013 (read at http://caselaw.lp.findlaw.com/scripts/getcase.pl?court=US&vol=000&invol=12-307).

OUTCOME: *Bowers:* There is no right to homosexual sodomy (5–4) (1986).

WINDSOR: The United States may not discriminate against legally married same-sex couples (5-4) (2013).

When the police came to Michael Hardwick's home looking for him, his roommate let them in. When the police got to Hardwick's room, they observed him engaged in sexual behavior with another male. They arrested him under Georgia's antisodomy statute, which prohibits "any sexual contact involving the genitals of one person and the mouth or anus of another." Hardwick argued that the statute violated the right to privacy that the Court established in the *Griswold* birth control case (1965), which the Court later held to protect rights that were "deeply rooted in this Nation's history and tradition."* Noting that prohibitions on sodomy had "ancient roots," the Court voted 5–4 against the claim, calling the argument that homosexual sodomy is among those traditions "facetious." Chief Justice Warren Burger concurred, approvingly citing medieval English sources that declared sodomy as an offense of "deeper malignity" than rape. At the time, only about 32 percent of the American public agreed with the opinion that homosexual relations should be legal."

The Supreme Court reversed that decision nearly twenty years later in *Lawrence v. Texas* (2003). With seven new members on the Court, the justices voted 6–3 that the Texas law prohibiting sodomy was unconstitutional, with the majority opinion resting the decision on the liberty protected by the due process clause of the Fourteenth Amendment.

In the *Windsor* case (2013), the Supreme Court struck down the part of the Defense of Marriage Act (DOMA) that prohibited the federal government from granting marriage benefits to same-sex couples. Under federal law, one spouse can leave unlimited amounts of money to a surviving spouse, but DOMA (1996) had declared that the federal government would only recognize marriages as being between one man and one woman. When Edith Windsor's lawful wife died, the federal government claimed that Windsor owed $363,053 in inheritance taxes, an amount Windsor would not have had to pay had she been married to a male. The Supreme Court ruled that the federal government could not discriminate against Windsor's legal same-sex marriage.

In fewer than thirty years, the Supreme Court had gone from holding that states could criminalize homosexual activity to determining that the federal government must recognize same-sex marriages that are lawfully performed in other states. These changes coincide with a near doubling of support for marriage equality in the United States during that time. Whether this new result was directly due to the change in public opinion or due to new justices from a different generation who reflected that changed opinion, the Court's decision aligned with changes in public opinion.§

1. Should the justices of the Supreme Court be influenced by public opinion?
2. How should the Court decide which rights, among those not specifically listed in the Constitution, should be protected as fundamental rights?

Griswold v. Connecticut, 381 U.S. 479 (1965); *Washington* v. *Glucksberg*, 521 U.S. 702, 721 (1997).
§ Homosexual relationships should be legal: http://www.gallup.com/poll/1651/Gay-Lesbian-Rights.aspx. Support for same-sex marriage: http://www.gallup.com/poll/162398/sex-marriage-support-solidifies-above.aspx. Both accessed April 14, 2014.

interests. It has generally declined over the past fifty years, with steeper declines following the beginning of the Iraq War in 2003 and the financial collapse that began in 2008. One estimate in January 2014 suggested that just 15 percent of the public trusted "the government in Washington to do what is right."[15]

Efficacy has also declined. It stood at more than 70 percent in 1960; by 1994, it had fallen by half. In other words, only one-third of Americans felt that their opinions mattered to government. The figure rebounded to 60 percent by 2002 but then declined again during the Iraq War and financial crisis. It has fallen well below 40 percent in the current environment.[16] There is little doubt, as President Obama said in his first inaugural address, that there has been a "sapping of confidence across our land."

Public trust and efficacy react to changes in government and whether the nation is experiencing good or bad times. Yet, through it all, Americans' commitment to the country and its core institutions has remained strong. Patriotism, for example, shows little decline. In 2014, 5 percent of Americans viewed themselves as unpatriotic.[17] Almost no one in the country favors overthrowing the government.[18]

→ KEY QUESTIONS:
What does a decline in efficacy and public trust mean for American democracy?

Checkpoint

CAN YOU:
- Define public opinion
- State the reasons public opinion has a powerful impact on the presidency
- Track efficacy and public trust in government

6.2 Public Opinion Polls

❭ Decide how well polls measure public opinion

Polls make it possible to gauge the public's thinking on a variety of issues or officials, but they have been scientifically conducted only since the 1930s. Even today, a poorly designed or executed poll can produce misleading results. Moreover, so much information is available from surveys that it is important to know which findings warrant attention and which warrant caution. Poll results can be biased, contradictory, and confusing.

Scientific Polling and the Growth of Survey Research

In the 1800s, newspapers and other organizations polled the people to assess public opinion, but these polls were of limited help because who was being surveyed was unclear. So-called straw polls, for example, sought to predict the outcome of elections. During the presidential campaign of 1824, the *Harrisburg Pennsylvanian* canvassed the opinion of newspaper readers and concluded that Andrew Jackson would get 63 percent of the vote and win easily.[19] As it turned out, Jackson received only about 40 percent of the popular vote.

Though straw polls were often inaccurate, newspapers and magazines continued to poll readers' opinions well into the twentieth century. During the 1936 presidential campaign, the *Literary Digest* conducted a poll that predicted Republican Alf Landon would win the election by 57 percent over President Franklin Roosevelt. The reverse happened: Roosevelt won with a landslide 61 percent of the vote. Why did the *Literary Digest* get it so wrong? It had sent out 10 million ballots. But it had sent them to names drawn from automobile registration lists and telephone books and asked recipients to mail the ballots back. The sample, as a result, was biased. First, in 1936 those who owned automobiles and had telephones were wealthier than average Americans and were more likely to be Republicans. Less wealthy Americans, responding favorably to Roosevelt's actions to end the Great Depression, were increasingly

to public sentiment but not be a slave to it. Instead, they would debate it in a way that would improve it and allow for better government. Over time, the amount of input by citizens has increased; now senators are voted into office by direct election, not by state legislatures. Literacy in 2014 stands at about 99 percent,[37] suggesting that citizens are better able today than in the eighteenth century to meet the demands of being "informed."

But are they? Political scientists went in search of the "informed voter," and they learned that citizens do not know many details about politics. Only 10 percent of the public knows the name of the Speaker of the House. Only about a third can name one U.S. Supreme Court justice. Only about half of Americans know which party controls Congress, and fewer than half know the name of their own congressional representative.[38] These facts suggest that average citizens do not possess the detailed information necessary to hold their government accountable.

Should these data be taken as evidence that the public is not able to meet its democratic responsibilities? Let us consider some findings that give reason for optimism. First, the public, collectively, seems to make reasonable choices. For example, when the economy is doing poorly, the party in power suffers. Voters hold presidents and legislators accountable; failures are punished, and successes are rewarded. Further, Americans do not favor costly wars, and they tend to reward candidates who pursue peace.[39]

→ **KEY QUESTIONS:**
How much information does the public need to possess to make self-government possible?

Second, although individuals do not know all the details about candidates' views on all the issues, they do tend to know candidates' views on the issues that are salient to them. Hunters know candidates' views on gun control; college students know candidates' views on student loans. One study estimates that when an issue is salient to an individual, that individual knows candidates' views on that issue correctly more than 90 percent of the time.[40]

Third, the public can learn quickly if an issue is salient enough to them and receives attention in the news media. The public quickly learned about AIDS when it started to become a public health crisis in the 1980s. Following 9/11, the public understood the need to consider some curtailment of civil liberties to ensure security (see Public Policy and Public Opinion).

Fourth, public opinion is more stable than is suggested by the shifting answers people give to the same question just a few months apart. The instability reflected in polls does not speak to a fickle or poorly informed public. Instead, it appears that polls themselves may be at fault.[41] That is, survey questions and the normal error associated with these questions make people's attitudes appear more unstable than they really are.

Finally, personal decision making is not always based on complete information, so why should political decision making be expected to conform to rational models that scholars use? Individuals often rely on cues and instincts to make decisions, rather than on analyses of detailed information. Scholars have termed such thinking low information rationality.[42] There are two famous examples from presidential campaigns. In 1976, President Gerald R. Ford (1974–77), campaigning in Texas, bit into a tamale with the husk still on, a gaffe suggesting that he knew little about the foods and habits of the people he hoped would vote for him. In 1992, President George H. W. Bush (1989–93) asked what milk cost in grocery stores. His admission that he did not know suggested that he was out of touch with

GERALD R. FORD LIBRARY

Campaigning in 1976, President Gerald Ford visited Texas and, as politicians almost always do, sampled the local food. When he bit into a tamale with the husk still on, it was more than a humorous incident. Many interpreted the gaffe as indicating that Ford did not understand the people he claimed, as president, to represent.

ordinary Americans, who do their own shopping. His competitor, William Jefferson (Bill) Clinton (1993–2001), knew the price of milk and other items, such as jeans. Simple things like not knowing how to eat a tamale or what groceries cost turned some voters against Ford and Bush. These individuals concluded that the candidates were not like them and were not likely to understand their problems.

It is easy to make any member of the public—even a president—look uninformed, and of course it would be better if the public knew more about politics. But individuals do appear to learn about the issues that matter to them. Gaining information is a gateway to influence because, individually, people learn what they need to know to advance their interests, and collectively voters do hold government officials accountable.

→ KEY QUESTIONS:
Does polarization prevent good policy making?

Is the Public Polarized?

The engaged and informed citizens of a democracy cannot be expected to agree on everything. They will naturally have different views on issues. When the differences become stark, however, the danger is that **polarization** will fuel controversy and personal attacks to the point that compromise and consensus become impossible. Congress has clearly become more polarized over the past thirty years. Figure 6.3 tries to capture the idea of polarization on a simple left–right continuum. In the 1970s, the parties adopted positions that were closer to the middle; forty years later, their positions are more at the extremes. In fact, Democrats and Republicans disagree on more issues now than at any time since the end of the Civil War.[43]

polarization:
Condition in which differences between parties and/or the public are so stark that disagreement breaks out, fueling attacks and controversy.

In the 1970s, there were numerous liberal Republicans and conservative Democrats. By 2008, these two groups were nearly extinct. In 2009, for example, Pennsylvania Senator Arlen Specter, one of the few moderate Republicans in Congress at the time, bolted from the Republican Party and became a Democrat. He switched parties because of what he saw as a swing to the right by the Republicans. The differences between the parties have continued to grow,[49] evidenced by victories by candidates from the Tea Party movement in the 2010 congressional elections.[50] There is little doubt that the parties have polarized since the 1970s, along the lines described in Figure 6.3.

→ KEY QUESTIONS:
Do political parties influence public opinion, or is it the other way around?

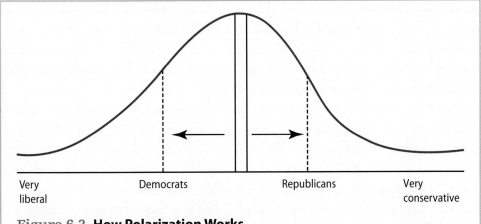

Very
liberal   Democrats   Republicans   Very
                                                                               conservative

Figure 6.3 How Polarization Works

When the parties are polarized, they move toward the tail of these distributions. When parties are depolarized, they adopt positions near each other. Currently the parties are polarized, but that was not the case in the 1970s.

Source: John G. Geer, © Cengage Learning®.

Public Policy and Public Opinion:
Antiterrorism

To see how public opinion affects the policies pursued by government, we examine foreign policy. In particular, we focus on antiterrorism. With continuing terrorist attacks around the world, it is important to consider the public's support for policies that advance our security and how public opinion impacts policy making in this area.

The September 11th, 2001, terrorist attacks prompted a huge increase in the government's efforts to secure U.S. citizens at home and abroad. In general, public opinion was highly supportive of the steps that President George W. Bush took to fight terrorism. These steps were taken with advice from Defense Department agencies, the Federal Bureau of Investigation, and the Department of Justice. The Bush administration authorized the detention of suspects, whether U.S. citizens or not, without charges or trials, and wiretapping (eavesdropping) without a warrant. With the onset of the 2003 war in Iraq, the measures employed in the name of antiterror security increased. Then, in 2004, CBS News and the *New Yorker* magazine broke the story about the Abu Ghraib facility in Iraq, where Iraqi prisoners were subject to activities that violated international norms of treatment and might be considered torture.[44] Subsequently, it was revealed that the U.S. interrogators used waterboarding, a near-drowning technique, as a means of getting information from prisoners about potential terrorist plots. The international community considers waterboarding to be torture, and many Americans were shocked by the news and demanded an end to the practice. The Bush administration also argued that suspected terrorists detained at the Guantánamo Bay facility located in Cuba, outside the United States, were not entitled to protections guaranteed to all prisoners of war by the Geneva Convention. In the 2006 *Hamdan v. Rumsfeld* case, the Supreme Court ruled that the detainees were protected by Article 3 of the Geneva Convention. Yet allegations of torture continued. The issue of treatment of detainees became a major issue in the 2008 presidential campaign. After he took office, President Obama declared that the United States would no longer engage in any practice that violated international norms. The president also announced that the Guantánamo Bay facility would be closed. Despite an early consensus in the White House to close this controversial facility, deciding what to do with existing detainees and how best to handle others who may be engaged in terrorism has proven difficult.[45]

One of the reasons that these policies are hard to pursue is that Americans remain conflicted about the type of force necessary to preserve national security. In 2013, an AP poll reported that 51 percent of respondents supported the use of harsh interrogation techniques on suspected terrorists, while 38 percent opposed these techniques.[46] The core dilemma is that antiterrorism policies must remain secret to be effective, and the only opportunity the public has to register an opinion about government action is after that action has been taken. If harsh interrogation techniques save American lives by uncovering and then preventing a terrorist attack, the public will support the use of these techniques. But how can we be sure that such efforts are really effective? Does the government go too far sometimes? These are tough questions.

Public uncertainty can also be seen in regards to the public's reaction to Edward Snowden's release of intelligence information. In January 2014, 46 percent of Americans thought what

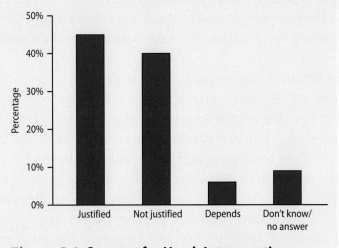

Figure 6.4 Support for Harsh Interrogation Techniques

A majority of the public supports the use of harsh interrogation techniques on terrorism suspects.

Source: Conducted by CBS News, November 6 – November 10, 2011, and based on 1,182 telephone interviews.

he had done was "bad for the country," and 40 percent thought it was good.[47] These are not easy issues, and the public's thinking reflects this kind of division. The public wants society to be open but yet realizes that security demands some secrecy. It is easy to see, therefore, why people can have different opinions about how to approach such a tough topic. Whether you agree or not with what Snowden did, he did remind Americans of an important debate that has been part of the country since its inception (see Figure 6.4).

The debate over secrecy is now taking place in a very different context than just a decade ago. The public is generally less inclined these days to get involved in international affairs. More than 50 percent of the public in 2013 wants the United States to "mind its own business," which represents an all-time high over the past fifty years. Following the 9-11 terrorist attacks in 2001, for example, the proportion of citizens who held such views stood just at 30 percent.[48] This broader context has important implications for U.S foreign policy and how we approach antiterrorism measures.

Construct Your Own Policy

1. Using modern technology, devise a way of accurately measuring public opinion so that the president and Congress consider it before deciding how best to fight terrorism.

2. Design a comprehensive antiterrorist policy that can effectively protect the United States from attack and safeguard individual liberty at the same time.

What is less clear is whether the public is also polarized. Some scholars have argued that the public has polarized along with parties, but there is also evidence that the public is more moderate, even though the choices the parties offer them are not.[51] For example, according to a series of surveys conducted by the Pew Research Center between 1987 and 2007, "the average difference between Republican and Democratic identifiers on forty political and social issues increased from 10 to 14 percent, a surprisingly small difference."[52] These data suggest that the public is more moderate than the choices that are laid before them in elections would suggest. But scholars disagree about the extent of differences among the electorate, with some suggesting that the political center has collapsed.[53]

Even some who think that the public is not as polarized as the parties are worried that polarization will yield more personal attacks and greater incivility. Others offer a more optimistic view, arguing that increasing polarization will activate people's interest in elections, which in turn will spur more interest in politics. In fact, the share of the public that cares about which party wins the presidential election has increased since 1988. Interest in elections, generally, also seems to be on the rise. In 1988, 44 percent of the public paid "a lot" of attention to the presidential campaign. In 2000, the proportion stood at 53 percent, a notable gain.[54] In 2012, around 70 percent of Americans indicated substantial interest in the presidential election.[55]

Having a clear choice engages people and gives them a stake in an election outcome. If the system became depolarized, as in the 1950s, the public would lack a choice. It would no longer matter whether Democrats or Republicans won because they would do the same thing once in office. For these reasons, many scholars in the 1950s called for parties that would offer the public a real choice (see Chapter 8, Political Parties). Citizens, under such conditions, can more effectively hold officials accountable for misdeeds and reward successes.

→ KEY QUESTIONS:
How would you explain the fact that political trust has declined in recent decades, yet interest in elections has increased?

Checkpoint

CAN YOU:

- Explain how partisanship relates to public opinion
- Explain the importance of political ideology
- Assess how well informed the American public is and whether it matters
- Describe polarization and its effects

6.4 Group Differences

❯ Describe how demographic characteristics influence public opinion

Public opinion is shaped by partisanship and ideology. Social scientists find that demographics also matter—that is, the tendency for certain groups within the American population to hold similar views. In this section, we look at the ways socioeconomic status, religion, gender, race and ethnicity, and education tend to organize public opinion.

Socioeconomic Status

Socioeconomic status is a combined measure of occupation, education, income, wealth, and relative social standing or lifestyle. It influences where one lives, what kind of work one does, whom one knows, the kinds of schools one attends, and the kind of opportunities one can take advantage of. These matters inevitably mold political attitudes. Working-class people are more likely than wealthier people to favor more government programs to help the poor and provide child care, more funding for public education, and more protection for Social Security. Around 70 percent of Americans earning between $15,000 and $35,000 support increased spending by government on such social services. Among those earning between $75,000 and $105,000, the proportion drops to about 55 percent.[56]

Age

Age also influences opinions on issues because the stage of one's life affects how one thinks about issues. For instance, 70 percent of people under 30 years of age favor increased spending on student loans. That drops to 42 percent among those over 55. This gap makes sense because younger people are more likely to need student loans. Younger people are much more likely to favor making marijuana legal than are older people. As of 2014, around 60 percent of those Americans 18–29 years old favor making marijuana legal. For those 65 and older, the percentage drops by nearly half to about 33 percent.[57] In general, older citizens are more socially conservative than are younger citizens,[58] and there is evidence that people tend to become more conservative as they age.

→ KEY QUESTIONS:
Does being a member of a demographic group shape opinion?

Religion

Religious affiliation is another indicator of opinion. Overall, for example, Protestants are more conservative than Catholics or Jews. Only 12 percent of Jews describe themselves as conservative, compared to 36 percent of Protestants. On some issues, Muslims have been found to be more liberal than the general population and significantly more liberal than Protestants and Catholics. For example, 70 percent of Muslims favor an activist government, whereas just 43 percent of the public as a whole subscribes to that view. On social issues, however, Muslims show a much more conservative tendency. When asked "Which comes closer to your view? Homosexuality is a way of life that should be accepted by society, or homosexuality is a way of life that should be discouraged by society," 61 percent of Muslims said that homosexual lifestyles should be discouraged. Only 38 percent of all Americans gave that response.[59]

CONNECT WITH YOUR CLASSMATES MindTap for American Government

Access the Public Opinion and Political Socialization Forum: Discussion– How Religion Shapes Public Opinion.

Gender

Starting in 1980, a **gender gap** emerged in U.S. politics. Before 1980, the differences in political attitudes among men and women were not large and did not draw much attention. However, in elections since Ronald Reagan's 1980 victory over Jimmy Carter (1977–81), women have been generally more supportive of Democrats than of Republicans. In 1980, the gap was 8 percentage points: 54 percent of men backed Reagan, and only 46 percent of women backed him. The gap has varied from 4 percent in 1992 to 11 percent in 1996. In 2008, Barack Obama secured 56 percent of the female vote and just 49 percent of the male vote. In April 2012, among women, Obama held a substantial lead in the polls over then-presumptive Republican nominee Mitt Romney—as much as 20 percentage points.[60] Such differences remind us that if only women were allowed to vote, the Democrats might have won every presidential election since 1980 save for Reagan's landslide against Walter Mondale in 1984.[61]

gender gap: *Differences in the political attitudes and behavior of men and women.*

In general, women are more liberal than men, and gender gaps are also evident on specific issues. Women tend to favor more spending on social programs than men. In 2013, more men favored cutting Medicare to reduce the deficit than did women.[62] Men are much more likely to support the death penalty than are women (62 percent versus 38 percent). This gap disappears when it comes to abortion. In 2013, around 20 percent of women and men thought abortion should be illegal in all circumstances.[63]

Race and Ethnicity

Another divide in public opinion involves race and ethnicity. The issue of slavery tore the nation apart, and more than one hundred years after the Civil War, Americans remained divided about issues involving race. In 1964, African Americans overwhelmingly endorsed desegregation, whereas white Americans were split on the issue. In 1974, only 23 percent of white Americans felt "government should help blacks," whereas 69 percent of African Americans believed that government should take that role.[64] Similar gaps exist today in regard to support for affirmative action policies that grant preferences to people (not only African Americans but also women) who have suffered discrimination in the past in job hiring, school admissions, and contracting. In 2012, only 14 percent of whites favored "preferences for hiring blacks." Three times as many African Americans favored affirmative action.[65]

The term *Latino* is used to describe a broad array of groups that do not necessarily share common experiences, so opinion among Latinos tends to be divided. Some Latino families have lived in the Southwest for centuries, since before the area became part of the United States in 1848. Others came to the United States within the past few years from homelands throughout Central and South America. Cuban immigrants, who left their homeland following the rise of Fidel Castro and the Communists in the late 1950s, tend to be much more conservative than Puerto Ricans and Mexican Americans. According to one study, about 60 percent of Cuban Americans are Republican identifiers, compared to only about 15 percent of Mexican Americans (see Global Gateways).[66] Latinos are divided in other ways as well. According to one group of prominent scholars:

> On many key domestic issues, significant majorities of each [Latino] group take the liberal position. On other issues, there is no consensus and, depending on the issue, Mexicans may be on the right, while Cubans and many Puerto Ricans are on the left of the nation's current political spectrum. Thus, labels such as liberal or conservative do not adequately describe the complexity of any one group's political views.[67]

→ **KEY QUESTIONS:**
Is your political opinion shaped by your social class, age, religion, gender, race and ethnicity, and/or education level?

Thus, both parties compete for the support of the Latino community. In 2004, Latino support for President George W. Bush helped him defeat John Kerry. In 2008, however, Barack Obama gained two-thirds of the Latino vote, a shift partly owing to actions by Republicans in Congress to block immigration reform. The importance of this group will only grow, as suggested by Figure 6.5. As Latinos comprise more and more of the electorate, issues salient to them will also become increasingly important. Latinos

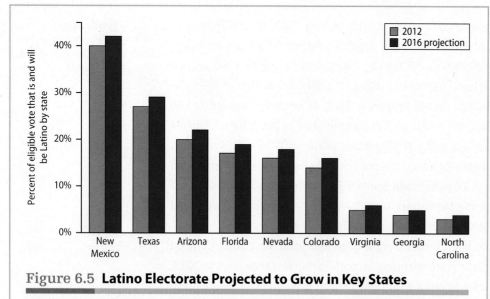

Figure 6.5 **Latino Electorate Projected to Grow in Key States**

Both parties need to find ways to reach out to Latino voters if they want to win elections in the coming years.

Source: Adapted from http://www.washingtonpost.com/blogs/plum-line/wp/2014/03/10/why-republicans-should-embrace-immigration-reform-in-one-chart/?hpid=z2.

7

Interest Groups

On forty campuses across the United States, college chapters of Common Sense Action (CSA) are attempting to take back politics for the Millennial generation. What began as an idea tossed around by Brown University undergrads Sam Gilman, Andrew Kaplan, and Heath Mayo, has turned into one of the most innovative student-run interest groups trying to change politics. Their mission is to expand "opportunities for Millennials by bringing our generation to the policy-making table and building a movement of Millennial voters committed to advancing generational fairness, investing in Millennial mobility, and repairing politics."

After working as an intern at the Bipartisan Policy Center in Washington D.C., Gilman realized the importance of workforce development. The Millennial generation had twice the unemployment rate of the national average, and yet members of Congress were not discussing this issue, mostly because it would not win elections. No community present in Washington D.C. was pushing for the interests of young people, so Gilman convinced Kaplan and Mayo to form their own bipartisan organization.

A key moment for Gilman occurred on September 11th, 2012, at 1:30 P.M., when his closest friend went to vote in the primary election on campus thirty steps from the campus center and told him that he was only the seventeenth voter that day. "And that really hit me. And when I voted in the general election two days before we officially launched CSA, I was the 130th voter at 10:15 A.M. The critical moment was realizing what happens if we can mobilize Millennials in and around primary elections for issues that impact our generation, in a world in which so few people vote in primary elections, and they are increasingly becoming the most important elections in our country, particularly as districts are becoming more polarized."

Through dorm meetings, Gilman, Kaplan, and Mayo were able to get a sense of the issues their generation cared about. At the subsequent CSA National Summit, the group established a core principle—respecting where people come from—so that liberals and conservatives alike can come together and find common ground on issues that affect their generation the most. Their bipartisan Agenda for Generational Equality seeks to advance generational fairness via a national entitlement solution, encourage Millennial mobility by making college more affordable, invest in the employment of Millennials, and repair politics through increased Millennial political participation.

Need to Know

7.1 Outline how interest groups have developed over time

7.2 Identify the types of interest groups that have evolved

7.3 Describe activities interest groups engage in

7.4 Analyze what balances out power among interest groups

7.5 Assess what makes an interest group successful

(▶) **WATCH & LEARN** MindTap for American Government
Watch a brief "What Do You Know?" video summarizing Interest Groups.

Their bipartisan approach has paid off. With their chapter model and grassroots organizing, CSA is active in community education, campus organizing, candidate education, voter empowerment, and bringing about change via primary elections in a bipartisan and inclusive manner.

CSA is tapping into the Millennial generation through its campus challenge, which seeks to empower students through education and network building. For CSA, finding strong leaders in the Millennial generation is key to not only running the group but also making real bipartisan changes in politics. The group's dedication to issues particular to their generation does not restrict the group. CSA recognizes the importance of intergenerational discussions, which have taken place through conversations with local senior facilities as well as with CSA's senior advisors: former U.S. Senators Pete Domenici (R-NM) and Byron Dorgan (D-ND). The grassroots origins and activities of CSA are current examples of students engaging in collective action to generate change and using university and political resources to raise awareness and support for issues relevant to the Millennial generation.[1]

Small or large, student-run or long-established national organizations, interest groups are a mechanism of representation in a democracy because they help translate individual opinions and interests into outcomes in the political system. Interest groups form for many reasons: to advance economic status, express an ideological viewpoint, influence public policy, or promote activism in international affairs. In a democracy, the most crucial role of interest groups is their attempt to influence public policy, which is one of the express interests of the student-run CSA. In this chapter, we examine the history of interest groups, why they form, what they do, and their impact on democratic processes. We also identify how and why some groups are more influential than others. Throughout the chapter, we focus on interest groups as gateways to citizen participation and, at the same time, point out how they can erect gates when they pursue narrow policy interests.

7.1 Interest Groups and Politics

> Outline how interest groups have developed over time

In 1831, the French political theorist Alexis de Tocqueville came to the United States to observe American social and political behavior. He stayed for more than nine months and later published his study as *Democracy in America,* a classic of political literature. He wrote, "The most natural right of man, after that of acting on his own, is that of combining his efforts with those of his fellows and acting together. Therefore the right of association seems to me by nature almost as inalienable as individual liberty."[2] Tocqueville noticed that Americans in particular liked to form groups and join associations as a way of participating in community and political life. To Tocqueville, the formation of group life was an important element of the success of the American democracy.

What Are Interest Groups?

Tocqueville used the term *association* to describe the groups he observed throughout his travels in America; today we call them interest groups. An **interest group** is a group of citizens who share a common interest—whether a political opinion, religious affiliation, ideological belief, social goal, or economic objective—and try to influence public policy to benefit its members. Other types of groups form for purely social or community reasons, but this chapter focuses on the groups that form to exert political influence.

Most interest groups arise from conditions in public life. A proactive group arises when an enterprising individual sees an opening or opportunity to create the group for social, political, or economic purposes. A reactive group forms to protect the interests of members in response to a perceived threat from another group, or to fight a government policy that the members believe will adversely affect them, or to respond to an unexpected external event.

interest groups:
Groups of citizens who share a common interest—a political opinion, religious or ideological belief, a social goal, or an economic characteristic—and try to influence public policy to benefit themselves.

Groups whose members share a number of common characteristics are described as homogeneous, whereas groups whose members come from varied backgrounds are described as heterogeneous. All interest groups are based on the idea that members joining together in a group can secure a shared benefit that would not be available to them if they acted alone.

Citizens most often join groups to advance their personal economic well-being, to get their voices heard as part of a larger group's efforts on an issue, or to meet like-minded citizens who share their views. There is no legal restriction on the number of groups that people can join, and citizens are frequently members of a number of organizations. On the large scale, citizens join groups as a gateway toward participating in democratic society.

The Right to Assemble and to Petition

The First Amendment states that Congress cannot prohibit "the right of the people peaceably to assemble, and to petition the Government for a redress of grievances." This right to assemble is the **right of association**. The Framers believed that the opportunity to form groups was a fundamental right that government may not legitimately take away. At the same time, however, they were fearful that such groups, which Madison called **factions**, might divide the young nation. Although Madison recognized that such groups could not be suppressed without abolishing liberty, he also argued in *Federalist* 51 that, in a large and diverse republic, narrow interests would balance out each other and be checked by majority rule. (See *Federalist* 10 and *Federalist* 51 in the Appendix.) Madison feared that factions could have the same divisive or polarizing effect in a democracy. Nevertheless, the Bill of Rights contains protections for the rights of association and petition because these rights are essential for citizens to be able to hold their government accountable, ensure the responsiveness of elected officials, and participate equally in self-government.

The **right of petition** gives individuals with a claim against the government the right to ask for compensation, and it also includes the right to petition to ask for a policy change or to express opposition to a policy. It was the earliest and most basic gateway for citizens seeking to make government respond to them, and it has been used from the beginning of government under the Constitution. For example, in the First Congress, cotton growers asked the government for direct payment of subsidies to allow them to keep their farms in years with low crop yields. Owners of shipping companies petitioned Congress to limit the amount of goods that foreign ships could deliver to the United States so they could maximize their share of the carrying trade. Even the makers of molasses got together to ask the government to impose higher taxes on imported molasses so they would face less competition.[3] In the nineteenth century, petitions were used for broader and more sweeping issues, such as appeals to end slavery, to ban alcoholic beverages, and to secure the right to vote for women. In the twenty-first century, groups such as change.org use the Internet to make it possible for individuals to directly "ask" Congress for a benefit via e-mail or to sign

right of association: *Right to freely associate with others and form groups, as protected by the First Amendment.*

faction: *Defined by Madison as any group that places its own interests above the aggregate interests of society.*

→ KEY QUESTIONS:
Do you think interest groups are divisive and polarizing? Or do they bring citizens together? Can you give examples to support your opinion?

right of petition: *Right to ask the government for assistance with a problem or to express opposition to a government policy, as protected by the First Amendment.*

THE GRANGER COLLECTION, NYC

Citizens have been using their right to petition to influence government since the earliest days of the democracy. Here female lobbyists in the late nineteenth century are trying to persuade members of Congress in the Marble Room of the U.S. Capitol. Although women did not yet have the right to vote, they still went to Washington to make their voices heard on issues that were important to them.

→ KEY QUESTIONS:
Have you ever signed a petition? What was it for?

lobbying: *Act of trying to persuade elected officials to adopt a specific policy change or maintain the status quo.*

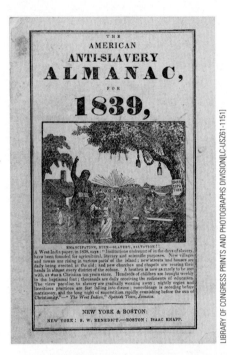

LIBRARY OF CONGRESS PRINTS AND PHOTOGRAPHS DIVISION[LC-US261-1151]

Abolitionists used stark imagery and words to rally citizens against slavery. In 1843, Lydia Maria Child compiled *The American Anti-Slavery Almanac.* **Its cover alone makes the case for abolition. Child was a writer and editor who was also active in the women's suffrage movement.**

→ KEY QUESTIONS:
How did interest groups work to end slavery? How long did it take women's suffrage groups to accomplish their goal?

→ KEY QUESTIONS:
Are groups representing manufacturers and corporations more or less powerful than citizens' interest groups? Do groups balance out each other?

a "virtual" petition that can be presented to Congress. Interest groups also use their high membership numbers as a proxy for the direct expression of support that once came from petitioners' personal visits to lawmakers.

Today the rights of association and petition most often take the form of **lobbying**, or trying to persuade elected officials to adopt or reject a specific policy change. Lobbying is a legitimate form of petitioning, and interest groups of all sizes and purposes engage in it, from CSA, to big corporations such as Microsoft and Google, to large-scale grassroots groups such as the Sierra Club. The term *lobbying* was coined more than three hundred years ago when individuals seeking favors from the British government would pace the halls, or lobbies, of the Parliament building, waiting for a chance to speak with members. The practice was immediately adopted in the new United States.

Interest groups lobby the legislative, executive, and even judicial branches of government at the state and federal levels. For example, when groups lobby Congress or state legislatures, they typically meet with members' staff aides to make the case for their policy goals. Lobbyists may also try to influence the executive branch by meeting personally with key bureaucrats and policy makers. Lobbying of the judicial branch takes the form of lawsuits against government policies that interest groups see as fundamentally unconstitutional or that go against the original intent of the law. Such lawsuits can be high profile and are initiated by groups of all political ideologies. For example, cases orchestrated by the National Association for the Advancement of Colored People (NAACP) and other liberal interest groups ended school segregation (see Chapter 5, Civil Rights). For other cases, interest groups can also submit *amicus curiae* briefs ("friend of the court") that record their opinions even if they are not the primary legal participants in a case. Interest groups also lobby for and against judicial nominees, especially Supreme Court appointments. Lobbying strategies and tactics differ according to the branch of government at the state and federal levels, but no government entity is outside the scope of lobbyists' efforts.[4]

The History of Interest Groups

As the nation expanded its geographic borders, its population, and its economic base, government took on more responsibilities that affected individual lives. Issues that were once considered local became nationally important, and improvements in travel and communications enabled citizens with a national concern to band together. Slavery was the most divisive of these national issues, and citizens who opposed slavery formed the American Anti-Slavery Society in 1833. Soon many other groups were urging the abolition of slavery, creating the abolitionist movement. Abolitionists held rallies, distributed pamphlets, and collected signatures on petitions to persuade Americans, specifically members of Congress, to abolish slavery.

Advocates for women's suffrage (the right to vote) paid close attention to antislavery efforts, seeing in them an example of the power of organization. In 1848, the women's suffrage movement was officially launched at Seneca Falls, New York.[5] To the members of this group, the refusal to allow women to vote was a gate that stood in the way of true political equality among all citizens. The abolitionist and the women's movements

global gateways

Amnesty International and Human Rights Watch

Amnesty International and Human Rights Watch are two of the most prominent human rights organizations in the world today and two of the most effective in bringing human rights issues to the attention of citizens and onto the desks of politicians.

Amnesty International was started in 1961 by Peter Benenson, an English lawyer, and today has more than 3 million supporters and volunteers worldwide. Its mission is to uphold the United Nations Universal Declaration of Human Rights to guarantee human rights to all citizens around the world. By informing the public through demonstrations and by lobbying members of political bodies throughout the world on the issue of human rights, Amnesty International has become one of the most widely recognized interest groups in the world. Most recently, it has been active in protesting human rights abuses committed by the Syrian government, including the use of chemical weapons to murder civilians, in attempting to put down a popular uprising. Additionally, it has taken a very active role in opposing the use of drone strikes by the United States in foreign lands.

Just over 30 years old, Human Rights Watch is also known worldwide for serving as a gateway to human rights by drawing public attention to injustices that occur on a daily basis in a wide range of countries. Similar to the watchdog role of the media, Human Rights Watch investigates human rights violations, including torture, and exposes those who have committed those violations.

The members of these groups are not necessarily fighting for benefits for themselves. Rather, they are working on behalf of individuals who live in countries where there are no protections against government abuses.

LLUIS GENE/AFP/GETTY IMAGES

In 2009, Amnesty International organized a protest in Barcelona, Spain, on behalf of human rights workers in Colombia who were killed, sent out of the country, or are missing. Each of the three hundred cutouts represents one of these individuals. International interest groups draw attention to problems in one country by planning protests such as this in as many places as they can.

1. How are Human Rights Watch and Amnesty International different from interest groups such as unions or trade associations?

2. Do you think Human Rights Watch and Amnesty International should receive direct support from the U.S. government for their efforts on behalf of human rights all over the world?

Sources: Information about Amnesty International was compiled from http://www.amnestyusa.org and a specific report on Syria by Amnesty International Staff, "Eyes on Syria," http://www.eyesonsyria.org/. Information about Human Rights Watch was compiled from Human Rights Watch, "About Us," http://www.hrw.org/about.

7.3 What Interest Groups Do

> Describe activities interest groups engage in

Interest groups perform a number of functions in the political process. They collect information about the implications of policy changes and convey that information to lawmakers and other policy makers. Their lobbying efforts aim to construct policies in ways that will most benefit their members. This section examines the tactics of lobbying, from providing information, to contributing to campaigns, to orchestrating grassroots movements that increase political participation on an issue. Lobbying is one of the fundamental gateways for expressing views and securing a favorable response from government officials.

Inform

All interest groups provide information about the issues they care about to their members, the media, government officials, and the general public. The type of interest group dictates the kind of information it disseminates. Before the Internet, groups provided members with information about government policies and new developments in their issue areas through newsletters and sessions at annual conventions. Today they disseminate such information on their websites and try to limit access by requiring members to register and sign in to the websites. Social media, such as Facebook and Twitter, also enable groups to keep members informed and to rally them to take action on the group's behalf.

Interest groups do more than merely report on current policy developments; they also provide members with interpretations of how the developments will affect their mission and goals. For example, in the area of environmental and energy policy, interest groups are very active in keeping their members up to date on policy developments. For example, in June 2014, when the EPA issued regulations to reduce carbon emissions from power plants by 30 percent, which was considered a strong stance against climate change, the Sierra Club posted a notice on its website informing its members and urging them to express their support.[19] (For more on the climate change issue, see Chapter 14, Economic, Domestic, and Foreign Policy.)

Interest groups also work hard to inform government officials about the impact of specific public policies. Most of the time, lobbyists have pro or con positions on a policy proposal, and their goal is to persuade government officials to agree with their perspective. Legislators and government officials are generally knowledgeable in their areas of expertise, but the vast size of the federal and state governments makes it hard to know the impact of policies on every citizen. Economic and ideological groups constantly monitor policies that might affect their members in a positive or negative way and strive to make legislators and government officials aware of the impact of policy proposals (see Public Policy and Interest Groups: Fracking).

→ KEY QUESTIONS:
When interest groups gather and disseminate information, are they performing a public service? Or do they do it just to advance their own causes? If so, is there anything wrong with that?

Lobby

Almost every kind of group with every kind of economic interest or political opinion—including business firms, trade and professional organizations, citizens' groups, labor unions, and universities and colleges—engages in one form of lobbying or another.[20] State, county, and city government officials maintain lobbying offices in Washington, D.C., both separately and as part of larger national groups such as the National Governors Association or the

United States Conference of Mayors. Lobbyists for these government entities frequently visit with the state's congressional delegation to keep the representatives informed about how federal programs are operating back home and to ask for legislation that will benefit their states. Mayors and county executives do the same thing, trying to influence their state legislators and governor by keeping them informed about how policies affect their constituents.

The Lobbyists. Groups can use their own employees as lobbyists or contract with firms that specialize in lobbying. According to the Center for Responsive Politics, in 2013, there were 12,279 individuals registered as active lobbyists in Washington, D.C. That amounts to nearly 23 lobbyists for each member of the

Here we see a hallway outside the state capitol in California where lobbyists gathered at the end of a legislative session to see how their proposals fared.

House and Senate.[21] The offices of many of these lobbyists are concentrated in an area of northwest Washington known as the K Street corridor; when people say they work on K Street, it is safe to assume that they are lobbyists.

Although lobbyists are frequently stereotyped as representing only the narrow interests of their clients, they are typically individuals who have held public service jobs at some point in their careers. There are three common pathways to becoming a Washington lobbyist: working on Capitol Hill, working in the executive branch, or working on a political campaign. Lobbyists may start out on a political campaign for a congressional candidate, work in a congressional office, and then leave to join a corporation, lobbying firm, or a law firm with a branch that lobbies on specific legal matters. Or lobbyists may start out as practicing attorneys, then go to work in Congress or the executive branch, and subsequently join a company or lobbying firm.

In 2013, interest groups and lobbying firms spent nearly $3.2 billion on a wide range of expenses associated with lobbying, including salaries for in-house lobbyists, consulting fees charged by lobbying firms, overhead for office space, and travel costs of staff [22] (see Table 7.2 on page 214). In the past, the costs of lobbying also included paid trips for members of Congress and their staffs (known as junkets), as well as expensive meals. Lobbyists justified these expenses as a way of getting to know members of Congress in a smaller and more relaxed setting, which they claimed would enable them to enhance their or their client's influence in the policy process. In 2007, congressional ethics reforms prohibited paid trips and meals for members and staff.[23] Still, lobbyists can use money to maintain their influence in other ways. For example, their salaries typically include allocations to make strategic campaign contributions to members of Congress who preside over issues that are important to their companies or clients.[24]

During a typical day, lobbyists phone, e-mail, or meet with congressional staffers, their clients, and possibly members of the media to gather information about relevant issues for their clients or to promote their clients' policy positions. Lobbyists also attend congressional

→ KEY QUESTIONS:
Why is the public perception of lobbyists so negative?

Public Policy and Interest Groups:
Fracking

The struggle for power over policy decisions is ongoing, and interest groups are always moving forward to accomplish their agendas within the larger policy-making arena. The issues within the energy and environmental arena are vast, and in this section, we focus on the interest group activity surrounding the use of hydraulic fracturing, otherwise known as fracking, which is a technique that extracts oil and natural gas. Since 1997, the use of fracking has expanded greatly, bringing with it increases in jobs and overall production of oil and gas nationwide, which has contributed to economic growth in some areas.[25] At the same time, there have been serious allegations that fracking poses a threat to the environment, particularly safe drinking water. In response to concerns expressed by residents in areas with fracking, in 2010 Congress requested that the Environmental Protection Agency conduct a study of the effects of fracking on drinking water. The EPA then launched a study and focused on locations in four states: North Dakota, Pennsylvania, Texas, and Colorado where fracking had already been occurring for some time.[26] As such, the issue of fracking presents a clear case study of the trade-offs between jobs, energy production, and environmental protection and how interest groups try to influence public policy in these areas.

Both America's Natural Gas Alliance (ANGA), a group that promotes the use of natural gas, and the Natural Resource Defense Council (NRDC), an environmental advocacy group that opposes fracking, have responded to this investigation in ways that advance their own perspective. ANGA is an example of a corporate interest group designed to advance the policies preferred by its industry members. NRDC is typical of a public interest nonprofit group that addresses issues of public policy which affect a wide group of citizens.

Each group is committed to representing the views of its members; for ANGA that consists of oil and gas companies, and for NRDC, that consists of

Fracking is becoming more widespread across previously undeveloped lands. Here a fracking site known as the Marcellus Shale Well sits among farmland in Pennsylvania.

MARK OVASKA/REDUX

To Know	To Test Yourself	To Participate

▶ Identify the types of interest groups that have evolved

Interest groups can be categorized as economic, ideological, and foreign policy and international, and each has different policy goals and strategies.	• Describe the different types of economic interest groups. • Explain how ideological and issue-oriented groups can lead to polarization. • Compare and contrast the missions of foreign policy and international interest groups.	• Create a set of interest groups that would represent different characteristics of voters such as gender, income, age, race, ethnicity, and ideology.

▶ Describe activities interest groups engage in

Generally, interest groups gather and disseminate information in their issue areas, lobby using various strategies such as meeting with staff and legislators as well as workers in the executive branch, and contribute to political campaigns and advertising to the extent that federal law allows.	• Explain how interest groups keep members informed. • Describe how interest groups lobby. • Define *political action committee*.	• Take the position as head of an interest group, and describe your policy goal and what strategy you would use to influence legislators, voters, and other groups to support your policy goals.

▶ Analyze what balances out power among interest groups

Scholars who study why interest groups form and their effects in a democratic society debate whether the wealthy have disproportionate power to use interest groups to their advantage, and so to the disadvantage of others. Scholars also debate whether interest groups balance out each other. Lobbyists, federal regulators, and members of Congress form networks that some describe as "iron" and closed to citizen influence and some describe as transparent and open to citizen influence. In today's democracy, elected officials, bureaucrats, and even the judiciary often act as intermediaries in interest group conflict.	• Compare the pluralist and elitist views of democratic society. • Explain why interest groups may be detrimental to the general public. • Recall the routes of influence that interest groups can use.	• Propose ways of balancing power across interest groups to make sure that government is equally responsive to as many people as possible on a given issue.

▶ Assess what makes an interest group successful

The success of interest groups can be measured in four ways: leadership accountability, membership stability, financial stability, and public influence. The longer an interest group exists, the more powerful it is. When a policy is debated, some interest groups will win by maintaining the status quo, and others might win by changing current policy.	• Explain the importance of leadership accountability in interest group success. • Describe issues in membership stability. • Name sources of financial stability. • Identify indicators of interest group influence.	• Consider how internally democratic interest groups really are. • Evaluate whether the free rider is a problem for democracy. • Debate whether an interest group can be too powerful.

"Self-government is not an easy thing to do. It requires a lot from citizens.... I believe it is my obligation, not a choice, to be informed about my local, state, and national government."

JOSH McKOON
Furman University,
Greenville, South Carolina

8

Political Parties

Josh McKoon, who was first elected to the Georgia senate in 2010, credits his experience at Furman University in Greenville, South Carolina, for launching "his lifetime commitment to conservative politics." As a political science and communications major, he volunteered on Republican Bob Dole's 1996 presidential campaign and worked for both a state representative running for Congress and a U.S. congressman running for the Senate. His wealth of campaign experience was one reason he was elected president of the College Republicans chapter at Furman. McKoon maintains that his time at Furman allowed him to become plugged into the Republican network. "I learned very early," he said in a phone interview, "that it is 90 percent about who you know, and making those contacts with the right individuals."

In 1999, McKoon met George W. Bush, the governor of Texas who was running for president. By making contacts with Bush's campaign team, McKoon landed a job as a director of field operations on Bush's primary campaign in South Carolina. As a field director, he coordinated campaign activities with Bush supporters at Clemson and Furman universities and built volunteer networks that facilitated Bush's get-out-the-vote efforts. After completing law school, McKoon headed back to Columbus, the Georgia city where he was born, reconnected with the Muscogee County Republican Party, and started a Young Republicans chapter, which he eventually chaired.

As party chair, McKoon sought to get more Republicans involved in state and local government using a three-pronged approach. First, he worked to expand grassroots campaign operations throughout Muscogee County to give Republican challengers the capacity to wage better campaigns. Second, he tried to recruit more viable Republican candidates with the talent and qualifications to challenge incumbent Democrats in the Georgia statehouse. Third, he used his fundraising skills to fill the party coffers to support local races. As it turned out, McKoon became one of the Republican candidates himself, running to represent the 29th district in the state senate; in 2014, he won reelection to his third term in office. McKoon got his start with the help of a lot of volunteer support from college students. One of them, Theresa Garcia, was quoted in a local newspaper as saying that she got involved "because of Josh's concerns about issues folks my age are concerned about. . . . Josh is concerned about jobs—and jobs are on everybody's minds. Will there be jobs when

Need to Know

8.1 Outline how political parties evolved in American politics

8.2 Identify which issues divided the first political parties

8.3 Explain why two parties dominate the U.S. political system

8.4 Define partisan affiliation and ideology

▶ **WATCH & LEARN** MindTap‑ for American Government

Watch a brief "What Do You Know?" video summarizing Political Parties.

we graduate? . . . We want to see Josh in the state senate because he is not far removed from us."

McKoon calls the Republican Party his "gateway." "In Columbus as a high school student and as an attorney," he says, "in Tuscaloosa as a law student, and in Greenville as a college student, the Republican Party offered me an access point to candidates, campaigns, and political experiences." Since joining the state senate, McKoon has introduced bills relating to health care, education, and criminal justice, and he is currently the chair of the Georgia Senate Judiciary Committee. His political career shows how young people can themselves run for elective office and generate support among young people who want to elect someone who can relate to and respond to their needs.[1]

Political parties offer every citizen in America the opportunity to participate in politics and even to run for elected office. In this chapter, we look at the role of political parties in the American constitutional system by examining what they do, how they formed and evolved over time, and what role they play in shaping electoral choices for candidates and voters alike.

LISTEN & LEARN

MindTap™ for American Government

Access Read Speaker to listen to Chapter 8.

8.1 The Role of Political Parties in American Democracy

> Outline how political parties evolved in American politics

A democratic government must be responsive to its citizens, and for government to be equally responsive, every citizen must have an equal opportunity to influence it. But mobilizing the more than 318 million people in the United States to take an active role in monitoring their government is a truly momentous challenge. In the United States, political parties fill an essential need by shaping the choices that voters face in elections, which serve as the key mechanism by which voters hold their government accountable. With so many public offices to fill, voters need some sort of road map to compare candidates and make the choices that will serve their best interests. The potential danger of relying on parties to shape these choices is that parties become interested only in winning office, not in serving the interests of the people. It takes action and vigilance on the part of voters to ensure that parties do not go in this direction.

In this section, we look at the role that parties play in the American democratic system, specifically at the way they organize the electorate, shape the elections that determine whether their candidates win office, and guide the actions of elected officials.

> **KEY QUESTIONS:**
In what ways are parties gateways for citizen participation? As you read this chapter, look for evidence.

What Are Political Parties?

A **political party** is a group of individuals who join together to choose candidates for elected office—whether by informal group voting or a formal nominating process. These candidates agree to abide by the **party platform**, a document that lays out the party's core beliefs and policy proposals. Parties operate through national, state, and county committees; members include party activists, citizen volunteers, and elected officials. A party's main purpose is to win elections in order to control governmental power and implement its policies; this fundamental goal distinguishes parties from interest groups, who also seek to influence electoral outcomes, but do not formally run candidates for office.

At the national level, the party issues its platform during presidential election years. In their 2012 platforms, for example, the Republican Party (www.gop.org) and the Democratic Party

political parties:
Broad coalitions of interests organized to win elections in order to enact a commonly supported set of public policies.

party platform:
Document that lays out a party's core beliefs and policy proposals for each presidential election.

how to govern. On the other hand, when the two parties together do not offer policy proposals that a significant number of voters want to see enacted, third parties form. These third parties can mount challenges so significant that the major parties are compelled to act, often by incorporating the third party's policy proposal into their platforms.

Theodore "Teddy" Roosevelt ran for president as the Progressive Party candidate. Roosevelt, a Republican, had served as president from 1901 to 1909. He decided to run for president again in 1912 to mobilize voters around a host of progressive reforms that would weaken party machines, most notably the idea of popular elections for U.S. senators. At that time, U.S. senators were elected in state legislatures rather than directly by the voters. Although Roosevelt lost, the Progressives were successful in getting Congress to pass and the states to ratify the Seventeenth Amendment on April 8, 1913, which allowed for the direct election of U.S. senators.

Since Teddy Roosevelt's run, five contenders representing significant third parties have entered presidential elections, but none has been able to build a sustained organization over time. Two of these candidates, Strom Thurmond (Dixiecrats) and George Wallace (American Independent Party), ran on segregationist platforms of parties that were splinter groups of the Democratic Party. John Anderson (National Unity Party) and Ross Perot (United We Stand) each ran on a platform that favored moderate social policy and strict fiscal discipline. Ross

Here we see members of Operation American Spring, a Tea Party affiliated group, marching in Washington to protest against the Obama Administration in 2014.

Perot was given credit for using his United We Stand Party to force the two major party candidates in 1992, President George H. W. Bush (1989–93) and William Jefferson (Bill) Clinton (1993–2001), to address the federal deficit, the amount by which annual government spending exceeds incoming revenue. Ralph Nader ran for president on the Green Party ticket in 2000, 2004, and 2008 promoting a platform that called for stronger environmental and consumer protections. Although Nader did not win, his messages of change and open government were clearly echoed by the mainstream Democratic candidate, Barack Obama, in his successful first campaign for president. For a compact list of significant parties in American politics, see Figure 8.4.

Though third parties have not fared well in national electoral contests, they sometimes find success in lower level elections. The Libertarian Party, for example, currently claims more than 140 elected officials.[21] Most are members of school boards and town councils, with mayors holding the highest offices. Another example of a third party that found success in local elections was the La Raza Unida Party (LRUP) in the 1970s.[22] The LRUP organized in 1970 in the south Texas counties of Zavala, Dimmitt, and La Salle, all near the U.S.-Mexico border. Its founders' goals were to advance the economic, social, and political interests of Mexican Americans. Their mobilizing efforts led to electoral victories in Crystal City, Cotulla, and Carrizo Springs school boards and town councils, all areas heavily populated by Latinos yet whose local offices Anglos had historically held. The La Raza Unida

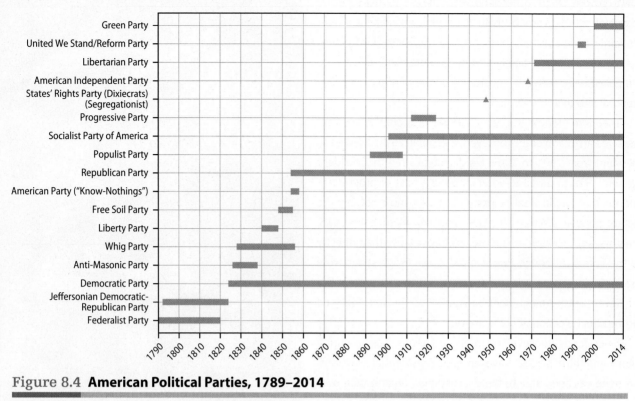

Figure 8.4 American Political Parties, 1789–2014

Note that the Democratic Party is the nation's oldest political party. The graph shows it beginning under President Andrew Jackson, but some argue that it actually began with President Thomas Jefferson's Democratic-Republicans.

Party spread throughout the Southwest into rural and urban areas from Texas to California, electing members to various local offices. Part of its legacy is the activation of Latinos into the political process and providing a gateway for Latinas; one notable veteran of the party is Rosie Castro, former Bexar County LRUP Chairwoman and mother of Secretary of Housing and Urban Development Julián Castro and his twin brother, Congressman Joaquín Castro (TX-20) (who is featured in Chapter 10, Congress).

The Tea Party

Third parties do not have to stand by themselves to have an impact on party politics; they can also be an influential force within one or more parties. For example, in 2010 and 2012, the Tea Party movement was very effective at supporting challengers to incumbents in primary elections in the Republican Party or supporting a third candidate in the general election. By one count, 129 candidates running for the House of Representatives and 9 candidates running for the U.S. Senate Congress in the 2010 elections affiliated themselves with the Tea Party.[23] Its message was fiscal responsibility, lower taxes, and paying down the national debt, and the Tea Party was successful in electing members of Congress, such as Senator Rand Paul (R-Ky.), who share its concern that the federal budget ought to be at the top of the American political agenda.[24]

More recently, the established wing of the Republican Party started to fight back against efforts to undermine incumbent Republicans or candidates that did not subscribe entirely to the Tea Party's agenda. In March 2014, Senator Mitch McConnell (R-KY), who was facing a Tea

→ KEY QUESTIONS:
What are the benefits and the risks of voting for a third-party candidate?

COMPARE WITH YOUR PEERS
MindTap™ for American Government

Access the Political Parties Forum: Polling Activity—Hurricane Sandy and Politics.

Party challenger in his primary, was quoted as saying, "I think we will crush them everywhere." The first test of that came in Texas where a Tea Party challenger, Representative Steve Stockman, was in fact overwhelmingly defeated by the incumbent Republican candidate, John Cornyn, in the Senate primary. In the face of the enormous resources of the mainstream Republican Party, the Tea Party had more difficulty in 2014 recruiting and funding strong challengers to Republican incumbents in the House and Senate.[25]

The Tea Party movement, although not officially a political party, illustrates how third parties can force the two major political parties to be more responsive; in this case, the Tea Party has given voice to more conservative voters. When they are large enough, these groups have the potential to move the party platforms in new directions and, in turn, to change federal laws.[26] The Tea Party movement's success in defeating incumbent Republicans in primaries and in electing Republicans who espoused more conservative views has created a more polarized and less effective governing environment in Congress (see Chapter 6, Figure 6.4, and Chapter 10).

Senator Rand Paul (R-KY) is a favorite of the Tea Party and an example of a candidate who was supported by a faction of the party who went on to win a Senate seat. In Kentucky, Rand Paul defeated a candidate for the U.S. Senate who was supported by the more established wing of the Republican Party and went on to win the general election. Since then, he has championed Tea Party issues such as smaller federal government, reduced spending, and freedom from government surveillance.

Obstacles to Third Parties and Independents

Because third-party candidates can act as spoilers, the two major parties do everything they can to discourage them, from challenging signatures for ballot access in court to preventing them from participating in presidential debates. The Democrats and Republicans have controlled state legislatures and Congress for so long that they have successfully established gates within state electoral laws that favor a two-party system over a multiple-party system. In addition, without the backing of a major party to get out the vote, collect campaign contributions, and arrange for media coverage, most third-party and Independent candidates do not stand much chance of being elected. Consequently, voters who consider themselves Independents do not have the opportunity to vote for candidates who might be closest to them in terms of policy preferences.

Candidates who are elected from third parties have little influence in legislatures because parties shape the internal power structure there. The party that wins the majority of seats in the legislature becomes the majority party and consequently controls the legislative process. After the legislative session begins, members are asked to express their opinions in subcommittees, committees, and on the floor by voting with or against their party's proposed legislation, and it is rare that an alternative to the major party proposal is considered (see Chapter 10). Those who are elected as Independents, such as Senator Bernie Sanders (I-VT), have no party organization to join in the legislature. Independents must pledge to support one of the two major parties in order to sit on committees and perform their other responsibilities as

→ KEY QUESTIONS:
Should laws that discourage third parties be changed? What would be the effects in terms of government responsiveness?

→ KEY QUESTIONS:
What are the advantages and disadvantages of being an Independent?

→ KEY QUESTIONS:
How do interest groups encourage citizen participation in political parties? How do they limit it?

© ISTOCKPHOTO.COM/EDSTOCK

Public Policy and Political Parties:
Assault Weapons Ban

In Chapter 4, we explained how the Supreme Court has interpreted the provisions of the Second Amendment to allow individuals to own firearms. As we noted, gun control is a highly contested public policy area, especially between the Democrats and the Republicans. However, tragic events such as the shooting of former Congresswoman Gabby Giffords and six other people in Arizona; the Aurora, Colorado movie theatre shootings; and the Newtown school shootings have precipitated a national discussion surrounding the specific issue of banning assault weapons.

Although not all party members agree, the majority of self-identified Democrats favor stricter gun possession laws, and the majority of self-identified Republicans oppose restrictions on gun possession. In an October 2013 Gallup Poll, 77 percent of Democrats said they favored stricter gun control while 23 percent of Republicans agreed.[27] On the question of an assault weapons ban, however, the margin is closer, with 68 percent of Democrats in support compared to 39 percent of Republicans.[28]

During the 2012 presidential election, the Democratic Party made gun control part of its party platform, stating that "We can focus on effective enforcement of existing laws, especially strengthening our background check system, and we can work together to enact commonsense improvements—like reinstating the assault weapons ban and closing the gun show loophole—so that guns do not fall into the hands of those irresponsible, law-breaking few."[29] The Republican Party had a contrasting statement in their platform about the assault weapon ban, stating that "We oppose legislation that is intended to restrict our Second Amendment rights by limiting the capacity of clips or magazines or otherwise restoring the ill-considered Clinton gun ban."[30] By including these statements in their party's platforms during a presidential candidate, each party was staking out a distinct policy position designed to attract support from their base.

In Congress, these party differences are also strongly visible. For example, in the 113th Congress, Senator Feinstein (D-CA) introduced a bill to reinstate the assault weapons ban that would outlaw a number of types of firearms capable of holding large amounts of ammunition. Her bill, the Assault Weapons Ban of 2013, had twenty-four Senate cosponsors, all of whom are Democrats. In the House of Representatives, Representative Carolyn McCarthy (D-NY) introduced a bill with the same language, and there were eighty-one House cosponsors, all of whom are Democrats. However, because the House of Representatives was controlled by the Republicans, and Republicans in the Senate could filibuster the legislation, there was little to no chance that it would have passed. Despite the odds against passage, the assault weapons ban was an important focal point for Democrats to mobilize supporters of gun control.

Interest groups influence gun policy as well. The National Rifle Association (NRA), which is a large grassroots group and one of the most effective in the nation, figures prominently in the national discussion on a ban on assault weapons. Like many interest groups, the NRA has formed a PAC to contribute to campaigns. Most PACs contribute to incumbents, current members of Congress who are much more likely to win than challengers. Most PACs support incumbents from both parties. Unlike many groups, however, the NRA's PAC contributes overwhelmingly to candidates from one party: the Republican Party. In the 2011–2012 congressional election cycle, the NRA's affiliated PAC contributed a total of $984,037 to congressional campaigns, with 87 percent going to Republicans and 13 percent going to Democrats. Safari Club International, a group that promotes wildlife conservation and protects the rights of hunters, also throws its support primarily behind Republican candidates. Its Arizona-based PAC contributed $381,563 with 92 percent going to Republicans and 8 percent going to Democrats. There was only one group, the Brady Campaign to prevent gun violence, that overwhelmingly supported Democrats, contributing a total of $4,018 to pro-gun-control Democrats, and no funds to Republicans.[31] Campaign contributions are important and so is the potential to bring voters out the door to vote for candidates who support their policy positions. Political parties depend on interest groups who agree with their policy stances to help mobilize voters; without them, that job becomes much more difficult.

The issue of thwarting gun violence through gun control, with specific measures such as the assault weapon ban, will likely remain a strong source of division in parties at the top levels of the organizations, among party identifiers, and among members of Congress.

Construct Your Own Policy

1. Write a version of an assault weapons ban that you believe might attract more support from Republicans who are currently opposed to it.
2. Construct a strategy of cooperation between parties on the issue of gun violence that does not involve any new restrictions on gun ownership.

legislators. When he was elected to the Senate in 2006 and reelected in 2012, Sanders chose to caucus with the Democrats. When Angus King was elected to the Senate from Maine in 2012 as an Independent, he chose to subsequently caucus with the Democrats as well.

Challenges to Party Power from Interest Groups

In addition to challenges from third parties, the two major parties face challenges from established interest groups and from broader social groups formed at the grassroots of American politics (see Chapter 7, Interest Groups). These groups and movements draw attention to each party's failings in specific issue areas and engage in activities from staging protest rallies to nominating alternative candidates to run in primaries in order to get parties to move closer to the policy positions the group or movement advocates.

Over the past two decades, interest and social movement groups have become more tightly aligned with specific political parties, and that alignment has undermined their capacity to serve as independent checks on—or competitors with—political parties. For example, unions such as the Service Employees International Union (SEIU) and environmental groups such as the Sierra Club are generally supportive of the Democratic Party, whereas business groups such as the Chamber of Commerce and the National Rifle Association are supportive of the Republican Party. For interest groups, the risk in continuously supporting one party is that the party will take their support for granted. In fact, parties are most responsive to interest groups when they threaten to withdraw their support or start their own party organizations. Consequently, interest groups maintain their influence with political parties by constantly expressing their preferences on policies to party leaders and providing support only when the party is responsive to their concerns.

For example, on the issue of gun control, interest groups on both sides of the issue have been very active in lobbying elected officials and trying to persuade the public to support their preferred policy position.

Checkpoint

CAN YOU:

- ▪ Explain the median voter theorem
- ▪ Describe how a single-member plurality system encourages two parties
- ▪ Summarize the role third parties have played in American politics
- ▪ Survey the obstacles to third parties and Independent candidates
- ▪ Explain how interest groups and political parties have become more closely aligned

8.4 Party Alignment and Ideology

> Define partisan affiliation and ideology

Throughout U.S. history, there have been long stretches of time during which the party affiliations of voters remained stable, but there have also been key elections in which parties lost or gained significant blocs of voters. Scholars have tried to identify the factors that explain why voters make large, permanent shifts from one party to another. Shifts in party allegiance can occur when there is an external shock to the nation, such as an economic depression or a foreign military attack. Shifts can also occur when public attitudes change considerably, and one party appears to respond more quickly to those changes than another.

The Parties after the Civil War

Following the Civil War, as we have seen, the Republicans were dominant in the Northeast and West, and the Democrats were dominant in the South and increasingly in large cities

Learning Outcomes: What You Need . . .

To Know	To Test Yourself	To Participate
▶ **Outline how political parties evolved in American politics**		
They have one primary purpose: to win elections in order to control government power and implement their policies. Parties organize the electorate by giving them choices of policies and candidates, and they also organize Congress and state legislatures into cohesive groups that consistently vote for the policies that they promise in their platforms. Parties nominate candidates for office in primary elections, which are open to all voters, although in some states voters must affiliate with a party before voting.	• Define political party. • Identify the three arenas in which parties operate. • Track the party nomination process.	• Design a system that allows the greatest number of voters to participate in choosing the party nominee.
▶ **Identify which issues divided the first political parties**		
The basic division between the Federalists and the Antifederalists over the ratification of the Constitution survived into the Washington administration to become factions; by the time of Jefferson's election in 1800, the factions had become political parties. Between 1800 and the Civil War, various parties rose and fell, but since the end of the war, the two major parties—the Democratic Party and the Republican Party—have dominated the American political system.	• Explain the differences between the Federalists and the Antifederalists. • Describe the events that opened up the presidential nomination process. • Explain how the Republican Party formed. • Connect patronage and party power. • Describe reforms that reduced party power.	• Design your own political party, identify which issues to focus on, and explain how you would attract members; explain why your party would be more accountable than the existing two other major parties.
▶ **Explain why two parties dominate the U.S. political system**		
The effects of the two-party system are to limit voter choices to "for" and "against" and to discourage third parties, although the issues third parties arise to address are frequently adopted by one of the major political parties.	• Explain the median voter theorem. • Describe how a single-member plurality system encourages two parties. • Summarize the role third parties have played in American politics. • Survey the obstacles to third parties and independent candidates. • Explain how interest groups and political parties have become more closely aligned.	• Imagine yourself as head of the Tea Party, and devise a strategy that would enable this third party to win the presidency.
▶ **Define partisan affiliation and ideology**		
Voter realignments occur when the parties readjust the focus of their policies, typically as a result of a major event such as an economic depression or a military conflict. Since Franklin D. Roosevelt's New Deal of the 1930s, liberals have generally aligned with the Democratic Party and conservatives with the Republican Party. The modern political landscape is marked by a partisan divide, with the parties taking on starker opposing positions and ramping up the rhetoric to the point that voters sometimes wonder if partisanship is taking precedence over policy making.	• Explain how voters align and realign with political parties. • Describe the impact of the New Deal on political ideology. • Explain how the Democratic Party came to be seen by African Americans as the party that supported civil rights. • Recall how Ronald Reagan's campaign strategy appealed to conservative Democrats. • Describe the general shift in the ideological core of the Democratic and Republican Parties since 1994.	• Identify three issues that you believe cut across ideological dividing lines. How would you encourage lawmakers to use these issues as examples of how to work together?

AP IMAGES/MATT YORK

BRIGHAM YOU

THE WORLD IS OUR C

"It's my hope I'll be reelected to serve this community. . . . There's a lot of work we still have to do to fight for the middle class and make sure every Arizonan has a shot at the American dream."

KYRSTEN SINEMA
Brigham Young University

9

Elections, Campaigns, and Voting

Congresswoman Kyrsten Sinema (D-AZ) is unconventional. Just consider her educational background. She graduated high school at the age of 16 in Arizona as valedictorian and graduated Brigham Young University (BYU) in 1995 at the age of 18. She earned a master's degree in social work in 1999, a JD in 2004, and her PhD in Justice Studies in 2012—all from Arizona State University. Sinema also has a strong bipartisan streak—again something unusual these days. She first ran for state legislature in 2002 as an independent, but after losing the race, ran as a Democrat in 2004 and won. In the Arizona State Legislature, she worked closely with Republicans on legislation tied to human trafficking. In her race for Congress in 2012, the *Arizona Republic*, the local Phoenix newspaper, endorsed her for her nonpartisan style, arguing that for "Sinema, it's always about the issue, not the personalities."[1] Finally, Sinema's personal choices make her unique: Although raised in a conservative Mormon family, she is the first openly bisexual person elected to Congress. In an era when the country has become quite use to openly gay politicians, her sexuality drew quite a bit of attention. She was not fond of the attention either, explaining that "I'm not a pioneer. I'm just a regular person who works hard."[2]

Yet Sinema is a pioneer. She uses the political process as a gateway to make a difference for the better. During her childhood, she faced some hard times as a child, living for a time in an abandoned gas station without electricity or running water.[3] Those early experiences shaped her life and convinced her to get involved and make the lives of people better. She supported the DREAM Act as a member of the Arizona State Legislature. She also fought to rein in

Maricopa County Sheriff Joe Arpaio's hard-line immigration stances, which often drew attention across the entire country.[4] She hired undocumented DREAM activist Erika Andiola (featured in Chapter 5, Civil Rights) on her staff—a strong signal about her position on that issue. Since being in the U.S. Congress, she has focused a good deal of attention on issues tied to veterans. She argues that "our country has a

Need to Know

9.1 Describe the ideas that molded the Framers' thinking about elections.

9.2 Outline the steps in presidential campaigns.

9.3 Identify the issues that shape presidential campaigns.

9.4 Determine which issues shape congressional campaigns.

9.5 Explain why there are battles over ballot access.

9.6 Outline how the right to vote has expanded.

9.7 Identify who tends to turn out in American elections.

9.8 Articulate the main theoretical approaches that explain voting.

9.9 Evaluate how low turnout is in American elections.

9.10 Analyze how changes in voting laws have affected participation rates.

▶ **WATCH & LEARN** MindTap™ **for American Government**
Watch a brief "What Do You Know?" video summarizing Elections and Campaigning for Office.

moral responsibility to do right by the men and woman who serve in our military."[5]

In 2012, she won an open seat for a new district that arose from the redistricting following the 2010 Census. In this fairly competitive district, she won the election with about 49 percent of the vote. Her Republican opponent, Vernon Parker, garnered 45 percent, and a Libertarian candidate secured about 6 percent of the vote. As a first-term member of Congress from a competitive district, she faced a tough battle for reelection. And having tackled the tough issues in Congress and being openly bisexual, she faced harsh attacks. But Simena knew from the moment she won in 2012 that 2014 would not be easy. Knowing that, she has raised a good deal of money to not only respond to any attacks but also to send signals to potential challengers that she is more than capable of competing for votes. Even in a Republican year, Sinema won 54 percent of the vote. Interestingly, her campaign only ran positive ads. She wanted to advance her reputation as an atypical politician. Sinema also benefited from that fact that her opponent, Wendy Rogers, would not even debate her. Sinema's ability to raise money was a huge advantage. She's a very successful fundraiser—a fact that should help her in future re-election efforts.

Elections, campaigns, and voting, as the experience of Kyrsten Sinema demonstrates, offer a gateway into the American political system. They provide many opportunities for participation, not only running for office but also volunteering and working at the polls. During campaigns, candidates offer competing visions of the role of government and promise to enact specific policies. The people decide to support a candidate and a campaign program when they go to the polls. Elections provide the most common (and easiest) gateway for the people to express their opinions and to hold elected officials accountable. In combination, elections, campaigns, and voting offer the public a chance to shape the course of government. In this chapter, we examine how elections, campaigns, and voting work, asking whether, and how, these institutions promote government responsiveness and equality for citizens. The chapter also addresses other forms of participation that help hold government accountable. Finally, we look at recent and future public policy concerning participation and voting.

9.1 The Constitutional Requirements for Elections

❯ Describe the ideas that molded the Framers' thinking about elections

→ KEY QUESTIONS:
Why did the Framers set up gates against popular participation in elections?

LISTEN & LEARN
MindTap for American Government

Access Read Speaker to listen to Chapter 9.

Given the importance of elections to the democratic process, it is surprising that the Constitution says so little about them. The requirements that the Constitution lays out for elections indicate that the Framers wanted to set up barriers against direct democracy. Only the House of Representatives was to be elected directly by the people. In elections for the president and for the Senate, the public's role was indirect and complex. Today, senators are elected directly by the people. Presidential elections also give citizens more say in the process, but these contests continue to be shaped by constitutional requirements that serve as a gate between the people and the presidency. In this section, we explain the constitutional requirements for American elections as background for understanding the ways in which presidential and congressional campaigns are run.

Presidential Elections

→ KEY QUESTIONS:
Why did the Framers give so much authority over presidential elections to the states?

The constitutional rules governing the selection of the president reflect three fundamental themes that guided the Framers' thinking. First, the states were given broad discretion on key matters regarding presidential elections to ensure their importance and to counterbalance the power of the national government. Second, the Framers designed the presidency

Figure 9.7 provides some clear data on Latino voting by comparing the rates of participation to other relevant groups. As the figure shows, Latino voting in presidential elections continues to lag behind the rates of both white and African American voters. Over the past four election cycles, whites have voted at rates between 60 percent and 70 percent, while African American turnout has increased from 52 percent to an historic 66 percent in the 2012 election. In the same time period, voting rates for Latinos have hovered in the range of 45–51 percent. The gap between black and Latino turnout has increased in recent years, surely reflecting the mobilization of the African American community with the Obama candidacy.

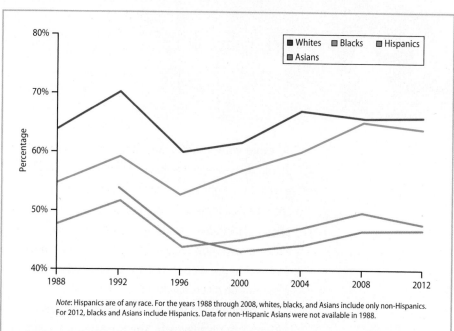

Note: Hispanics are of any race. For the years 1988 through 2008, whites, blacks, and Asians include only non-Hispanics. For 2012, blacks and Asians include Hispanics. Data for non-Hispanic Asians were not available in 1988.

Figure 9.7 **Voter Turnout Rates in Presidential Elections by Race and Ethnicity, 1988–2012**

Source: Pew Resource Center, http://www.pewresearch.org/fact-tank/2013/05/08/six-take-aways-from-the-census-bureaus-voting-report/

This lower turnout masks, however, the fact that Latinos comprise an ever growing segment of the total voting population. While turnout rates have been pretty flat, the number of eligible Latino voters has grown from 13.2 million to 23.7 million since the year 2000. While the 2000 Latino turnout rate of 45 percent brought around 6 million people to the polls, the 2012 turnout rate of 48 percent resulted in around 11 million Latino voters. Latinos now constitute about 10 percent of the electorate,[58] and the percentage will only grow in the coming years.[59]

Checkpoint

CAN YOU:

- Survey the expansion of suffrage between 1790 and 1860

- Describe how minorities and immigrants have at times been prohibited from voting

9.7 Who Votes?

> Identify who tends to turn out in American elections

Voting is an important gateway to influence, but not everyone has the inclination or the desire to participate. Failure to vote has real implications for the political process; it affects which representatives govern and make laws, and who governs has policy consequences that affect everyone in the United States. Low turnout raises questions about government's responsiveness, and unequal turnout by various demographic groups suggests that government's response is unequal, too. Low turnout among young people, for example, in contrast to older Americans, means that elected officials may give more attention to issues affecting senior voters, such as Social Security, than to issues affecting

Public Policy, Voting, and Participation: Voter ID Laws

To avoid voter fraud, many states have instituted voter identification requirements. As of 2014, thirty-one states have identification laws in force.[60] Of these, eight states require voters to show a photo ID, and three states require a nonphoto ID, such as a bank statement with the voter's address. Other states ask voters to show ID with or without a photo but do not prevent the individuals from voting if they do not present a ballot ID at the polling stations. Voter ID laws, however, are controversial as some argue that it creates a gate to participation. The poor and less educated, for example, may find it harder to meet these new standards and, if so, may be disenfranchised.

Opponents of Indiana's 2005 photo identification law sought to block its implementation through a lawsuit. The fundamental issue in this case was whether state laws that were intending to prevent voter fraud had the result of preventing citizens who were legally entitled to vote from doing so. Indiana argued that the requirement of a photo ID was not unduly burdensome because the state provided voter identification cards to citizens who had no other photo IDs. But opponents argued that the process of getting such a card was too complicated and that the overall effect of the law would be to disenfranchise thousands of citizens. In 2008, the Supreme Court upheld the Indiana law by a 6–3 vote. Justice John Paul Stevens wrote on behalf of the majority, "The state interests identified as justifications for [the law] are both neutral and sufficiently strong to require us to reject" the lawsuit. However, Justice David Souter wrote in dissent that the law "threatens to impose nontrivial burdens on the voting right of tens of thousands of the state's citizens."[61]

Today, the issue is still not settled. In 2012, the American Civil Liberties Union filed suit against Pennsylvania's new strict voter ID law, and the State Supreme Court struck down the law.[62] In addition to not "[assuring] fair and free elections," as the Pennsylvania judge wrote, these laws may have a disproportionate effect on some groups of voters.

For example, elderly, poorer citizens, and even women whose surnames may change as they marry, divorce, or simply maintain their maiden names[63] may not have acceptable forms of photo identification. Latinos may also be less likely than other voters to have valid photo identification. In Wisconsin, for example, scholars showed that not only were Latinos less likely to have such IDs, but they were also less likely to have the documents necessary to obtain them (see Figure 9.8).[64] In a federal court case brought by the League of United Latin American Citizens (LULAC), the courts used such evidence to strike down a Wisconsin law requiring citizens to present photo identification to vote. At issue was whether the Wisconsin law violated Section 2 of the Voting Rights Act that prohibits voting practices or procedures that discriminate on the basis of race, color, or membership in one of the language groups identified in the VRA.[65]

These are all complicated issues and as such must be thoughtfully assessed, especially as they affect differentially the ability of certain groups to influence the political process.

Political considerations also come into play. The two political parties may see their electoral fortunes tied to either increased or decreased voter participation and thus have different incentives to cooperate with each other on voting requirements.

With the Hamiltonian and Jeffersonian views of voting in mind, it is important to decide what standards should be imposed for citizens to vote. Clearly, the federal government has taken steps to make the voting process easier and more convenient. But ultimately states and localities administer and oversee elections, and states have responded inconsistently to the federal efforts. Some appear to have made it easier to vote, but others, such as Indiana, have made it harder by requiring photo identification at the polling place. It would seem that, in a democracy, all citizens should have an equal opportunity to cast their votes because voting is the fundamental mechanism by which we hold government accountable. As states introduce more laws regarding identification, disparities in the opportunity to vote may be growing.

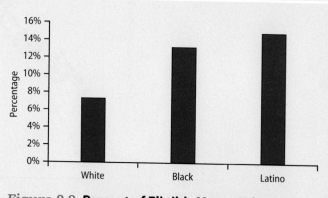

Figure 9.8 **Percent of Eligible Voters Who Lack Photo ID by Race and Ethnicity**

Source: Matt A. Barreto, and Gabriel R. Sanchez, "Rates of Possession of Accepted Photo Identification, Among Different Subgroups in the Eligible Voter Population, Milwaukee County, Wisconsin," Expert Report Submitted on Behalf of Plaintiffs in *Frank v. Walker*, Civil Action No. 2:11-cv-01128(LA), April 23, 2012, https://www.aclu.org/files/assets/062-10-exhibitjexpertreport.pdf.

Construct Your Own Policy

1. Write a set of requirements that you think citizens should meet to in order vote and that balances concerns for voter fraud with easing access to voting.

2. Construct a strategy for cooperation regarding voting requirements that addresses voter fraud concerns mostly voiced by Republicans as well as easy access for voters that Democrats embrace.

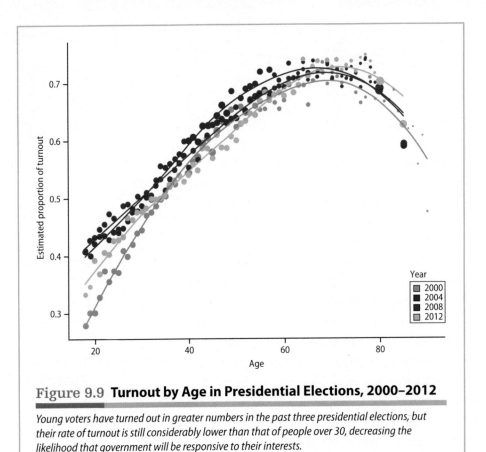

Figure 9.9 **Turnout by Age in Presidential Elections, 2000–2012**

Young voters have turned out in greater numbers in the past three presidential elections, but their rate of turnout is still considerably lower than that of people over 30, decreasing the likelihood that government will be responsive to their interests.

Source: Census Current Population Surveys.

younger voters, such as the costs of education. Figure 9.9 documents that the youngest voters have the lowest turnout and that voters turn out more often as they age. In this section, we examine turnout rates generally and then look at turnout rates by various demographic groups.

Turnout

Even with widespread opportunity to cast ballots and shape the course of government, Americans often choose not to vote. In 1996, fewer than half of eligible voters (about 48 percent) took the time to vote in the presidential contest between William Jefferson (Bill) Clinton (1993–2001) and Senator Robert Dole (R-Kans.). In 2012, the rate of participation improved to about 58 percent.[66] While that proportion was higher than in 1996, it was less than in 2008. Presidential elections are high-stimulus events that generate more interest and voting than any other American election. In midterm congressional elections, which are low-stimulus elections, turnout is usually less than 40 percent. For primary elections during presidential nominations, turnout is even lower. In 2012, in the all-important New Hampshire presidential primary, turnout was less than 31 percent, and it was lower still in other states. Illinois had a turnout of just 11 percent, and Florida had only 13 percent.[67] For local school board elections, the electorate is even smaller: Often fewer than 10 percent of eligible citizens vote in such contests. A general assessment of turnout in the United States is offered later in the chapter. Here, we turn to the demographics of turnout.

→ KEY QUESTIONS:
When some groups vote less frequently than other groups, what is the effect on government?

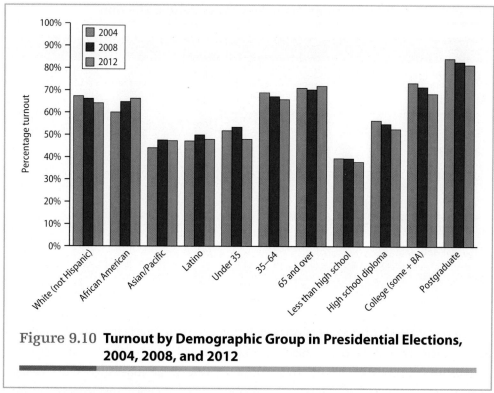

Figure 9.10 Turnout by Demographic Group in Presidential Elections, 2004, 2008, and 2012

Source: Census Current Population Surveys.

The Demographics of Turnout

Given the important power that voting brings in a democracy, the following becomes a central question: Who votes? Do various demographic groups vote in equal proportions? If not, what are the consequences for government responsiveness?

The data suggest that people who are most likely to vote tend to be better educated, better paid, and older than those who are unlikely to vote (see Figure 9.10). There are some modest race, ethnicity, and gender differences, but when scholars control for differences in education and income, differences in race pretty much disappear.[68] The key lesson is that the driving force of participation is the development in young people of the kinds of skills and habits that prepare an individual for active citizenship.

Sex. Women turn out at a slightly higher rate than men, by perhaps 3 to 5 percentage points. According to one estimate, 59 percent of women reported voting in 2012 compared to 54 percent of men.[69] The gender gap is important in American politics, but it relates to the tendency of women to support Democrats over Republicans, not to the difference in turnout between women and men.

Age. Age affects rates of participation. Turnout peaks once voters are about 60 years old (see Figure 9.9 on page 290). Even when differences in education and income are controlled for, participation remains higher for older Americans. In 2012, around 70 percent of citizens older than 65 claimed to have voted. The proportion is just 41 percent for those 24 and younger, and it is even lower for those 21 and younger.[70] Such findings are tied to the fact that younger citizens are often more mobile and less integrated into the community than are older citizens.[71]

It is worth noting that participation by the very youngest voting-age citizens (18–24) climbed to more than 49 percent in 2008, from 36 percent in 2000. Much of this gain was

→ **KEY QUESTIONS:**
Why do better-educated, better paid, and older people vote at higher rates than less-educated, more poorly paid, and younger people? What is the effect on government?

→ **KEY QUESTIONS:**
What can you do to get young people in your community to vote? Why is it important?

Table 9.1 Turnout by Income in the 2012 Presidential Election

	Percent Turnout
Less than <$15	48%
$15,000–19,999	52%
$20,000–29,999	56%
$30,000–39,999	58%
$40,000–49,999	62%
$50,000–74,999	66%
$75,000–99,999	70%
$100,000–150,000	74%
Over $150,000	76%

© CENGAGE LEARNING®

among young blacks, whose rate of participation jumped in response to Obama's candidacy. But the excitement of the youth faded four years later with 41 percent turnout in 2012.[72,73] One has to be cautious in making too much of these changes, but it does suggest that younger people can, under some conditions, become more active in politics. The general shift from the mid-1990s, where turnout was about 35 percent, to now being over 40 percent is in line with some of the early patterns of greater participation that have been found among the Millennials—the youngest cohort of voting-age citizens.

Income.   The higher one's income, the more likely one is to vote. More income generally means that people believe they have more at stake and thus more reason to vote. Individuals with higher incomes are also likely to be in environments in which politics is frequently discussed and that provide greater opportunities for learning about the political process. Political knowledge is strongly correlated with the propensity to vote. Further, individuals with higher incomes are more likely to be able to arrange to vote than are those with low-paying jobs, who may be less able to take time off from work to go to the polls.

Data from the U.S. Census Bureau in Table 9.1 strongly confirm this relationship. In 2012, about 75 percent of people with total family incomes between $100,000 and $150,000 reported that they went to the polls. For people whose incomes fell in the range that represents the annual median family income in America—$40,000 to $50,000—turnout was 62 percent. For the least-well-off (those earning less than $15,000), the proportion who claimed to have voted was 48 percent.

Education.   Although race and ethnicity, sex, age, and income have some effects on the propensity of people to vote, the number of years of formal education seems to be the most important influence. Social science research has documented the connection between education and voting.[74] The youngest voting-eligible citizens (18- to 24-year-olds) who have college degrees have turnout rates 13 percentage points higher than the rates of older citizens (65–75) who do not have a high school education.[75] Table 9.2 shows the propensity to vote by educational level from 1988 to 2012. The gap between people with the least education

Table 9.2 Turnout by Education in Presidential Elections, 1988–2012

Years of Education	1988	1992	1996	2000	2004	2008	2012
				Turnout			
8 years or fewer	37%	35%	30%	27%	24%	23%	22%
Less than high school	41%	41%	34%	34%	34%	27%	32%
High school	55%	58%	49%	49%	50%	50%	49%
Less than college	65%	69%	61%	60%	66%	65%	61%
College or more	78%	81%	73%	72%	74%	73%	72%

Source: Harold Stanley and Richard Niemi, *Vital Statistics on American Politics* (Washington, D.C.: CQ Press, 2013).

and those with the most was 50 percentage points in 2012—a huge difference. Nearly three-fourths of college-educated people vote, whereas less than a quarter of those with just a grade school education do so.

The relationship between education and voting may not be as simple as these data suggest, however. New evidence indicates that going to college does not matter as much as childhood socialization, which imbues the values of citizenship and similarly affects the decision to attend college. It is not, therefore, spending four years in college that makes college graduates more likely to vote; rather, it is having been raised in an environment that stresses the importance of education that shapes willingness to vote.[76]

The gap in turnout between people who are more educated and those with little education has increased over the past forty or so years. The increase can be explained by expanded access to education. Individuals who lack a high school education are at a much larger disadvantage than in the past. These patterns suggest that inequalities may result as government responds more effectively to those who vote than to those who do not.

Checkpoint

CAN YOU:
- Generalize about turnout in the United States
- Identify the characteristics of individuals who are more likely to vote

9.8 Why Citizens Vote

> Articulate the main theoretical approaches that explain voting

With the right to vote guaranteed and widely available, why do some people choose not to vote? Perhaps we can start to answer that question by reversing it, that is, by looking at why people *do* vote. Political scientists have developed three approaches to explain why eligible voters choose to cast ballots. One model draws from the field of economics, the second draws from psychology, and the third focuses on the rules and context of the election. In this section, we present these explanations as well as some new ideas about the relationship of genetics and voting.

> **KEY QUESTIONS:**
> Did you vote in the 2014 midterm elections? Why or why not?

An Economic Model of Voting

The economic model of voting starts with the assumption that all choices involve calculations about self-interest that balance costs and benefits. In choosing a college, students consider the price of tuition, the location of the school and its reputation, the quality of the education, and the potential social life. The decision to vote is no different. According to the economic model, citizens consider the costs and benefits of voting; when the benefits exceed the costs, they turn out to vote. So, according to this model, if voting becomes less costly to all citizens, there should be an increase in participation. If it becomes more costly, fewer people will turn out. Under this model, voters act in a rational, self-interested fashion.

However, economic voting is not straightforward. In *An Economic Theory of Democracy* (1957), Anthony Downs describes **rational voting** as a puzzle. He points out that there are some costs tied to voting, such as the time it takes to become informed, to register to vote, and to go to the polls.[77] Costs could also involve lost work time and the cost of gas to drive to the local polling place. These costs are not huge, but they are real.

The conclusion of the economic model is that voting is not in one's self-interest and in fact is irrational. If the decision to vote is driven by a self-interested assessment of costs and benefits, people should not take the time to vote. That is a troubling conclusion for the workings of democratic government. Obviously, if citizens do not bother to vote, government cannot be responsive, and public officials will not be held accountable.

Downs understood the troubling implications of his model and claimed that people voted because they knew that the system would collapse if no one voted. To save the system from collapse, it was rational to vote. This observation has appeal at first glance, but the logic is flawed: One vote will not save the system from collapsing. So even if the system is about to crumble, it remains rational to abstain from voting.

The prediction from Downs's model has drawn much attention from scholars. William Riker and Peter Ordeshook sought to save the model by introducing the idea of civic duty as a benefit of voting. The notion of civic duty is important, but the argument describes a psychological attitude voters might have.[78] Thus Riker and Ordeshook's argument does not solve the problem in Downs's model.[79] Narrow self-interest does not explain why people vote. As a consequence, political scientists tend to view voting as more of a psychological process than as a narrow economic or self-interested process.

A Psychological Model of Voting

The psychological model views participation in elections as a product of citizens' attitudes about the political system. These attitudes are often a product of socialization and early political experiences. People who are raised in households in which voting is important are likely to think that participation matters. Those who have a strong sense of trust in government or believe that their votes matter are more likely to participate. The focus here is on what we called civic interest in Chapter 1, Gateways to American Democracy.

Riker and Ordeshook's concept of civic duty fits well in this psychological model of voting. Many people who vote recognize that being a citizen in a democracy carries the obligation to vote. In 2012, for example, 90 percent of the public believed that "it's my duty to always vote."[80] The act of voting makes citizens feel good and feel that they are part of the political system. Surveys have found a strong correlation between civic-mindedness and the propensity to vote. In fact, there is often guilt associated with not voting, so much so that people tend to over-report the frequency with which they go to the polls.[81]

rational voting: *Economic model of voting wherein citizens weigh the benefits of voting against the costs in order to take the most personally beneficial course of action.*

→ KEY QUESTIONS:
Should the government adopt laws that advance the Jeffersonian or Hamiltonian approach to participation?

→ KEY QUESTIONS:
Do you feel like you have a civic duty to vote? If so, where did you get that sense of duty?

Another psychological component tied to the act of voting is partisanship. Citizens who align themselves with the Democratic Party or the Republican Party are more likely to vote. Being a partisan implies an engagement in politics, and partisans see importance in the outcomes of elections. Partisanship increases the prospects that an individual will vote.

Both civic duty and partisanship are attitudes formed in childhood. One survey found that a person's attitude about citizenship expressed in 1965 was a powerful predictor of his or her voting in the 1980 presidential election.[82] The relationship between socialization and voting holds even after education and other important variables that drive participation are taken into account. In addition, parents' electoral activism in 1965 also explains their children's willingness to vote in 1980. Much has changed since 1980, but socialization continues to have a long and powerful reach.

It is also clear that citizens who express greater trust in government are more willing to participate. In addition, people who think they have a voice in government are more likely to vote. Political scientists call this attitude **efficacy**—the belief that one's involvement influences the course of government.

efficacy: *Extent to which people believe their actions can affect public affairs and the actions of government.*

An Institutional Model of Voting

A third explanation of voting looks at political context. In the **institutional model**, voting is understood to be shaped by the rules of the system, by political party behavior, by the ways candidates run their campaigns, and by the context of the election.[83] This model does not ignore individuals' personal resources or psychological attitudes; it simply points out that the political environment is a factor that shapes participation.

institutional model: *Model of voting that focuses on the context of the election, including whether it is close and whether the rules encourage or discourage participation.*

It is clear, for example, that the popularity and appeal of the candidates affect turnout.[84] Contenders who are viewed as unexciting, even boring, offer voters few reasons to participate. But both very popular and very unpopular candidates might spur turnout. A highly controversial candidate might lead people who are strongly opposed to show up in great numbers on election day. A highly popular candidate likewise brings out supporters.

The competitiveness of an election also influences motivation. Elections that look to be close draw voters' interest and attention, especially if they think their votes might influence the outcome. A close race is exciting, and people like to be part of it. But elections often are not competitive, lessening citizens' incentive to make time to cast their ballots.

Because voting takes time, the efforts by parties, interest groups, and civic organizations to bring people to the polls can make a difference. Get-out-the-vote drives seem to pay big dividends, especially at the local level.

JUSTIN SULLIVAN/GETTY IMAGES

Musician Kid Rock performs during a campaign rally for Mitt Romney at the Royal Oak Music Theatre in Royal Oak, Michigan, on February 27, 2012. Campaigns try many ways to encourage younger citizens to participate.

For example, direct personal contact, such as going door to door, may increase the rate of voting by 7 to 10 percentage points in local elections.[85] Even text messaging seems to increase turnout by about 3 percentage points, according to a recent study.[86] The size of these effects is not likely to apply to presidential elections because many people are already inclined to vote in these high-stimulus elections. Parties, too, can increase turnout by mobilizing their base to participate.[87] Canvassing by telephone or in person not only may lower information costs but also may activate citizens' sense of civic duty. In some cases, parties or other organizations pick up people and bring them to the polls, lowering the costs of voting.

Is Voting in Your Genes?

It makes sense that voting is a product of psychological forces or perhaps of the costs and benefit of participating. But might the choice to be active in politics have a deeper cause? Might it be in your genes? More than two thousand years ago, Aristotle contended that "man is by nature a political animal." Political scientists have tended to believe that citizens are "blank slates," nurtured by socialization, education, and environment. Recent evidence, however, has suggested a genetic component to participation. James Fowler and his colleagues found a strong relationship between genes and turnout.[88] Another study reported "that two extensively studied genes are significant predictors of voter turnout."[89] These new data are important because they suggest that scholars may need to move beyond looking at the nurture side of the equation and start to consider the role nature plays in shaping individuals politically.

Checkpoint

CAN YOU:

■ Describe the economic model of voting

■ Describe the psychological model of voting

■ Describe the institutional model of voting

■ Address the genetic model of voting

9.9 Assessing Turnout

❯ Evaluate how low turnout is in American elections

As this chapter has established, most Americans do not vote in most elections. Even in presidential elections, for which turnout is highest, only slightly more than half of eligible voters go to the polls. In this section, we assess turnout in the United States. Is it too low for responsive and responsible government? Even more important, does turnout increase the prospects of governmental action that ensures equality?

Is Turnout Low?

There is a widespread belief among political scientists, political observers, and journalists that turnout in American elections is low. Consider the titles of the following books on the topic of voting in the United States: *Why Americans Still Don't Vote, Where Have All the Voters Gone?*, and *The Vanishing Voter.*[90] When just 37 percent of the American public took the time to vote in the 2014 congressional elections, the concern about low turnout expressed in these books seems justified. Even with all the attention and interest surrounding the 2012 presidential elections, turnout of the voting-age population was about 58 percent.[91] Such data strike many as disappointing. But further investigation of turnout can offer a different way to interpret the situation.

The United States Compared to Other Democracies.

Compared to other democracies, turnout in the United States is low. Between 1948 and 2012, the average rate of turnout in U.S. presidential elections was about 57 percent,[92] while in other democracies it was 90 percent or more.[93] These numbers compel an assessment of why U.S. turnout is so low.

One reason has to do with the rules for voting. Australia has **compulsory voting**—citizens are required by law to vote. Those who do not vote must pay a $20 fine, and the fine increases to $50 if the nonvoter does not answer the Australian Election Commission's inquiry about why he or she did not vote. New Zealand requires all citizens to register to vote. In most of the countries of Western Europe, the government is responsible for registering citizens to vote. In the United States, by contrast, both voting and registering are voluntary, and only about 70 percent of the public is registered. That means that nearly one-third of potentially eligible voters cannot cast votes on election day even if they want to do so.

Another reason has to do with the convenience of voting. Most European countries lessen the costs of voting by allowing it to take place on Sunday. In the United States, voting takes place on Tuesday, a workday for most people. Federal law stipulates that the first Tuesday after the first Monday in November is the day on which voting for president and members of Congress will take place, and most states have also selected Tuesdays as the day for voting in primaries and in state and local elections. The costs of voting are increased because people may be at work and may have difficulty finding the time to vote.

According to one estimate, turnout in the United States would be 27 percentage points higher (or more than 80 percent) if the nation had laws and rules that foster voting.[94] At the least, this figure suggests that comparisons of turnout in various democracies require a careful accounting of the rules and institutions that shape the willingness of citizens to go to the polls.

Trends in Turnout.

A second problem is noted regarding turnout trends in the last fifty years. One of the lines in Figure 9.11 (see page 299) represents the percentage of turnout in presidential elections measured against the **voting-age population (VAP)**, an estimate of those old enough to vote. In the United States, all citizens 18 or older constitute the VAP. The graph shows a lot of change—a decline in the 1970s, a surge in 2004 and 2008, a drop off in 2012. This pattern is much the same for midterm elections. In 1962, turnout for congressional elections was 48 percent. It fell to a low of 38 percent in 1986, with a slight rebound to about 41 percent in 2010. But regardless of how you want to interpret these shifts, one thing is clear: Turnout today is less than it was fifty years ago.

This pattern becomes more worrisome in light of rising levels of education since 1960, as education is one of the strongest predictors of turnout. Even though education levels have increased over the past fifty years (see Table 9.2 on page 293), the rate of participation in elections has not increased.

compulsory voting:
Practice that requires citizens to vote in elections or face punitive measures such as community service, fines, or imprisonment.

→ KEY QUESTIONS:
Should the United States adopt compulsory voting?

→ KEY QUESTIONS:
Should the United States vote on Saturday or Sunday instead of a weekday?

voting-age population (VAP):
Used to calculate the rate of participation by dividing the number of voters by the number of people in the country who are 18 and over.

generational replacement: *Cycle whereby younger generations replace older generations in the electorate.*

→ KEY QUESTIONS:
What effect do negative ads have on you?

These kinds of data have led political scientists to study why fewer Americans seem to be voting.[95] Explanations have varied. One explanation looks at the difference between those who enter the electorate and those who leave. The concept of **generational replacement** describes a trend in which older voters who pass away are replaced in the electorate by less reliable young voters.[96] It is very difficult, however, to sort out generational differences from changes in self-interest. That is, do older voters turn out to vote because of the generation they were part of, because they are older and have more experience in dealing with politics, or because they want to protect their interests or expand the benefits that directly affect them, such as Medicare and low payments for prescription drugs?

A second explanation has been the decline of party organizations.[97] Local parties have been less able to turn out the vote on election day than they were in the late nineteenth and early twentieth centuries, and therefore the voting rate has declined. Some scholars have estimated that half of the decline in turnout can be attributed to the drop in mobilization efforts.[98] This explanation has appeal, but parties in many ways are stronger today than they were in the past, although the days of big city bosses and urban political machines are gone. Obama and the Democratic Party were successful in turning out the vote in 2012, especially in key states such as Ohio, and citizens are voting along party lines more than any time since scientific surveys began in the 1950s. So a decline in party strength (perceived or real) is not an adequate explanation for low turnout.

A third explanation for declining turnout is the increasingly harsh tone of political campaigns. Some argue that negative campaigns have fueled voter apathy. It is clear that negative advertising on TV often fosters voters' disgust with politics. About 80 percent of people say they do not like these campaign tactics.[99] Initial studies suggested that negative campaigns could decrease turnout by about 5 percentage points.[100] In addition, there is clear evidence that negativity in campaigns has been on the rise since the 1960s, so there has been an apparent correlation between the two trends.[101] Scholars and pundits rushed to endorse this hypothesis. But subsequent studies have called the hypothesis into question.[102] A harsh campaign is likely to be competitive, and competitive campaigns draw interest and therefore increase turnout. Further, negative attacks can activate partisanship, which also increases turnout. People often choose to affiliate with a party in part because they do not like members of the opposite party. An attack ad by the Republicans can remind their supporters why they oppose the Democrats, giving them more reason to participate. A recent comprehensive study of all research on this topic shows clearly that negativity is not responsible for lowering turnout.[103]

A New Way to Measure Voting.   There is another explanation that actually contends that turnout has *not* declined over the past forty years: The VAP measure has been in error because it does not take into account increases in the number of immigrants and convicted felons who are ineligible to vote. Over the few decades, there has been a steep increase in the number of undocumented immigrants. With the sagging economy of the past few years, the numbers have declined, but even so, in 2011 the number of illegal immigrants was estimated to be nearly 12 million (or about 4 percent of the population).[104] Over the past twenty years, there has also been nearly a threefold increase in the

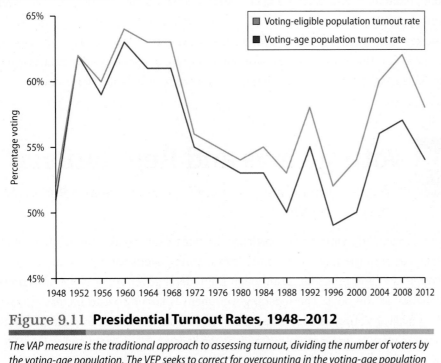

Figure 9.11 Presidential Turnout Rates, 1948–2012

The VAP measure is the traditional approach to assessing turnout, dividing the number of voters by the voting-age population. The VEP seeks to correct for overcounting in the voting-age population by removing noncitizens and people in jail who are not eligible to vote. Until 1972, this correction made only a modest difference. But given the surge of immigration and the growth in the number of convicted felons since then, the VEP measure is more accurate. Turnout in the 2004 and 2008 elections is actually comparable to turnout in the 1950s and 1960s, but dropped in 2012.

Source: "Presidential Turnout Rates, 1948–2012," United States Elections Project, accessed January 28, 2014, http://elections.gmu.edu /voter_turnout.htm. Copyright © 2012 by Michael McDonald. Reproduced by permission.

number of people in prison (from 585,000 to 1.6 million), reflecting tougher sentencing in American courts of law.[105]

A new measure called the **voting-eligible population (VEP)** corrects for these trends. The top line in Figure 9.11 presents the VEP estimates for turnout. It indicates that aggregate turnout in the 2008 presidential election was actually about 62 percent. By this measure, turnout has not declined over the past thirty years. In fact, turnout is now a full 10 percentage points higher than in the presidential election of 1948, when it was 52 percent. These revised estimates put a new spin on what has been perceived as a problem with U.S. elections, suggesting that Americans are not less willing to vote than in the past or than citizens in other democracies.[106]

Do Turnout Rates Create Inequality?

Voting is a hallmark of democratic politics and is certainly a cherished American value. The idea is simple. Each person has one vote, and each vote should be equal. The fact that those who are better educated or better off participate at a greater rate is a potential source of concern (see Table 9.1 on page 292 and Table 9.2 on page 293). That the wealthy are more likely to vote than the poor is an especially troubling trend because the income gap between the rich and the poor is increasing.[107] As the rich become richer, they become better able to

⭐ **voting-eligible population (VEP):**
Used to calculate the rate of participation by dividing the number of voters by the number of people in the country who are eligible to vote rather than just of voting age.

→ KEY QUESTIONS:
Do Americans have equality in voting? Explain.

Checkpoint

CAN YOU:

■ Explain why turnout is lower in the United States than in some other democracies

■ Address the issue of turnout and inequality

contribute more money to parties and candidates.[108] Such donations only further advance their potential influence.

It makes sense that politicians respond to people who participate and do not respond to those who do not. That is why it is so important for people to get involved in politics and also why the increasing rate of participation in the past decade or so is such good news.

9.10 Voting Laws and Regulations

> Analyze how changes in voting laws have affected rates of participation

The rules surrounding voting alter participation rates. Policy making regarding voting is undertaken at both the federal and state levels. State governments continue to manage most voting laws and procedures, although the federal government steps in to prevent discrimination at the polls. The federal government is committed to increasing participation by making voting as easy as possible. At the same time, both state and federal governments work to prevent voter fraud, as we saw when we examined voter ID laws. Thus, policy making regarding voting has the effect of both expanding and potentially contracting turnout. This section reviews policies that have altered the way voting works in the United States.

Reforms to Voting Laws in the 1890s

Rules matter, as the institutional model of voting suggests. Any change in the laws governing voting (or any process related to voting) will alter how that process works. A classic example of the power of rules can be found in the late nineteenth century, when the Progressives called for a series of reforms to the voting process to end corrupt practices. The reforms affected who was eligible to vote and the way people actually voted. In other words, they altered who participated in elections.

Corrupt voting practices needed to end. Big-city political machines routinely "stuffed" the ballot box,[109] and party members manipulated the results to ensure victory. Turnout in some cities exceeded 100 percent, meaning that not only were some people voting who should not have been but also that some were voting multiple times. Party members often rounded up people and brought them, in sequence, to various polling precincts around the city, making sure they voted in each one. Someone who had died would remain on the rolls, and the party machine would "allow" that person to vote. This corrupt practice has been referred to as **graveyard voting**.[110]

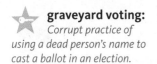

graveyard voting:
Corrupt practice of using a dead person's name to cast a ballot in an election.

In response to these excesses, Progressives called for voter registration.[111] The idea was that voters would have to preregister with a government official to be placed on an official list of voters. The list would be updated when someone died, and it would be used at the polls on election day to ensure that a potential voter had the right to vote and had not already voted. This reform spread rapidly. Today, all states except North Dakota require voter registration. The specific rules of registration vary a great deal among the states. For example, only in Idaho, Iowa, Maine, Minnesota, Montana, North Carolina, New Hampshire, Wisconsin, and

→ KEY QUESTIONS:
If you are a registered voter, what was your experience with registration? Was it a gate or a gateway?

Wyoming can a person register and vote on election day.[112] All other states require registration before the actual voting.

The National Voter Registration Act

In 1993, Congress sought to streamline voter registration procedures so that more Americans would exercise their right to vote, at least in federal elections. The National Voter Registration Act, commonly known as the "Motor Voter" law, requires states to allow citizens to register to vote at the same time they apply for or renew their driver's licenses. This law also requires states to inform citizens who are removed from the approved voter rolls and limits removal to a change of address, conviction for a felony, and, of course, death. These requirements were in response to charges that local governments, controlled by political parties, improperly removed voters from the voter rolls without their knowledge; under the guise of updating voter registration lists, officials of one party were disqualifying voters who would tend to vote for the other party's candidates. The 1993 law imposes criminal penalties on anyone who tries to coerce or intimidate voters on their way to the polling place or tries to prevent registered voters from casting their ballots.[113]

New Forms of Voting

As indicated earlier, some states are experimenting with laws that make voting easier. Some have instituted early voting, allowing voters to cast ballots before the Tuesday on which a general election is held. This flexibility helps working people, who might find it hard to find time to vote on a Tuesday. It also provides more than a single day for voting, so that schedule conflicts (such as a dental appointment or a sick child) do not interfere. In Texas, for example, citizens can vote any time between seventeen and four days before election day, so "you don't have to stand in long lines on election day."[114] Other states, such as Oregon, have started to make use of a **vote-by-mail (VBM) system**. Voters get ballots in the mail two weeks before the election, giving them a chance to research the candidates and cast their ballots. They can make their choices at home and avoid the often long lines at the polling booth. This innovation, proponents argue, lowers the cost of voting, and there is some evidence it has increased participation. Oregon has had a very high rate of voting, although it did drop from about 70 percent in 2008 to about 64 percent in 2012.[115] California has had less success with voting by mail. Some now worry that, under the rules of VBM systems, less-educated people are less likely to vote.[116]

Over the past three decades, nearly two-thirds of states passed "early voting" provisions that allow citizens to cast ballots prior to election day (see Figure 9.12).[117] The idea was that limiting participation to a single day kept many people from participating. The idea seemed sensible, and a lot of states followed suit. Although there is little evidence that early voting increases turnout, the provisions clearly lower the costs of voting.[118] Recently, however, some states have begun to reverse those laws and reduce the availability of early voting, eliminated same-day voter registration, and enacted new strict photo identification requirements.[119] These new laws increase the cost of voting, making it more

→ KEY QUESTIONS:
How can the government prevent fraud and still encourage citizens to vote?

COMPARE WITH YOUR PEERS
MindTap for American Government

Access the Voting Forum: Polling Activity—Voter Registration.

→ KEY QUESTIONS:
Should the government take steps to increase voting? Why?

vote-by-mail (VBM) system: *Method of voting in an election whereby ballots are distributed to voters by mail, and voters complete and return the ballots by mail.*

CONNECT WITH YOUR CLASSMATES
MindTap for American Government

Access the Voting Forum: Discussion—Election Day.

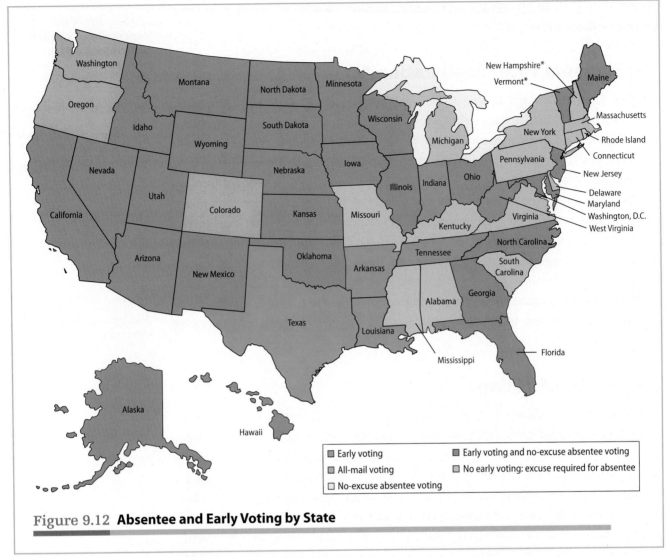

Figure 9.12 Absentee and Early Voting by State

Legend:
- Early voting
- All-mail voting
- No-excuse absentee voting
- Early voting and no-excuse absentee voting
- No early voting: excuse required for absentee

Source: http://www.ncsl.org/research/elections-and-campaigns/absentee-and-early-voting.aspx

→ KEY QUESTIONS:
What are the risks and benefits of early voting? Of voting by mail?

→ KEY QUESTIONS:
Aside from voting, how have you participated in politics and civic life?

difficult for some citizens to vote. Others say the laws are necessary to protect the integrity of the ballot box.

Nevertheless, new technologies, including the Internet, Twitter, and cell phones, may be used in the future, and they could make it easier for some people to vote—elderly and disabled, for example—thus increasing turnout. However, opponents of using these technologies argue that they would be too susceptible to voter fraud for two reasons: First, there would be no way to identify the person who is casting the vote, unless citizens are given individual pin codes or use their Social Security numbers. Given the number of Internet security breaches, opponents argue that such a system would not guard personal privacy. Second, votes at polling places are counted by election officials, but Internet and cell phone voting data would likely be collected and counted by computer servers, which are vulnerable to hacking and other security breaches.

In considering the effects of voting by new technologies, the beneficial effects on community and civic life of having everyone vote on a single day should also be considered.

The act of standing in line and talking with fellow voters, or discussing the act of voting with friends and family at the end of the day, can reinforce the sense of political efficacy and provide a foundation for the democratic process. Voting by mail, cell phone, or via twitter may detract from this shared experience, and that cost must be weighed against the added benefits of increased voter participation.

Checkpoint

CAN YOU:

- Identify the goals of the Progressive voting reforms
- Assess how the Motor Voter law, vote-by-mail, and early voting have affected voter turnout

Elections, Campaigns, Voting, and Democracy

American elections and the campaigns that precede them are the means by which citizens participate in selecting those who will govern them. It is inevitable that they are at the center of concerns about American democracy. Many observers worry that campaigns are too long, that candidates spend too much money, and that the voters are not very well informed. These concerns often focus on the fairness of the process and of the outcome. In the long term, the process has worked reasonably well. In the short term, it is those who lose who see the process as unfair.

In any assessment of the American political system, your own partisanship needs to be set aside. The general lesson is that elections and campaigns, although imperfect, provide a real chance to ensure government responsiveness and have done so over many years and decades. The public digests information and chooses a candidate. People's votes are a blunt instrument, but they help to forge accountability. It is through this competitive struggle that American democracy works. Critics worry that the public does not know many of the details of candidates and their platforms, and that is clearly true. But the American public should not be underestimated. The fact that the public collectively seems to act in reasonably coherent ways is testimony to political scientist V. O. Key's classic observation that "voters are not fools."[120]

Moreover, the U.S. government has lasted more than two centuries. This longevity is not an accident and is attributable, in large part, to the fact that Americans have, collectively, taken the time to participate. There have been many barriers, from limited suffrage to rules that discourage voting, but the long-term trend has been increased participation, which speaks to the health of American democracy. Now suffrage—the right to vote—is available to all citizens except those convicted of a felony (see Chapter 5).[121] The rate of voting in the United States is not as low as many observers tend to assert. Further, looking at participation more broadly, Americans do more than just vote in elections. They are engaged in political campaigns and in making their communities better at the local level.

There is a danger to a democracy from a distortion in turnout; the rich participate more than the poor, and this gap seems to be growing. With nonvoters being poorer and less educated, their failure to participate may help explain why government is not as responsive to their needs. Put another way, the government may be overly responsive to the needs of the well-off. This disparity in responsiveness threatens the underpinnings of a democratic and egalitarian society. If the political system responds to one segment of the population and systematically ignores other segments, general support for democracy, based on principles of fairness, could drop significantly.

With the Internet's growing influence, there may be other dangers to democracy. Wealthier citizens have more access to the information and resources on the Internet and therefore become even more informed and better able to make government responsive to their needs. The rich have always had advantages, but their advantages may be growing. At the same time, the Internet might be used to extend participation. As recent presidential campaigns have demonstrated, this technology can be used to expand the number of contributors to include people who have only a few dollars to contribute or who might want to show up at a local meeting to learn about an issue of relevance to them.

Let us now return to Figure 9.5 (page 284), which offered two models of participation. The Hamiltonian model argued that more participation is not always a good thing and that government works best with limited involvement from the public. The Jeffersonian model contended that greater participation improves both the quality of the input and the lives of citizens. Within our book's gateway approach, the participatory model of voting has more appeal than the elite model. Democracy becomes more responsive, more accountable, and more equal if more people participate. The cycle is reinforcing. Citizens themselves need to do all they can to encourage participation; doing so is in their self-interest and their civic interest. Democracy rests on the active and healthy participation of the citizenry. In other words, as the number of gateways increase, so does the quality of American civic life.

Master the Concept
of Elections and Campaigning for Office with MindTap™ for American Government

 REVIEW MindTap™ **for American Government**
Access Key Term Flashcards for Chapter 9.

 TEST YOURSELF MindTap™ **for American Government**
Take the Wrap It Up Quiz for Chapter 9.

 **STAY CURRENT** MindTap™ **for American Government**
Access the KnowNow blog and customized RSS for updates on current events.

 STAY FOCUSED MindTap™ **for American Government**
Complete the Focus Activities for Elections and Campaigning for Office.

Key Concepts

battleground state (p. 277). Why do presidential candidates focus on battleground states?

compulsory voting (p. 297). Should the United States make voting compulsory?

efficacy (p. 295). How should democracy increase people's sense of efficacy?

Electoral College (p. 267). Is the Electoral College a gate or a gateway to democracy?

generational replacement (p. 298). What changes in turnout can be expected as young people become eligible to vote and older citizens no longer can?

gerrymandering (p. 272). Does gerrymandering weaken responsiveness?

graveyard voting (p. 300). How was graveyard voting curtailed?

institutional model (p. 295). What are the weaknesses of the institutional model of participation?

invisible primary (p. 273). What is the importance of the invisible primary?

microtargeting (p. 278). Why do politicians engage in microtargeting?

negativity (p. 279). What are the benefits of negativity for voters?

permanent campaign (p. 273). Why is the permanent campaign a problem for Congress?

position issues (p. 279). Why are position issues uncommon in campaigns?

rational voting (p. 294). Why might rational voting be bad for democracy?

redistricting (p. 271). What is the difference between redistricting and gerrymandering?

safe seat (p. 281). Are safe seats a sign of government responsiveness or unresponsiveness?

swing states (p. 277). Is your state a swing state?

swing voters (p. 277). Why are swing voters less common today?

suffrage (p. 283). When were women first extended the right of suffrage?

Super PACs (p. 276). What was the effect of Super PACs on the 2012 presidential election?

term limits (p. 282). What are the advantages and disadvantages of term limits?

valence issues (p. 279). Why are valence issues common in campaigns?

vanishing marginal (p. 281). Why do vanishing marginals mean elections are less competitive?

vote-by-mail (VBM) system (p. 301). Why might VBM increase turnout?

voting-age population (VAP) (p. 297). How is VAP different from VEP?

voting-eligible population (VEP) (p. 299). Explain the merits of this measure.

wedge issue (p. 279). Why do politicians like to use wedge issues?

Learning Outcomes: What You Need ...

To Know	To Test Yourself	To Participate

▶ **Describe the ideas that molded the Framers' thinking about elections.**

The constitutional requirements for elections set up gates against direct democracy by allowing only the House of Representatives to be elected by the people. State legislatures chose both senators and the electors who would elect the president. Today senators are elected directly by the people. The Electoral College enhances the influence of small states over states with large populations and affects the strategy of presidential campaigns. Because of the structure of the Electoral College, the candidate with the highest number of popular votes sometimes does not win the presidency.	• Summarize the constitutional requirements for presidential elections. • Summarize the constitutional requirements for congressional elections.	• Argue that the constitutional requirements for elections create citizen inequality. • Vote in a local or state election this year.

To Know	To Test Yourself	To Participate

▶ **Outline the steps in presidential campaigns.**

Presidential campaigns are demanding on the candidates and are shaped by constitutional requirements, interparty struggles, and strategies for attracting votes.	• Compare and contrast nineteenth-century and twenty-first-century presidential campaigns. • State the importance of the invisible primary to candidate momentum. • Explain how caucuses and primaries work. • Tell what happens at national conventions.	• Debate whether the permanent campaign increases government responsiveness or impairs government performance. • Attend a caucus or vote in a primary.

▶ **Identify the issues that shape presidential campaigns.**

Campaigns make public engagement possible but are very expensive. Strategies for winning states crucial to winning the electoral vote introduce inequalities, as does the shaping of appeals to voters.	• Track trends in fundraising for presidential campaigns. • Describe the impact of the Electoral College on presidential campaigns. • Explain microtargeting as a campaign strategy. • Compare and contrast valence issues and position issues. • Describe the role of negativity in campaign strategies.	• Evaluate the role of money in presidential elections. • Assess whether the Electoral College creates citizen inequality. • Evaluate the pros and cons of negative advertising.

▶ **Determine which issues shape congressional campaigns.**

Campaign promises, including those in party platforms, are the measure against which citizens can evaluate the performance of the president and Congress. The presidency and the composition of Congress change in response to economic conditions and foreign relations, and the pattern of party gains and losses indicates that voters use elections to hold officials accountable and that the presidency and Congress are responsive institutions.	• Explain how fundraising needs restrain candidates. • Describe the role of political parties in congressional campaigns. • Give reasons for incumbency advantage.	• Decide if campaigns are too expensive. • Decide if incumbents are too entrenched.

▶ **Explain why there are battles over ballot access.**

Participation is essential to the functioning of democracy, and voting is the most common means by which people get involved. The Constitution gives states authority over the "Times, Places and Manner of holding Elections." State rules vary, introducing some inequalities in access. Because voting shapes the outcome of elections and the conduct of government, there have always been debates over who gets access to the ballot. The Hamiltonian model of participation sees risks in the extension of the franchise to groups that may be uninformed and favors a larger role for elites. The Jeffersonian model of participation maintains that greater participation produces better outcomes and encourages citizens to get more involved in self-government.	• Explain why it matters that the Constitution delegated authority over voting to the states. • Compare and contrast the Hamiltonian and Jeffersonian models of participation.	• Debate the relationship between citizen voting and democratic government.

▶ **Outline how the right to vote has expanded.**

Today Americans enjoy almost universal opportunities to vote, but in the past, the vote was denied to African Americans, women, Native Americans, and immigrant groups denied citizenship.	• Survey the expansion of suffrage between 1790 and today. • Describe how minorities and immigrants have at times been prohibited from voting.	• Appreciate your right to vote. • Investigate the status and causes of disfranchisement today.

To Know	To Test Yourself	To Participate

▶ **Identify who tends to turn out in American elections.**

Unequal turnout by various demographic groups suggests that government's response is unequal. Most troubling for democracy is the tendency for people with higher incomes to vote at higher rates than the poor. Older people and those with more education also tend to vote at higher rates than younger people and those with less education.	• Generalize about turnout in the United States. • Identify the characteristics of individuals who are more likely to vote.	• Critique citizen equality in light of turnout.

▶ **Articulate the main theoretical approaches that explain voting.**

Political scientists explain why people vote (and choose not to vote) using theoretical models. The economic model examines the costs and benefits of voting. The psychological model examines attitudes, including the idea of civic duty and the influence of partisanship. The institutional model examines the rules and regulations surrounding voting, including political party behavior, campaign strategy, and the context of the election. Genetic factors are a new consideration.	• Describe the economic model of voting. • Describe the psychological model of voting. • Describe the institutional model of voting. • Address the genetic model of voting.	• Analyze your own reasons for voting. • Assess the impact of civic duty, partisanship, and the competitiveness of elections in turning out the vote.

▶ **Evaluate how low turnout is in American elections.**

Turnout in the United States is lower than in many other democracies, but it can be explained by the institutional model.	• Explain why turnout is lower in the United States than in some other democracies. • Address the issue of turnout and inequality.	• Evaluate whether low turnout invalidates the idea of self-government. • Assess whether higher turnout among the wealthy than among the poor has an impact on public policy.

▶ **Analyze how changes in voting laws have affected rates of participation.**

From the 1790s to the 1870s, voting rights expanded. From the 1870s to the 1920, barriers to voting, especially for African Americans, increased. After 1920, voting rights expanded again and were increasingly protected by the federal government. The overall trend has been toward constant expansion of the right to vote. Voter registration helps prevent fraud in elections but also poses a gate that decreases turnout.	• Identify the goals of the Progressive voting reforms. • Assess how the Motor Voter law, vote-by-mail, and early voting have impacted affected voter turnout.	• Propose ways to increase turnout in the United States.

"Just as there are streets and highways that help us get to where we want to go on the road, there is an infrastructure of opportunity in America that allows us to get to where we want to go in life."

JOAQUÍN CASTRO
Stanford University

10
Congress

Very few people can claim that their sibling is the Secretary of Housing and Urban Development, but even fewer can say this while they are already a sitting member of the U.S. House of Representatives. Joaquín Castro (TX-D) from Texas's 20th district was born in 1974 to a community activist mother and a schoolteacher father. As a second generation Mexican American, Representative Castro and his identical twin brother Julián were well aware of the sacrifices their grandparents had to make to give their children a better life in America. His family history has deeply affected how he serves his congressional district.

Public service did not come naturally for one of the Castro brothers: Joaquín Castro was uninterested in politics and public service despite growing up in a political household. Only after they left Texas and went to school at Stanford did both the Castro brothers recognize the importance of public service. After earning law degrees from Harvard Law School, the Castro brothers went back home and joined a private law firm. Representative Castro fulfilled his interest in public service by running for the state legislature in District 125, while Julián Castro entered into city politics, running for the city council seat his mother lost three decades before. During his five terms in the state legislature, Joaquín Castro took a deep interest in education and health care, and he served as the vice chairman of the Higher Education Committee.

During his 2012 campaign for the U.S. House, Representative Castro promised to pursue his "Infrastructure of Opportunity," a program that Castro believes "allows each of us to pursue our American dreams." Castro wants to see the United States build an infrastructure of exemplary public schools and universities, a strong health care system, and an economy that pays people well so they can support their families.

As Representative Castro passionately declared from the House floor after he won his seat with nearly 64 percent of the vote, the infrastructure of opportunity is just as important for the future of America as is a sound transportation infrastructure. Representative Castro has put his support behind bills that will help improve the infrastructure of opportunity, such as his sponsorship of the Student Aid Expansion Act of 2013 and the Paycheck Fairness Act. He even spends a large portion of his free time improving education opportunities in his home district, which includes parts of San Antonio. He has helped to raise money for underprivileged youths to go to college through the Trailblazers College Tour, and he created SA READS, which has provided more than 200,000 books to more than 150 schools and shelters in San Antonio.

Need to Know

10.1 Describe how Congress has developed

10.2 Define the powers of Congress

10.3 Outline how Congress is structured

10.4 Explain how a law is made in Congress

10.5 Assess what a member of Congress does

(▶) **WATCH & LEARN** MindTap for American Government
Watch a brief "What Do You Know?" video summarizing The Congress.

309

Beyond education and health care, Representative Castro also cares deeply about the nation's defense and military needs. Through his assignments on the House Armed Services Committee and the House Foreign Affairs Committee, Representative Castro was able to visit Afghanistan as they were holding elections in March 2014. During his visit, Castro was able to personally thank Texas service members and present them with a Texas flag. Castro's service on the House Armed Services Committee is particularly important for his constituents, as the city of San Antonio has three military bases, and the state of Texas has more than 120,000 active military personnel and 1.7 million veterans. Representative Castro's committee service as well as his prior service in the state legislature have uniquely positioned him as a trusted leader willing to give voice to the needs of his constituents and act as an advocate for the many servicemen and women whom he represents.[1]

In this chapter, we explain how members of Congress navigate the gates and gateways embedded in the legislative branch to best serve the interests of their constituents. The fact that members of Congress must repeatedly return home to ask the voters to reelect them helps keep them responsive to their constituents, who hold them accountable for the policies they enact into law. But the process of congressional representation—that is, of putting good ideas into practice as law—is difficult and complex. Structural gates are embedded in a separation of powers system of government and in a democratic legislative process that encourages competition among groups with conflicting interests. Navigating this terrain is not easy, but Joaquín Castro's efforts to represent his district show how an individual member of Congress seeks to be an advocate as well as a legislator.

10.1 Congress as the Legislative Branch

> Describe how Congress has developed

→ KEY QUESTIONS:
Is Congress a gateway to democracy, or a gate?

LISTEN & LEARN
MindTap for American Government

Access Read Speaker to listen to Chapter 10.

In Chapter 2, The Constitution, we discussed the ideas of representation that shaped the Framers' thinking. They believed that a democratic government had to be responsive and accountable to the people. In such a government, leaders would not inherit power; rather, they would be chosen by the people at regular intervals, and these elections would be the key way that voters would hold government officials accountable for their actions. The Framers of the Constitution designed Congress to be the legislative branch of the federal government, and they gave it broad powers to enact laws. At the same time, they wanted the process of lawmaking to be complex and deliberative so that members of Congress would not succumb to impulsive actions that might harm constituents or violate fundamental constitutional rights. Over time, Congress has increased the scope and range of its powers, but the new responsibilities have added a layer of complexity that makes it harder than ever to pass laws.

Representation and Bicameralism

→ KEY QUESTIONS:
What did the Framers do to control Congress's power?

Essential to understanding how Congress facilitates representation in the American democracy is to recognize that it is bicameral; that is, it is divided into two separate chambers: the House of Representatives and the Senate. This structure reflects the Framers' fear that the power of the legislative branch might grow to the point where it could not be controlled by the other two branches. Because the legislative branch is closest to the people—its members represent specific population groups, by region, and can be removed by election—the Framers believed that Congress would have a democratic legitimacy that neither the executive nor the judicial branches would possess.

The solution, according to James Madison, was to divide the legislature into two parts that would check each other. In *Federalist* 51 he explained that this would "render them . . . as little connected with each other, as the nature of their common functions, and their common dependence on the society, will admit." The House of Representatives would be a large body that reflected population size within states and was directly elected at frequent intervals (every two years). The Senate would be an elite chamber, with two senators for every state regardless of population size elected by state legislatures for six-year terms. In that way, both the popular opinions of average voters and the elite opinions of the well educated and the wealthy would be represented in Congress. This arrangement also guaranteed that large states could not overwhelm smaller states in determining the content of laws. The specific differences between the two parts of Congress are discussed in the next section.

Constitutional Differences between the House and Senate

To accomplish Madison's goal, the Constitution establishes four key differences between the two chambers of Congress: qualifications for office, mode of election, terms of office, and constituencies (see Table 10.1).

Qualifications for Office. To serve as a member of the House of Representatives, an individual must be at least 25 years old, reside in the state that he or she represents, and have been a U.S. citizen for seven years before running for office. The qualifications for the Senate are that an individual must be at least 30 years old, reside in the state he or she represents, and have been a U.S. citizen for nine years before running for office. Senators are expected to be older and to have lived in the United States for a longer period of time than House members because the Framers believed those characteristics would make the Senate the more stable partner in the legislative process.

The Framers created the House of Representatives and the Senate as separate chambers of Congress, but both are located in the U.S. Capitol. In this view from the National Mall, the Senate chamber is on the left, and the House chamber is on the right. There are six office buildings for members of Congress and their staff members, three on each side of the Capitol.

© ISTOCK.COM/VISUALFIELD

Table 10.1 Comparison of House and Senate Service

	House	Senate
Minimum age	25 years old	30 years old
Citizenship	7 years	9 years
Term of office	2 years	6 years
Geographic constituency	District	State
Redistricting	Every 10 years	—
Mode of election until 1914	Direct	Indirect through state legislatures
Mode of election after 1914	Direct	Direct

© CENGAGE LEARNING®

Although the members of the First Congress (1789–91) were all white men, no provision in the Constitution delineates a specific race, gender, income level, or religion as a prerequisite for serving in Congress. Twenty-first-century Congresses have been much more diverse, with female, African American, Hispanic, Pacific Islander, and Native American members in the House (see Figure 10.1). Nevertheless, note that women held only 18 percent of the seats in the 113th Congress (House and Senate combined), although they constituted 51 percent of the nation's population. African Americans hold forty House seats and two Senate seats, while Latinos hold thirty-one House seats and four Senate seats. Despite the advancements made by underrepresented groups in electing members to Congress, it is still predominantly white and male.[2] The average House and Senate member is older than 57. House members tend to serve an average of five terms (ten years) and Senators an average of two terms (twelve years).[3] The twenty-first-century House has included members from the Protestant, Catholic, Jewish, Greek Orthodox, Mormon, Buddhist, Quaker, and—for the first time—Muslim faiths. The religious background of senators has been slightly less varied but has also included members from the Protestant, Roman Catholic, Mormon, and Jewish faiths.[4]

House members have more varied prior experience than their Senate colleagues. A majority of House members served in their state legislatures before coming to Congress; others were mayors, law enforcement officers, teachers, doctors, ministers, radio talk show hosts, accountants, business owners, and even three airline pilots. Just as House members use state legislatures as stepping-stones, senators use the House of Representatives to launch their bids for the Senate. In the 113th Congress, fifty-one senators had previously served in the House of Representatives, and others had been mayors, governors, and attorneys general or had held executive branch positions.

Mode of Election.   House members are elected directly by citizens. Senators are elected directly as well, but that is a more recent development. From 1789 to 1914, the mode of election for the Senate was indirect: Citizens voted for members of their state legislatures, who then selected the U.S. senators. The mode of election for the House and Senate was different on purpose. The House was supposed to be more immediately responsive to the opinions of the people, but the Framers designed the Senate to insulate senators from the direct voice of the people, in other words, to make them less directly responsive to the people.

The mode of election for the Senate was changed from indirect to direct with the ratification of the Seventeenth Amendment in 1913. At the end of the nineteenth century, in

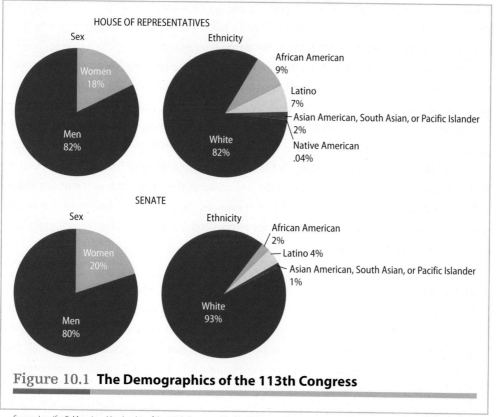

Figure 10.1 **The Demographics of the 113th Congress**

Source: Jennifer E. Manning, *Membership of the 113th Congress: A Profile,* CRS Report for Congress, R42964 (Washington, D.C.: Congressional Research Service, March 14, 2014).

response to charges of deadlock and corruption during the election of U.S. senators in state legislatures, Progressives led a movement to allow voters to directly elect their senators.[5] The amendment opened up a much more direct gateway of influence for constituents over their U.S. senators.

Terms of Office. A term of office is the length of time that an elected official serves before facing the voters again in an election. The term of office for House members is two years, and the term of office for U.S. senators is six years. The difference in term of office leads to key differences in how each chamber operates. House members have a shorter amount of time to demonstrate their effectiveness before they face reelection, so the House of Representatives as a whole is usually in a greater hurry to pass legislation than is the Senate. Senators know they have six years before they have to face their voters, so they have a bit more flexibility in working out disagreements among their constituents and balancing

Barbara Mikulski (D-Md.) is the longest serving woman in Congress. She served in the House of Representatives from 1977 to 1986, when she was elected to the Senate. Throughout her career, she has championed women's health and labor issues. She has also been a strong advocate for her home state of Maryland.

constituents' interests against the interests of the nation as a whole. Because senators know they have a longer time in which to establish a good reputation among their home state voters, the Senate takes more time to deliberate over legislation.

In any given election year, the entire membership of the House of Representatives must face the voters, but only one-third of senators stand for reelection. To guarantee that the whole Senate would never stand for reelection all at once, the Constitution divided the first Senate, which met in 1789, into three classes of senators who would be elected at different six-year intervals.[6] To this day, the maximum number of senators who stand for regularly scheduled reelection in the same year is thirty-four (out of a possible 100), thereby ensuring that a majority of the Senate is never up for reelection at the same time as the entire House of Representatives.[7] This electoral condition reinforces the stability of the Senate's membership; it also limits the electoral incentives for House and Senate members to cooperate with one another to pass legislation.

Constituencies. A constituency is the set of people that officially elects the House or Senate member; in the United States, constituency is defined geographically. Each member of the House of Representatives represents a congressional district with established geographic boundaries within the state (except for seven states with populations so small that they have just one congressional district; see Figure 10.2). Each U.S. senator represents an entire state, and two U.S. senators are elected from each state.

→ KEY QUESTIONS:
Which congressional district do you live in? Which congressional district is your college in?

In 1789, the average size of a congressional district was about 30,000 people, and the average size of a state was about 300,000 people; in 2014, a congressional district had about 711,000 people, and the nation's largest state, California, had approximately 38 million residents.[8] Because the Framers knew that the country's population would change, they required a count, or census, of the population every ten years. Following the census, the number of congressional districts in each state would be adjusted to reflect population changes. The House started with 65 members and, when capped by Congress at 435 in 1929, had increased by 670 percent.[9] Congress was concerned that if the House grew any larger it would not be possible to conduct legislative business.[10] Today, because there is an absolute limit on the total number of House members, population growth or decline has a direct bearing on a state's representation, increasing or decreasing the state's number of representatives and thus its relative influence in the House.

Redistricting. Only the House of Representatives is subject to redistricting, which is the redrawing of the boundaries of congressional districts in a state to make them approximately equal in population size. Because the size of the House is limited to 435, the overall number of congressional seats per state must be adjusted following a census if there have been population changes. Based on the state's allocation of congressional districts, the state legislature redraws the districts, and the only real limitation on redistricting is that the boundaries of the district must be contiguous (uninterrupted). During redistricting, the majority party in the state legislature tries to influence the process to construct each district in such a way that a majority of voters favors its party, thereby making it easier for its candidates to win, in a process known as gerrymandering. Sometimes the majority party will combine two existing districts that have House members from the other party, forcing them to run against each other.

→ KEY QUESTIONS:
With each state having the same number of senators, what are the consequences for citizen equality across small and large states?

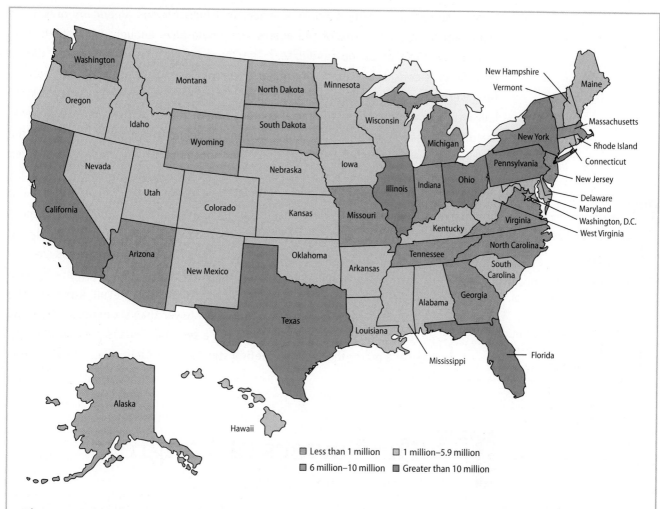

Figure 10.2 States by Population, 2013

The U.S. Senate has two senators for every state, regardless of population. This arrangement makes states equal in Senate votes: Wyoming has the same number of votes as California. But it also means that the 582,658 citizens of Wyoming have the same voice in the Senate as the 38,332,521 citizens of California. Equal representation in the Senate did not seem as imbalanced when states had more similar population sizes, but today, with such huge differences, some observers think representation in the Senate is inherently unfair.

Source: © Cengage Learning®; data from U.S. Census Bureau, "Population Estimates," http://www.census.gov/popest/data/state/totals/2013/index.html, accessed May 12, 2014.

Redistricting has also been used as a tool to achieve greater minority representation in the House of Representatives following the theory of descriptive representation, whereby an individual represents a constituency not just in terms of geography but also in terms of race or ethnicity. The Voting Rights Act of 1965 prohibits states and political subdivisions from denying or limiting "the right of any citizen of the United States to vote on account of race or color"; it was later amended to protect the voting rights of non-English-speaking minorities—referring to Latinos—as well. This act is discussed in detail in Chapters 5, Civil Rights and 9 Elections, Campaigns, and Voting; here we focus on the fact that many states initially responded to the law by redrawing congressional districts to group minority voters in a way that would deny them the voting strength to elect a minority member of Congress. In 1982, Congress amended the Voting Rights Act to prevent this kind of manipulation. In response, some state legislatures

→ KEY QUESTIONS:
How do majority-minority districts provide a gateway for better representation of minority interests?

created so-called majority-minority districts in which African Americans or Latinos would constitute a majority of the voters and would have enough votes to elect an African American or Latino candidate.[11] The Texas district that Congressman Castro represents is considered a majority-minority district, with 70 percent of the population there identifying as Latino.[12] Since then, the federal courts have ruled that state legislatures overemphasized the racial composition of these districts to the point that the districts made no geographic sense. Current guidelines on redistricting call for the consideration of race in drawing district lines but not to the extent that it was employed in the past.[13]

Because representation in the Senate is related to state boundaries, not to population size, some scholars have argued that the Senate is less responsive than the House. It is true that there are vast differences in population size among the states[14] (see Figure 10.2). As we explore later in this chapter, the rules of the Senate amplify this imbalance of influence by granting each senator equal power to delay, or block, legislation. As a result, a senator who represents a state such as Wyoming, with fewer than six hundred thousand people, can delay, or in the final day of a session, actually prevent, the passage of a policy that might benefit a state such as California, with 38 million people.

Checkpoint

CAN YOU:

■ Explain the reasons for and consequences of bicameralism

■ Explain the constitutional differences between the House and Senate

10.2 The Powers of Congress

> Define the powers of Congress

As Chapter 2 describes, the Framers granted Congress powers that were necessary to construct a coherent and forceful federal government. Some of these, such as the power to tax and to regulate commerce among the states, had been denied to Congress under the Articles of Confederation, and their absence had weakened the new republic. At the same time, the Framers worried that the legislative branch would grow too powerful. So they limited the powers of Congress to a list in Article I, Section 8, of the Constitution, together with a few stated responsibilities in other sections. The following discussion highlights the most important powers of Congress. It also examines the ways that Congress has used its constitutional powers to expand its role in the policy-making system and ways that Congress is balanced and checked by the executive and judicial branches.

→ KEY QUESTIONS:
How have the powers of Congress increased? Why did they increase?

Taxation and Appropriation

Congress has the power "To lay and Collect Taxes." In a division of this important power, the Constitution states that all bills for raising revenue should originate in the House of Representatives, but the Senate "may propose or concur with Amendments, as on other Bills." Initially, the Framers thought that tax revenue would come primarily from levies placed on imported goods. As the industrial economy grew, so did the need for government services and programs that cost money. With the Sixteenth Amendment, ratified in 1913, Congress gained the power "to lay and collect taxes on incomes," whatever the source. This amendment overturned prohibitions on certain types of income taxes.

Paralleling the power to tax, Congress also has the power to spend—"to pay the Debts and to provide for the common Defence and general Welfare." The general welfare clause has proven to be a major means by which Congress's power has expanded. Congress **appropriates** (or allocates) federal monies on programs it **authorizes** (or creates) through its lawmaking power. This "power of the purse" has been instrumental in the expansion of Congress's relative strength among the branches of government.[15] The Constitution also gives Congress the authority to borrow money, to coin money, and to regulate its value, and it requires a regular accounting of revenue and expenditures of public money.

War Powers

The Constitution gives Congress authority to "provide for the common Defence." In reality, the war powers are shared with the president. For example, Congress has the sole power to declare war, but this power is typically used only after the president has requested a declaration of war. In many cases, the president may ask Congress for specific authorization to take military action; under its power of taxation and appropriation, Congress has the authority to fund or refuse to fund military operations. Generally, Congress also has the power "to raise and support Armies," "to provide and maintain a Navy," "to provide for calling forth the Militia," and to make rules and regulations regarding the armed forces and their organizations. Relations between Congress and the president over war powers have sometimes been harmonious, but in recent decades, they have become contentious. The struggle between the president and Congress over the war powers is examined in detail in Chapter 11, The Presidency.

Regulation of Commerce

The Constitution gave Congress an important power that it did not have under the Articles of Confederation: the power "to regulate Commerce with foreign Nations, and among the several States, and with the Indian Tribes." Using the power in this commerce clause, Congress established a national set of laws regulating commerce that are applicable to all states equally.[16] In time, the authority to regulate interstate commerce has allowed Congress to expand its power to the point that almost no economic activity is beyond its reach. In 2012, the Court ruled that Congress's requirement, set forth in the Patient Protection and Affordable Care Act, that individuals purchase health insurance went beyond Congress's commerce clause authority but upheld most of the act as within Congress's taxing authority (see Supreme Court Cases: *National Federation of Independent Business et al. v. Sebelius*).

Appointments and Treaties

In recognition of the Senate's perceived wisdom and stability, the Framers gave the Senate, and not the House, the power of advice and consent. In the appointment of high-level executive branch appointees, such as cabinet secretaries and ambassadors, this power allows the Senate to evaluate the qualifications of a presidential nominee and, by majority vote, to approve

→ KEY QUESTIONS:
Why do you think the Framers gave the House, rather than the Senate, the authority to originate revenue bills?

appropriate: *Congress's power to allocate a set amount of federal dollars for a specific program or agency.*

authorize: *Congress's power to create a federal program or agency and set levels of federal funds to support that program or agency.*

→ KEY QUESTIONS:
What is meant by the term "general welfare" with respect to Congressional power? How would you define it today?

COMPARE WITH YOUR PEERS
MindTap for American Government

Access The Congress Forum: Polling Activity—The Power to Declare War.

supreme court cases

National Federation of Independent Business et al. v. Sebelius (2012)

QUESTION: May Congress impose a mandate to purchase health insurance on those who do not wish to carry it? Did Congress exceed its spending authority with the Medicaid expansions?

ORAL ARGUMENT: March 26–28, 2012 (listen at http://www.oyez.org/cases/2010-2019/2011/2011_11_400)

DECISION: June 28, 2012 (read at http://www.oyez.org/cases/2010-2019/2011/2011_11_400)

OUTCOME: Yes, the authority is within Congress's taxing power (5–4). Yes, Congress exceeded its spending authority (7-2). Overall, however, the law is constitutional.

The Obama administration argued that because the decisions of individuals not to purchase health insurance have a substantial effect on hospitals and insurance companies involved in interstate commerce, Congress has the right to mandate the purchase of such insurance. Those opposed to the act argued that if Congress could make people purchase health insurance because of the substantial effect it has on interstate commerce, why couldn't it, under the same reasoning, make people buy broccoli? As a fallback, the administration argued that even if the act was not itself a regulation of commerce, it was necessary and proper to the regulation of commerce (see Supreme Court Cases: *McCulloch v. Maryland* in Chapter 3, Federalism). As a second fallback, the administration argued that the mandate was a valid exercise of Congress's authority to tax to provide for the general welfare. Opponents pointed out that when Congress was debating the bill, the Obama administration insisted that the payments for not purchasing health insurance were a penalty and not a tax, so that members of Congress could not be accused of passing unpopular tax increases. Additionally, opponents claimed that the threat states faced of losing all Medicaid funding if they did not voluntarily expand their Medicaid coverage was coercive, in violation of the Tenth Amendment (see Chapter 3).

In a complicated decision, Chief Justice John Roberts, joined by the Court's four more conservative justices (Samuel Alito, Anthony Kennedy, Antonin Scalia, and Clarence Thomas), declared that Congress did not have the authority under the commerce clause or the necessary and proper clause to mandate that individuals enter the insurance market. This part of the opinion weakens Congress's commerce clause powers. Crucially, however, Chief Justice Roberts, joined by the Court's four more liberal justices (Stephen Breyer, Ruth Bader Ginsburg, Elena Kagan, and Sonia Sotomayor), ruled that the penalty for not purchasing insurance could be considered a tax, and that as a tax, it was well within Congress's authority.

Finally, by a 7–2 vote, all justices except Ginsburg and Sotomayor, argued that Congress cannot rescind previously committed funds to states that refuse to accept the new Medicaid requirements, imposing the first limits on Congress's spending power in seventy-five years. But by a 5–4 vote, with Roberts joining the liberal bloc, the Court upheld the withholding of new funds from states that did not accept the new Medicaid expansion, as well as the rest of the law. In November 2014, the Supreme Court agreed to review the section of the Affordable Care Act that provides insurance subsidies only to the states that have established insurance exchanges (16) and not to the residents of the 34 states that chose not to establish exchanges. Without the subsidies, the law may be unworkable.

1. Why does it matter whether the payment for not having health insurance is a "penalty" or a "tax"?
2. What was unusual about the Court's decision involving Congress's spending authority?

or reject the nominee. Similarly, the appointment of all federal judges, from district courts to the Supreme Court, is subject to the approval of the Senate (see Chapter 13, The Judiciary, for more details on this process). Additionally, the Senate acts as a check on the president's power to make treaties with foreign nations: Treaties must be approved by a two-thirds vote, or they fail to take effect (see Chapter 11 for more on treaty negotiation and ratification). The advice and consent role of the Senate acts as a gateway for citizen influence over presidential appointments and treaties because senators are more likely to block appointments and treaties that they believe are unpopular with their constituents.

The Senate exercises its advice and consent powers when it holds hearings on presidential nominees and then votes to approve or reject them. In the summer of 2009, senators questioned President Barack Obama's first Supreme Court nominee Sonia Sotomayor, an appeals court judge from New York. She was confirmed on August 6, 2009, by a vote of 68 to 31, and she is the first Latina Supreme Court justice.

Impeachment and Removal from Office

Congress's ultimate check on the executive and judicial branches is its power to remove officials and judges from office by impeachment. The president, vice president, and high-level officials are subject to impeachment for "Treason, Bribery, or other high Crimes and Misdemeanors." This power is rarely used. In Chapter 11, we examine the two cases in which presidents have been impeached, but not removed from office. In the case of President Richard Nixon (1969–74), the threat of impeachment was credible enough that he resigned from office.

The process of impeachment and removal from office takes place in two steps. First, a majority of the House of Representatives votes to bring formal charges against the president or other federal official, an action called impeachment. Then the Senate conducts the trial, with the chief justice of the United States presiding in the case of the president's impeachment, and votes to convict or acquit. If two-thirds of the senators present vote to convict, the president or the federal official will be removed from office.

Lawmaking

Congress, as the legislative branch, is responsible for lawmaking. Unlike the enumerated powers listed at the beginning of Article I, Section 8, and explained previously, the final paragraph of Section 8 gives Congress broad authority "to make all Laws which shall be necessary and proper for carrying into Execution the foregoing Powers." In combination with the general welfare clause and the commerce clause, this necessary and proper clause allows Congress a great deal of leeway to carry out its responsibilities under the assumption that additional powers are implied in these clauses, although not explicitly stated in the Constitution. Over time, Congress has made full use of this flexibility to expand its

> → KEY QUESTIONS:
> Why did the Framers give the Senate the power of advice and consent?

authority in a wide range of areas, such as regulating interstate railroads, establishing civil rights protections, funding school lunch programs, limiting greenhouse gases, and providing student loans. Essentially, if an argument can be made that a service or program is reasonably tied to an enumerated power, Congress has used its powers to create that service or program.

Authorization of Courts

In Article I, the Constitution also gives Congress the power to "constitute Tribunals inferior to the Supreme Court." Article III, the section on the judiciary, reiterates congressional control by saying that Congress may "ordain and establish" courts at levels lower than the Supreme Court. In 1789, Congress used this power to pass the Judiciary Act, which established federal district courts and circuit courts of appeal. Today, there are ninety-four district courts and thirteen appellate circuits.[17]

The federal judicial branch asserted more authority over the other two branches in the Supreme Court case of *Marbury v. Madison* (see Chapter 2). This case established judicial review, which is the federal judiciary's power to declare laws passed by Congress as unconstitutional. The *Marbury* decision gave the courts the power to interpret the Constitution and determine how congressional laws (and even executive branch actions) conform to its explicit language and its intent (see Chapter 13 for further explanation of this decision).

In recent years the Senate has tried to reassert its influence over the federal courts through the nomination process.[18] As we discuss later in the chapter, individual senators can try to defeat presidential nominees for federal judgeships with whom they disagree on key constitutional questions.

Oversight

After a bill becomes a law, the executive branch, headed by the president, is supposed to carry out the law according to Congress's wishes. But the executive branch is a bureaucracy with many departments and agencies that have authority to implement laws. The sheer size and complexity of the federal bureaucracy make it difficult for Congress to determine whether laws are being administered according to the intent behind them (see Chapter 12, The Bureaucracy, for more details). Over time, Congress has asserted its oversight authority to monitor the ways in which the executive branch implements law. This authority stems from Congress's responsibility to appropriate money to provide for the general welfare of the nation. Congress constantly exercises this authority, but less so under unified government, when the same party controls Congress and the White House, than under **divided government**, when the party that controls Congress is not the party of the president. Under unified government, members of Congress assume that because they share the same partisan affiliation as the president, his administration is more likely to implement laws according to congressional intent.

In contrast, legislatures in countries that have parliamentary systems typically choose their executives from among the members of the majority party so that the executive and legislative branches always share the same policy goals. Consequently, legislative oversight is not a fundamental element of those political systems (see Global Gateways: The Parliamentary System of the United Kingdom).

divided government:
Situation in which one party controls the executive branch, and the other party controls the legislative branch.

→ KEY QUESTIONS:
Think about the power to investigate. Which branch should have this power?

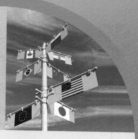

All democracies have a legislature and an executive, but their relationship to each other produces differences in the way people are represented. The United States has separate legislative and executive branches. In the United Kingdom, the executive and the legislative branches are intertwined. The United Kingdom is a limited monarchy democracy, with a queen as the head of state and a parliament for its legislature. The British Parliament is bicameral; the House of Commons has 650 members, and elections are held in single-member districts, as they are in the United States. The party that wins the most seats wins control of the chamber. The House of Lords has 779 members; some members inherit their seats, and others are appointed by the queen. The approval of both branches of the legislature, in the same year, is necessary to pass legislation.

In the British system, the prime minister, who is the chief executive of the government, is an elected member of the House of Commons chosen by the majority party and officially recognized by the queen. He appoints ministers and advisers to his cabinet without the formal approval of the legislature. Because the prime minister comes from the majority party in the legislature, the executive and the legislature typically agree on the legislation that needs to be passed to accomplish the party's goals. As party leader, the prime minister is responsive to the party's voting base. There are no regularly scheduled parliamentary elections, but elections must be held at least once every five years, and the campaigns last for less than three weeks. The prime minister calls for elections either when the majority party is very popular, so that it can retain power, or when it is so unpopular that the public calls for a change.

In 2010, Prime Minister Gordon Brown, a member of the Labour Party, had lost popularity, and in the May 6 election the Conservatives, led by David Cameron, won more seats than the Labour Party did but fell short of a working majority. As a result, the Conservatives joined with members of a third party, the Liberal Democrats, to form a working majority party in Parliament, producing a complete change in the coalition of parties that constitute the majority.

Source: UK House of Commons, http://www.parliament.uk/mps-lords-and-offices/mps/current-state-of-the-parties/ and UK House of Lords, http://www.parliament.uk/mps-lords-and-offices/lords/composition-of-the-lords/ accessed April 16, 2014.

1. How does the British parliamentary system differ from the U.S. separation of powers system?

2. Compare citizen control in elections that are regularly scheduled and in elections that are scheduled by the majority party in power.

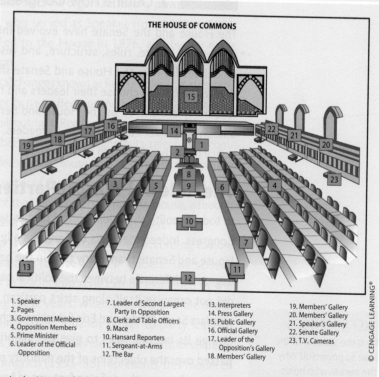

THE HOUSE OF COMMONS

1. Speaker
2. Pages
3. Government Members
4. Opposition Members
5. Prime Minister
6. Leader of the Official Opposition
7. Leader of Second Largest Party in Opposition
8. Clerk and Table Officers
9. Mace
10. Hansard Reporters
11. Sergeant-at-Arms
12. The Bar
13. Interpreters
14. Press Gallery
15. Public Gallery
16. Official Gallery
17. Leader of the Opposition's Gallery
18. Members' Gallery
19. Members' Gallery
20. Members' Gallery
21. Speaker's Gallery
22. Senate Gallery
23. T.V. Cameras

© CENGAGE LEARNING®

In the House of Commons, members of the two major parties sit on opposite sides, as in the U.S. Congress, but they are identified as "government" and "opposition."

KEVIN DIETSCH/UPI/LANDOV

Nancy Pelosi (D-CA) was elected the first female Speaker of the House of Representatives in 2007. She was generally considered a strong Speaker because she exerted control over committee chairs and the conditions under which bills were considered on the House floor.

was willing to give Gingrich strong powers to accomplish policy goals. However, just three years later, Gingrich resigned the Speakership after the 1998 midterm elections; the Republicans lost seats as a result of an unpopular attempt to impeach President Clinton (see Chapter 11).

After Gingrich, the Republicans chose a less powerful Speaker, Dennis Hastert (R-Ill.), and moved from a conditional party government system to what scholars call a party cartel system. According to Gary Cox and Mathew McCubbins, in this system, the power of party leaders rests on their ability to set the legislative agenda and provide services, such as campaign finance funds, and organizational positions, such as committee positions, to party members in exchange for their loyalty.[24] This type of cartel system worked better for the Republicans after 2001, when a Republican was elected to the White House and set the policy agenda for members of the party. Typically under unified government, members of the majority party in the House use the president's agenda as a starting point. As a result, the Speaker can lose independence in setting the policy direction for the House. A case in point is the Hastert Rule, named after former Speaker Dennis Hastert. The Hastert Rule states that when the Republicans are in majority control of the House, they will not bring a bill to the House floor without a majority of Republicans (i.e., a majority of the majority) agreeing to do so. In adopting that rule, the House Republican Party as a whole was ensuring that the Speaker would only bring bills to the House floor that followed their preferences.

After the Democrats won control of the House in the 2006 elections, Nancy Pelosi was elected the first female Speaker of the House. She lost that post after the Republicans gained a House majority in 2010 and elected John Boehner as Speaker. The ability of the Speaker to make the most of party power depends a great deal on how unified the party is on any given issue, or a whole range of issues, and on whether he or she represents the same party as the president. In the 112th and 113th Congresses, Speaker Boehner, with an opposite party president, had the most difficulty holding his majority party together on votes related to federal spending and deficit reduction. On these issues, he faced both an internal party division and a small wing of the Republican majority, led by Tea Party affiliated members, that did not want to cooperate with President Barack Obama under any circumstances. In fact, cooperation broke down so severely over the federal budget and national debt in late 2013 that the government shut down for sixteen days (see Chapter 14, Public Policy, for a full discussion). To resolve this impasse, Speaker Boehner had to violate the Hastert Rule in order to make sure the government was funded, and the debt ceiling was increased.

Whether he or she works with a same- or an opposite-party president, the Speaker's most important responsibility is to maintain power in the House for the majority party, and that means getting the members of the majority party reelected. To do so, the Speaker supports a set of policies that he or she believes are popular with voters, and he or she tries to get those policies enacted into law. For example, during the consideration of health care reform in the House, the Democrats shared the goal of passing a health care reform bill, so they allowed the Speaker to use all the tools at her disposal to get the bill passed. The Democrats suffered big losses in the 2010 elections in part due to voter backlash on this issue. For Speaker Boehner, the 2012 elections represented his first test of holding onto power in the House, and he focused his efforts on bringing bills to the House floor on issues such as federal aviation, transportation, and insider trading in Congress, all of which he knew had support within Congress and were popular with voters. By the time the 2014 elections came around, Boehner and the Republicans were more secure in holding the majority. Still, Pelosi and Boehner share the dubious distinction of presiding over Congresses with some of the lowest approval ratings ever recorded; in early 2014, only 12 percent of Americans approved of the job that Congress was doing.[25]

House Party Leaders.

The **House majority leader**, as second in command, works with the Speaker to decide which issues the party will consider. He or she also coordinates with committee leaders on holding hearings and reporting bills to the House floor for a vote. The House majority leader must strike a compromise among many competing forces, including committee chairs and external interest groups. He or she is also expected to raise a significant amount of campaign contributions for party members, and that role produces more pressure to appease as many interest groups as possible. The majority leader also has nine majority whips to help "whip up" support for the party's preferred policies and keep lines of communication open between the party leadership and the rank-and-file membership. The majority leader and whips work hard to track members' intended votes—in a process called the whip count—because they want to bring to the floor only those bills that will pass; any defeat on the floor could weaken voter confidence in the majority party.[26]

John Boehner (R-OH) replaced Pelosi as Speaker in 2011 after the Republicans won control of the House in the 2010 elections. Boehner has faced more internal party division than Pelosi did, but the Republicans still managed to hold on to the House in the 2012 and 2014 elections.

The minority party in the House is the party that has the largest number of House members who are not in the majority party. The highest-ranking member of the minority party is the **House minority leader**, and his or her main responsibility is crafting the minority party's position on an issue and serving as the public spokesperson for the party. If the minority party is the same as the president's party, the House minority leader is also expected to garner support for the president's policies among minority party members. The House minority leader works with minority whips who are responsible for keeping all the minority members in line with the party's public positions.

The challenge for the minority party in the House of Representatives is that it has very little institutional power; the majority party uses its numerical advantage to control committee and floor actions. Because of its institutional disadvantages, the minority party in the modern House of Representatives rarely has the power to stop majority party proposals from passing. Minority party members can vote no, but their real power lies in making speeches, issuing press releases, and stirring up grassroots opposition to majority party proposals.

⭐ **House majority leader:** *Leader of the majority party in the House and second in command to the Speaker.*

⭐ **House minority leader:** *Leader of the minority party in the House.*

→ **KEY QUESTIONS:**
Does the institutional structure of the House promote party dominance? Responsible lawmaking? What can be done about the structure of Congress?

The Senate

The Senate has always been a smaller chamber than the House because it is based on the number of states in the union and does not adjust according to population growth. Since 1959, when Hawaii and Alaska joined the union, the Senate has had 100 members, and the magic number to secure majority control in the Senate has been fifty-one senators. Not until the 1910s did senators formally appoint individual senators to speak for them as majority and minority party leaders. However, the Senate majority leader has fewer formal powers to advance the party's agenda compared to the Speaker of the House. Because the Senate never grew to be as large and unwieldy as the House, the individual members have rarely seen the benefit of giving up power to party leaders to make the Senate run efficiently or enact the party's agenda.

President Pro Tempore. Article I, Section 3, of the Constitution states that the vice president shall be the president of the Senate, but that in his absence the Senate may appoint a president pro tempore (temporary president) to preside over the Senate. For most of the Senate's history, the vice president presided over the Senate, and his main functions were to recognize individual senators who wished to speak and to rule on which procedural motions were in order on the Senate floor. The vice president can also break a tie vote in the Senate, a power that can give the president's party control of the outcome on the floor. But in the 1950s, the vice president became more active in executive branch business and less active in the Senate. Subsequently, the Senate began appointing the oldest serving member from the majority party as the president pro tempore to serve as the temporary presiding officer. The president pro tempore is closely advised by the Senate parliamentarian, who is responsible for administering the rules of the Senate.

Senate majority leader: *Leader of the majority party in the Senate.*

Senate Party Leaders. The majority party elects the **Senate majority leader**, but unlike the Speaker of the House, this position is not written into the Constitution. The job of the Senate majority leader is to make sure the Senate functions well enough to pass legislation. To accomplish that goal, the Senate majority leader tries to craft legislation as close to the preferred policies of his or her party as possible, necessitating a great deal of compromise and the "power of persuasion."[27]

→ KEY QUESTIONS:
Does the institutional structure of the Senate promote party dominance? Responsible lawmaking? Individual careers? What can be done about the structure of Congress?

Still, the Senate majority leader does have several formal powers. For instance, he or she is the official scheduler of Senate business and is always recognized first to speak on the Senate floor. Every senator has the right to speak on the Senate floor, but senators must speak one at a time. Being recognized first, before any other senator, gives the majority leader the power to control the floor and prevent any other senator from speaking. But because the Senate majority leader relies on the senators' voluntary cooperation to conduct the business of the Senate, there are limits on how tough he or she can be on Senate colleagues. If a Senate majority leader tries to bully senators, they might retaliate by constantly using their individual floor powers to try to delay or block key legislation.

The **Senate minority leader** is the leader of the minority party in the Senate and is expected to represent minority party senators in negotiations with the majority leader on which bills are brought to the Senate floor and under what circumstances. Similar to the House counterpart, the Senate minority leader's job is to organize minority party senators into a coherent group that can present viable alternatives to the majority party's proposals.

Senate minority leader: *Leader of the minority party in the Senate.*

The extended leadership structure of the Senate looks similar to that of the House (see Figure 10.3). It consists of an assistant majority leader, majority and minority whips, and conference chairs, all of whom are responsible for uniting the senators in their respective parties and crafting legislative proposals that can garner enough support to pass the Senate.

The Committee System

Almost all legislation that passes the House or Senate goes through a committee. The House and Senate are organized into separate committees to deal with the different issues, such as agriculture, energy, and education. The party that has the majority in the entire House or Senate also has the majority of seats on each committee, and the committee chair is chosen from the majority party, with the approval of the party caucus. Typically, each House member or senator gives the party leadership a list of desired committee assignments, and the leadership assigns committee seats according to seniority and the availability of seats on specific committees.

House of Representatives

Majority Party

Speaker of the House → Majority Leader → Majority Whip → Caucus Chair → Caucus Vice Chair

Majority Leader → Congressional Campaign Committee Chair

Minority Party

Minority Leader → Minority Whip → Conference Chair → Policy Committee Chair

Minority Leader → Congressional Campaign Committee Chair

Senate

Majority Party

President Pro Tempore → Majority Leader → Assistant Majority Leader → Conference Vice Chair → Policy Committee Chair → Conference Secretary

Majority Leader → Senatorial Campaign Committee Chair

Minority Party

Minority Leader → Minority Whip → Conference Chair → Policy Committee Chair → Conference Secretary

Minority Leader → Senatorial Campaign Committee Chair

Figure 10.3   The Structure of Party Leadership in Congress

Each chamber of Congress has its own separate party leadership structure designed to help party leaders keep rank-and-file members united and accomplish the party's policy goals.

The House and Senate each have several types of committees. A standing committee is a permanent committee with the power to write legislation and report it to the full chamber. Select committees, joint committees, and special committees are usually focused on a more narrow set of issues, such as aging or tax policy, but none has the same legislative clout and authority as a standing committee. In the House, there are twenty standing committees, and the average House committee has forty-three members. In the Senate, there are sixteen standing committees, and the average Senate committee has twenty members. The committee system is the central hub of legislative activity in Congress.[28] Committees hold hearings to consider members' bills, to conduct oversight of the executive branch, or to draw attention to a pressing issue. Committees also write the legislation that is eventually considered on the House and Senate floors. Table 10.2 lists the standing committees in each chamber.

During committee hearings, committee members hear testimony on the content and impact of a bill from other members of Congress, executive branch officials, interest groups, businesses, state and local government officials, and citizens' groups. For the public, hearings are a direct gateway for influence on members of Congress because important information is conveyed in a public setting. Committee hearings serve five basic functions for members of Congress: They draw attention to a current problem or issue that needs public attention, inform committee members about the consequences of passing a specific bill, convey constituents' questions and concerns about an issue, exert oversight of the executive branch to determine whether congressional intent is being honored, and provide an arena in which individual members make speeches to attract media attention that is often used later in a campaign as evidence that the member is doing his or her job. Committee chairs decide which bills receive hearings and which

Table 10.2 Standing Committees in Congress

House of Representatives (20 committees)	Senate (16 committees)
Agriculture	Agriculture, Nutrition, and Forestry
Appropriations	Appropriations
Armed Services	Armed Services
Financial Services	Banking, Housing, and Urban Affairs
Budget	Budget
Education and the Workforce	Health, Education, Labor, and Pensions
Energy and Commerce	Commerce, Science, and Transportation Energy and Natural Resources Environment and Public Works
Foreign Affairs	Foreign Relations
Homeland Security	Homeland Security and Governmental Affairs
Oversight and Government Reform	
House Administration	Rules and Administration
Judiciary	Judiciary
Natural Resources	
Transportation and Infrastructure	
Rules	
Science, Space, and Technology	
Small Business	Small Business and Entrepreneurship
Ethics	
Veterans' Affairs	Veterans' Affairs
Ways and Means	Finance

Source: U.S. House of Representatives, http://www.house.gov/committees/; and U.S. Senate, http://www.senate.gov/pagelayout/committees /d_three_sections_with_teasers/committees_home.htm. See the committee membership lists.

go on to **markup,** a meeting in which committee members write the version of the bill that they may send to the entire chamber for a vote. In both the hearing and markup process, the committee chair gives preference to the views of the majority party members of the committee.

markup: *Process by which bills are literally marked up, or written, by the members of the committee.*

Committee chairs have powerful roles. The chair is typically the majority party member who has the most seniority (longest time) on the committee. However, the Speaker or the Senate majority leader reserves the right to suggest a less senior member as chair if he or she believes that person will better serve the party's interests. In 2010, the Republicans selected Fred Upton (R-Mich.) as chair of the same committee, passing over Joe Barton (R-Tex.), who had served as **ranking member**—the member of the committee from the minority party with the greatest seniority—since 2006. The party leadership believed that Congressman Barton's views were out of sync with the party majority, especially after his public apology to the BP oil company for the federal government's demand for a monetary settlement to pay for the cleanup of the Gulf oil spill in 2010. This case illustrates the steps that party leaders will take to maintain control over committee agendas through the selection of committee chairs. Additionally the Republicans have a three-term limit on committee chairmanships; the Democrats do not. Term limits on chairmanships sustain the party's power to make a change in leadership of committees on a regular basis.

ranking member: *Leader of the minority party members of a committee.*

In general, when a bill is referred to a committee, it is assigned to a subcommittee, a smaller group of committee members who focus on a specific subset of the committee's issues. Subcommittees can consider legislation, but only the full committee can report a bill to the chamber floor for consideration.

Advocacy Caucuses

In addition to committees in the House and Senate, there are also advocacy caucuses, groups whose members have a common interest and work together to promote it. Members might have similar industries located in their districts and states, such as coal mining; or share a background, such as the Congressional Black Caucus or the Hispanic Caucus; or hold similar opinions on issues, such as abortion or land conservation. Members join an advocacy caucus because it gives them an opportunity to work closely with colleagues to represent specific interests and to draw attention to issues of concern to them and to their constituents. Many advocacy caucuses are bipartisan, that is, both Democrats and Republicans join as members. Advocacy caucuses are important to the interactions of Congress because they bring together members from different parties and regions that might not otherwise work closely with each other.[29]

→ KEY QUESTIONS:
How do advocacy caucuses counteract the role of parties in Congress? How can they be a gateway for citizen influence?

Nearly three hundred advocacy caucuses are registered with the Committee on House Administration. In contrast, the Senate has only one official caucus, on International Narcotics Control. However, the Senate has a number of informal caucuses, such as the Senate Air Force Caucus and the Senate Steel Caucus, with members from both parties.

Advocacy caucuses have no formal legislative power, but they can be influential on a bill, especially in the House, because they represent a bloc of members who could vote together in support or opposition. As an alternative to joining a caucus, senators can join together in a temporary coalition and call a press conference to draw attention to the group, industry, or issue that unites them. Senators can also join a congressional caucus even though it is lodged in the House. When he was a senator from Illinois (2005–2008), Barack Obama joined the Congressional Black Caucus.

Checkpoint

CAN YOU:

- Describe the role parties play in Congress
- Explain the role of party leaders in the House of Representatives
- Compare and contrast the functioning of the Senate and House
- State how the committee system works
- Identify the role of advocacy caucuses in Congress

10.4 The Lawmaking Process

› Explain how a law is made in Congress

In this section, we examine the lawmaking process. The process by which a policy proposal becomes a bill and then a law is long and winding, and the Framers designed it deliberately to ensure that laws were reasonable and well thought out. The gates against passage are almost too successful. In the 112th Congress (2011–2012), members introduced 7,837 bills in the House of Representatives and 4,461 bills in the Senate. Of the total 12,298 bills, Congress enacted only 283—or 2.3 percent—into law.[30] It requires compromise and cooperation for a bill to become a law. For an overview of the process, see Figure 10.4.

The Procedural Rules of the House and Senate

→ **KEY QUESTIONS:**
Do the procedural rules of the House and Senate serve as gates or gateways to legislation? Why would there be gates that prevent Congress from fulfilling its fundamental responsibility to pass laws?

rule: *Guidelines issued by the House Rules Committee that determine how many amendments may be considered for each bill.*

Just as the roles of political parties and leaders differ in the House and Senate, so do the internal rules of these chambers. Over time, House and Senate members have adopted different procedures for considering legislation, and these procedures can make compromise between the two chambers more difficult.

The House Committee on Rules. To proceed from committee to the House floor, all bills must pass through the House Rules Committee. Because the House is so large, bills cannot proceed to the floor from committee unprotected; otherwise, the number of legislative amendments that could be offered by the 435 members of the House would overwhelm lawmaking.

The Rules Committee maintains control before the bill goes to the floor by issuing a **rule** dictating how many amendments may be considered. A closed rule means that no amendments may be offered; a modified closed rule allows a few amendments; and an open rule, as its name suggests, allows any number of amendments. The most typical rule is a modified closed rule, which allows the minority party to offer at least one alternative to the bill supported by the majority party. The rule is voted on by all members of the House; if it is approved, debate on the bill begins. If the rule is defeated, the bill is returned to the House Rules Committee or the originating committee for further consideration.

The majority party has learned over time how to use the Rules Committee to maintain policy advantages over the minority party. The majority party uses its numerical advantage on the Rules Committee (9–4 in the 113th Congress) to structure floor debate to limit the minority party's opportunity to amend or change a bill. The Speaker appoints all the majority party members to the Rules Committee, and they are expected to use their powers to advance the party's preferred version of a bill.

Agenda-Setting Tools in the Senate.

The Senate does not have a gatekeeper committee like the Committee on Rules in the

AP IMAGES/SENATE TELEVISION

All senators have the right to speak on the Senate floor, and sometimes they use this power to delay or block legislation, or draw attention to an issue they see as important. Here we see Senator Rand Paul (R-KY) using his power to speak indefinitely on the Senate floor.

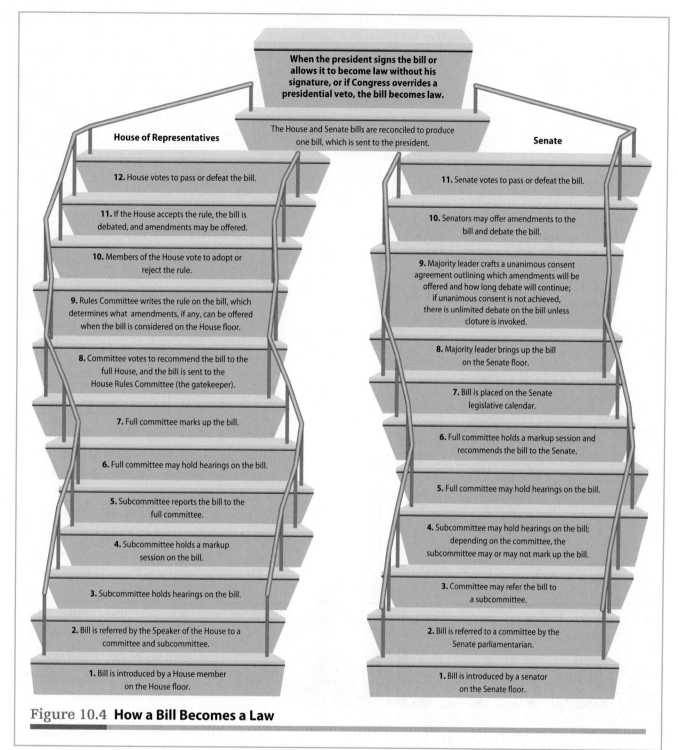

When the president signs the bill or allows it to become law without his signature, or if Congress overrides a presidential veto, the bill becomes law.

The House and Senate bills are reconciled to produce one bill, which is sent to the president.

House of Representatives

12. House votes to pass or defeat the bill.

11. If the House accepts the rule, the bill is debated, and amendments may be offered.

10. Members of the House vote to adopt or reject the rule.

9. Rules Committee writes the rule on the bill, which determines what amendments, if any, can be offered when the bill is considered on the House floor.

8. Committee votes to recommend the bill to the full House, and the bill is sent to the House Rules Committee (the gatekeeper).

7. Full committee marks up the bill.

6. Full committee may hold hearings on the bill.

5. Subcommittee reports the bill to the full committee.

4. Subcommittee holds a markup session on the bill.

3. Subcommittee holds hearings on the bill.

2. Bill is referred by the Speaker of the House to a committee and subcommittee.

1. Bill is introduced by a House member on the House floor.

Senate

11. Senate votes to pass or defeat the bill.

10. Senators may offer amendments to the bill and debate the bill.

9. Majority leader crafts a unanimous consent agreement outlining which amendments will be offered and how long debate will continue; if unanimous consent is not achieved, there is unlimited debate on the bill unless cloture is invoked.

8. Majority leader brings up the bill on the Senate floor.

7. Bill is placed on the Senate legislative calendar.

6. Full committee holds a markup session and recommends the bill to the Senate.

5. Full committee may hold hearings on the bill.

4. Subcommittee may hold hearings on the bill; depending on the committee, the subcommittee may or may not mark up the bill.

3. Committee may refer the bill to a subcommittee.

2. Bill is referred to a committee by the Senate parliamentarian.

1. Bill is introduced by a senator on the Senate floor.

Figure 10.4 **How a Bill Becomes a Law**

House, and all senators have the power to try to amend legislation on the floor. The tool that they use is Rule XIX of the Standing Rules of the Senate, which grants senators the right to speak on the Senate floor. Over time, senators have used this right to make speeches, offer amendments to bills, object to consideration of a bill on the floor, or engage in **filibusters**, extended debates that members start with the purpose of delaying or even preventing the passage of bills.[31] All senators in the majority and the minority parties can use the filibuster.

filibuster: *Tactic of extended speech designed to delay or block passage of a bill in the Senate.*

Throughout Senate history, a wide range of bills, from civil rights legislation to product liability legislation, have been delayed or defeated by filibusters.[32]

cloture: *Vote that can stop a filibuster and bring debate on a bill to end.*

The only way to stop a filibuster is by invoking **cloture**, a motion to end debate that requires a supermajority of sixty votes to pass. In November 2013, the Democratic majority, led by Senator Harry Reid (D-Nev.), changed the threshold for cloture on presidential nominations and judicial nominations for district and appeals court judges to fifty-one rather than sixty. This made it easier for President Obama to get his nominees confirmed because the Democrats had a working majority of fifty-five members, which meant that approval for these nominees was virtually guaranteed and could not be blocked by the Republicans. This was an historic change; the Senate had not changed the cloture threshold since 1975 when it lowered it from two-thirds of the Senate (67) to three-fifths (60).

However, this cloture change was not without significant controversy. Typically major rules changes in the Senate require two-thirds of Senators to agree but in this case, the majority party used procedural tools to get around this requirement. When the Republicans blocked an Obama judicial nominee for the Court of Appeals, the majority leader, Senator Harry Reid (D-Nev.) made a motion to reduce the threshold for cloture for judicial nominations other than for the Supreme Court to fifty-one votes, rather than sixty votes. The presiding officer of the Senate, who chairs the proceedings, ruled that Senator Reid's motion was out of order. Reid in turn asked for a roll call vote; it takes only a majority of the Senate to accept or reject the ruling of the chair. The Democrats had fifty-five votes, and fifty-two of them voted to reject the ruling of the chair, which allowed Senator Reid's motion to replace existing rules, and effectively eliminated the filibuster on presidential executive branch nominees and federal judges (except for the Supreme Court).[33] However, it is important to note that the Democrats did not seek to eliminate the sixty-vote threshold for filibustering legislation. Given that the majority control of the Senate and the White House can change hands, it was deemed too risky to shut off the option just in case the Democrats became the minority party in the Senate, and lost the White House in 2016. It is clear from the action by the Democrats that a simple majority of the Senate has the authority to eliminate the filibuster at any point that it desires. After cloture has been invoked on a bill, no more than thirty additional hours of debate are permitted. All amendments must be germane to the bill's issues, and a time for a final vote is set. Figure 10.5 illustrates the variation in the number of cloture motions in the Senate over time.

In addition, Senate rules no longer require those seeking to block a bill to speak continuously

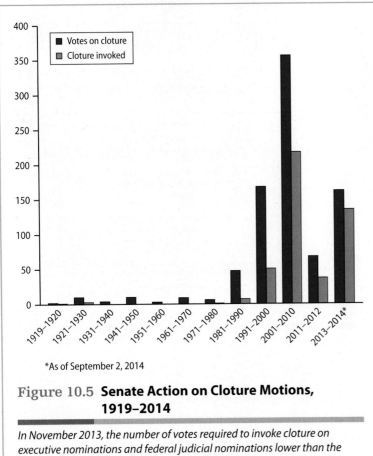

*As of September 2, 2014

Figure 10.5 Senate Action on Cloture Motions, 1919–2014

In November 2013, the number of votes required to invoke cloture on executive nominations and federal judicial nominations lower than the Supreme Court was lowered from sixty votes to fifty-one votes.

Source: United States Senate, http://www.senate.gov/pagelayout/reference/cloture_motions/clotureCounts.htm.

on the floor. Senators who oppose a bill can merely state their intention to filibuster, and that will be sufficient to block the bill from consideration on the floor. Senators also use the threat of a filibuster to block the president's judicial nominations, a practice that has come under increasing scrutiny. Filibusters of this type are an expression of partisanship or ideology, and they can disrupt the operation of the federal courts.[34] To counteract the filibuster in recent years, the Senate has resorted to a two-track system in which a bill that is being filibustered can be set aside to allow the Senate to proceed to other bills. But even with this two-track system, the filibuster has imposed substantial costs on the Senate, both in terms of the legislation that has failed to pass and the legislation that could not be brought to the floor.

Some scholars have argued that the filibuster has been used too frequently as a way of blocking action on important public policies and is not a legitimate democratic instrument of power. Others argue that filibustering is a responsive and effective means of representation in Congress; if there is intense opposition to a bill in a senator's state, or from a minority of voters nationwide, the senator may consider it a responsibility to block the bill's passage.[35]

Without a gatekeeper like the House Committee on Rules and with the constant threat of a filibuster, there are few restrictions on a bill when it comes to the Senate floor. When the Senate majority leader wishes to bring a bill up for consideration, he or she must ask unanimous consent. Consequently, the Senate typically operates under **unanimous consent agreements** to establish guidelines for debating a bill. Senators strike a deal about how a bill will be debated on the Senate floor, how and when amendments will be offered, how much time will be allocated to debate and vote on amendments, and at what time on what date the final vote on the complete bill will take place. Senators have accepted this form of limitation on their rights to amend or block a bill because it requires their consent and enables the Senate to move forward and pass key legislation.

Nevertheless, a senator can object to a unanimous consent request to bring a bill to the Senate floor in a practice known as a **hold**. A hold is a less drastic measure than a filibuster, but it can be used by any senator to delay a bill for a minimum of twenty-four hours. The majority leader can circumvent a hold by requesting a vote on cloture; if sixty senators agree, the Senate proceeds to consider the bill. Typically, senators hold up bills to extract concessions from Senate leaders or from the administration on the legislation being considered. They also use the hold to draw increased attention to a bill in the hope that public opposition will develop.

Legislative Proposals

The lawmaking process starts with an idea. Ideas for legislation can come from a number of sources, including constituents, interest groups, local or national newspaper stories, state or local governments, staff members, and the members' own personal interests.[36] When an idea is agreed on, the House or Senate member's staff consults with the Office of Legislative Counsel, which turns the general outlines of a bill into the technical language that will alter the U.S. Code, the set of federal laws that governs the United States. After approving the final legal language of a bill, the member introduces the bill into the respective chamber (House or Senate), an action known as bill sponsorship. After a bill is introduced, other members can sign on to be cosponsors (sponsorship of legislation is discussed in more detail later in this chapter). In reality, many freestanding bills that are introduced separately are later incorporated into larger omnibus bills that are passed by Congress. Combining bills into omnibus

→ KEY QUESTIONS:
Is the filibuster a legitimate means of protecting minority rights?

⭐ **unanimous consent agreement:** *Agreement among all 100 senators on how a bill or presidential nomination will be debated, changed, and voted on in the Senate.*

⭐ **hold:** *Power available to a senator to prevent the unanimous consent that allows a bill or presidential nomination to come to the Senate floor, which can be broken by invoking cloture (sixty votes).*

→ KEY QUESTIONS:
How can you as a citizen influence legislation in Congress?

→ KEY QUESTIONS:
How do omnibus bills make accountability more difficult?

legislation can be useful, especially in periods of divided government. These big bills allow Congress to pass numerous provisions that might not pass if each were presented separately.[37]

Committee Action

After a member introduces a bill, it is referred to one or more committees or subcommittees that have jurisdiction over its subject matter. The first step in getting the bill enacted into law is to secure a hearing on a bill in subcommittee or full committee. In general, a committee tends to act first on bills that are sponsored by the chair of the committee, then on those sponsored by the subcommittee chairs, and last on bills sponsored by regular members of the committee. If the sponsor is not on the committee to which the bill is assigned, it is much harder to get action on the bill. This arrangement also makes sense because committee members are more likely to have expertise on the issues covered by the committee than are other legislators, so their bills are taken more seriously by their fellow committee members.[38] In rare cases, however, as a result of intense interest group lobbying or media pressure, a committee might hold a hearing on a bill sponsored by someone who is not a committee member, but the committee typically drafts its own bill to address the same issue.

After the hearings, the committee may move to the markup. At this point, the stakes intensify in terms of what the bill will ultimately look like, so the stakeholders in the policy process try to exert influence. In this era of increased partisanship and party leadership control, committees have less freedom to craft legislation that differs from the leadership's goals. After the full committee approves a bill, it and an accompanying committee report are sent to the full House or Senate for consideration by all members.

Floor Action and the Vote

→ KEY QUESTIONS:
What is the purpose of floor debate? Does it change minds and votes?

When a bill is sent to the full House or Senate—commonly known as "going to the floor"—all the members of the chamber gather to debate and vote on it. Debate takes different forms in each chamber. In the House, it is heavily structured, and most members are allowed no more than five minutes to speak on a measure, leaving almost no time for actual deliberation among members. In contrast, the Senate has few limits on the time allowed for members to speak on an issue on the floor. If the Senate is operating under a unanimous consent agreement or cloture, time is limited; otherwise, senators can make speeches and even engage in active debate on an issue for much longer than their House counterparts. Unfortunately for the current political system, real debate rarely occurs on the floor; instead, representatives and senators use their opportunity to speak to make partisan speeches or to direct their remarks to their constituents back home, knowing that the proceedings are televised by C-Span, and C-Span2.

During a roll call vote, the clerks of the House or Senate call the name of each member, who registers his or her vote electronically. Members cast up or down votes on legislation (to pass or reject), to table (set aside) legislation, or to approve a motion to recommit (send it back to committee with instructions to rewrite it). In addition to individually recorded votes, general voice votes can be taken when a consensus exists and there is no perceived need to record each member's vote.

→ KEY QUESTIONS:
Who are your representatives and senators? Do you want them to be trustees or delegates?

A roll call vote is the most fundamental way that a member of Congress represents constituents. When members of Congress cast their votes, they can act as trustees who exercise independent judgment about what they believe is best for the people or as delegates who do exactly as the people wish. Over time, congressional representation has evolved into a hybrid of both types of representation; thus, members of Congress act as both trustees and delegates. Roll call voting is therefore a key gateway for citizen influence in the legislative process.

Scholars have long characterized roll call voting by partisan dimension and by ideological or spatial dimension because in the past both the Democratic and Republican parties contained both liberals and conservatives.[39] Currently, the vast majority of Democratic members are liberal, and the vast majority of Republican members are conservative. Consequently, scholars now can examine roll call voting through both the partisan and ideological lens simultaneously. They confirm that most members of the House and Senate vote along party lines; in the 112th Congress, in the House, 90.5 percent of Republicans and 87 percent of Democrats voted with their party; in the Senate, 83 percent of Republicans and 92 percent of Democrats voted with their party. Overall, 73 percent of all votes taken in the House and 60 percent of all votes in the Senate divided along party lines.[40] Party leaders in Congress frame the content of bills and the choices for roll call votes along the lines of party platforms and ideology. Essentially, they are engaging in what is called message politics, designing legislation to push members into casting votes that may later be used in campaigns against them.[41] This framework reflects a responsible parties system (see Chapter 8) in which voters can clearly distinguish Democratic and Republican legislative policy goals. Although the increased emphasis on partisanship makes it easier for citizens to more clearly hold Congress accountable, it decreases the likelihood of bipartisan cooperation and makes passing legislation more difficult.

Conference Committee

For a bill to become law, the House and Senate have to pass an identically worded version of it to send to the president for signature. The last stage in the congressional legislative process takes place when the House and Senate meet in conference committee to resolve any differences in the versions that passed each chamber. The Speaker of the House and the Senate majority leader typically appoint the chairs and ranking members from the committees that originated the bills, plus other members who have been active on the bill. If the bill is very important to the party leaders, they also have the power to appoint themselves to the committee. If the conferees can reach agreement, the conference committee issues a conference report that must be voted on by the entire House and Senate. Because the conference report represents the end of the negotiation process between the two chambers, members cannot offer amendments to change it. However, if a majority of members of the House or Senate are displeased with the final results of the conference, they can defeat the report outright or vote to instruct the conference committee to revise the agreement.

In the past twenty years, Congress has decreased its use of conference committees. Instead, party leaders take on the responsibility of producing a final bill themselves. In choosing this path, they concentrate power in the hands of fewer members of Congress than in the traditional conference committee system.[42] Although this alternative provides a more streamlined way of legislating, it also acts as a gate against input from committee members who wish to represent their constituents' views on the final version of the bill.

The Budget Process and Reconciliation

Although the federal government tries to spend about as much money as it takes in from revenues, it does not typically succeed. Instead, it usually runs a **federal budget deficit**, which

federal budget deficit: *Difference between the amount of money the federal government spends in outlays and the amount of money it receives from revenues.*

national debt: *Sum of loans and interest that the federal government has accrued over time to pay for the federal deficit.*

requires it to borrow money to meet all its obligations (see Chapter 14 for more detail on current deficits and national debt). Although the process is complex, essentially this means that the federal government pays interest on outstanding loans, and the loans and interest that accumulate over time constitute the **national debt**.

The modern Congress operates under a budget process created in the Congressional Budget and Impoundment Control Act of 1974, which was enacted to give Congress more power over the federal budget.[43] It was passed at a time of relatively low deficits, but many new government programs were being implemented, and government financial obligations were steadily rising. The act created the House and Senate Budget Committees and the Congressional Budget Office so that Congress could construct its own budget blueprint as an alternative to the president's annual budget.

concurrent budget resolution:

Congressional blueprint outlining general amounts of funds that can be spent on federal programs.

The federal government's fiscal year begins on October 1 and ends on September 30, and the key aspect of the budget process is that the congressional budget, known as the **concurrent budget resolution**, is supposed to be approved by both chambers by April 15. Because the budget resolution does not have the force of law, it is not sent to the president for his signature; rather, it serves as general instructions to congressional committees about how much money can be allocated for federal programs in the fiscal year. The authorizing committees take this blueprint into account when they reauthorize existing programs or create new ones, and the appropriations committees in the House and Senate use it to allocate funds in twelve separate bills. They typically begin their work in May in the hope of enacting all appropriations bills by September 30. If Congress and the president fail to agree on any one of the twelve appropriations bills, Congress enacts a **continuing resolution** that funds the government temporarily while disagreements about spending are worked out.

→ KEY QUESTIONS:
Does the congressional budget process help or hurt deficit reduction efforts?

From 2009 to 2012, the House of Representatives passed a budget resolution, but the Senate did not. This failure to produce a concurrent budget resolution left the appropriations process less structured. As a result, Congress relies more heavily on continuing resolutions than on passing separate appropriations bills. Congress's failure to produce a budget resolution makes it harder for voters to hold it accountable for federal budget policy. In December 2013, Congress broke the trend and passed a concurrent budget resolution, which allowed them to subsequently pass an omnibus appropriations bill that would last until October 1, 2014. For more details on the conflicts surrounding these bills, see Chapter 14.

continuing resolution: *Measure passed to fund federal programs when the appropriations process has not been completed by September 30, the end of the fiscal year.*

The 1974 Budget Act also created a parallel budget bill, known as **reconciliation**, which does require the president's signature. Reconciliation was specifically designed as umbrella legislation to bring all bills that contain changes in the tax code or entitlement programs in line with the congressional budget. Entitlement programs, such as Social Security, Medicare, and Medicaid, are considered mandatory because they pay out benefits to individuals based on a specified set of eligibility criteria. When Congress wants to make a change to one of these programs, it must pass a reconciliation bill. The reconciliation bill has special procedural protections in the Senate: It cannot be filibustered, and it can be debated for no more than twenty hours. A bill that cannot be filibustered was a tempting target for those who wanted to add nonbudget-related provisions. Consequently, in 1985, the budget process was modified to include the Byrd rule, which required that reconciliation be used only to reduce the federal deficit, which at the time was $212.3 billion.[44] In subsequent years, the Byrd rule has been interpreted to mean that all provisions of reconciliation must be directly related to the budget.[45]

reconciliation: *A measure used to bring all bills that contain changes in the tax code or entitlement programs in line with the congressional budget.*

→ KEY QUESTIONS:
Why did the Framers give Congress the final say in whether a bill should become a law?

Despite the Byrd rule, Congress has found ways to use the reconciliation process to pass controversial legislation. In 2010, the Democratic majority in Congress used it to pass part of its comprehensive health care reform, commonly known as Obamacare. Both Democrats and Republicans have used the reconciliation process to go beyond changes in the tax code, or to balance the budget, on issues ranging from welfare reform to children's health insurance.[46]

Presidential Signature or Veto, and the Veto Override

In the last step in the legislative process, the bill is sent to the president for his approval or rejection. A president can actively reject, or veto, a bill. If Congress will be going out of session within ten days, the president can wait for the session to end and simply not sign the bill, a practice known as a pocket veto. If Congress remains in session, and the president neither vetoes the bill nor signs it, the bill becomes law.

The veto is a powerful balancing tool for the president against the overreach of Congress; however, the Framers also gave Congress the **override**, which is the power to overturn a presidential veto with a two-thirds vote in each chamber. When the president vetoes a bill, it is returned to the chamber from which it originated; if two-thirds of the members of that chamber vote to override the veto, it is sent to the other chamber for a vote. A two-thirds vote by each chamber, rather than just a majority vote, is required for an override because the Framers wanted to enable the president to block a bill passed by Congress if he does not believe that it is in the best interest of the nation as a whole. The president can use the veto either to prevent a bill from becoming law or to pressure Congress into making changes that are closer to his policies.[47]

override: *Congress's power to overturn a presidential veto with a two-thirds vote in each chamber.*

Checkpoint

CAN YOU:
- Compare the procedural rules in the House and Senate
- State how a bill is proposed
- Describe what happens to a bill in committee
- Characterize floor action and voting
- Explain what happens in conference committees
- Identify the key components of the congressional budget process
- Define the president's role in the lawmaking process

10.5 The Member of Congress at Work

> Assess what a member of Congress does

The cardinal rule of succeeding in the House or Senate is simple: Never forget where you came from. Representative Joaquín Castro has shown how a member tries to balance the competing demands of legislating with the core responsibility of serving constituents. The following sections describe exactly what the job of a House or Senate member entails.

Offices and Staff

For all newly elected members in the House and Senate, the first steps are to set up an office and hire staff members. In the House, each representative receives about the same amount of money for office operations. In the Senate, the office budget is determined by the population size of the senator's home state, based on the reasoning that senators from larger states have more constituents and more issues to deal with than their smaller-state colleagues. Most members bring some of their campaign workers to Washington to work on their staffs

Public Policy and Congress:
Unemployment Insurance

In times of economic difficulty, Congress is often asked to act quickly to help individuals in need of income support. During the Great Depression, President Franklin Delano Roosevelt (1933–45) proposed a number of programs that would try to help workers get back on their feet, and provide a safety net for their retirement years. The Social Security Act of 1935 set out to accomplish a number of these goals, and we discuss it in depth in Chapter 14. As part of the Social Security Act, Congress enacted a program designed to provide temporary cash payments to unemployed workers who have lost their jobs, due to downsizing or layoffs, known as Unemployment Insurance. Workers who quit their jobs or are fired from their jobs are not eligible for Unemployment Insurance. In nearly all states, Unemployment Insurance is funded by a tax on employers, which is collected by the federal government and placed in the Unemployment Trust Fund, but the program is administered by state governments. Although the federal government gives states the power to run the program, it sets basic rules for its administration.

Since its creation, the Unemployment Insurance program has grown from covering businesses that employ eight or more workers to any business that employs one or more workers, essentially covering the entire workforce. Typically, unemployment benefits are available for twenty-six weeks before an individual exhausts his or her benefits. However, during economic crisis periods, Congress has agreed to extend unemployment insurance for longer periods of time and provide federal funding to states to pay for the extra weeks of benefits for unemployed workers.

Such was the case in 2008 when the housing and stock market declines left a lot of people without work. President George W. Bush worked with a Democratic-controlled House and Senate to pass a federally funded extension program, called Emergency Unemployment Compensation (EUC), which allowed workers to collect UI for up to seventy-three weeks on top of the twenty-six weeks normally allowed, for a total of ninety-nine weeks of eligible benefits. In February 2009, shortly after President Obama took office, unemployment stood at 8.3 percent, and he requested that Congress extend EUC as part of the American Recovery and Reinvestment Act of 2009, otherwise known as the stimulus package.[48] The Democratic-controlled Congress passed that bill, and the extended time frame for benefits lasted until June 1, 2010. However, the unemployment rate had increased in the intervening year and after several short-term renewals, in December 2010, President Obama worked with Congress to renew EUC through June 2012.

After the House Republicans took control of the House of Representatives in 2011, it was unclear whether future renewals of extended unemployment would be possible because of their general opposition to longer term government relief programs. Proponents of extended unemployment benefits argue that by giving cash benefits to individuals who are out of work, the government is helping to keep the economy afloat. By some estimates every dollar paid out in unemployment benefits generates $1.60 in return.[49] However, opponents argue that extending unemployment benefits beyond twenty-six weeks discourages individuals from taking jobs that might pay less than the value of their unemployment benefits. In turn, individuals who stay out of the workforce for longer periods of time have a more difficult time finding jobs, thereby creating an entrenched cycle of long-term unemployment.

Despite these objections, the Republicans in the House did agree to renew EUC through January 2, 2013, because unemployment continued to be very high, but they insisted on reducing the total number of weeks a recipient could receive benefits.[50] As it was set to expire at the end of 2012, Congress and President Obama agreed to renew the program for one more year as part of a larger bill that also extended tax cuts that were enacted in the Bush administration.

However, in December 2013, as EUC was again set to expire, the unemployment rate stood at 6.7 percent, and Republicans in the House and Senate argued that it was no longer necessary to extend unemployment benefits past the traditional twenty-six weeks. Because the Republicans controlled the House of Representatives, it was not possible to renew the program without their support. In the months that followed in 2014, President Obama negotiated with the U.S. Senate, which was controlled by the Democrats, and asked for bipartisan support from Republican Senators to put pressure on the House Republicans to support a limited extension of EUC. The Senate did pass a temporary UI extension in April 2014, but the House did not take up the measure; with unemployment rates falling steadily through September 2014, the Congress adjourned without passing the UI extension.

Construct Your Own Policy

1. Construct an unemployment safety net that would help those who lose their jobs but not discourage people from seeking employment.
2. Create a government work program that would employ individuals who have no other job and who have run out of unemployment benefits. How long could people stay employed by such a program?

Master the Concept
of The Congress with MindTap™ for American Government

 REVIEW MindTap™ **for American Government**
Access Key Term Flashcards for Chapter 10.

TEST YOURSELF MindTap™ **for American Government**
Take the Wrap It Up Quiz for Chapter 10.

 STAY CURRENT MindTap™ **for American Government**
Access the KnowNow blog and customized RSS for updates on current events.

STAY FOCUSED MindTap™ **for American Government**
Complete the Focus Activities for The Congress.

⭐ Key Concepts

appropriate (p. 317). What is the difference between appropriation and authorization?

authorize (p. 317). How is authorization a part of Congress's "power of the purse"?

cloture (p. 332). How is cloture invoked?

concurrent budget resolution (p. 336). How is a concurrent budget resolution used by congressional committees?

continuing resolution (p. 336). When is a continuing resolution used?

divided government (p. 320). How does divided government make it harder to compromise?

earmark (p. 341). Why did Congress ban earmarks?

federal budget deficit (p. 335). What causes the federal government to run a budget deficit?

filibuster (p. 331). How does the filibuster give power to individual senators?

hold (p. 333). How is a hold used in relation to unanimous consent agreements?

home style (p. 342). How does a member of Congress use home style to help get reelected?

House majority leader (p. 325). What is the House majority leader's role within the House?

House minority leader (p. 325). What is the role of the House minority leader in policy making when he or she shares the president's party?

markup (p. 329). What is the committee chair's role in relation to markup?

national debt (p. 336). How is the national debt related to the federal budget deficit?

override (p. 337). How does the override strengthen Congress's power over the president?

ranking member (p. 329). Who gets to serve as ranking member on a committee?

reconciliation (p. 336). Why was the reconciliation process created?

rule (p. 330). What are the different types of rules and their implications?

Senate majority leader (p. 326). What is the primary means through which the Senate majority leader wields power?

Senate minority leader (p. 326). How does the Senate minority leader represent his or her party members?

Speaker of the House (p. 323). How did Thomas Brackett Reed increase the power of the Speaker of the House and the majority party in the House of Representatives?

unanimous consent agreement (p. 333). What does a unanimous consent agreement do?

Learning Outcomes: What You Need . . .

To Know	To Test Yourself	To Participate
▶ Describe how Congress has developed		
The Framers designed Congress as a bicameral legislature so that the House of Representatives and the Senate—with different qualifications for office, modes of election, terms of office, and constituencies—would check and balance each other. Although its enumerated powers are limited, Congress has built on its implied powers to become the powerful legislative branch it is today. Differences in size, rules, structure, and responsibility have molded the House and the Senate into very different institutions.	• Explain the reasons for and consequences of bicameralism. • Explain the constitutional differences between the House and Senate.	• Weigh the gridlock caused by bicameralism against the checks and balances it provides.

To Know	To Test Yourself	To Participate

▶ Define the powers of Congress

The Framers structured Congress to give it the powers necessary to govern the newly formed union, especially the powers to tax and spend and declare war. Over time, the powers of Congress have evolved under the separation of powers system. In some ways, congressional powers have expanded, especially in the area of advice and consent, but at the same time congressional productivity has declined.

- State what the general welfare clause allows Congress to do.
- Recall why war powers are shared with the president.
- Define the commerce clause and explain its power.
- Explain the power of advice and consent.
- Describe the process of impeachment.
- Compare and contrast the enumerated and implied powers.
- Explain Congress's role in the authorization of courts.
- Characterize how Congress uses its powers of oversight on the other two branches.

- Debate whether Congress's power over interstate commerce should be limited but its power over going to war should be strengthened.
- Consider whether Congress's power over the executive and judicial branches should be expanded, and, if so, how.

▶ Outline how Congress is structured

Political parties play a stronger role in the organization and operation of the House than of the Senate. In the Senate, each member has relatively equal power, and passing legislation requires compromise and cooperation. In recent years, intense partisanship, including party-line voting and message politics, has decreased the likelihood of bipartisan cooperation and made it more difficult for Congress to pass legislation.

- Describe the role parties play in Congress.
- Explain the role of party leaders in the House of Representatives.
- Compare and contrast the functioning of the Senate and House.
- State how the committee system works.
- Identify the role of advocacy caucuses in Congress.

- Is Congress too partisan? If so, how would you change the structure of the House and the Senate to encourage bipartisan cooperation? Would you have to change our electoral structure?

▶ Explain how a law is made in Congress

The procedures through which a bill becomes a law are different in the House and Senate, but each chamber engages in committee work, hearings, floor debate, and voting. Following passage by each chamber individually, a formal conference committee or an informal group of party leaders resolves differences between the two bills to produce a single bill that is presented to the president for signature. If the president vetoes a bill, Congress can override the veto with a two-thirds majority in each house.

- Compare the procedural rules in the House and Senate.
- State how a bill is proposed.
- Describe what happens to a bill in committee.
- Characterize floor action and voting.
- Explain what happens in conference committees.
- Identify the key components of the congressional budget process.
- Define the president's role in the lawmaking process.

- Map out ways you could influence the content of legislation as it is being considered in Congress.
- Design a federal budget that does not create a deficit.

▶ Assess what a member of Congress does

Members of Congress try to balance the competing demands of legislation and constituent service, and they are always anticipating the next election. A successful legislator seeks to be responsive to constituents by engaging in committee work, sponsoring and voting on bills, and securing federal funds for his or her district or state.

- Explain the importance of constituent services.
- Recall the four legislative responsibilities of congressional members.
- Describe the key ways in which members of Congress communicate with constituents.
- State how elections shape the work of members of Congress.

- Identify three policies you believe your representative and senators should address, and devise a plan to communicate to them about your interests.

"As a second-generation Greek immigrant, I was raised to be thankful for the gifts that this great nation gave to me and to my parents before me. Throughout my childhood in Hinton, West Virginia, my father, an optometrist and small business owner, and my mother, a teacher, were both engaged in service through our community and church. And so, with this core commitment to service and passion for impact, I am humbled and excited by this next challenge. . . . I look forward to working alongside the remarkable men and women of the Department [of Health and Human Services] to continue to ensure that children, families, and seniors have the building blocks of healthy and productive lives."[1]

SYLVIA MATHEWS BURWELL
Harvard University

11

The Presidency

From a very young age, Sylvia Mathews Burwell showed a keen interest in politics. In elementary school, she helped campaign for a friend's father, and at age 11, she volunteered for Jay Rockefeller's bid for governor. Later Sylvia's mother ran for the mayoral election of her hometown, Hinton, West Virginia, at age 65. She won, without ever having run for public office before. Sylvia graduated from Harvard with a degree in government and became a Rhodes Scholar at Oxford University, which introduced her to the world of professional politics. In 1992, Sylvia worked on the Clinton presidential campaign. She led Clinton's economic transition team, and after he won his election, became a staff director on the National Economic Council (NEC).

Sylvia Mathews Burwell was promoted to the chief of staff for the Treasury Secretary and then served the president as his deputy chief of staff. In 1998, she assumed the position of deputy director in the Office of Management and Budget (OMB). When Republican candidate George W. Bush won the 2000 presidential election, she turned her focus to the world of nonprofit foundations, initially working for the Bill and Melinda Gates Foundation. As president of the Walmart Foundation, she tackled global health issues. Her past experience with the OMB put her on the top of a short list of candidates to head the agency after Democratic President Barack Obama was reelected in 2012. In 2013, Obama nominated her for the position. Burwell's appointment as OMB director was impressively smooth, and she was confirmed by the Senate in a 96-0 vote on April 24, 2013. On April 11, 2014, President Obama nominated Burwell as the next Health and Human Services (HHS) Secretary.

The president put one of his most important policy legacies—the Affordable Care Act (ACA)—in her hands. Although this confirmation process was also relatively smooth, Burwell did have to answer questions about how she would improve the implementation of the ACA. The Senate Finance Committee approved her nomination by a vote of 21-3 on May 21, 2014, and the full Senate confirmed her on June 5, 2014 by a vote of 78-17.

Sylvia Mathews Burwell's career exemplifies the gateways that open when you get involved in politics: the political networks that talented and hardworking volunteers establish on campaigns. Burwell's experience demonstrates how campaign work can be the beginning of a lifetime of

Need to Know

11.1 Outline the requirements to serve as president

11.2 Identify the powers of the president and explain how they are limited

11.3 Describe the growth of executive influence

11.4 Analyze why the president is so powerful during wartime

11.5 Summarize how the White House is organized

11.6 Assess presidential greatness

▶ WATCH & LEARN MindTap for American Government
Watch a brief "What Do You Know?" video summarizing The Presidency.

349

public service. As Secretary of HHS, Burwell will be carrying out the remainder of the health care law that has yet to be implemented, and Republicans used her nomination to reiterate their criticisms of the law. Burwell's appointment is also the perfect example of how the gates of Congress can get in the way of executive branch policy implementation, even for laws that have already passed through their chambers.[2]

In this chapter, we examine how the president governs and how responsive he can be to the people. We look at his constitutional powers and the way he uses the executive power to achieve his policy goals, from nominating appointees such as Sylvia Mathews Burwell to issuing executive orders to accomplish policy goals. We also look at the limits on presidential power. As presidential scholar Charles Jones has argued, successful presidents work within a separation of powers system and alongside the legislative and judicial branches, compromising, persuading, and overcoming opposition. The most successful presidents are strong leaders with clear policy visions and excellent communication and negotiation skills. In the twenty-first century, the American president has to implement existing law and, equally important, leads the effort to turn his policy goals into law and achieve his visions for the nation.

LISTEN & LEARN
MindTap for American Government

Access Read Speaker to listen to Chapter 11.

11.1 Presidential Qualifications

> Outline the requirements to serve as president

The American presidency was invented at the Constitutional Convention in 1787. The Framers had no definitive models to help them determine what sort of person should serve as a democratically elected head of state because nations were still run by monarchs whose power to rule was hereditary. But the Framers had George Washington, the hero of the Revolutionary War, in mind for the office, and he helped shape the idea of what a president should be. Still, they left the qualifications as open as possible, and men with diverse experiences have served as president.

Constitutional Eligibility and Presidential Succession

Article II, Section 1, of the Constitution states that the president must be a natural-born citizen (or a citizen at the time the Constitution was adopted), at least 35 years old, and a resident of the United States for at least fourteen years. The original Constitution did not specify eligibility for the vice presidency, as the person who came in second in the vote for president would be vice president. But in 1800, Thomas Jefferson (1801–1809) and Aaron Burr ended up in a tie in the Electoral College when in fact supporters wanted to elect them as a team, with Jefferson as president and Burr as vice president. The Twelfth Amendment, ratified in 1804, changed the process so that candidates are elected for president and vice president separately. The amendment also directs that the vice president must meet the same eligibility requirements as the president and that electors cannot vote for both a president and a vice president from the elector's home state. This requirement makes it difficult for parties to nominate presidents and vice presidents from the same state.

The Constitution also states that when the president is removed from office by death, resignation, or inability to perform the duties of the office, the vice president becomes president. It stipulates that if neither the president nor the vice president is able to complete the elected term, Congress should designate a successor by law. In 1792, Congress passed the Presidential

Succession Act, which designated the president pro tempore of the Senate as next in line, and then the Speaker of the House. In 1841, John Tyler (1841–45) became the first elected vice president to succeed a president when President William Henry Harrison insisted on giving a two-hour inaugural speech in freezing rain while wearing no hat or coat, and consequently came down with a cold. Besieged by candidates hoping that he would appoint them to public office, he had little time to rest. Only one month after assuming office, the new president died after his cold developed into pneumonia. The order of succession today is illustrated in Table 11.1.

There was no constitutional provision for replacement of the vice president, and in the course of the nation's history, the office has occasionally been vacant. Eventually, the Twenty-Fifth Amendment, ratified in 1967, required the president to nominate a replacement vice president, who must be approved by a majority vote of the House and the Senate. The first vice president to assume office in this manner was Gerald R. Ford, nominated by President Richard M. Nixon (1969–74) in 1973, following the indictment and subsequent resignation of Vice President Spiro T. Agnew on charges of tax fraud.

The amendment also allows for a temporary transfer of power from the president to the vice president in cases of incapacity when invoked by either the president or vice president and a majority of the cabinet. To date, only the president has invoked this clause and then only when he has had to have surgery that would require sedation. For example, in 1985, when President Ronald Reagan (1981–89) had a colonoscopy, Vice President George H. W. Bush was acting president for eight hours.[3] In contrast, no one invoked the clause when President Reagan was shot in a failed assassination attempt in 1981; Vice President Bush stood in for him at official functions and meetings for approximately two weeks but did not serve as the official acting president during this time.

Today another constitutional amendment, the Twenty-Second (1951), limits the president to two elected terms. For a century and a half, presidents followed the precedent established by George Washington (1789–97) when he stepped down after two terms. But in 1940, President Franklin Delano Roosevelt (1933–45) chose to run for a third term and won and also won election to a fourth term in 1944. Though the dangers of World War II were a factor in his staying in office, many Americans, especially Republicans, worried that a long-standing president could expand executive branch power too much, so they sought a way to limit presidential terms of service. In 1946, Republicans captured a majority in the House and Senate, and on the very first day the new Congress met, they proposed a constitutional amendment limiting the president to two full terms in office.[4] For a list of constitutional amendments that pertain to the presidency, see Figure 11.1.

Table 11.1 Presidential Order of Succession

1. Vice president
2. Speaker of the House
3. President Pro Tempore of the Senate

Cabinet Secretaries

4. State
5. Treasury
6. Defense
7. Attorney General
8. Interior
9. Agriculture
10. Commerce
11. Labor
12. Health and Human Services
13. Housing and Urban Development
14. Transportation
15. Energy
16. Education
17. Veterans' Affairs
18. Homeland Security

© CENGAGE LEARNING®

→ KEY QUESTIONS:
How do term limits make the president less responsive to public opinion?

Figure 11.1 Constitutional Amendments Pertaining to the Presidency

Twelfth	1804	Requires that electors cast separate votes for president and vice president and specifies requirements for vice presidential candidates
Twentieth	1933	Declares that presidential term begins on January 20 (instead of March 4)
Twenty-Second	1951	Limits presidents to two terms
Twenty-Fifth	1967	Specifies replacement of the vice president and establishes the position of acting president during a president's disability

© CENGAGE LEARNING®

★ **lame duck:** *Term-limited official in his or her last term of office.*

→ KEY QUESTIONS:
Unlike members of Congress, presidents represent all the people of the United States. How can a president represent all the people?

Presidential term limits enforce turnover and open opportunity for new leadership, but they also act as a gate that prevents voters from reelecting a popular president whom they want to keep in office. Because a president in his second term cannot seek reelection, he is commonly referred to as a **lame duck**. Lawmakers know that the president's time in office is limited, so they are less likely to cooperate or compromise with him. On the other hand, a president who wants to chart a policy course that is unpopular may be more likely to do so when he does not have to face the voters. Lame duck status therefore has the advantage of giving the president more political freedom, but the disadvantage of making him less directly responsive to public opinion.

Background and Experience

In keeping with the democratic spirit of the founding of the United States, the Framers did not specify qualifications for the presidency beyond age and citizenship, and in the ensuing two centuries, men of varying backgrounds have served in the office. Presidents have come from all walks of life and from almost all regions of the country. The clearest path to the White House is through the office of the vice president, but most presidents have some combination of service in the military, in a state legislature, or as governor; in the U.S. House of Representatives and Senate; or in a prior presidential administration. For example, James Monroe (1817–25) was a soldier in the Revolutionary War, a U.S. senator, minister to France, secretary of state, and secretary of war. Herbert Hoover (1929–33) was an international food relief worker and secretary of commerce.[5]

There are advantages and disadvantages for presidents, depending on their prior experience. Lyndon Baines Johnson (1963–69) was very successful in passing his domestic policy agenda in large part due to his experience as a House member, U.S. senator, and Senate majority leader. His prior

THE GRANGER COLLECTION, NYC

George Washington was a successful military general who led American troops in the Revolutionary War. He was widely admired and was chosen to be the first president of the United States because it was believed that his experience and personal characteristics would be a model for the future. He took the oath of office on April 30, 1789, on the balcony of Federal Hall in New York City, then the nation's capital.

experience taught him crucial negotiating skills with members of Congress, and he used his skills to their fullest extent. In contrast, Jimmy Carter (1977–81) was generally considered to have failed in getting his domestic policy agenda enacted because of his lack of experience in Washington. He came to the White House from the governor's mansion in Georgia, where he exercised executive power with little challenge from the legislature. When he faced a Congress that did not embrace his agenda, he lacked the negotiating skills to be successful. Of course, no single set of qualifications or experiences can guarantee success as a president. When voters cast their ballots for president, they take a leap of faith that the person who wins will be trustworthy, accountable, and responsive to their needs and will implement the laws equally for every citizen. For a list of the presidents of the United States, see Table 11.2.

Table 11.2 **The Presidents of the United States, 1789–2014**

President	Term Dates	Party	Prior Experience
1 George Washington	1789–97		General
2 John Adams	1797–1801	Federalist	Vice president
3 Thomas Jefferson	1801–1809	Democratic-Republican	Vice president, secretary of state
4 James Madison	1809–17	Democratic-Republican	Secretary of state, U.S. House, state legislator
5 James Monroe	1817–25	Democratic-Republican	Secretary of war, secretary of state, U.S. Senate
6 John Quincy Adams	1825–29	Democratic-Republican	Secretary of state, U.S. Senate
7 Andrew Jackson	1829–37	Democrat	U.S. Senate, general, U.S. House
8 Martin Van Buren	1837–41	Democrat	Vice president, U.S. Senate
9 William Henry Harrison	1841 (died in office)	Whig	U.S. Senate, general, territorial governor
10 John Tyler	1841–45	Whig	Vice president, U.S. Senate, governor, U.S. House
11 James K. Polk	1845–49	Democrat	Governor, U.S. House
12 Zachary Taylor	1849–50 (died in office)	Whig	General
13 Millard Fillmore	1850–53	Whig	Vice president, U.S. House
14 Franklin Pierce	1853–57	Democrat	U.S. Senate, U.S. House, state legislator
15 James Buchanan	1857–61	Democrat	Secretary of state, U.S. Senate, U.S. House
16 Abraham Lincoln	1861–65 (died in office)	Republican; National Union	U.S. House
17 Andrew Johnson	1865–69	Democrat; National Union	Vice president, U.S. Senate, U.S. House
18 Ulysses S. Grant	1869–77	Republican	General
19 Rutherford B. Hayes	1877–81	Republican	Governor, U.S. House, general
20 James A. Garfield	1881 (died in office)	Republican	U.S. Senate, general, U.S. House, state legislator
21 Chester A. Arthur	1881–85	Republican	Vice president, collector of the port of New York
22 Grover Cleveland	1885–89	Democrat	Governor, mayor
23 Benjamin Harrison	1889–93	Republican	U.S. Senate
24 Grover Cleveland	1893–97	Democrat	U.S. President, governor, mayor
25 William McKinley	1897–1901 (died in office)	Republican	Governor, U.S. House

Table 11.2 (*Continued*)

President	Term Dates	Party	Prior Experience
26 Theodore Roosevelt	1901–1909	Republican	Vice president, governor
27 William Howard Taft	1909–13	Republican	Secretary of war, governor general of the Philippines, federal judge
28 Woodrow Wilson	1913–21	Democrat	Governor, university president
29 Warren G. Harding	1921–23 (died in office)	Republican	U.S. Senate, lieutenant governor, state legislator
30 Calvin Coolidge	1923–29	Republican	Vice president, governor
31 Herbert Hoover	1929–33	Republican	Secretary of commerce
32 Franklin Delano Roosevelt	1933–45 (died in office)	Democrat	Governor, assistant secretary of the navy, state legislator
33 Harry S. Truman	1945–53	Democrat	Vice president, U.S. Senate
34 Dwight D. Eisenhower	1953–61	Republican	University president, general
35 John F. Kennedy	1961–63 (died in office)	Democrat	U.S. Senate, U.S. House
36 Lyndon Baines Johnson	1963–69	Democrat	Vice president, U.S. Senate, U.S. House
37 Richard M. Nixon	1969–74 (resigned)	Republican	Vice president, U.S. Senate, U.S. House
38 Gerald R. Ford	1974–77	Republican	Vice president, U.S. House
39 Jimmy Carter	1977–81	Democrat	Governor, state legislator
40 Ronald Reagan	1981–89	Republican	Governor, actor
41 George H. W. Bush	1989–93	Republican	Vice president, CIA director, U.S. House
42 William J. Clinton	1993–2001	Democrat	Governor, state attorney general
43 George W. Bush	2001–2009	Republican	Governor
44 Barack Obama	2009–	Democrat	U.S. Senate, state legislator

© CENGAGE LEARNING®

The Expansion of the Presidency

President George Washington had the enormous responsibility of setting the standard for how a president should govern in a democracy, and he was very careful not to infuse the office with airs of royalty or privilege. The Framers anticipated that the executive branch would be led by one person whose primary responsibility would be the defense of the United States. As commander of the Continental Army during the Revolutionary War, Washington had military experience, but he was also a cautious and thoughtful statesman who wanted to establish a precedent for how the chief executive should operate.

In the course of the nineteenth century, from the presidencies of Thomas Jefferson, to Andrew Jackson (1829–37), to Abraham Lincoln, and finally to William McKinley (1897–1901), the nation grew in size, population, and economic power. The job of the chief executive grew accordingly, but, though increasingly demanding and complex, it remained essentially focused on national defense and economic growth. In the twentieth century, however, the United States became a leading international military and economic power. Its role in World War II and the subsequent Cold War against the Soviet Union expanded the authority of the presidency. Historian and presidential adviser Arthur Schlesinger Jr. used the term **imperial presidency** to describe

→ KEY QUESTIONS:
What defines an imperial presidency?

★ **imperial presidency:**
Power of the president to speak for the nation on the world stage and to set the policy agenda at home.

the power of the president to speak for the nation on the world stage and to set the policy agenda at home.[6] Schlesinger's view suggests that as long as the United States is engaged in military conflicts all over the world to promote and protect its interests, the president will be considered the most important figure in American politics. However, after two very long wars, public opinion has shifted against intervening in foreign conflicts (see Chapter 6, Public Opinion and the Media), which leaves less support for presidential military action on foreign soil. As the public looks more inward and focuses on domestic policy, Congress and the president stand on more balanced scales.

11.2 Presidential Power: Constitutional Grants and Limits

> Identify the powers of the president and explain how they are limited

As we saw in Chapter 10, Congress, the Framers enumerated Congress's powers, both to assert powers that were missing under the Articles of Confederation, such as the powers to collect taxes and to regulate commerce, and to constrain the branch they anticipated would be the most powerful. The Framers expected the executive branch to be smaller and less powerful and did not believe it necessary to enumerate the executive powers as they did the legislative powers (see Table 11.3). Instead, in the very first sentence of Article II, they "vested" the president with a general grant of "executive Power" and then, later in the article, stated certain additional powers and responsibilities. The general grant of executive power has allowed the presidency to become the powerful office it is today. In this section, we look at the constitutional sources of the president's powers, the ways in which presidents have sought to expand their constitutional powers, and the ways in which the other branches, especially Congress, act to check and balance the president.

Commander in Chief

The president is the **commander in chief** of the armed forces of the United States, which includes the Army, Navy, Air Force, Marine Corps, and Coast Guard, plus their Reserve and National Guard units. An elected commander in chief, rather than an appointed military officer, is a distinctly important element of American democracy. The president directs all war efforts and military conflict. Congress, however, has the power to officially declare war and to authorize funding for the war effort. Because the war powers that are divided between the president and Congress are so contentious, we examine them later in the chapter.

commander in chief: *Leader of the armed forces of the United States.*

→ KEY QUESTIONS:
Why is it important that the commander in chief of the U.S. military is a civilian?

Power to Pardon

The president has the power to grant clemency, or mercy, for crimes against the United States, except in the case of impeachment from federal office. Clemency is a broad designation that includes a **pardon**, which is forgiving an offense altogether, and a commutation,

pardon: *Full forgiveness for a crime.*

Table 11.3 A Comparison of Legislative and Executive Authority under the Constitution

While the Constitution grants specific legislative authority to Congress, it provides a general grant of authority to the president that does not require specific enumerated grants of power, nor is there an executive equivalent of Article I, Section 9, which specifically limits congressional authority.

	Legislative	Executive
Authority	"All legislative Powers herein granted shall be vested in a Congress of the United States"	"The executive Power shall be vested in a President of the United States"
Specific Powers	Article I, Section 8, including: • lay and collect taxes • provide for the common defense • regulate interstate and foreign commerce • authorize courts • set uniform rules for naturalization and bankruptcy • establish post offices • make all laws that are "necessary and proper" for carrying out the listed powers	Article II, Section 2, including: • act as commander in chief of armed forces • grant pardons • make treaties • receive foreign ministers • appoint ambassadors, judges, cabinet-level officials Article II, Section 3: • ensure that the laws are faithfully executed Article I, Section 7: • veto legislation
Limits on Power	Explicit limits on powers: Article I, Section 9, including: • no bills of attainder • no ex post facto laws • no titles of nobility Bill of Rights: • substantive limits of the First through Eighth Amendments Ninth Amendment: • enumeration of rights does not grant general authority Tenth Amendment: • people and states retain reserved powers not granted to Congress	Mostly through checks and balances: • veto override • Senate confirmation on appointments • Senate treaty ratification • removal by impeachment

© CENGAGE LEARNING®

which is shortening a federal prison sentence; in general, pardoning someone is considered a more sweeping act of clemency than commuting a sentence. Election considerations can also come into play because presidents who are in their first term may want to appear tougher on crime than in their second term, when they will not be seeking reelection. For example, in his first term in office, President George W. Bush issued nineteen pardons and commuted two sentences, but in his second term, Bush granted 170 pardons and commuted seven sentences. In comparison, President Barack Obama issued 22 pardons and commuted one sentence in his first term, and by September 2014, he had already issued 52 pardons and commuted ten sentences.[7]

→ **KEY QUESTIONS:**
Should the president have the power to pardon? What impact does this power have on citizen equality?

Treaties and Recognition of Foreign Nations

The president or his designated representative has the power to negotiate and sign treaties with foreign nations, but he must do so with the "Advice and Consent of the Senate," as specified by the Constitution. For a treaty to be valid, two-thirds "of the Senators present" must approve. Historically, the Senate has refused to approve some notable treaties, ranging from the Treaty of Versailles ending World War I signed by President Woodrow Wilson (1913–21), to the Kyoto Protocol on climate change signed by Vice President Albert Gore Jr. who was representing President William Jefferson (Bill) Clinton (1993–2001). These examples illustrate how the requirement that the Senate approve treaties serves as a gateway for public input into presidential actions, and how it can be a gate that blocks a president's attempt to reach agreements with foreign nations. Today, with the expansion of globalization, the president's representatives negotiate treaties over a wide range of areas, such as military alliances, human rights accords, environmental regulations, and trade policies (see Global Gateways: The World Trade Organization and Global Trade). The president also enters into executive agreements, which do not require Senate approval and tend to be less expansive in scope than treaties.

The president's authority in foreign affairs includes the power to "receive Ambassadors and other public Ministers," which allows the president to recognize the legitimacy of foreign regimes. Such decisions are frequently based on the internal political system of the foreign nation. For example, revolutionaries overthrew Russia's czarist regime in 1917, but the new Soviet Union, a Communist nation, was not recognized by the United States until 1933, through the action of President Franklin Delano Roosevelt. In contrast, in 2008, when the young democracy of Kosovo declared its independence from Serbia, President George W. Bush immediately recognized it as an independent nation.[8] However, the president also reserves the power not to recognize self-declared independent nations as in the case of Russian separatists who took over control of the Crimean peninsula and eastern parts of Ukraine.

Executive and Judicial Nominations

The president has the power to appoint all federal officers, including cabinet secretaries, heads of independent agencies, and ambassadors. The presidential appointment process has two steps: nomination, and subsequent approval by a majority of the Senate. The appointed officers are typically referred to as political appointees, and they are expected to carry out the president's political and policy agenda (in contrast to civil servants, who are hired through a merit-based system and are politically neutral; see Chapter 12, The Bureaucracy). During Senate recesses, the president can make appointments that will expire when the Senate officially adjourns at the close of a Congress (adjourns *sine die*), unless the appointee is subsequently confirmed. Presidents have sometimes used recess appointments to bypass the Senate, as President Obama did in appointing Richard Cordray director of the Consumer Financial Protection Bureau in 2012. Obama used the recess appointment power to get around strong Republican opposition to Cordray's appointment and the creation of the bureau he was nominated to lead (for more on this bureau, see Chapter 12). In order to prevent the president from making recess appointments when the Senate is on short breaks, the Senate has taken to officially staying in session but not conducting any business. In response, President Obama has acted as if the Senate was in recess and made a set of appointments to several agencies, including the NLRB. In the 2014 case *National Labor Relations Board v. Noel Canning*, the Supreme Court ruled that only the Senate can decide when it is in recess, thus striking down three NLRB appointments.

globalgateways

The World Trade Organization and Global Trade

One of the areas in which the president can exercise his power is through global trade because the executive branch negotiates trade agreements, which are then approved by Congress. For example, in 2014, President Obama spent considerable time and energy negotiating the Trans-Pacific Partnership trade agreement with twelve nations, foremost Japan, but the agreement was not finalized. With globalization, trade has become increasingly important to the U.S. domestic economy in two ways. First, as U.S. companies expand by manufacturing and selling goods overseas, they press the president to forge trade agreements with other countries. Likewise, foreign companies have started to locate in the United States, and this development makes it all the more important for the president to remove trade barriers that might deter investment in the United States.

From 1948 to 1994, world trade was governed by the General Agreement on Tariffs and Trade (GATT), which was the gateway through which nations set up trade agreements, sometimes bilaterally but frequently on a multi-country basis. The first round of GATT involved only 23 nations; in 1994, at the final round, 123 nations participated. That year these nations agreed to form the World Trade Organization (WTO), a neutral body responsible for settling trade disputes among member countries.*

U.S. membership in the WTO presents an opportunity and a challenge to presidential power. On the one hand, it provides a means for resolving trade disputes, but, on the other, it constrains the United States, which must abide by WTO rulings even when they are detrimental to U.S. trade interests.

Another check on the president's power is the requirement that Congress approve global trade agreements. Moreover, because Congress is elected by the people, it serves as a gateway for public opinion to influence global trade. Indeed, Congress has required that trade agreements include environmental protections and meet certain labor standards to ensure that the countries doing business with the United States follow the same rules as U.S.-based companies.

1. Should the president be able to use unilateral action when it comes to trade agreements with foreign nations?
2. Is U.S. involvement in international trade organizations such as the WTO good for American democracy?

Leaders of major industrialized countries meet in various locations in high-level meetings, known as summits, to discuss global trade and other economic issues. Here President Obama is a guest of Prime Minister David Cameron of Great Britain when that country hosted the G-8 summit in 2013.

*Information in this paragraph is from the World Trade Organization, http://www.wto.org. For more on trade politics, see David Karol, "Divided Government and U.S. Trade Policy: Much Ado about Nothing?" International Organization 54, no. 4 (2000): 825–44, and Jeanne J. Grimmett, "Why Certain Trade Agreements Are Approved as Congressional-Executive Agreements Rather Than as Treaties," CRS Report for Congress, 97-896 (Washington, D.C.: Congressional Research Service, November 3, 2011), http://www.fas.org/sgp/crs/misc/97-896.pdf.

SAUL LOEB/AFP/GETTY IMAGES

TITLE IMAGE: © KLETR/SHUTTERSTOCK.COM

this privilege is that the president must make difficult choices and, without the guarantee of privilege, may not receive or deliver the fullest information in the course of his deliberations.

The Supreme Court created an exception to this privilege in *United States v. Nixon* when on July 24, 1974, it unanimously ruled that executive privilege is not absolute and must give way when the government needs the information for a trial. The tapes showed that Nixon and his aides had conspired to cover up the Watergate break-in. Three days later, the House Judiciary Committee approved three articles of impeachment against Nixon.[15] With the full House of Representatives ready to vote on the articles, President Nixon resigned on August 9, 1974.

In 1975, Nixon's successor, former Vice President Gerald R. Ford (1974–77), pardoned Nixon of all federal offenses he might have committed. The Watergate scandal had a negative impact on the American presidency, raising public mistrust of the office and of the federal government more generally. However, the process leading up to Nixon's resignation also revealed the ways in which members of both parties can work together in Congress to exercise congressional oversight of the executive.

Impeachment is not a power to be used lightly, but it does serve as a gateway for the public, through its elected officials in Congress, to hold the president, cabinet officials, and federal judges accountable for abuses of power.

Checkpoint

CAN YOU:
- Characterize the presidential power of commander in chief
- Compare pardon and commutation
- Describe the role of the Senate in the president's power to negotiate and sign treaties
- Recall the steps to presidential appointments
- Survey the power of the veto
- Explain how the State of the Union address has evolved as a tool for the president
- Compare and contrast examples of impeachment (or impending impeachment)

11.3 The Growth of Executive Influence

❯ Describe the growth of executive influence

→ KEY QUESTIONS:
Should the president be subjected to civil lawsuits while he is in office? State the reasons for your answer.

With all the formal constitutional restrictions on the president, one has to wonder how the modern presidency became so powerful. The answer lies in the general grant of executive power and the constitutional provision that the president "take Care that the Laws be faithfully executed," which he promises to do when he takes the oath of office. Presidents have found ways to unlock the enormous powers inherent in these constitutional provisions to expand their informal powers over policy making and implementation. The president's veto power and Congress's power to override and to impeach the president counteract each other and help ensure that each branch remains responsive to its governing responsibilities. However, Congress has no formal means to balance and check the president's growing executive power, though at times the judicial branch has been able to do so.

→ KEY QUESTIONS:
What should be done about the growth of executive power? Is it a problem for checks and balances among the separate branches?

Presidential Directives and Signing Statements

Presidents use the executive power to issue **presidential directives** that give specific instructions on a federal policy and do not require congressional approval. Recent presidents have used this unilateral power much more frequently than previous presidents, especially under conditions of divided government or interbranch policy conflict.[16] Presidential directives

presidential directive: *Official instructions from the president regarding federal policy.*

might take the form of executive orders, proclamations, or military orders. They are the primary way that presidents shape policy implementation, and they are the instruments presidents use to act quickly in national emergencies.[17]

The best-known type of directive is the **executive order**, which can be used for a wide range of purposes. Typically, executive orders instruct federal employees to take a specific action or implement a policy in a particular way. Some scholars argue that executive orders are an important source of "independent authority" that is used solely at the discretion of the president.[18] Even though presidents since Washington have issued executive orders, the orders were not officially numbered until 1862 and not published in the *Federal Register* until 1935.[19] In 1948, President Harry Truman integrated the armed forces with Executive Order 9981, stating "there shall be equality of treatment and opportunity for all persons in the armed forces, without regard to race, color, religion, or national origin."[20] Truman used the power of executive order to bypass congressional and some military opposition to integration of the armed forces because he believed it was the right thing for the country.

Still, a presidential directive is not completely immune from scrutiny or accountability. In 1952, during the Korean War, the United Steelworkers union threatened to stop work at steel mills. In response, President Truman used his executive powers to order the seizure of steel mills and put them under the control of the United States government. Although the steel workers were willing to put off the strike and work in the newly government-controlled mills, the steel mill owners sued to challenge the legality of the seizure. In *Youngstown Sheet and Tube Co. v. Sawyer,* better known as the Steel Seizure case, the Supreme Court ruled against the president, claiming he had no statutory authority from Congress to seize the mills and that his commander in chief status did not allow him to seize domestic property when the United States was at war in a foreign land (see Supreme Court Cases: *Youngstown Sheet and Tube Co. v. Sawyer*).

In foreign and military affairs, presidents can issue presidential directives on national security, which have a similar purpose to executive orders but are not published in the *Federal Register,* which is the official record of government regulations (see Chapter 12). These directives can announce specific sanctions against individuals who are considered enemies of the United States or make larger statements about U.S. policy toward a foreign country. President George W. Bush used this power frequently in what he described as a war on terror and in the conduct of the wars in Afghanistan and Iraq. For example, he issued an order in 2001 to create military tribunals that would try suspected enemy combatants and terrorists, rather than allowing them to be tried in a regular military court. He also created a special subcategory called homeland security presidential directives, which are not as widely publicized as other directives and deal only with homeland security policy.

When a president signs a bill into law, he can issue **signing statements**, written remarks that reflect his interpretation of the law that are not required or authorized by the Constitution. Signing statements can be classified as nonconstitutional and constitutional. Nonconstitutional statements are typically symbolic, celebrating the passage of the law or providing technical instructions for implementing a new law. Constitutional statements are more serious in that the president uses them to indicate a disagreement with Congress on specific provisions in the law. In constitutional signing statements, the president may go so far as to refuse to implement specific provisions of laws. This kind of statement is a challenge to Congress's constitutional authority to legislate.[21] Even when the presidency and the Congress

executive order:
Presidential directive that usually involves implementing a specific law.

signing statements:
Written remarks issued by the president when signing a bill into law that often reflect his interpretation of how the law should be implemented.

are controlled by the same party, signing statements can be used to shift the implementation of policy toward presidential preferences. President Obama recognized the controversy over signing statements, and he issued a memorandum early in his administration stating that he would use signing statements "to address constitutional concerns only when it is appropriate to do so as a means of discharging my constitutional responsibilities."[22] In issuing this memorandum, President Obama was trying to alleviate concerns about abusing executive power but at the same time preserving the presidential power to interpret legislation that is inherent in signing statements. As of September 2014, President Obama had issued twenty-eight signing statements and 187 executive orders.[23]

Presidential directives and signing statements create tension between the president and Congress and between the president and the judiciary because they are an expansion of presidential power. At times they have been deemed illegal.[24] Many presidents, from Lincoln to Franklin Delano Roosevelt to George W. Bush, have taken temporary actions that have violated constitutional rights in the name of national security, from suspending *habeas corpus* to interning Japanese Americans to eavesdropping on U.S. citizens (see Chapter 4, Civil Liberties, and Chapter 5, Civil Rights, for expanded discussions of these actions). Judging the merit of such actions is difficult because citizens have to decide whether the president is acting in good faith on behalf of the country or seeking to expand his own power and agenda.

Power to Persuade

Presidents understand that communicating well with the public is essential to building support for their policies. They also face the challenge of using their personal reputations and negotiating skills to generate support among members of Congress. President Theodore Roosevelt (1901–1909) described the office of the president as a **bully pulpit**, where presidents could use the attention associated with the office to make a public argument in favor of or against a policy.[25] The key to using the bully pulpit effectively is to explain a policy in simple and accessible terms, to get the public's attention, and to frame an issue in a way that is favorable to the president's policy position. Using the bully pulpit can accomplish the president's goals only if he already has a receptive audience. In today's highly partisan and divided political climate, there is no guarantee that the president's detractors will listen to his message.[26]

A president's relationship with the members of the news media is a crucial factor in successful communication, and it has evolved dramatically over time. Samuel Kernell, a presidential media scholar, argues that over the past seventy years, presidents have increased the extent to which they control their interactions with the press. Press conferences are one important way of sustaining a relationship with the news media, and presidents have tried to use them to their advantage. Some presidents are more comfortable with the

→ KEY QUESTIONS:
What limits can Congress, the courts, and/or the American people place on the president?

bully pulpit:
Nickname for the power of the president to use the attention associated with the office to persuade the media, Congress, and the public to support his policy positions.

President Theodore Roosevelt was a larger-than-life figure who challenged corporate monopolies, sought to strengthen U.S. international power, and increased federal efforts at land conservation. He was known for using the office of the president as a bully pulpit to persuade the public to support his policies.

supreme court cases

Youngstown Sheet and Tube Co. v. Sawyer (1952)

QUESTION: Can the president seize steel mills to prevent a strike during wartime?

ORAL ARGUMENT: May 12, 1952

DECISION: June 2, 1952 (read at http://caselaw.lp.findlaw.com/scripts/getcase.pl?court=US&vol=343&invol=579)

OUTCOME: No, the seizure was overturned (6–3).

After North Korea's invasion of South Korea in June 1950, President Harry Truman sought and received a United Nations resolution permitting intervention on behalf of South Korea. In 1952, with the Korean War still raging, the United Steelworkers announced plans for an April strike. President Truman feared that the strike would severely harm America's war effort. One alternative for putting off the strike was to seek a temporary court order prohibiting a strike when national security is at stake, a provision allowed under the Taft-Hartley Labor Act.

Uncomfortable with what was perceived to be an anti-labor policy, Truman instead ordered Secretary of Commerce Charles Sawyer to seize the steel mills and run them under the flag of the United States. Because the steelworkers preferred working at the steel mills under the government to the Taft-Hartley alternatives, they agreed to come back to work after the seizure.

The steel mill owners then brought suit challenging the seizure. Truman claimed the authority to do this under his power to make sure that the laws were faithfully executed and under his power as commander in chief of the armed forces. The Court's decision rejected the president's authority to seize the steel mills, noting that Congress had not passed a law allowing the seizure, so there were no laws involving the seizure to be faithfully executed.

The Court also ruled that the president's authority to rule as commander in chief did not extend to domestic seizures during foreign wars. Without congressional authorization, the president could not seize the steel mills. A separate concurring opinion, since treated as the heart of the case, noted that the president's authority is at its peak when he acts under the express authority of Congress, is in a middle category when Congress has not acted, and is at its lowest when the president acts contrary to congressional will. As Congress had rejected granting the president the authority to seize property in labor disputes, Truman was acting under the lowest level of authority. Without congressional authorization, the president could not seize the steel mills.

The Steel Seizure case still stands as the leading decision on presidential authority. The Supreme Court relied heavily on it in deciding that President George W. Bush did not have the authority to hold enemy combatants from the war in Afghanistan at the U.S. naval base at Guantanamo Bay, Cuba, without a hearing, since Congress had not authorized the action.*

1. Why did the Court block President Truman's seizure of the steel mills?
2. Did the decision place the president above Congress, below Congress, or equal to Congress in terms of making policy?

* *Hamdan v. Rumsfeld*, 548 U.S. 557 (2006).

his first obligation is to take any and all steps that he believes will protect Americans. After signing a type of presidential directive known as a Presidential Policy Guidance statement on the use of drones in May 2013, the president said this:

> Nevertheless, it is a hard fact that U.S. strikes have resulted in civilian casualties, a risk that exists in every war. . . . But as commander in chief, I must weigh these heartbreaking tragedies against the alternatives. To do nothing in the face of terrorist networks would invite far more civilian casualties—not just in our cities at home and our facilities abroad, but also in the very places like Sana'a and Kabul and Mogadishu where terrorists seek a foothold. Remember that the terrorists we are after target civilians, and the death toll from their acts of terrorism against Muslims dwarfs any estimate of civilian casualties from drone strikes. So doing nothing is not an option.[44]

Presidents weigh the costs of ensuring the safety of American citizens, both in terms of dollars and the lives of American soldiers, against the costs of using tactics that may result in civilian deaths.

The American Civil Liberties Union (ACLU) and the Center for Constitutional Rights has filed lawsuits on behalf of Al-Awlaki both before and after his death in an attempt to block the president and the executive branch from targeting American citizens. However, federal courts have dismissed these suits. Moreover, American public opinion indicates strong bipartisan support for drone strikes, with 69 percent of Republicans and 59 percent of Democrats approving Obama's decision.[45] In such an atmosphere, President Obama is likely to continue to use this advanced technology, which he believes is effective and justified in the interests of national security.

Construct Your Own Policy

1. Devise a more transparent policy on reporting the use of drones and the number of casualties associated with this type of weapon.
2. Create a set of guidelines for the executive branch to follow in determining who will be the subject of a drone attack.

GENYA SAVILOV/AFP/GETTY IMAGES

Here we see the conflict in Ukraine where separatists waged protests in favor of breaking free of Ukraine and aligning with Russia. In 2014, the conflict escalated from protests to civil war.

The U.S. led a coalition of nations in air strikes against ISIL, and provided weapons to groups fighting against ISIL.

Tensions with Russia intensified when Ukrainian rebels ousted their pro-Russian president. Ukraine, Russia's neighbor to the West, is home to many individuals of Russian heritage. Subsequently, Russian separatists staged takeovers of Ukrainian government buildings in southern and eastern Ukraine, essentially declaring them part of Russia. The Ukrainian government was not well prepared to stop these takeovers, which Russia actively supported. In response, President Obama and leaders of European nations imposed economic sanctions on Russia in an effort to pressure them to withdraw their support of these separatists. In September 2014, the Ukrainian government and the separatists declared a cease fire, but fighting continued, with both military and civilian casualties.

President Obama and Congress understand that the United States is expected to take the lead in responding to this crisis. However, it is also clear to both Obama and Congress that the American public are weary of war and international conflict. Still, Americans view global instability as a threat to their safety. In 2014, it became increasingly clear to both Obama and Congress that public opinion among American people at this time leaned strongly against intervention in foreign conflicts. In contrast, after the 9/11 terrorist attacks in 2001, for example, only 30 percent of Americans said that the U.S. should "mind its own business."[46] This broader context has important implications for U.S. foreign policy because presidents, and members of Congress, recognize the difficulty of waging a military intervention without public support.

These examples demonstrate that tension between the presidency and Congress over war powers compels the president to make the case to Congress that military action is necessary. Moreover, as in the case with Ukraine and Syria, presidents face challenges in persuading a war-weary nation to intervene militarily. In such cases, the Obama administration has sought to actively intervene only with strong international support and with as limited U.S. ground troop involvement as possible.

Power Struggles between the President and the Judiciary

Power struggles between the president and the judiciary in wartime generally focus on civil liberties. In Chapter 4, we examined the Court's rejection of Abraham Lincoln's argument about the suspension of *habeas corpus*, and in Chapter 5, we discussed the Court's acquiescence in President Franklin Delano Roosevelt's executive order on the internment of Japanese Americans. In this chapter, we have already noted the limits on presidential actions imposed by the Steel Seizure case.

→ KEY QUESTIONS:
What limits should the judiciary impose on presidential actions in wartime? Give examples.

To Know	To Test Yourself	To Participate

▶ **Identify the powers of the president and explain how they are limited**

Among the president's constitutional powers are those associated with being commander in chief. The president also has the power to pardon, to negotiate and sign treaties and recognize foreign nations, to veto bills passed by Congress, and to appoint federal officers.	• Characterize the presidential power of commander in chief. • Compare pardon and commutation. • Describe the role of the Senate in the president's power to negotiate and sign treaties. • Recall the steps to presidential appointments. • Survey the power of the veto. • Explain how the State of the Union address has evolved as a tool for the president. • Compare and contrast examples of impeachment (or impending impeachment).	• Evaluate the president's power over the military. • Design a way to make appointments and judicial selection less partisan. • Evaluate the role of partisanship in impeachment.

▶ **Describe the growth of executive influence**

The Constitution vests the president with a general grant of executive power and requires that he "take Care that the Laws be faithfully executed." These responsibilities have been used by presidents to vastly increase presidential power. The president uses his executive power to issue presidential directives. He also uses the office to persuade the people and Congress and to set the agenda for domestic and foreign policy.	• Recall the different types of presidential directives. • List the tools available to a president as he uses his power to persuade. • Describe how the president can set the public agenda.	• Determine whether you think the presidency has become too powerful.

▶ **Analyze why the president is so powerful during wartime**

As presidential power has grown, the president has come into increasing conflict with the other two branches of government, particularly during wartime. The War Powers Act has proven to be weak because when Congress authorizes military action, the president has sole powers as commander in chief.	• Track trends in the struggle between the president and Congress over war powers. • Describe issues in the struggle between the president and the judiciary in wartime.	• Design a way to broaden Congress's power to limit intervention in foreign conflicts. • Evaluate the importance of civil liberties in wartime.

▶ **Summarize how the White House is organized**

The Executive Office of the President has great influence over budgetary, military, and economic policies. The roles of vice president and first lady have grown in recent years.	• Track the growth of the executive staff. • Explain how the role of the vice president has evolved over time.	• Evaluate whether the vice president should be given an expanded set of formal powers.

▶ **Assess presidential greatness**

Presidential leadership is generally judged on how successful a president is in getting his preferred policies passed into law and in getting the bureaucracy to be effective and efficient. Americans also judge their presidents on their communication and negotiation skills.	• Explain how Franklin D. Roosevelt had such a large impact on public policy. • Recall the programs of Lyndon B. Johnson's Great Society and how they were passed. • Describe the impact of Ronald Reagan on the economy with his support of tax cuts.	• Develop criteria for judging presidents. • Describe the ideal president for the twenty-first century.

"If front-line, non-intelligence government employees cannot disclose wrongdoing to the public that was never classified and then that information can be stamped years later with a classified TSA marking, the First Amendment is now meaningless."[1]

ROBERT MACLEAN
Air Force

To Know	To Test Yourself	To Participate

▶ **Outline the essential elements of a bureaucracy**

Each bureaucratic organization has a clear mission, a hierarchical decision-making process, an area of expertise, and a bureaucratic culture. Aside from cabinet departments, there are various types of organizations within the bureaucracy, some designed to be more or less independent of the president.	• Explain how the mission of a bureaucracy shapes its goals. • State the advantages and disadvantages of the hierarchical decision-making process. • Characterize bureaucratic expertise. • Describe bureaucratic culture.	• Evaluate the degree of accountability associated with a bureaucratic mission. • Design a bureaucracy that is more efficient and responsive.

▶ **Describe the growth of the bureaucracy over time**

Since 1789, the bureaucracy has grown from three to fifteen executive departments as government's responsibilities have grown, primarily in the area of the economy. The first regulatory agency was established in 1887 to regulate railroad practices. Federal employment has developed from a corps of wealthy elites with political connections to members of the Congress and the president into a merit- and performance-based civil service designed to be protected from political influence. The president appoints cabinet secretaries and other high-level political appointees who are expected to carry out the president's agenda.	• Equate the establishment of cabinet departments with developments in the U.S. economy and society. • Describe what regulatory agencies do. • Explain how and why the civil service evolved. • Survey the types of jobs career civil servants perform. • Recall why political appointees have increased in number over time. • Explain the growth of the use of private-sector contract workers.	• Evaluate the bureaucracy in terms of government responsiveness. • Assess why merit-based employment is better than patronage in a democracy. • Consider whether you would like to work for the government. • Evaluate the accountability of private-sector contract workers.

▶ **Assess how the bureaucracy is both accountable and responsive, and how it can fail**

Following a consistent regulatory process, agencies draft regulations, which are open to comment by citizens, members of Congress, interest groups, and relevant businesses and industries before they are finalized. Congress exercises influence over policy through its oversight responsibilities and power to authorize and allocate funds. Lawsuits can involve the judicial branch in the interpretation of public policy. The bureaucracy is subject to criticism for acting slowly, but in a democracy, the need for efficiency is counterbalanced by the need for transparency. Reform efforts have improved transparency by providing protections for whistleblowers. The policy-making process and regulatory process together exemplify government responsiveness and accountability to citizens even as they also reflect the concerns of competing interests.	• Explain ways the legislative and judicial branches can check the bureaucracy. • Examine how the need for bureaucratic efficiency and transparency can counteract each other. • Describe what it means to be a whistleblower. • Relate the consequences of bureaucratic failure.	• Describe how you can influence the bureaucracy. • Evaluate the importance of offering protection to whistleblowers.

"Theresa, I think this fish hás found her pond."

SONIA SOTOMAYOR, TO A PROFESSIONAL FRIEND AFTER OVERCOMING HER FEARS ABOUT BEING A JUDGE
Princeton University

In 1996, a Court of Appeals Court in Texas declared affirmative action unconstitutional within the Fourth Circuit.[10] The University of Texas responded by implementing a program that guarantees admission to the University of Texas to anyone who graduates in the top 10 percent of his or her high school class. Because public schools are highly segregated in Texas, the university believed this would be an effective means of obtaining a diverse student body.

In the meantime, the Supreme Court revisited the *Bakke* decision in a pair of 2003 cases (*Gratz* and *Grutter*), discussed in this chapter. Despite surpassing the average qualifications required by the University of Michigan to gain entrance, Jennifer Gratz and Barbara Grutter were both rejected—Gratz from the undergraduate program and Grutter from the law school. With the legal assistance from the Center for Individual Rights, a conservative legal group that actively sought students looking to fight affirmative action, both women sued the university. As we saw earlier, the Supreme Court struck down the undergraduate and upheld the law school admissions policy.

In the case of the law school, Justice Sandra Day O'Connor expressed the belief that the Constitution required affirmative action programs to be temporary solutions only and the hope that by 2028 they would no longer be necessary. Opponents of affirmative action, such as Ward Connerly, chair of the American Civil Rights Institute, hope that such plans will not last that long. Connerly has launched state-level initiatives in Arizona, California, Colorado, Michigan, Nebraska, and Washington to let voters decide whether such programs should be allowed. Voters rejected affirmative action in all those states except Colorado.

California voters passed their amendment in 1996. Since that time, and despite fears that the initiative would reduce the number of underrepresented minorities in colleges and universities, Latino students have become the largest ethnic group at the University of California.[11]

In 2014, the Michigan case reached the Supreme Court, which declared in *Schuette v. Coalition to Defend Affirmative Action* that the people of Michigan had the right to pass a constitutional amendment via initiative that prohibits the state's public universities from using race as a factor in admissions or public employment.[12]

Construct Your Own Policy

1. Construct an employment policy that maintains equal opportunity but does not explicitly consider race, ethnicity, or gender.
2. Revise the judicial nomination and confirmation process to reduce the emphasis on ideology as a legitimate consideration.

is, have gone through their last appeal at the state level, can file a writ of *habeas corpus* with a U.S. District Court, which then allows the court to determine whether one or more of the defendant's federal legal rights have been violated. Second, any parties who have exhausted their state appeals can file a request for review, known as a **petition for a writ of *certiorari***, directly with the Supreme Court.

The District Courts

The Judiciary Act of 1789 established thirteen district courts for the thirteen states. Today, there are ninety-four districts. Many states have more than one district, but no district covers more than one state. Districts that cover only part of a state receive geographical names, such as the Northern District of Illinois. Altogether there are 667 district judgeships. Many districts have only one judge, but the Southern District of New York has twenty-eight, and the Central District of California has twenty-seven. Nevertheless, with rare exceptions, district judges oversee trials alone, not in panels.

Trials in the district courts are either criminal or civil. In civil suits, plaintiffs (the parties bringing the suit) often request monetary damages to compensate for harm done to them, such as by a broken contract or a defective product. When rights are alleged to have been violated, they may ask that the practice be stopped. Litigants filed more than 278,000 civil suits in the district courts in 2012, and the federal government initiated nearly 71,000 criminal prosecutions.[13]

When Gratz and Grutter sued the University of Michigan over its admissions policies, the first stop for each was the U.S. District Court. Both had standing to sue, as their rejections by the university were real injuries, and because they claimed that their rights to equal protection under the Fourteenth Amendment had been violated, their cases raised a constitutional issue and entered the federal court system. Gratz and Grutter sought not only their own admission to the University of Michigan but also an end to the university's use of race in admissions decisions. The district courts allowed both suits to move forward as **class action lawsuits**, meaning that Gratz and Grutter were suing not only on behalf of themselves but also on behalf of all people denied admission at Michigan on account of their race. Class action lawsuits can open the gateways of access to groups of citizens in the same circumstances, thus broadening the impact over the possible result of an individual lawsuit.

Civil Procedure. The overwhelming majority of lawsuits filed in federal court settle out of court with a negotiated agreement between the plaintiff and the defendant. In 2012, the district courts terminated nearly three thousand civil cases.[14] Litigants settled nearly 99 percent of these cases before going to trial. Of the few cases that went to trial, nearly two-thirds were decided by juries. The other third were bench (nonjury) trials, as the *Gratz and Grutter* cases were.

After a case is assigned to a judge, the next step in a civil suit is discovery. Discovery grants each side access to information relevant to its suit held by the other side. Crucial to the *Gratz* and *Grutter* suits were University of Michigan documents showing differential admission rates for whites and minorities who had similar grades and standardized test scores. During discovery, the attorneys for each side can also question witnesses for the other side in a process known as deposition. Following discovery, litigants file briefs with the court, laying out their arguments.

To Know	To Test Yourself	To Participate

▶ **Explain how state and lower federal courts operate**

State cases that contain issues of federal law or that contain particular types of parties can be appealed from state courts to the federal courts. District courts conduct civil and criminal trials, while courts of appeals hear appeals from district courts. Cases from the courts of appeals can be appealed to the Supreme Court.	• Explain how state court cases can end up in federal court. • Give an overview of the responsibilities and procedures in district courts. • Give an overview of the responsibilities and procedures in courts of appeals.	• Understand what would happen if federal courts could not review state court decisions on questions of federal law. • Evaluate whether average citizens are able to use the gateway of filing lawsuits.

▶ **Review the procedures the Supreme Court uses**

Supreme Court decisions are made by a majority, though the justices sometimes write concurring opinions that agree with the majority but give a different rationale. The minority who disagree may write dissents.	• Explain how cases reach the Supreme Court. • Describe the process of oral argument.	• Read and critique a recent majority opinion (http://supreme.lp.findlaw.com).

▶ **Identify factors that influence judicial rulings and the impact those decisions have**

Judicial policy making can be explained by both legal and extralegal approaches, with legal approaches having more sway at lower levels and extralegal approaches at higher levels, where judicial activism can be problematic for a democracy. Although the Supreme Court is not directly accountable to the public, it is to some degree responsive to public opinion.	• Survey how the Court reaches and issues decisions. • Discuss the impact Court decisions do and do not have.	• Evaluate why and whether Supreme Court decisions might have limited impacts. • Identify the gateways that create responsiveness of Supreme Court decisions to public opinion.

▶ **Discuss how federal judges get selected**

The president appoints federal judges with the advice and consent of the Senate. The higher the court, the more likely the Senate is to scrutinize nominees and refuse consent on the basis of nominees' ideology and/or qualifications. The Supreme Court, which once contained only white male Protestants, has increasingly diversified with respect to religion, race, and gender. This more-equal access to the Supreme Court may also make the Court more responsive to an increasingly diverse nation.	• Explain senatorial courtesy. • Describe issues in nominations to courts of appeals. • Discuss the ways in which partisanship and ideology influence Supreme Court nominations.	• Consider the merits of diversity in the courts.

▶ **Outline how the Supreme Court has expanded and contracted national powers**

Through the Court's history, its interpretations have expanded, then contracted, and once again expanded national powers, especially with regard to economic regulation. After a long and slow start, the Court has also moved, fairly consistently, toward greater protections of equality.	• Describe the ways in which the Marshall Court expanded national power. • Explain how the Supreme Court acted to limit equality between the 1830s and 1930s. • Discuss what might have led the Supreme Court to accept greater national authority starting in 1937.	• Understand why it is important for courts to protect minority rights.

"Get involved. You have no idea what you can accomplish until you become unstoppable.... If I had a nickel for every time someone said we would fail, I would never have to work again."

KATE HANNI
College of the Redwoods, Eureka, California

TRUSTEE MEMORIAL PLAZA

14

Economic, Domestic, and Foreign Policy

When Kate Hanni was a student at the College of the Redwoods, she was a theater arts major who dreamed of being a rock star—"to be in front of a gazillion people with their lighters on," as she put it. Today she is a different kind of rock star, founder and first president of Flyersrights.org, a coalition group that claimed a major victory when the Department of Transportation ruled that domestic airlines must allow passengers who have been stuck on a stranded plane for more than three hours to get off the plane. Since that rule was passed, it has been extended to international airlines that operate in the United States for delays lasting more than four hours. Flyersrights has become a powerful gateway organization for advocacy on behalf of travelers seeking safe and well-regulated modes of transportation.

Hanni had not planned to be a political activist. For years, she was a successful real estate broker in Napa County, California, who enjoyed spending time with family and friends and still sang on occasion with her rock band, the Toasted Heads. But in 2006, her life took a new direction. With 134 other passengers, she and her family were stranded for nine hours and sixteen minutes in a jet parked at the airport in Austin, Texas. There was little food or water, and the lavatories reeked. "People got so angry they were talking about busting through the emergency exits," Hanni recalled. "I was fuming. It was imprisonment."

When Hanni got home, she drafted an online petition demanding legal rights for airline passengers. The following month, when an ice storm at New York's Kennedy International Airport stranded thousands of passengers in planes for up to eleven hours, her cause took off. She gave up her real estate business, and she and her husband took out a line of credit on their house to build a website. Soon her petition had eighteen thousand signatures, and people in her e-mail network wrote to Congress and the Federal Aviation Administration and posted videos of the stranded flight experience on YouTube. Hanni got media attention, promoting passengers' rights in radio and TV interviews. Her coalition gained support from airline labor unions, air traffic controller unions, and consumer groups. She talked her congressman, Mike Thompson (D-CA), into introducing legislation. The following year, Hanni staged a "strand-in" near the Capitol in Washington D.C., with a tent outfitted to resemble the interior of an airplane and invitations to members of Congress to see what it felt like to be trapped. As the movement's theme song, she got the Toasted Heads to rewrite the Animals' 1965 hit, "We've Gotta Get Out of This Place."

Need to Know

14.1 Outline the steps in the policy-making process

14.2 Identify the key federal programs that comprise domestic policy

14.3 Explain how the federal government intervenes in the economy

14.4 Evaluate the effectiveness of U.S. foreign policy

▶ **WATCH & LEARN** MindTap for American Government
Watch brief "What Do You Know?" videos
summarizing Domestic Policy and Foreign Policy and National Security.

In response, the airlines fought back by claiming that conditions were not as bad as reported. The Air Transport Association argued that deplaning would only cause delays and cancellations and might compromise passenger safety. A version of Congressman Thompson's bill passed the House, but a similar bill introduced by Barbara Boxer (D-CA) did not pass the Senate. New York and California passed airline passenger laws, but a federal court of appeals struck down New York's law on the grounds that only the federal government has the authority to regulate airline service.

In the end, that's exactly what happened. On December 21, 2009, Transportation Secretary Ray LaHood announced new airline regulations. After two hours on the tarmac, airlines must give passengers food and water. After three hours, they must let them off or face stiff fines—$27,500 per passenger. In an e-mail to supporters, an elated Hanni called the regulations "an early Christmas present" but reminded them that "we're not done yet!" Five years later, in 2014, Hanni and the organization she founded is still active; citing fees for checked bags and chronically delayed or canceled flights, she continues to advocate for passengers' rights and push for formal legislation to more strictly oversee airline travel.[1]

The story of Kate Hanni is remarkable because she, as an ordinary citizen, demanded that the federal government live up to its responsibility of ensuring the safe travel of passengers. She took matters into her own hands and used the gateways of citizen influence on policy making to draw attention to the issue. Her activism changed federal policy on transportation.

Through this book, we have looked at examples of activists and how they and the groups they joined have transformed the policies that affect each of our daily lives. We have examined the minimum wage, fracking, the assault weapons ban, the use of drones, the death penalty, voter ID laws, and unemployment laws—just to name a few. In this chapter, we will bring it all together, giving these issues a wider context and providing an in-depth description of the policy-making process in the domestic, economic, and foreign arenas and examples of the process in each of these arenas. We will look at the formal process of policy making, the ways in which the government interacts with the private sector in implementing domestic and economic policy, and the effectiveness of foreign policy in promoting U.S. values and interests around the globe. A fundamental question for students of American government is whether public policy making serves as a gate or a gateway to effectively serving the peoples' interest.

14.1 Public Policy under a Constitutional System

> Outline the steps in the policy-making process

public policy:
Intentional actions of government designed to achieve a goal.

Public policy can be described as the set of laws and regulations that govern American political and social life to meet a specific need and accomplish a goal. It is in the arena of public policy—in determining who gets what, when, and how, and with what result—that we can see whether the constitutional system created by Madison and the Framers really works. Can the people pursue policies that advance their own interests? Can the people's representatives, while pursuing policies that advance their constituents' interests, produce a nation that looks out for the welfare of all the people?

With a government deliberately designed to represent competing interests, public policy has tended to cycle. One argument gains favor, driving policy in one direction. But new problems arise, calling for a redirection of policy. In the early years of the American republic, for example, Congress raised tariffs (taxes on imports) to help support new manufacturing enterprises, which could then undersell foreign competitors. But when agricultural interests complained about having to pay high prices for foreign goods, Congress lowered tariffs. Banking policies were similarly adjusted, sometimes to favor debtors and other times to favor creditors.

The Process of Policy Making

The development of good public policy is always difficult and complex. A policy, for example, of providing tax benefits to homeowners to spur home ownership sounds like a good thing, as would policies that make it easier for people to obtain mortgages. It would help homeowners, support the home construction industry, and create jobs, building more stable communities. But what sounds simple rarely is that simple because there are usually unintended consequences. A policy of tax benefits for homeowners can also encourage sprawl that turns agricultural land into suburbs, thus decreasing crop yields and altering food production, while leaving cities with vacant housing and declining tax bases. Making it easier for people to obtain mortgages means more people default on their loans when the economy goes into a downturn, as happened during the most recent recession (2007–2009). Subsequently, government responds to these new problems by developing additional policies to revitalize agriculture, urban infrastructure, and the banking system.

With so many competing interests and the potential for unintended negative consequences, government seeks to pursue policy making that maximizes benefits and minimizes costs. This is not easy and often does not happen. Political scientists—scholars who study politics and the processes of government—have categorized the steps in policy making to make the process more understandable.

The main stakeholders in the policy process include members of Congress, the president, the executive branch agency that deals with the issue, the courts, political parties, interest groups, and interested citizens. These stakeholders attempt to formulate a policy that will address the problem (see Figure 14.1).

Although presidents and members of Congress formally appear to be in command of the federal policy-making process, they face a complex set of gates standing in the way of implementing policy. In Chapter 3, Federalism, we explained how governmental powers are shared among the federal, state, and local governments. Frequently, policy changes at the federal level require cooperation from these other governmental units, and that can be a complicated task across all fifty states. Encouraging all the states to adopt the same policy is not always possible, at which point, the federal government must step in and implement the policy itself. In this chapter, we discuss economic, domestic, and foreign policy and show how public policy is an outcome of all the actions taken by a wide array of stakeholders at the federal, state, and local levels.

The first step is **problem identification** of the problem. For example, constituents might complain to members of Congress that the cost of college is too high. The second step is for the issue of the cost of higher education to make it to the **policy agenda** of policy makers.[2] Of all the problems that government might be able to solve, only a small fraction can receive attention at any one time. Those that get on the policy agenda get the attention of Congress, the president, the executive branch agency that deals with the issue, the courts, political parties, interest groups, and interested citizens. These stakeholders attempt **policy formulation** that will solve the problem (see Figure 14.1). In the example of the

★ **problem identification:** *The first step in the policy-making process, in which a problem in politics, the economy, or society is recognized as warranting government action.*

★ **policy agenda:** *The second step in the policy-making process, in which a problem that has been identified gets the attention of policy makers.*

★ **policy formulation:** *The third step in the policy-making process, in which those with a stake in the policy area propose and develop solutions to the problem.*

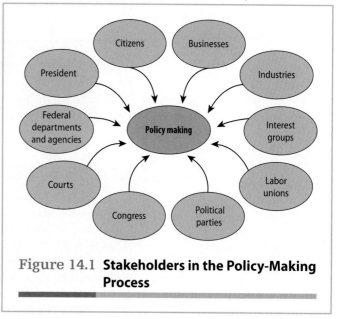

Figure 14.1 Stakeholders in the Policy-Making Process

© CENGAGE LEARNING

high cost of college, the stakeholder network considered three proposals: direct federal loans to college students; promoting private loans by paying banks the interest on student loans while the student is in college; and guaranteeing the loans if students are unable to repay them.

In a fourth step, **policy enactment**, the legislative branch passes a law that enacts one or more of those proposals, as Congress did with student loans in 2010. Following passage, the legislature grants the executive branch **policy implementation** authority over the program. In this case, the Department of Education was given the authority to direct the student loan program. After a few years, Congress may engage in **policy evaluation** of the program. Following this policy evaluation, the cycle of policy making might begin again with new legislation to adjust the program to make it work better (see Figure 14.2).

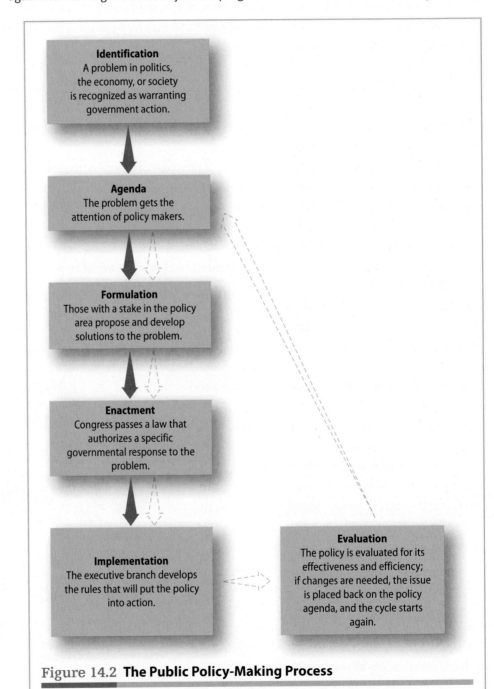

Identification
A problem in politics, the economy, or society is recognized as warranting government action.

Agenda
The problem gets the attention of policy makers.

Formulation
Those with a stake in the policy area propose and develop solutions to the problem.

Enactment
Congress passes a law that authorizes a specific governmental response to the problem.

Implementation
The executive branch develops the rules that will put the policy into action.

Evaluation
The policy is evaluated for its effectiveness and efficiency; if changes are needed, the issue is placed back on the policy agenda, and the cycle starts again.

Figure 14.2 The Public Policy-Making Process

© CENGAGE LEARNING

In this chapter, we will focus on domestic, economic, and foreign policies. In each of these domains, the stakeholders mentioned earlier wield influence in different ways, depending on the characteristics of the issue being considered. In most cases, the origins of an implemented policy start with Congress when it passes a law, and the president approves it (discussed in more depth in Chapter 10, Congress). But in other cases, the president can use his executive regulatory power to effect change without a new congressional law, or Congress can decide to change funding allocations for specific programs in order to slow down or prevent their implementation. In the next section, we will examine more closely this second method of policy implementation.

The Regulatory Process

For laws to be implemented, there must be rules to instruct policy makers, government officials, organizations, and businesses. The formal responsibility for policy implementation falls to the bureaucracy in what is commonly called the **regulatory process** (see Figure 14.3). The current framework for the regulatory process has its foundation in the Administrative Procedures Act (APA) that Congress passed in 1946 to provide a consistent blueprint for all federal agencies in the issuing of regulations.

The federal government typically issues regulations when a law is first enacted and when a new circumstance or policy need arises that requires updates to the way the law is implemented. One such circumstance might be a change in the political control of the White House. Frequently, an incoming president of a different party issues new regulations to reverse the previous administration's policies. More commonly, a new president instructs federal agencies and the Office of Management and Budget (OMB), which oversees budgetary and regulatory issues, to revise existing regulations to better reflect his policy preferences. For example, in April 2014, President Obama issued an executive order requiring private contractors doing business with the federal government to pay the men and women they employ equal wages for equal work.

The bureaucracy produces these regulations by working within a process that begins with identifying the agency that has jurisdiction. The agency in charge will then offer preliminary **regulations** during which the political appointees of the agency will determine whether they are in line with the president's policy views. Although the bureaucracy is theoretically supposed to be insulated from direct political pressure, the reality is that the president's policy preferences are considered during this process.

When there is some agreement on the content of the preliminary regulations, they are submitted to the Office of Information and Regulatory Affairs (OIRA) within the OMB for approval to be printed in the ***Federal Register***, the official published record of all executive branch rules, regulations, and orders. As noted previously, the OMB must review all regulations before they take effect. When preliminary regulations appear in the *Federal Register*, a period for public comment is defined (typically outlined in the originating legislation) ranging from thirty to ninety days. During this period, ordinary citizens, interest groups, and relevant industries and businesses can submit their opinions to the agency about the regulations. In

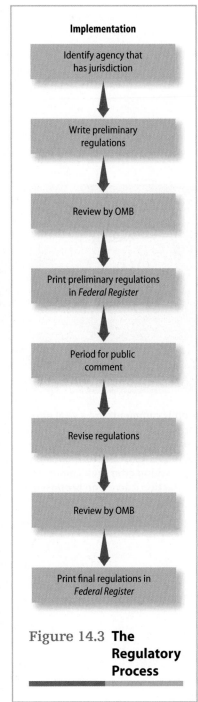

Implementation

Identify agency that has jurisdiction

Write preliminary regulations

Review by OMB

Print preliminary regulations in *Federal Register*

Period for public comment

Revise regulations

Review by OMB

Print final regulations in *Federal Register*

Figure 14.3 **The Regulatory Process**

© CENGAGE LEARNING

Federal Register:
Official published record of all executive branch rules, regulations, and orders.

→ KEY QUESTIONS:
What role can citizens play in the regulatory process?

addition, the agency or its local affiliate can hold public hearings in locations across the country to solicit opinions on the regulations.

Based on all the responses it receives, the responsible agency revises the preliminary draft regulations and issues final regulations. These are once again sent to the OMB and then are published in the *Federal Register* thirty days in advance of taking formal effect. Once the final regulations are issued, the program is officially ready to be implemented. A current example of this process concerns the disposal of coal ash from coal-burning power plants. After a major coal ash spill into local rivers and streams in Tennessee, environmental groups pushed the EPA to issue new regulations outlining the requirements for safe coal ash disposal. The preliminary regulations were issued in October 2009, but after the public comment period was up, the EPA still had not issued final regulations. In response, environmental groups, led by Earthjustice, sued the EPA, and a judge forced the agency to agree to issue the final regulations by December 19, 2014. Only a few days later, a second major coal ash spill occurred in North Carolina, adding more pressure for the EPA to act in a timely manner.[3] Such extreme delays in issuing final regulations are not typical, but this example shows how the regulatory process itself can act as a gate to effective oversight of industry and environmental protection.

Public comments are a vital part of the regulatory process because they are a gateway by which citizens can communicate their opinions about the impact of policy to regulators. Here residents of communities affected by fracking offer their comments to the Environmental Protection Agency on proposed regulations.

Blocking Implementation

Even after final regulations are issued, groups can challenge the legality of them in the federal court system. For example, in 2014, the Supreme Court considered a challenge to regulations issued requiring the inclusion of contraception in employer-sponsored health insurance plans under the Affordable Care Act. In the case, *Hobby Lobby v. Kathleen Sebelius, Secretary of Health and Human Services et al.*, the Court ruled in favor of Hobby Lobby being able to opt out of the guidelines in the final regulations for some forms of contraception (see Chapter 4, Civil Liberties, for more on this case). In addition to court action, the House or Senate can pass appropriations bills with language that prevents an agency or department from using federal money to implement the regulations. However, the president typically threatens to veto the bill if this type of language is included because it undermines his policy priorities and, more broadly, his executive power to implement laws. As a result, legislative leaders usually remove such language in the final version of appropriations bill sent to the president (see Chapter 10 for more on the appropriations process).

State Governments and Public Policy

As we noted in Chapter 3, it is important to understand how the federal government interacts with state government in implementing policy and, at the same time, how states interact with each other. In this section, we will take a closer look at how states can influence each other through processes referred to as policy diffusion and the race to the bottom.

Policy Diffusion. In a 1932 opinion, Supreme Court Justice Louis Brandeis wrote, "It is one of the happy incidents of the federal system that a single courageous State may, if its citizens choose, serve as a laboratory; and try novel social and economic experiments without risk to the rest of the country."[4] The main benefit of states serving as laboratories of change is that other states can learn about successful programs and copy them or learn what not to do if an experimental program fails. This takes place through a process known as **policy diffusion**, and it typically starts with states that border one another. Examples are numerous, including the Children's Health Insurance Program,[5] regulation of air pollution,[6] school choice plans (allowing students to choose which school in a district to attend),[7] health care reform,[8] and Indian gambling casinos.[9] States learn not only from neighboring states but also from their local governments. Such was the case with antismoking ordinances, which cities and towns successfully adopted before states did.[10]

The federal system of government requires cooperation between the national and state governments, and federal policy is frequently implemented by state governments. Here governors meet to discuss proposed changes to federal educational guidelines during a meeting of the National Governors Association.

AP IMAGES/CLIFF OWEN

policy diffusion: *Process by which policy ideas and programs initiated by one state spread to other states.*

The Race to the Bottom. If diffusion is the good side of policy making in a federal system, the race to the bottom can, depending on one's point of view, potentially involve negative consequences. A race to the bottom exists when states compete against each other to reduce taxes, environmental protections, or welfare benefits in order to create incentives for businesses to come to the state or disincentives for poor people to come. For example, lower tax rates draw people to a state, yet to keep people there, the state cannot raise taxes even when the public might desire more spending.[11] When states compete economically with one another, if one state decreases environmental enforcement, a neighboring state may be forced to do so as well.[12] In terms of welfare benefits, individuals seeking benefits move to the most generous states. This situation led states to establish residency requirements for welfare until the Supreme Court prohibited them.[13] Consequently, states that want to increase welfare benefits for their own citizens hesitate to do so unless neighboring states also do so, lest they attract an overload of recipients from those other states.[14] Alternatively, the Obama administration established a "Race to the Top" (RTTP) in education, whereby states that implement education reforms, such as increasing the number of charter schools, receive more federal aid. This action coincides with increasing federal involvement in education over the past fifty years.

→ KEY QUESTIONS:
How does policy diffusion serve as an example of policy making in a federal system?

Checkpoint

CAN YOU:
- Identify the steps in the policy-making process
- Summarize the stages of the regulatory process
- Describe how regulations can be blocked from taking effect
- Explain what is meant by policy diffusion

14.2 Domestic Policy

> Identify the key federal programs that comprise domestic policy

The term domestic policy covers a wide range of policy areas in which the government plays a role, at the federal, state, and local levels, in the lives of average citizens. Table 14.1 lists the major federal programs generally considered under the category of domestic policy, when they were originally enacted into law at the federal level, and a brief description of what they do.

Throughout the book, we have covered major issues in domestic policy, including public education (see Chapter 3), affirmative action (Chapter 13, The Judiciary), and workplace equality (Chapter 5, Civil Rights). In this chapter, we explore three major areas of domestic policy that are sparking intense debate today: entitlement programs, income security, and health care; immigration; and energy and environmental policy. In each of these issue areas, we will provide an overview of public policy and then analyze an example of how a specific policy has been crafted and implemented (see Public Policy features).

Table 14.1 **Major Federal Programs**

Names	Year	Description
Social Security	1935	Old age retirement insurance program that pays a monthly amount to retired workers
Unemployment Insurance	1935	Temporary replacement income for job loss
Social Security Disability Insurance	1935	Payments to individual who can no longer work due to disability
Supplemental Security Income	1972	Subsidy for low-income individuals who are over 65, or blind, or disabled
Medicare	1965	Health care insurance for elderly and disabled
Medicaid	1965	Health care insurance for low-income individuals
Temporary Aid to Needy Families	1935	Subsidy for low-income individuals with children; originally known as Aid to Families with Dependent Children but replaced in 1996 by TANF
Food Stamps	1964	Subsidy for low-income individuals for food purchase
Public Housing Assistance	1937	Subsidy for low-income individuals for housing
Immigration and Nationality Act	1952	Laws governing documented entry and citizenship into the United States
Clean Air Act	1963/1970	Laws requiring minimum standards for air quality; amended in 1970 to create the Environmental Protection Agency
Clean Water Act	1972	Regulations for the discharge of potential contaminants into water sources
Affordable Care Act	2010	Mandate requiring every individual to have health insurance coverage and providing access and subsidies through exchanges and expanded Medicaid

© CENGAGE LEARNING

Entitlement Programs, Income Security, and Health Care Overview

During the twentieth century, the federal government enacted laws to create a social safety net to provide income stability for the elderly and disabled, and assistance with food, health care, and housing for the poor. **Social Security** is one of the largest and likely best-known federal domestic policy programs; it is essentially a federally guaranteed pension program funded by taxes imposed by employers and workers. Social Security was created in 1935 as part of the set of policy programs known as the New Deal proposed by President Franklin Delano Roosevelt (1933–45) (see Chapter 11, The Presidency). The New Deal represented a major change in the relationship between the federal government and individuals by establishing a set of programs that would guarantee payment to an individual if he or she met certain criteria, for example, age, children, low income, or disability. This type of program is commonly known as an **entitlement program**, which means that an individual is "entitled" to receive the benefit as long as they qualify under these criteria. The passage of the Social Security Act marked the beginning of the transformation of the role of the federal and state governments in providing a social safety net for individuals in need of financial assistance as well as aid to secure food, housing, and health care.

Social Security itself is a mandatory retirement account for all workers that is funded by taxes paid by both employers and workers. The amount of Social Security retired workers receive is calculated based on the amount of time they worked while paying into the program; when they retire, they receive a monthly payment direct from the federal government. The drive to provide this kind of income security for individuals was in large part a response to the dire effects of the Great Depression, which left millions of people without jobs and income. At the same time, the federal government created Unemployment Insurance, which is run by state governments according to federal guidelines; it provides short-term payments to workers who lose their jobs and is funded by taxes imposed on employers.

In addition to these programs, which are targeted at the working population, the Social Security Act of 1935 and its subsequent legislative expansions have created several other programs that are designed to help individuals who need assistance supporting themselves or their families. Two of these, Social Security Disability Insurance and Supplemental Security Insurance, are designed to help those who are no longer able to work, or who have a disability that prevents them from working full time. Another major program is Temporary Aid to Needy Families (TANF), which is a program to provide payments to women in poverty with children (it was originally called Aid to Families with Dependent Children). The majority of this program's costs are funded by the federal government through a single amount of funding per year, known as a block grant, although states are expected to contribute a minimum amount of money to help administer the program.

In addition to income security, as part of the New Deal, the federal government also put in place sets of programs to help individuals get mortgages to buy housing through the Fannie Mae Corporation and to build affordable housing by offering subsidies to developers. These programs were aimed at helping people buy houses because that was believed to help ensure financial stability and help the economy through new housing construction.[15]

In the 1960s, under President Johnson's Great Society initiative (see Chapter 11), these types of income security programs were expanded to include health care, food security, and expanded

Social Security: *Federal pension program that makes a monthly payment to retired elderly workers and disabled persons.*

entitlement programs: *Federal programs, such as Social Security, Medicare, or Medicaid, that pay out benefits to individuals based on a specified set of eligibility criteria.*

COMPARE WITH YOUR PEERS
MindTap™ **for American Government**

Access the Economic Policy Forum: Polling Activity—Reforming Social Security.

→ **KEY QUESTIONS:**
What policy goals do entitlement programs address?

AP IMAGES/J. SCOTT APPLEWHITE

Senior citizens who are recipients of Social Security and Medicare are very vocal in seeking to protect their benefits. Here a group of elderly activists traveled to Capitol Hill in Washington D.C. to oppose proposed cuts to those programs.

Medicare: *Federal health insurance program for the elderly and disabled.*

Medicaid: *Shared Federal and state health insurance program for low-income persons.*

→ KEY QUESTIONS:
Why has the implementation of the Affordable Care Act been so complicated?

housing assistance. In terms of health care, **Medicare** was created as a federal program, funded through a payroll tax that provided health insurance to people over the age of 65. **Medicaid** was created as a shared program between the federal and state governments, funded through general taxation, to provide health care coverage for low-income people.[16] The Food Stamp Program, today known as Supplemental Nutritional Assistance Program, was designed to provide money to low-income families to purchase food and household items and is fully funded through general taxation. Lastly, federal housing assistance was expanded under the Section 8 program to provide payments to housing developers to cover the rental costs of housing for low-income individuals who typically must pay a minimum of $25 or 30 percent of their income toward rent under the program.[17]

It has been nearly eighty years since the passage of the Social Security Act, and the federal government has expanded many of the programs the Act first established, but not without controversy and opposition. When the Social Security Act was first passed, opponents claimed it was an overreach of federal power to take money from individuals only to give it back to them in their later years. Moreover, establishing other anti-poverty subsidies that would be paid directly to lower income individuals might create a dependency on that payment that would discourage them from securing independent financial security. Lastly, opponents of expanding the role of the federally guaranteed safety net have argued that as the population expands and lives longer, the cost of these programs is unsustainable. Currently, the net cost of entitlement programs is $1.22 trillion, which is nearly 34 percent of the federal budget for fiscal year 2014.

The federal bureaucracy, specifically the Department of Health and Human Services (HHS), is largely responsible for administering these programs in conjunction with state and local government. We provide a brief overview of HHS in Chapter 12 (The Bureaucracy), but here we embed it in the larger context of the expansion of the federal role in health care over the past decade. The most recent such expansion came with the Affordable Care Act, which was enacted in 2010 and requires all individuals to purchase health insurance, either on their own, or if they are low-income, with subsidies from the federal government.

The American health care system includes private and public health care insurance components. Most Americans receive health insurance through their employment or purchase it independently from private insurance companies; as noted previously, federal programs are available to help cover the costs of health insurance. At the federal level, the Department of Health and Human Services is responsible for overseeing these programs, as well as implementing new ones. Each state also has a department of health, as do many cities and counties, and, importantly, states also have the power to regulate insurance providers who provide coverage there.

The process by which the Affordable Care Act (ACA), otherwise known as Obamacare, moved from proposal to bill to law was long and winding, as lawmaking always is, and it was especially complicated because of the fragmented nature of America's health care system, party politics and partisanship, and the heightened political rhetoric that surrounded the effort (see Chapter 10 for details). Ultimately, the Democrats used their majority party power in the House and Senate to pass the law, with no Republican support.

The primary impetus of the law was to provide access to health insurance to the nearly 10 percent of Americans who did not have it. They did not have health insurance for a range of reasons: their employer did not offer it; they were self-employed and could not afford to purchase it; they were unemployed but not poor or old enough to qualify for a government program; or they were deemed ineligible by private insurance companies because they had health conditions that made them high risk and expensive to cover.[18]

The ACA established a number of new programs, the most notable of which extended access to health insurance coverage to uninsured citizens and legal immigrants through an expansion of Medicaid eligibility and the provision of federal subsidies to workers to purchase private health insurance through health insurance exchanges that would be set up by states, or if the states refused, by the federal government directly.[19] The act provided for increased regulation of the medical services covered by private health insurance companies, mandated that individuals carry health insurance, required that young adults under the age of 26 be able to stay on a parent's insurance policy, and banned the denial of health insurance or an increase in premiums based on a preexisting condition. The act also increased payment levels to doctors who participate in the Medicaid program and helped senior citizens by closing a loophole in Medicare coverage for prescription drugs. The ACA is an important example of how the domestic policy process works, from the passage of the law to its implementation.

The Affordable Care Act (ACA)

The implementation of the act came in stages, with some of the regulations issued very soon after the bill passed, and others taking much longer to finalize. Part of the delay was attributable to a key lawsuit filed against the bill claiming that provisions included in it were unconstitutional. Twenty-six state attorneys general signed onto a lawsuit challenging the constitutionality of the federal health insurance mandate included in the law. The lawsuit made its way to the Supreme Court, which ruled in June 2012 and upheld the mandate (see Chapter 10).

The Court case cleared the way for implementation of the insurance provision through health care exchanges under ACA. However, only fourteen states set up their own health insurance exchanges; the federal government established exchanges in the remaining thirty-six states. The federal government established a six-month sign-up period to obtain coverage through the federal website, www.Healthcare.gov, or state websites that linked to the federal site. The federal website opened for business on October 1, 2013, but there were major problems from the start. The website crashed frequently, and concerns were raised about the security of the information people entered into the website. Ultimately, the problems with the website were resolved, but in the meantime, consumers had become wary of both the website and the program. Opponents of the program kept up a relentless attack both at the state and federal levels, and the negative communications were thought to have depressed enrollment numbers.[20] At the same time, and despite President Obama's oft-repeated declaration, "If you like your health insurance, you can keep it," health insurance policies for millions of Americans were canceled by insurance companies because these policies did not meet the minimum standards of coverage mandated by the ACA. In response to the public outcry over these cancelations, the Obama administration extended the timeline for switching to more comprehensive policies.

The ACA also encourages states to expand Medicaid to cover individuals at or below 138 percent of poverty because the federal government will pay the extra costs of the expansion for up to three years. As of September 2014, twenty-seven states agreed to the Medicaid expansion, with twenty-one refusing it, and two states still considering it.[21] Additionally, individuals who make between 100 percent and 400 percent of poverty level are eligible for subsidies where the federal government will help pay for part of the cost of their premiums.[22] Traditionally underserved communities, such as Latinos, are estimated to comprise nearly 25 percent of those eligible for coverage under ACA, and the Obama administration made it a point to engage in targeted outreach to encourage enrollment among them.[23]

In terms of overall costs of health insurance premiums under the ACA, Figure 14.4 shows how the costs can vary across states, income levels, and the extent of available federal

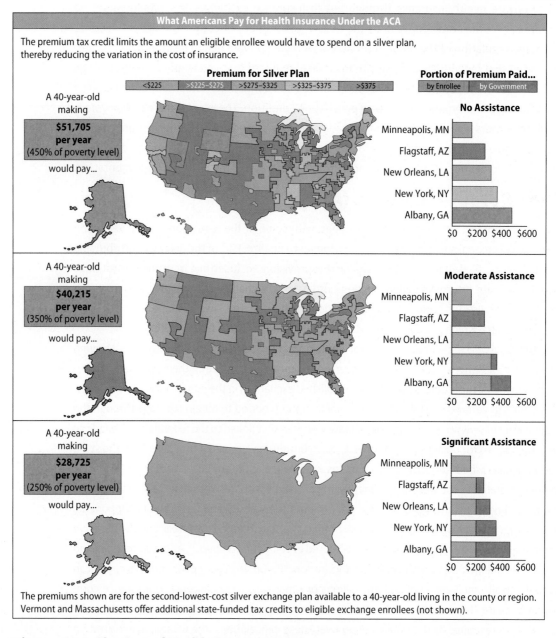

Figure 14.4 The Cost of Health Care Insurance

The Affordable Care Act expanded the opportunity for individuals who were previously unable to purchase health care insurance to buy it through state or federal run insurance exchanges. Figure 14.4 shows the estimated costs of health care insurance to individuals depending on personal circumstances.

Source: Kaiser Family Foundation, "Visualizing Health Policy: What Americans Pay for Health Insurance under the ACA," March 19, 2014, accessed March 19, 2014, http://kff.org/infographic/visualizing-health-policy-what-americans-pay-for-health-insurance-under-the-aca/.

subsidies.[24] The dynamics surrounding the ACA reflect the complexity of implementing health care policy for millions of Americans across states. At the end of the first enrollment period, as we noted in Chapter 8, Political Parties, more than 8 million people had signed up to get health insurance through the ACA, a number which was above the Obama administration's target. Despite the rollout pitfalls and intense opposition, the program was up and running in 2014. However, Secretary of Health and Human Services Kathleen Sebelius ultimately took the blame for all the problems surrounding the initial implementation of the ACA; she resigned her post in April 2014 after serving for five and a half years and was replaced by Sylvia Mathews Burwell (our vignette subject in Chapter 11). The ACA brings up the larger question of whether major policy overhauls can be accomplished without bipartisan support in the American federalism structure because states are so vital in the implementation process. Without their full cooperation, it becomes much more difficult for a federal program to succeed.

Immigration Policy Overview

Another very important and often contentious issue in the public policy sphere is immigration policy—for both legal and unauthorized immigration. The Department of Homeland Security, the Department of Justice, and the Department of State share jurisdiction over immigration policy. Immigration has fueled U.S. population growth since the nation's founding, and the United States now comprises citizens with ancestries from many different foreign lands. In 2012, there were 13.3 million legal permanent residents in the United States—people born outside of the United States who have been granted legal status and reside in the United States.[25] The largest percentage of foreign-born people come from Latin America (mostly Mexico), followed by Asia and then Europe. Immigration laws serve simultaneously as gates regulating entry into the United States and as gateways to eventual citizenship. For those individuals who entered the United States without authorization and have put down roots, there is no current pathway to legal citizenship available. However, children who are born to unauthorized immigrants living in the United States are legal citizens because of the Fourteenth Amendment to the Constitution.

The Legal Immigration Process. The legal immigration process is jointly administered by the Department of State and the U.S. Citizenship and Immigration Services (USCIS), an agency of the Department of Homeland Security. Immigrants seeking to come to the United States apply for visas, which are granted by the Department of State; once they arrive, their journey toward citizenship is overseen by USCIS.[26]

To come to the United States with the intention of staying on a permanent basis, individuals can apply for a general immigration visa, a family relations visa, or an employment visa. The Immigration and Nationality Act of 1990 sets an annual limit of between 416,000 and 675,000 on these types of visas; in addition, 50,000 visas are set aside for people born in countries that have recently had the lowest numbers of immigrants to the United States.[27] In 2013, 459,751 individuals entered the United States as legal permanent residents.[28]

→ KEY QUESTIONS:
How do immigrants become naturalized citizens?

To become a naturalized citizen, an immigrant must first apply to be a legal permanent resident (LPR) of the United States, a step known as getting a green card, which is the permanent resident card issued to those who are eligible. (The green card is no longer green, but the name has remained.) To get a green card, an individual must secure a sponsor who will attest that the individual has some means of financial support. The individual must also take a medical

Immigrants go through a long and complex process to become a naturalized U.S. citizen. In this photo, immigrants who have come from many different nations are sworn in as U.S. citizens.

exam and secure proof of employment if he or she intends to hold a job in the United States. This criterion can present a significant barrier to permanent residency: The federal government requires an individual seeking permanent residence to have talents or skills for a particular job that a current U.S. citizen could not provide. Marriage to an American citizen can also serve as a gateway to a green card, although the federal government has imposed stricter oversight on such marriages to counteract fraud. In 2013, the federal government also extended this gateway to apply to same-sex marriages, in response to the Supreme Court ruling in the DOMA case, which struck down discrimination against same-sex partners under federal law.[29] To become a fully naturalized U.S. citizen, a green card holder must reside in the United States continuously for at least five years; be able to read, write, and speak English; pass a citizenship test on the history and government of the United States (see Chapter 5); and pledge support for the United States.[30]

The Debate over Unauthorized Immigration.

In recent years, pressure to reform immigration laws to address the issue of unauthorized immigration has mounted because of the millions of individuals who have entered the United States outside the legal immigration process.[31] Proponents of reform argue that individuals who arrived illegally but have since established productive lives should be legally incorporated into society and have the opportunity to be full and active citizens, a position that opponents refer to as "amnesty." Opponents tend to counterargue that individuals who broke the law to enter the United States must be forced to return to their country of origin and apply for legal immigration status, and that without stronger border security, the hope of amnesty will just drive greater unauthorized immigration. The Republican and Democratic Parties are split along these lines as well; Democrats are stronger supporters of immigration reform that includes amnesty, while Republicans support a stronger border enforcement program with no amnesty.

The last major piece of legislation to deal specifically with unauthorized immigration was the 1986 Immigration Reform and Control Act, which passed with bipartisan support and was signed into law by President Ronald Reagan (1981–89). The act granted amnesty, or forgiveness, to almost 2.8 million individuals who had entered the country without authorization and wished to stay as legal residents.[32] The 1986 reform bill did not stem the flow of unauthorized immigrants to the United States. In 2007, President George W. Bush (2001–2009), a Republican, and the Democratic-controlled Congress tried to produce a new immigration reform bill that would give unauthorized immigrants who were already in the United States an opportunity to become citizens but would, at the same time, discourage future unauthorized immigration. They failed to reach agreement.

> → KEY QUESTIONS:
> Why is immigration the responsibility of the federal government? Should that change—why or why not?

One reform bill that gained traction was the Development, Relief, and Education for Alien Minors proposal, known as the DREAM Act, which would allow children who entered the country illegally with their parents to get on a path to legal citizenship at age 16 if they have been in the country for five years, have graduated from high school, and have no criminal record.[33] In his first term, President Obama announced his support for the DREAM Act. By June 2012, Congress had not passed it, so, using his authority over border control and national security, President Obama ordered the Department of Homeland Security to stop the deportation of young people who met the criteria of the DREAM Act and allow them to apply for temporary work permits. Although it did not create a full path to citizenship, President Obama's action did partially implement the policy goals of the DREAM Act.[34]

Local and Federal Action on Unauthorized Immigration. States and localities, especially those along the border with Mexico, have tried to address unauthorized immigration in their own ways and in opposite policy directions. States with Republican-dominated legislatures have taken more punitive action than those controlled by Democrats. The most publicized effort took place in Arizona, where in April 2010 then-Governor Jan Brewer signed a law, S.B. 1070, that allowed police officers to ask about immigration status when they stopped individuals for any other police inquiry. Under the law, it was a crime to fail to show documentation establishing legal residence in the United States, and police officers could hold someone until their immigration status was verified.[35] Later that year, the U.S. Justice Department sued to get the law struck down in federal court on the basis that the state was infringing on the proper role of the federal government on immigration. The case made its way to the Supreme Court in 2012, and in *Arizona v. United States*, the court struck down the law because it assumed state powers over immigration that are granted to the federal government.

Not all state responses to unauthorized immigration have been punitive. For example, California, Texas, and New Mexico each adopted policies that allow unauthorized immigrants to receive private and public aid to attend state colleges and universities. Their justification is that it is better to educate residents who are in the United States so that they can contribute to society than it is to put up gates against their educational and economic advancements.

Ultimately it will be a major challenge for policy makers in both major political parties to construct a holistic immigration policy that is both fair and practical. Although there is general agreement within the core membership of each party, there are enough dissenting voices on how to best cope with illegal immigration that a clear policy position may not emerge. One factor that might affect the future of immigration reform is the growing number of Latinos in the United States who typically express strong opposition to punitive measures on unauthorized immigration. As the number of Latino voters grows, the United States may see more convergence on a single policy position by the parties in an effort to win this increasingly important voting bloc.

Energy, Environmental Policy, and Climate Change Overview

The public policy sphere of energy and environmental issues is ever expanding, from the domestic production of energy in the coal, oil, and natural gas sectors, to the protection of clean air and water, to the cleanups of toxic waste, to the global concern over climate change. Over the course of the twentieth century, these issues became ever more important with the expansion

supreme court cases

Arizona v. United States (2012)

QUESTION: Does the supremacy clause prevent the state of Arizona from supplementing federal immigration law?

ORAL ARGUMENT: April 25, 2012 (listen at http://www.oyez.org/cases/2010-2019/2011/2011_11_182)

DECISION: Decided June 25, 2012 (read at http://caselaw.lp.findlaw.com/scripts/getcase.pl?court=US&vol=000&invol=11-182)

OUTCOME: 5–3. The Supreme Court struck down three restrictions in the law.

As noted in Chapter 3, the national government has only those powers granted to it in the Constitution. While the remaining powers remain with the states, the supremacy clause declares that where federal and state laws conflict, federal law is supreme.

In response to a large influx of undocumented persons across the border with Mexico into Arizona, the Arizona State Legislature passed S.B. 1070. The United States believed that the law encroached on federal power to regulate immigration and sought to prohibit enforcement of its provisions. A federal district court found four provisions to be beyond the constitutional authority of Arizona to regulate: (1) creating a state-law crime for being unlawfully present in the United States, (2) creating a state-law crime for working or seeking work while not authorized to do so, (3) requiring state and local officers to verify the citizenship or alien status of anyone who was lawfully arrested or detained, and (4) authorizing warrantless arrests of aliens believed to be removable from the United States.

All eight of the justices hearing the case (Justice Kagan did not participate due to her prior work on issues related to the case while in the Justice Department) agreed that the provision requiring local police officers to check the immigration status of anyone lawfully arrested was constitutional. With Justices Scalia, Thomas, and Alito dissenting in part, a majority of the justices held that the rest of the provisions violated the supremacy clause given Congress's regulation of the subject.

The Court, in an opinion by Justice Kennedy, held that the Constitution's grant to Congress to "establish an uniform Rule of Naturalization," combined with Congress's extensive regulation of immigration deprives states of the authority to 1) make it illegal under state law for people to enter the United States without legal documentation, 2) make it illegal under state law for people without proper documentation to find employment, or 3) allow warrantless arrests of people believed to be in the United States without proper documentation. In all three provisions, the Court ruled that Congress's regulation of those facets of immigration were so extensive that states were "preempted" from adding to those regulations.

1. Why do you think the Arizona legislature might have passed the law in question?
2. Do you think any of the Arizona provisions were in fact unconstitutional; that is, they would be invalid even if Congress had not extensively regulated the areas in question?

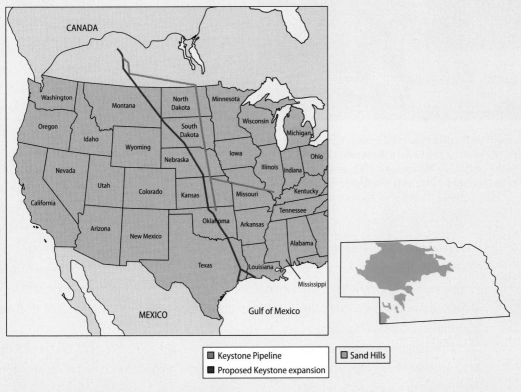

Figure 14.6 Keystone Pipeline Map

Legend: Keystone Pipeline | Proposed Keystone expansion | Sand Hills

© Cengage Learning, *Source:* Laris Karklis/The Washington Post. http://www.washingtonpost.com/national/health-science/canadian-firm-to-push-ahead-with-part-of-keystone-pipeline/2012/02/27/glQAvJftdR_story.html/; for the state of Nebraska, http://www.montrealgazette.com/technology/route+Keystone+pipeline+proposed+through+Nebraska/6486974/story.html.

XL Pipeline. In an interesting twist, labor and energy interest groups were allies, as both supported the construction of the pipeline. Environmental groups vigorously voiced their objections against the pipeline. In contrast, both the House and Senate passed resolutions calling for the approval of the pipeline. In fact, the amount of public response was so great that President Obama announced in 2014 that he had to delay his final decision on the Keystone XL Pipeline because the public comments on the project numbered in the millions, and the administration needed more time to consider all the views expressed on both sides of this issue.

Construct Your Own Policy

1. Propose a policy review process for energy-related proposals that you believe is more efficient than current practice.
2. Suggest alternative routes for the delivery of oil from Canada that would address environmentalists' concerns.

A number of Federal Reserve chairmen have served multiple terms, and under different presidents. The chair of the Federal Reserve is Janet Yellen, who was nominated by President Obama in October 2013, confirmed by the Senate, and took office in January 2014; she is the first female Federal Reserve chair in history.

agency that serves as the nation's central bank, increasing or decreasing the money supply by changing the reserve requirements—the amount of cash reserves that banks must keep on hand. To control the flow of money in the economy, Congress created the Federal Reserve in 1913 as a system of twelve regional banks in one national banking system. The Federal Reserve System is led by a seven-member board of governors, each nominated by the president and confirmed by the Senate. Members serve fourteen-year terms, and the president selects the board chair, who serves a four-year term, with the option of reappointment.

When the Federal Reserve increases reserve requirements, banks have less money to lend, and the money supply decreases. This action tends to raise interest rates. When the Federal Reserve decreases reserve requirements, banks have more money to lend, and thus the money supply increases (see Table 14.2). This move tends to lower interest rates. The Federal Reserve Board also controls the money supply through the discount rate, which is the interest rate that the Federal Reserve charges other banks on loans. When the discount rate is lower, banks are not able to charge high interest rates on the money they lend to consumers and businesses.

Although the president can name people to the Federal Reserve, he cannot fire them if they promote monetary policy that differs from his policy preferences. His only power over them comes from the nomination process.

The power of the federal government to steer the economy has been debated since our nation's founding. In times of crisis, the president and Congress can enact programs that target specific problems, as in the case of the auto industry bailout and stimulus

→ KEY QUESTIONS:
What roles do fiscal and monetary policy play in the economy?

Table 14.2 Comparison of Fiscal and Monetary Policy

Actions by Congress and the president affect fiscal policy, while actions by the Federal Reserve Board affect monetary policy.

Type of Policy	Policy Maker	Action	Direct Effect	Effect on Money Supply
Fiscal	Congress, president	Increase spending or cut taxes	Consumers have more money to spend.	Increases
	Congress, president	Decrease spending or increase taxes	Consumers have less money to spend.	Decreases
Monetary	Federal Reserve Board	Increase reserve requirement	Banks have less money to loan.	Decreases
	Federal Reserve Board	Decrease reserve requirement	Banks have more money to loan.	Increases
	Federal Reserve Board	Increase the discount rate	Loans are more expensive.	Decreases
	Federal Reserve Board	Decrease the discount rate	Loans are less expensive.	Increases

© CENGAGE LEARNING

package. But more generally, it is the Federal Reserve that has a strong role in setting monetary policy by setting interest rates, which in turn controls the flow of money to businesses and individuals seeking to take out loans.

Trade Policy

International trade—the exchange of commerce with other nations—is also an integral component of our nation's economic policy. In the twenty-first century, trade remains an important gateway to economic, political, and cultural relationships with other nations, though in recent years the nation has begun to import more goods than it exports.

Protectionism versus Free Trade.   Trade policy has long been aligned with foreign policy and has been used by the United States to export both capitalism and democracy. International trade policy is complex because each nation wants to negotiate deals that give its industries the greatest advantages either to sell their goods abroad or to be protected from cheaper imports from foreign nations. A policy that protects against foreign imported goods more than it promotes exports is known as **protectionist**, and a policy that strikes down barriers on imported foreign goods is known as **free trade**. A third and relatively recent policy, **fair trade**, encourages foreign trade as long as there are comparable working conditions and wages within the industries in the trading nations. Environmental regulation has also become increasingly important in trade negotiations. If one nation exploits its workers with long hours, unsafe conditions, environmental pollution, and low pay to produce and sell goods more cheaply than another, it violates fair trade practices. When a nation violates fair trade practices, individuals may boycott its products, or, more significantly, other nations may refuse to trade with it.

The president takes the lead in negotiating international trade agreements, either bilaterally (with one other country) or multilaterally through the office of the United States Trade Representative (USTR), an office created within the Executive Office of the President by President John F. Kennedy (1961–63) in 1963. The USTR is responsible for negotiating the terms of international trade agreements. To present a balanced position on behalf of the U.S. government, the USTR solicits information and feedback about the potential impact of the trade agreement from import- and export-related industries, cabinet departments, and members of Congress. Gathering such information is helpful not only in crafting an agreement that benefits U.S. industries but also in building the necessary support to get the trade agreement ratified by Congress.

During the late nineteenth and twentieth century, protectionist trade policies enabled U.S. industries to corner the consumer market and make huge profits. Businesses reinvested those profits in developing technology and in expanding so that the United States became the major supplier of manufactured goods throughout the world. It did not face strong competition in the world marketplace until the late 1980s, when Japan, China, and India developed their industrial capacity sufficiently to become competitive in a number of economic sectors. They replicated the U.S. policy of exporting their goods while maintaining trade barriers against the import of U.S. goods.

In the decades since, the United States has forged multilateral trade agreements designed both to expand export markets for U.S. goods and to allow more imported goods. The Canada Free Trade agreement, followed by the **North American Free Trade Agreement (NAFTA)**, created a free trade zone of goods and services across the northern and southern borders of the United States, creating jobs nationwide. However, some industries, such as the domestic textile

protectionist: *Policy designed to raise import barriers for goods that are domestically produced.*

free trade: *Policy designed to lower import barriers to encourage trade across nations.*

fair trade: *Policy designed to make sure that the working conditions are relatively equal in nations that trade with each other.*

→ KEY QUESTIONS:
What are the advantages and disadvantages of free trade over protectionism?

NAFTA: *Comprehensive multi-nation trade agreement ratified in 1994 that knocked down trade barriers among Canada, the United States, and Mexico.*

globalgateways

The Rise of the European Union

The European Union today consists of twenty-eight member nations that cooperate on economic and political issues such as monetary policy, trade subsidies, immigration, and international criminal justice. Although each EU member nation retains its own separate government and control over its military, all member nations agree to abide by the decisions of the European Union. In joining together under a single formal institution, these nations now constitute a powerful trading partner. Many of the EU nations also share a common currency, the euro, although the United Kingdom, Sweden, and Denmark are among those that have retained their own currencies.[44] By adopting a common currency that is not tied to a single nation's economy, the EU has achieved a greater role in shaping international monetary policy. However, when one EU member nation suffers a major financial crisis, as Greece and Spain recently did, there can be widespread negative effects on financial markets across the globe.

For the United States, the expansion of the European Union means that it must now consider the effects of its trade and monetary policies on a number of countries simultaneously, rather than working out agreements with each nation separately or in smaller groups. Indeed, in 2014, the United States forged ahead with a proposed trade agreement, known as the Transatlantic Trade and Investment Partnership (TTIP), which treats the EU as a single collective trading partner.

1. What is the European Union and why was it formed? Does it have its own currency?

2. Is the formation of the European Union as a trading bloc a good development for the United States' economy? Why or why not?

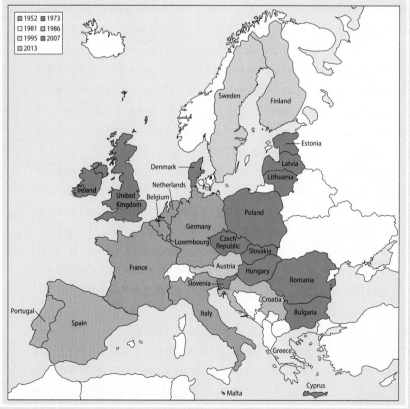

© 2016 CENGAGE LEARNING

and steel industries, were adversely affected and lost jobs. Many business executives moved their production facilities to Mexico, where it was less expensive to produce goods. These goods could then be sold cheaply in the United States because, under the free trade agreement, no import duties could be charged. The impact of NAFTA is an example of the consequences of policies that are designed to integrate the U.S. economy into the global world of trade.

Six years after the passage of NAFTA, the United States normalized trade status with China, which reduced trade barriers and opened up Chinese markets to U.S. goods; in doing so, it also encouraged American producers of goods such as textiles, apparel, steel, and electronics to relocate their production facilities to China. More than a decade later, the United States has a large trade imbalance with China; for the first seven months of 2014, U.S. imports exceeded exports to China by nearly $186 billion.[45] A large trade imbalance means that the American consumers are buying far more goods made in China than Chinese consumers are buying goods made in the United States. Such an imbalance in trade can harm U.S. manufacturers who are trying to compete with Chinese imported goods (see Figure 14.7).

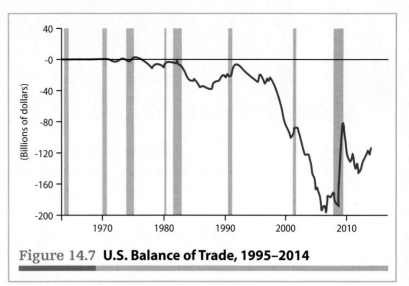

Figure 14.7 U.S. Balance of Trade, 1995–2014

Source: Adapted from Economic Research from the Federal Reserve Bank of St. Louis.

The increase in the number of economically developed nations as producers and consumers of goods, combined with the presence of U.S.-owned industries in these nations, has created a strong incentive for the United States to be a supportive partner in the international economy in order to encourage other countries to allow U.S. goods to be sold there.

Trade and International Economic Organizations. In addition to the unilateral trade agreements that it has struck with other nations, the United States also participated in the General Agreement on Tariffs and Trade (GATT), which governed multinational trade agreements between 1948 and 1994. In 1994, during the eighth round of GATT, the **World Trade Organization (WTO)** was created to deal with the explosive expansion of the global trade community and to establish a single international organization with the authority to resolve trade disputes.[46] If one country claims that another country is engaged in unfair trading practices, it can bring its case to the WTO; each party to the dispute must abide by the WTO's ruling or face monetary fines and trade limitations. For example, in 2009, China imposed a ban on broiler products, which covers chicken, from the United States, and the United States lodged a formal complaint with the WTO citing unfair trade practices, and the WTO formed a panel to resolve the issue.

⭐ **World Trade Organization (WTO):** *International organization that considers and resolves trade disputes among member nations.*

It took nearly four years for the WTO to return a decision, and it ruled that China had violated fair trade practices and had to remove the barriers to imported chicken from the United States.[47] The slow pace of the WTO deliberation illustrates how an international organization can serve as a gate or obstacle to efficient resolution of economic disputes. Entering the WTO was a major change in U.S. trade policy because it required the United States to relinquish its right to act unilaterally in trade disputes. At the same time, by agreeing to abide by WTO rulings, the United States gave assurance to foreign nations that it would respect international rules and would be a fair and reliable trading partner while expecting other nations to do the same.

Public Policy and the Economy:
Federal Deficit and the Debt Ceiling

Although many experts credit President Obama's policies with warding off an even deeper recession, or depression, they temporarily increased the federal deficit, which in turn increased the federal debt. As we noted in Chapter 10, the federal deficit is the difference between the amount of money that the government takes in and the amount of money that the government spends. When the federal government runs a deficit, it must borrow money to make up the shortfall. Consequently, the federal government pays interest on this borrowed money, and the combined amount of the borrowed money and the interest that accumulates over time constitutes the national debt.

As the federal debt has risen in recent years, Americans have become increasingly concerned about burdening future generations with the task of paying it back. There are two components to the federal debt: public debt, which is the money that comes from issuing debt instruments, such as U.S. Treasury bonds, that investors buy with a promise of getting a set amount of interest on the bonds at a later date; and intragovernment held debt, which is the amount of money that the federal government borrows from itself when it transfers money from one program to another or uses built-up reserves in one program as collateral for borrowing. The **debt ceiling** is a cap on the amount of money that Congress authorizes the president to borrow to pay the federal government's bills. Before 1917, there was no legal limit on the government's ability to issue such debt. However, to fund operations for World War I, Congress passed the Second Liberty Bond Act, which allows the federal government to issue longer-term debt as long as Congress issues its approval for doing so.[48] Consequently, today the president must ask to raise the debt ceiling and cannot do so without congressional approval.

The issue of the debt ceiling has become a major source of contention between the president and Congress. When President Obama first took office, he inherited a federal deficit of $1.4 trillion and a total national debt of $11.9 trillion dollars (see Figure 14.8); both were the cumulative effect of past presidential policy making, including the Bush tax cuts and the Iraq and Afghanistan wars. But during the first two years of the Obama administration, the national debt climbed to $13.5 trillion.[49] In the 2010 midterm congressional elections, the Tea Party movement became active within the Republican Party in order to strengthen the GOP's existing commitment to reduce taxes and federal spending. When the Republicans won control of the House of Representatives, those members who were elected with Tea Party support stayed adamant in their position against raising the debt ceiling. As noted in Chapter 10, the majority of those members were reelected in 2012, as was President Obama, which maintained divided party control between Congress and the presidency. Since then, the Tea Party factions in the House and the Senate have maintained their opposition to increased federal spending.

In September 2014, the end of fiscal year 2014, the projected federal deficit stood at $486 billion, which was less than half the size of what President Obama inherited in 2009, but the national debt had risen to $17.9 trillion. During his term, the issue of the federal debt ceiling caused standoffs with Congress on two separate occasions.

In 2011 President Obama proposed a "grand bargain" that would have cut the debt by $4 trillion over ten years with a combination of spending reductions and increased taxes. Republicans in

debt ceiling:
The congressionally authorized limit on federal borrowing.

with numerous regional conflicts. Since the end of WWII, many nations in addition to Vietnam and Iran had gained independence from such former colonial powers as France and the United Kingdom. Some of these nations—India and Indonesia, for example—had risen to prominence by attempting to remain neutral in the superpower struggle, forming the nonaligned movement (NAM). Modernization in China gave that huge nation new international stature. In the Middle East, tensions between Israel and the Arab states went unresolved. In Africa, decolonization had created a patchwork of new states across tribal lines struggling against corruption, poverty, and disease. And in the old Soviet bloc, especially in central Asia, new states struggled to suppress regional, religious, and ethnic hostilities and to resist Russian dominance. As we saw in 2014, Cold War tensions still resonate when issues of sovereignty emerge as they did with the Russian takeover of the Crimean peninsula, which was part of the country of Ukraine. In that case, the majority of residents in Crimea were of Russian descent and welcomed the aggressive takeover by the Putin-led government. Western nations responded by imposing economic sanctions on Russia, but tensions only escalated when Russian sympathizers in Eastern Ukraine waged war against the government. Russia kept control of Crimea, but a tentative cease fire was imposed in September 2014, in the eastern part of Ukraine.

CONNECT WITH YOUR CLASSMATES
MindTap for American Government

Access the Foreign Policy and National Security Forum: Polling Activity—U.S. as the World's Superpower.

Foreign Policy Tools

Nations have a wide array of policy tools available to them. Some involve cooperation through bilateral or multilateral treaties, diplomatic relations, and aid; others entail conflict through the use of force or the threat of military action. In this section, we will examine how the United States uses these tools.

Military Action.   The president, as commander in chief, has always made the decision to engage in military action. Although Congress has formally declared war only five times, U.S. troops have been sent into conflicts and potential conflicts about 250 times since the beginning of the nation.[52] Today, in making the decision to engage in military action, the president is heavily influenced by the recommendations of the secretary of defense, the national security adviser, and the director of the Central Intelligence Agency.

For military missions that are publicized, not secret, a president usually enjoys widespread support if the mission can be clearly tied to preserving national security. In cases in which the United States is attacked on its own soil, support for a military response is even higher. This so-called **rally-around-the-flag effect** is a surge in patriotic sentiment that translates into presidential popularity.[53] For example, when President George H. W. Bush commenced the first Gulf War, his approval ratings shot up to 89 percent.[54] His son, President George W. Bush, experienced a similar spike in popularity after 9/11; his job approval ratings went from 52 percent to 90 percent, and they remained above 70 percent for almost an entire year.[55]

The public's influence on the president's decision to engage in military action is always limited because the amount of information available to the public is purposely restricted, both to ensure the safety of the troops involved and to preserve military advantages in conflict. Simply put, the president and his military advisers have access to far greater amounts of information than does the average citizen, and in turn, the average citizen expects the president to act on this information in a way that preserves national security. Even when Congress debates sending troops or funding military action, most classified information is held in secret and not revealed to the public (but see Chapter 4 on the Snowden NSA revelations).

rally-around-the-flag effect: *Surge of public support for the president in times of international crisis.*

The fundamental imbalance of information held by the government and what the general public understands poses a major problem for the assumptions of a democracy because the people cannot hold the government fully accountable if they are not fully informed. Nevertheless, when a president decides to send troops, he has to anticipate public reaction and hope that the public maintains its trust and confidence in his decision to take such action.

The twenty-first century had ushered in new weaponry and new levels of violence committed by nations and **nonstate actors**, such as terrorist groups who take up violence against civilians as a means of attacking the United States and other Western nations.

The Bush administration used this new reality to justify military action against the Taliban regime in Afghanistan. President George W. Bush went one step further to launch a preemptive attack—that is, an attack prior to an act of aggression by another—against Iraq in 2003 to remove Saddam Hussein from power and dismantle alleged weapons of mass destruction that might be used against the United States and its allies (see Chapter 11 for more on the Iraq and Afghanistan wars). In invading Afghanistan and Iraq, Bush was trying to leverage the full strength of the U.S. military to combat terrorism.

However, many critics argue that in conflicts between a state and nonstate actors, traditional military weapons and strategies are ineffective, and new tools, such as surveillance, intelligence gathering and analysis, and the use of unmanned drones, are the only way to prevent future attacks. The policy infrastructure dedicated to addressing terrorism has grown dramatically over the past decade, with a greater reliance on cooperation among the Department of Homeland Security (see Chapter 12), Department of Defense, Department of Justice, and the president's National Security Council. Coordinating across such a vast portion of the federal government can produce both gates and gateways to effective antiterrorism policies, both at home and abroad (see Chapter 4 and Chapter 6, Public Opinion and the Media, for more on U.S. anti-terrorism policy).

Anti-Nuclear Proliferation Measures. Compounding the challenges of fighting terrorism is the fear of nuclear proliferation among established nations and nonstate terrorist groups. In addition to the United States and Russia, the United Kingdom, France, China, India, North Korea, Pakistan, and Israel have nuclear capabilities. Because India and Pakistan have experienced border clashes and are generally unfriendly toward each other, their possession of nuclear weapons poses a threat to the stability of Southeast Asia. Most recently, the United States has focused intense concern on nuclear weapons development in Iran (see Figure 14.10).

As the preeminent international peacekeeping organization, the United Nations has long led efforts to curb nuclear proliferation through treaties that would ban the testing of nuclear weapons and set up an official verification system whereby countries would be regularly inspected to make sure they were not developing nuclear capabilities. The Nuclear Non-Proliferation Treaty that went into effect in 1970 was designed to discourage nations from developing nuclear weapons technology; currently, 190 nations are signatories.[56] The key element of this treaty is the use of the International

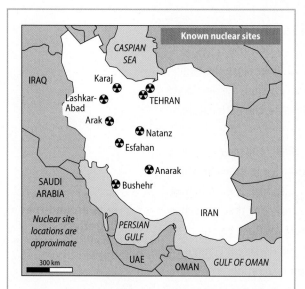

Figure 14.10 **Map of Nuclear Facilities in Iran**

Iran has been developing the capability to produce nuclear weapons, but has not yet finished the process. Here we see the sites in Iran that are believed to contain components in nuclear weapons production.

Atomic Energy Commission to monitor and inspect nations' weapons capability. The United States and the rest of the international community rely on this organization and its powers to monitor nuclear facility development in countries that do not currently have nuclear weapons, such as Iran. To that end, President Obama instructed his Secretary of State, John Kerry, to participate in multilateral negotiations with Iran to limit their progress toward acquiring a nuclear weapon.

Diplomacy and Humanitarian Assistance.

In addition to military actions, another cornerstone of U.S. foreign policy is diplomacy. The Department of State is responsible for formulating foreign policy using nonmilitary methods; these efforts

The U.S. Agency for International Development provides humanitarian assistance around the world. In 2014, USAID workers were sent to the front lines of the effort to treat and contain the Ebola virus in West Africa.

are conducted by diplomatic personnel in U.S. missions, consulates, and embassies around the world. There are also agencies within the Department of State that oversee a key component of our foreign policy—the provision of humanitarian assistance. The interdependence of nations today provides an opportunity for Americans, from the average citizen to the president, to participate on a wider level and improve living conditions everywhere. A world with more stable nations that treat their citizens equally and with dignity benefits the United States because it means that fewer internal conflicts will emerge that warrant military intervention. Governmental and nongovernmental organizations that provide funds for economic, health, and educational development provide an avenue for the U.S. government, groups, and individual citizens to take an active role in international life.

For example, within the U.S. federal government, the U.S. Agency for International Development (USAID) is an independent agency with the mission of providing gateways for the provision of training, education, and materials to developing nations and of promoting democracy.[57] It is led by an administrator appointed by the president who works closely with other federal departments, including the Department of State, on international aid issues. USAID was created by President John F. Kennedy in 1961 as part of the Foreign Assistance Act. Today its activities include disaster relief, child health and nutrition, and disease treatment and prevention. For example USAID Disaster Assistance Response Teams were very involved in fighting the Ebola virus in West Africa. In fiscal year 2014, USAID had an operating budget of $1.57 billion.[58]

In addition to unilaterally promoting economic development, the United States is also a member of the World Bank and the International Monetary Fund, two global economic organizations. The **World Bank** was founded in 1944 as an international aid and reconstruction organization to help rebuild nations that had been badly damaged during WWII.[59] Today it has 186 members, known as shareholders, and five divisions that work together to provide low-interest loans, grants, and investment capital to build and improve infrastructure and

→ KEY QUESTIONS:
What goals can the United States accomplish through humanitarian aid?

★ **World Bank:**
International organization that distributes grants and low-income loans in developing countries.

Public Policy and International Relations: **Promotion of Democracy**

President Woodrow Wilson's idea was that the United States should make the world "safe for democracy," and President Truman's view was that the United States should intervene militarily to promote and defend against Communist takeovers. Truman's approach drew strength from the theory of "democratic peace," which holds that the world is a safer place if nations are democratic. The core contention is that democracies, reflecting the will of the people, have almost never gone to war against other each other.[62] The public's desire for peace simply makes that outcome rare.

The federal government attempts to export democratic values through diplomatic and cultural programs. The Voice of America broadcasts news and programming in more than forty different languages across the world and cooperates with private organizations, such as Radio Free Asia, that provide a forum for democratic activists in Myanmar, China, and other nondemocratic states. American interest groups and nonprofit organizations also promote democracy abroad. Freedom House supports nonviolent civil initiatives in societies where freedom is denied or threatened. Since 1972, the organization has issued reports on every country around the world, classifying countries as free, partially free, or not free based on a freedom index that takes into account the electoral process, civil liberties, and human rights (see Figure 14.11).

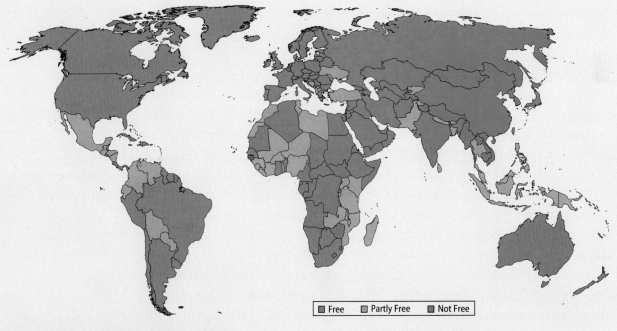

Figure 14.11 Freedom House Map

Today, the question of what is justified in the name of preserving and promoting the American form of democracy remains unresolved, especially in the face of old and new conflicts in nations such as Iraq, Egypt, and Syria where internal forces are battling for control of their governments. Making the case to the American people that direct U.S. intervention is necessary in distant regions with long histories of conflict, such as the Middle East, is difficult to do, as we saw with the debate over punishing Syria for its use of chemical weapons. America's international reputation was tarnished by its unilateralism in the Iraq War, making it more difficult for the United States to gain cooperation from the international community for intervention.

For these and other reasons, President Obama tried to reshape U.S. foreign policy by becoming more reliant on international organizations such as the United Nations, and using the international economic system to impose financial penalties and block trade with nations that violate international law or harbor terrorist groups. In an address to West Point, Obama made it clear that the United States would intervene when its interests were directly threatened, but that it could not be expected to send forces to engage in every military action occurring around the world. However, as the upheaval in Iraq shows, the United States remains involved in military conflicts even after the formal cessation of its role in war. The promotion of democracy is a long and unstable process, and when countries in which the United States has had a military presence devolve into civil war, there is enormous pressure to reengage to prevent further bloodshed.

Construct Your Own Policy

1. Outline guidelines for active U.S. engagement in foreign conflicts.
2. Devise a policy that only allows peaceful or nonmilitary U.S. involvement in promoting democracy.

alleviate poverty. The United States is the largest shareholder in the World Bank and consequently has leadership responsibilities; the president nominates the head of the bank, who serves a five-year renewable term.[60] The World Bank funds specific projects to improve transportation, provide clean water, build energy utilities, modernize medical care, initiate crop development programs, and provide start-up money for new businesses in poor and developing countries. In fiscal year 2014, the World Bank provided $39.6 billion in grants, loans, and investment capital to nations around the world.[61]

The **International Monetary Fund (IMF)** was created alongside the World Bank in 1944 with a different mission. The IMF focuses on preserving economic stability, including currency values, among nations and makes short-term loans to nations that cannot balance their budgets or are in need of immediate funds.[63] The IMF also works with nations to try to reduce their government debt by renegotiating loans or by providing loans on better terms. The IMF has the same set of members as the World Bank, and each member makes a financial contribution to the fund based on its share of the global economy. The IMF has a board of governors, which includes a governor from each member nation, but the daily operations of the fund are overseen by a managing director and a twenty-four-member executive board. In contrast to its role in the World Bank, the United States does not play a prominent role in directing IMF operations and does not nominate the managing director. However, the United States pays the largest single share (17 percent) of the IMF's fund, so it wields significant influence over lending decisions. In 2014, the IMF had $87.3 billion in outstanding loans to countries around the world.[64]

The United States supports organizations that send individuals to foreign nations for peace-keeping, educational, and cultural purposes. The **Peace Corps** is perhaps the best known of these organizations. The Peace Corps was established in 1961; since then, more than 195,000 U.S. citizen volunteers have lived and worked in seventy-six countries all over the world.[65] The mission of the Peace Corps is to help train citizens of other nations in essential skills, establish communication about Americans with other nations, and bring more knowledge about foreign peoples back to America through the volunteers. Today the Peace Corps operates on a budget of $378.8 million, and it still attracts recent college graduates and others who work in seventy-six countries in wide ranging fields, including teaching, agriculture, HIV/AIDS prevention, medicine, engineering, communications, environmental conservation, and construction.[66] The model of the Peace Corps has spurred the creation of domestic volunteer organizations including AmeriCorps and Teach for America, which operate within the United States but pursue similar goals of education and economic development in underserved areas.

However, the fact that nations are more connected to each other in our global world does not mean that they share political systems, religions, or culture. The differences that do exist have come into the forefront through regime change in recent years, which has resulted in political, social, and military conflict. America has objective strategic interests that it must protect, but it also has a strong commitment to human rights and democratic principles of government, and sometimes these guiding principles clash in the formulation of our foreign and military policy. Where the line should be drawn in international relations is decided by each presidential administration, in consultation with Congress; in that way, every presidential election is a gateway through which the American voters have the opportunity to render their opinions on whether to reset the boundaries of engagement.

⭐ **International Monetary Fund (IMF):** *International organization that works to stabilize currency values and government debt for nations in economic difficulty.*

⭐ **Peace Corps:** *U.S. government-funded organization that sends individuals on educational and cultural missions around the world.*

Checkpoint

CAN YOU:

- Describe the goals of U.S. foreign policy
- Assess the roles of military and diplomatic actions in U.S. foreign policy
- Evaluate U.S. efforts to promote democracy around the world

Public Policy and Democracy

Public policy covers a lot of territory in the language of American politics. It is essentially the set of outputs by federal, state, and local governments that address the interests and opinions of citizens. In this chapter, we have presented an overview of the federal regulatory system that serves as the main vehicle to implement the laws that Congress and the president enact. Once a law is passed, the executive branch produces a set of guidelines for how the law will work, and the public has a chance to comment on those regulations before they are finally put into place.

The three broad policy areas discussed in this chapter—domestic, economic, and foreign—all differ in the ways that policy outcomes can be directly controlled by policy makers. In domestic policy, our federal system of government has expanded over the past century to provide direct and indirect assistance to individuals in the area of income security, food security, housing, and health care. Our system of federalism allows states some leeway in how they implement federal law, especially when the policy overlaps with areas that are solely controlled by the states. The different ways that the Affordable Care Act has been implemented or blocked at the state level illustrate the variation in the potential impact of federal policy.

In the economic sphere, the president, Congress, and the Federal Reserve all have a role to play in how much money the government spends and how cheaply consumers can borrow money, but the independent business cycle also has a strong impact on whether those policies succeed in contributing to economic growth and stability.

In the area of foreign policy, the United States has always had to balance its own principles regarding human rights and freedoms with its military and economic self-interest around the world. Additionally, military and humanitarian crises emerge frequently and fall out of direct U.S. control; however, the United States is still faced with the choice of whether to intervene and to what extent. As recent events in Libya, Syria, and the Ukraine have shown, choosing the right policy is no easy task.

At times, it seems that there are more gates to influencing public policy in our system of government than there are gateways. Policy makers can be well intentioned and sincerely interested in reflecting the interests and concerns of the majority of the people, but the process itself can be slower and less inefficient than most of us would like. The policy-making process is complicated because it involves elected officials in multiple branches of government at all levels (federal, state, and local), the business community, interest groups, and private citizens who choose to make their opinions heard. Our system has about as much participation as James Madison would have expected; the question remains as to whether it is enough to address the pressing needs of the twenty-first century.

CONNECT WITH YOUR CLASSMATES
MindTap for American Government

Access the Domestic Policy Forum: Discussion—The Public's Impact on Policy Making.

Master the Concept
of Economic, Domestic, and Foreign Policy with MindTap for American Government

 REVIEW MindTap for American Government
Access Key Term Flashcards for Chapter 14.

 TEST YOURSELF MindTap for American Government
Take the Wrap It Up Quiz for Chapter 14.

 STAY CURRENT MindTap for American Government
Access the KnowNow blog and customized RSS for updates on current events.

 STAY FOCUSED MindTap for American Government
Complete the Focus Activities for Economic, Domestic, and Foreign Policy.

Key Concepts

Clean Air Act (p. 471) What role does the Clean Air Act play in U.S. environmental policy history?

Cold War (1946–91) (p. 483) What were the causes of the beginning and end of the Cold War**?**

Communism (p. 483) What is Communism?

debt ceiling (p. 480) What is the relationship between the debt ceiling and the federal deficit?

entitlement programs (p. 463) What is the definition of an entitlement program?

European Union (p. 482) What is the European Union, and what role does it play in international economics?

fair trade (p. 477) How does fair trade try to promote economic equality around the world?

Federal Register (p. 459) Where are all official federal government regulations published?

Federal Reserve Board (p. 473) When was the Federal Reserve created, and what does it do?

free trade (p. 477) What is the definition of free trade?

globalization (p. 482) How has globalization emerged as an international process over time?

International Monetary Fund (IMF) (p. 487) How does the IMF help stabilize nations that are in economic difficulty?

Medicaid (p. 464) Who is eligible for Medicaid, and what does it do?

Medicare (p. 464) Who is typically served through the Medicare program?

multipolar (p. 484) What does it mean to have a multipolar world?

NAFTA (p. 477) How did NAFTA affect trade among Canada, the United States, and Mexico?

nonstate actors (p. 486) How do nonstate actors complicate international peacemaking efforts?

Peace Corps (p. 490) When and why was the Peace Corps created?

policy agenda (p. 457) How do issues get on the policy agenda?

policy diffusion (p. 461) How do policy ideas spread across states?

policy enactment (p. 458) What does it mean when a policy is enacted?

policy evaluation (p. 458) What is the role of evaluation in the policy process?

policy formulation (p. 457) How does formulation work as the third step in the policy-making process?

policy implementation (p. 458) How does the executive branch implement public policy?

protectionist (p. 477) Who benefits from protectionist trade policy?

problem identification (p. 457) How does identification work as the first step in the policy-making process?

public policy (p. 456) Define public policy.

rally-around-the-flag effect (p. 485) Why do citizens tend to increase their support for government when facing a military threat?

recession (p. 472) How did the government react when the economy went into a recession in 2007–2008?

regulations (p. 459) How do regulations help government officials and individuals follow federal law?

regulatory process (p. 459) How would you describe the role of the regulatory process in our public policy system?

Social Security (p. 463) How is Social Security funded?

United Nations (p. 483) When and why was the United Nations created?

World Bank (p. 487) What function does the World Bank serve in international economic development?

World Trade Organization (WTO) (p. 479) When was the WTO created and why?

Learning Outcomes: What You Need . . .

To Know	To Test Yourself	To Participate
▶ **Outline the steps in the policy-making process**		
The path from idea to a policy involves five key steps. First a problem has to be identified, then it has to be on the congressional and executive agenda, then it has to be formulated into a policy according to federal guidelines, then it has to be enacted into law, then it has to be implemented (put into practice), and finally it has to be evaluated to see if the policy is accomplishing its stated goals.	• Describe how an idea becomes a policy proposal. • Identify the three key parts of the regulatory process. • Explain how the judiciary can be used to block implementation of policy. • Outline the role of state governments in implementing federal policies.	• Evaluate how the average citizen can get an idea on the policy agenda. • Design a way to streamline policy implementation.

14. Garry Wills, *Negro President: Jefferson and the Slave Power* (Boston: Houghton Mifflin, 2003), 5–6.

15. Wendy J. Schiller and Charles Stewart III, *Electing the Senate: Indirect Democracy before the 17ᵗʰ Amendment* (Princeton, NJ: Princeton University Press, 2014).

16. See Allison M. Martens, "Reconsidering Judicial Supremacy: From the Counter-Majoritarian Difficulty to Constitutional Transformations," *Perspectives on Politics* 5 (2007): 447–59.

17. James Madison, "*Federalist 47*," in *The Federalist Papers*, U.S. Constitution Online, accessed April 10, 2012, http://www.constitution.org/fed/federa47.htm.

18. James Madison, "*Federalist 39*," in *The Federalist Papers*, U.S. Constitution Online, accessed May 3, 2012, http://www.constitution.org/fed/federa39.htm.

19. Brutus, "Antifederalist 1," U.S. Constitution Online, accessed May 10, 2012, http://www.constitution.org/afp/brutus01.htm.

20. James Madison, "*Federalist 41*," in *The Federalist Papers*, U.S. Constitution Online, accessed April 10, 2012, http://www.constitution.org/fed/federa41.htm.

21. *Furman v. Georgia*, 408 U.S. 238 (1972).

22. *Gregg v. Georgia*, 428 U.S. 153 (1976).

23. "States with and without the Death Penalty," Death Penalty Information Center, accessed February 24, 2014, http://www.deathpenaltyinfo.org/states-and-without-death-penalty.

24. See http://www.gallup.com/poll/1606/death-penalty.aspx.

25. "Federal Death Penalty," Death Penalty Information Center, accessed April 10, 2012, http://www.deathpenaltyinfo.org/federal-death-penalty?scid=29&did=147.

26. Matt Apuzzo, "U.S. Is Seeking Death Penalty in Boston Case," *New York Times*, January 31, 2014, A1.

27. David Baldus, Charles A. Pulaski Jr., and George Woodworth, *Equal Justice and the Death Penalty* (Boston: Northeastern University Press, 1990).

28. *McCleskey v. Kemp*, 481 U.S. 279 (1987).

29. *Roper v. Simmons*, 543 U.S. 551 (2005); *Kennedy v. Louisiana*, 554 U.S. 407 (2008).

30. See http://www.innocenceproject.org/know/, accessed March 12, 2014.

31. *District Attorney's Office v. Osborne*, 174 L. Ed. 2d 38 (2009).

32. *Wickard v. Filburn*, 317 U.S. 111 (1942).

33. *National Federation of Independent Business v. Sebelius*, 11–393 (2012).

Chapter 3

1. This story was written by Dana K. Glencross of Oklahoma City Community College and compiled from information on the Oklahoma County website, http://www.oklahomacounty.org; Bryan Painter, "Local community service project helps area SHINE," *The Oklahoman*, October 11, 2010, 1A; Bryan Painter, "Community Service Project helps area SHINE," *The Oklahoman*, November 14, 2010, 9J; and telephone and e-mail interviews with Brian Maughan, February 29, March 28, and April 5, 2012, conducted for this textbook; chapter-opening quotation from March 13, 2012, e-mail.

2. Colin Bonwick, *The American Revolution* (Charlottesville: University of Virginia Press, 1991), 194.

3. "The First Political Cartoons," Archiving Early America, accessed April 13, 2012, http://www.earlyamerica.com/earlyamerica/firsts/cartoon/.

4. William Riker, *Federalism: Origin, Operation, Significance* (Boston: Little Brown, 1964), 5.

5. Article 6, the Virginia Plan, accessed August 7, 2014, http://avalon.law.yale.edu/18th_century/vatexta.asp

6. *Revenues and Expenditures for Public Elementary and Secondary Education: School Year 2010-11 (Fiscal Year 2011)* (Washington, D.C.: National Center for Education Statistics, 2014), accessed March 22, 2014, http://nces.ed.gov/pubs2013/2013344/findings.asp.

7. Michael B. Berkman and Eric Plutzer, *Ten Thousand Democracies* (Washington D.C.: Georgetown University Press, 2005).

8. 247 U.S. 483 (1954)

9. 404 U.S. 1211 (1971).

10. Joy Resmovits, "No Child Left Behind Waivers Granted to 33 U.S. States, Some with Strings Attached," *Huffington Post*, July 19, 2012, accessed July 20, 2012, http://www.huffingtonpost.com/2012/07/19/no-child-left-behind-waiver_n_1684504.html.

11. Alan Greenblatt, "Q and A with Paul Posner: July/August 2010," National Conference of State Legislators, 2010, accessed June 6, 2014, http://www.ncsl.org/bookstore/state-legislatures-magazine/q-and-a-with-paul-posner.aspx.

12. See http://www.ed.gov/news/press-releases/education-department-announces-next-rounds-race-top-including-another-key-invest.

13. James Madison, "*Federalist 39*," in *The Federalist Papers*, U.S. Constitution Online, accessed April 13, 2012, http://www.constitution.org/fed/federa39.htm.

14. *Cohens v. Virginia*, 19 U.S. 264 (1821).

15. *Chisolm v. Georgia*, 2 U.S. 419 (1793).

16. Elinor Ostrom, *Governing the Commons: The Evolution of Institutions for Collective Action* (New York: Cambridge University Press, 1990), 106–10.

17. *United States v. Windsor*, 133 S. Ct. 2675 (2013).

18. "Gay Marriage." ProCon.org., 2014, accessed April, 4, 2014, http://gaymarriage.procon.org/view.resource.php?resourceID=004857.

19. Chrissie Thompson, "Ohio Will Have to Recognize Gay Marriages, Judge Says." *USA Today*, April 4, 2014, accessed April 5, 2014, http://www.usatoday.com/story/news/nation/2014/04/04/ohio-gay-marriage/7304753/.

20. *McCulloch v. Maryland*, 17 U.S. 316 (1819).

21. *Gibbons v. Ogden*, 22 U.S. 1 (1824).

22. *Dred Scott v. Sandford*, 60 U.S. 393 (1857).

23. "Confederate States of America—Declaration of the Immediate Causes Which Induce and Justify Secession of South Carolina from the Federal Union," December 24, 1860, Avalon Project, Yale University, Lillian Goldman Law Library, accessed April 30, 2012, http://avalon.law.yale.edu/19th_century/csa_scarsec.asp.

24. See http://www.civil-war.net/pages/ordinances_secession.asp.

25. Andrew Johnson, "Veto of the Civil Rights Bill," March 27, 1866, Teaching American History, accessed April 13, 2012, http://teachingamericanhistory.org/library/document/veto-of-the-civil-rights-bill/.

26. Morton Grodzins, *The American System: A New View of the Government of the United States* (New York: Rand McNally, 1966), 8.

27. Wendy J. Schiller, "Building Careers and Courting Constituents: U.S. Senate Representation, 1889–1924," *Studies in American Political Development* 20 (2006): 1.

28. *Carter v. Carter Coal Co.*, 298 U.S. 238 (1936).

29. *National Labor Relations Board v. Jones & Laughlin Steel Corporation*, 301 U.S. 1 (1937).

30. *United States v. Darby Lumber Company*, 312 U.S. 100 (1941).

31. Grodzins, *American System*, 8–9.

32. "American Independent Party Platform of 1968," October 13, 1968, online by Gerhard Peters and John Woolley, The American Presidency

Project, accessed April 13, 2012, http://www.presidency.ucsb.edu/ws//index.php?pid=29570#axzz1rwnAcK5P.

33. Sean Nicholson-Crotty, "Rational Election Cycles and the Intermittent Political Safeguards of Federalism," *Publius: The Journal of Federalism* 38 (2008): 295–314.

34. Timothy Conlon, *New Federalism: Intergovernmental Reform from Nixon to Reagan* (Washington D.C.: Brookings Institution, 1988).

35. "Ronald Reagan, First Inaugural Address," January 20, 1981, American Rhetoric, accessed April 13, 2012, http://www.americanrhetoric.com/speeches/ronaldreagandfirstinaugural.html.

36. Tim Conlan and John Dinan, "Federalism, the Bush Administration, and the Transformation of American Conservatism," *Publius: The Journal of Federalism* 37 (2007): 279–303.

37. Scott F. Abernathy, *No Child Left Behind and the Public Schools* (Ann Arbor: University of Michigan Press, 2007), 23.

38. John Schwartz, "Obama Seems to Be Open to a Broader Role for States," *New York Times*, January 29, 2009, http://www.nytimes.com/2009/01/30/us/politics/30federal.html/; "DEA Pot Raids Go On; Obama Opposes," *The Washington Times*, February 5, 2009, http://www.washingtontimes.com/news/2009/feb/05/dea-led-by-bush-continues-pot-raids/?page=1.

39. *Younger v. Harris*, 401 U.S. 37 (1971).

40. *United States v. Lopez*, 514 U.S. 549 (1995).

41. *South Dakota v. Dole*, 483 U.S. 203 (1987) at 211.

42. *National Federation of Independent Business v. Sebelius*, 132 S. Ct. 2566 (2012).

43. *Gonzales v. Raich*, 545 U.S. 1 (2005).

44. *National Federation of Independent Business v. Sebelius*, 183 L. Ed 2d 450 (2012).

45. U.S. Census Bureau, "Local Government and Public School Systems by Type and State: 2012," accessed March 21, 2014, http://www.census.gov/govs/go/index.html.

46. See http://www.washingtonpost.com/blogs/the-fix/post/arizona-recall-why-russell-pearce-lost/2011/11/09/gIQALj6a5M_blog.html.

47. National Conference of State Legislatures, "Initiative, Referendum, and Recall," NCSL.org, http://www.ncsl.org/legislatures-elections/elections/initiative-referendum-and-recall-overview.aspx.

48. *Hollingsworth v. Perry*, 133 S. Ct. 2652 (2013).

49. http://www.iandrinstitute.org/BW%202014-2%20Election%20results%20(v1)%202014-11-04.pdf, and http://www.iandrinstitute.org/BW%202014-1%20Preview%20(v1)%202014-10-15.pdf. Accessed November 5, 2014.

50. Colorado Marijuana-Legalization Amendment Spending Tops $3 Million," *The Denver Post*, accessed April 6, 2014, http://www.denverpost.com/ci_21820068/colorado-marijuana-legalization-amendment-spending-tops-3-million.

51. Reid Wilson, "The Most Expensive Race of 2014 Could Be This California Ballot Measure," *The Washington Post*, March 25, 2014, accessed April 6, 2014. http://www.washingtonpost.com/blogs/govbeat/wp/2014/03/25/the-most-expensive-race-of-2014-could-be-this-california-ballot-measure/.

Chapter 4

1. Brutus, "*Antifederalist* 2," U.S. Constitution Online, accessed May 9, 2012, http://www.constitution.org/afp/brutus02.htm.

2. *West Virginia Board of Education v. Barnette*, 319 U.S. 624 (1943).

3. Annals of Congress, H439 (June 8, 1789), American Memory, Library of Congress, accessed May 18, 2012, http://memory.loc.gov/cgi-bin/ampage?collId=llac&fileName=001/llac001.db&recNum=221.

4. *Schenck v. United States*, 249 U.S. 47 (1919).

5. Judith A. Baer, *Equality under the Constitution* (Ithaca, N.Y.: Cornell University Press, 1983).

6. *Chicago B & Q Railway Company v. Chicago*, 166 U.S. 226 (1897).

7. *Gitlow v. New York*, 268 U.S. 652 (1925).

8. *Palko v. Connecticut*, 302 U.S. 319 (1937).

9. *Schenck v. United States*, 249 U.S. 47 (1919); *Debs v. United States*, 249 U.S. 211 (1919).

10. *Hirota v. MacArthur*, 338 U.S. 197 (1948).

11. *Hamdan v. Rumsfeld*, 548 U.S. 557 (2006).

12. See http://www.fas.org/irp/agency/doj/fisa/#rept.

13. Robin Toner and Neil A. Lewis, "A NATION CHALLENGED: CONGRESS; House Passes Terrorism Bill Much Like Senate's, but with 5-Year Limit, *New York Times*, October 12, 2011. accessed April 27, 2014, http://www.nytimes.com/2001/10/13/us/nation-challenged-congress-house-passes-terrorism-bill-much-like-senate-s-but.html.

14. Robert McMillan, "Obama Administration Defends Bush Wiretapping," *PC World*, July 15, 2009, http://www.pcworld.com/article/168502/obama_administration_defends_bush_wiretapping.html.

15. *Al Haramain Islamic Foundation v. Obama* 690 F.3d 1089 (2012), accessed April 28, 2014, http://cdn.ca9.uscourts.gov/datastore/opinions/2012/08/07/11-15468.pdf.

16. *Smith v. Maryland*, 442 U.S. 735 (1979).

17. See http://www.nytimes.com/2013/06/08/us/mining-of-data-is-called-crucial-to-fight-terror.html?nl=todaysheadlines&emc=edit_th_20130608&_r=0.

18. See http://www.nytimes.com/2014/03/25/us/obama-to-seek-nsa-curb-on-call-data.html.

19. See http://epic.org/privacy/wiretap/stats/fisa_stats.html.

20. See http://afgeneralcounsel.dodlive.mil/2014/01/14/u-s-judiciary-weighs-in-on-special-advocates-before-fisa-court/.

21. Charlie Savage, "U.S. Law May Allow Killings, Holder Says," *New York Times*, March 5, 2012.

22. See http://www.foxnews.com/politics/2014/04/21/federal-court-obama-administration-must-release-targeted-killings-memo/.

23. *Brandenburg v. Ohio*, 395 U.S. 444 (1969).

24. *Chaplinsky v. New Hampshire*, 315 U.S. 568 (1942).

25. David L. Hudson Jr., "Hate Speech and Campus Speech Codes," First Amendment Center, September 13, 2002, accessed May 9, 2012, http://www.firstamendmentcenter.org/hate-speech-campus-speech-codes.

26. Alan Charles Kors and Harvey Silvergate, *The Shadow University: The Betrayal of Liberty on America's Campuses* (New York: Free Press, 1998).

27. "Warning: College Students, this editorial may upset you," *Los Angeles Times*, March 31, 2014, http://www.latimes.com/opinion/editorials/la-ed-trigger-warnings-20140331,0,6700908.story#ixzz2yaSoYsXi.

28. See http://chronicle.com/blogs/conversation/2014/03/10/trigger-warnings-trigger-me.

29. *Virginia v. Black*, 538 U.S. 343 (2003).

30. *Tinker v. Des Moines School District*, 393 U.S. 503 (1969). The quotation in the caption on page 99 is from this decision, at 506.

31. *Bland et al. v. Roberts*, E.D. Va. (Apr. 24, 2012).

32. *United States v. O'Brien*, 391 U.S. 367 (1968).

33. *Hill v. Colorado*, 530 U.S. 703 (2000). The pro-protest decision in 2014 is *McCullen v. Coakley* (citation not yet available).

34. *West Virginia Board of Education v. Barnette*, 319 U.S. 624 (1943).

35. *Texas v. Johnson*, 491 U.S. 397 (1989).

36. *Morse v. Frederick*, 551 U.S. 393 (2007).

37. *Grayned v. City of Rockford*, 408 U.S. 104 (1972).

38. William Blackstone, *Commentaries on the Laws of England*, 1769 (Chicago: University of Chicago Press, 2002), 4:151–53.

39. *New York Times v. United States,* 403 U.S. 713 (1971).

40. *United States v. Progressive*, 467 F. Supp. 990 (1979).

41. See http://www.wikileaks.org.

42. Adam Liptak and Brad Stone, "Judge Shuts Down Web Site Specializing in Leaks," *New York Times*, February 20, 2008.

43. *Hustler Magazine v. Falwell*, 485 U.S. 46 (1988).

44. Anna Badkhen, "Web Can Ruin Reputation with Stroke of a Key," *San Francisco Chronicle*, May 6, 2007.

45. *Miller v. California*, 413 U.S. 15 (1973).

46. See http://thecolbertreport.cc.com/videos/49r39y/pussy-riot-pt--1.

47. *Ibid.*

48. Joe Nocera, "Pussy Riot Tells All," *New York Times*, February 7, 2014, http://www.nytimes.com/2014/02/08/opinion/nocera-pussy-riot-tells-all.html?_r=0.

49. *Jenkins v. Georgia*, 418 U.S. 153 (1974).

50. *New York v. Ferber*, 458 U.S. 747 (1982).

51. *Ashcroft v. Free Speech Coalition*, 535 U.S. 234 (2002).

52. *Reno v. American Civil Liberties Union*, 521 U.S. 844 (1997).

53. *Brown v. Entertainment Merchants Association*, 131 S. Ct. 2729 (2011).

54. *United States v. Stevens*, 559 U.S. 460 (2010).

55. Ontario Consultants on Religious Tolerance, "Religious Laws," ReligiousTolerance.org, accessed May 9, 2012, http://www.religioustolerance.org/lawmenu.htm.

56. *Rosenberger v. University of Virginia*, 515 U.S. 819 (1995).

57. *Church of Lakumi Babalu Aye v. City of Hialeah*, 508 U.S. 520 (1993).

58. *Reynolds v. United States*, 98 U.S. 145 (1878).

59. Bill Mears,"Judge Strikes Down Part of Utah Polygamy Law in 'Sister Wives' Case," *CNN*, December 16, 2013, http://www.cnn.com/2013/12/14/justice/utah-polygamy-law/.

60. *Clay, aka, Ali v. United States,* 403 U.S. 698 (1971).

61. *Employment Division v. Smith*, 494 U.S. 872 (1990).

62. *City of Boerne v. Flores*, 521 U.S. 507 (1997), at 536.

63. *Hosanna-Tabor Evangelical Lutheran Church and School v. Equal Employment Opportunity Commission*, 132 S. Ct. 694 (2012).

64. See "Rethinking the Incorporation of the Establishment Clause: A Federalist View," *Harvard Law Review* 105 (1992): 1700.

65. *Everson v. Board of Education*, 330 U.S. 1 (1947).

66. *Lemon v. Kurtzman*, 403 U.S. 602 (1971).

67. *Engel v. Vitale*, 370 U.S. 421 (1962) (prayer); *Abington School District v. Schempp*, 374 U.S. 203 (1963) (Bible reading).

68. *Epperson v. Arkansas*, 393 U.S. 97 (1968).

69. *Edwards v. Aguillard*, 482 U.S. 578 (1987).

70. *Lee v. Weisman*, 505 U.S. 577 (1992).

71. *Santa Fe Independent School District v. Doe*, 530 U.S. 290 (2000).

72. *Board of Education v. Allen*, 392 U.S. 236 (1968).

73. *Meek v. Pittenger*, 421 U.S. 349 (1975).

74. *District of Columbia v. Heller*, 554 U.S. 570 (2008).

75. *McDonald v. Chicago*, 561 U.S. 3025 (2010).

76. *Florence v. County of Burlington*, 10-945 (2012).

77. *Riley v. California*, 134 S. Ct. 999 (2014).

78. *Schneckloth v. Bustamonte*, 412 U.S. 218 (1973).

79. *Missouri v. McNeely* 133 S. Ct. 1552 (2013).

80. *Maryland v. King*, 133 S. Ct. 1958 (2013).

81. See Jeffrey A. Segal, "Predicting Supreme Court Decisions Probabilistically: The Search and Seizure Cases, 1962–1981," *American Political Science Review* 78 (1984): 801.

82. *California v. Ciraolo*, 476 U.S. 207 (1986).

83. *Florida v. Jardines*, 133 S. Ct. 1409 (2013).

84. *Kyllo v. United States*, 533 U.S. 27 (2001).

85. *Virginia v. Moore*, 553 U.S. 164 (2008).

86. *Prado Navarette v. California,* accessed April 28, 2014. http://www.supremecourt.gov/opinions/13pdf/12-9490_3fb4.pdf.

87. *United States v. Jones*, 132 S. Ct. 945 (2012).

88. *Vernonia School District 47J v. Acton*, 515 U.S. 646 (1995); *National Treasury Union v. Von Raab*, 489 U.S. 656 (1989); *Chandler v. Miller*, 520 U.S. 305 (1997).

89. *Mapp v. Ohio,* 367 U.S. 643 (1961).

90. Priscilla H. Machado Zotti, *Injustice for All: Mapp v. Ohio and the Fourth Amendment* (New York: Peter Lang, 2005).

91. *United States v. Leon*, 468 U.S. 897 (1984).

92. *Nix v. Williams*, 467 U.S. 431 (1984).

93. *Miranda v. Arizona*, 384 U.S. 436 (1966).

94. *Dickerson v. United States*, 530 U.S. 428 (2000).

95. *Powell v. Alabama*, 287 U.S. 45 (1932).

96. *Gideon v. Wainwright*, 372 U.S. 335 (1963).

97. *Argersinger v. Hamlin*, 407 U.S. 25 (1972).

98. *Williams v. Florida*, 399 U.S. 78 (1970); *Johnson v. Louisiana*, 406 U.S. 356 (1972).

99. *Georgia v. McCollum*, 505 U.S. 42 (1992); *J. E. B. v. Alabama*, 511 U.S. 127 (1994).

100. Peter Johnson, "Decisions Uncertain in Civil Rights Charges against Zimmerman," ABC News, March 19, 2014, http://www.abc57.com/news/national-world/Decision-uncertain-in-civil-rights-charges-against-Zimmerman-251100481.html.

101. Akhil Amar, *The Bill of Rights* (New Haven, Conn.: Yale University Press, 1998), 82.

102. *Rummel v. Estelle*, 445 U.S. 263 (1980).

103. *Furman v. Georgia*, 408 U.S. 238 (1972).

104. *Gregg v. Georgia*, 428 U.S. 153 (1976).

105. *District Attorney's Office v. Osborne*, 557 U.S. 52 (2009).

106. *Herrera v. Collins*, 506 U.S. 390 (1993).

107. *Griswold v. Connecticut,* 381 U.S. 479 (1965).

108. *Eisenstadt v. Baird*, 405 U.S. 438 (1972).

109. Gerald Rosenberg, *The Hollow Hope* (Chicago: University of Chicago Press, 1991), 262.

110. *Roe v. Wade*, 410 U.S. 113 (1973).

111. *Planned Parenthood of Southeastern Pennsylvania v. Casey*, 505 U.S. 833 (1992).

112. *Bowers v. Hardwick*, 478 U.S. 186 (1986).

113. National Opinion Research Center, General Social Survey, University of Chicago.

114. *Lawrence v. Texas*, 539 U.S. 558 (2003).

115. *Cruzan v. Director, Missouri Department of Health*, 497 U.S. 261 (1990), at 278.

116. *Washington v. Glucksberg*, 521 U.S. 702; *Vacco v. Quill*, 521 U.S. 793 (1997).

117. *West Virginia State Board of Education v. Barnette*, 319 U.S. 624 (1943).

118. Robert Dahl, "Decision-Making in a Democracy: The Supreme Court as a National Policy-Maker," *Journal of Public Law* 6 (1957): 279–95.

119. Anthony Lewis, *Freedom for the Thought That We Hate: A Biography of the First Amendment* (New York: Basic Books, 2007).

120. John L. Sullivan, James Pierson, and George Marcus, *Political Tolerance and American Democracy* (Chicago: University of Chicago Press, 1973); James L. Gibson, "Enigmas of Intolerance: Fifty Years after Stouffer's *Communism, Conformity, and Civil Liberties*," *Perspectives on Politics* 4 (March 2006): 22.

Chapter 5

1. Information for this vignette came from Anna Fifield, "Tough Talk over Illegal Immigrants Leaves 'Dreamers' Disillusioned," *Financial Times*, February 27, 2012, accessed April 29, 2014 via LexisNexis Academic Universe; Lawrence Downes, "Questions for a Young Immigration-Rights Activist," *New York Times*, April 10, 2013, http://www.nytimes.com/2013/04/11/opinion/questions-for-a-young-immigration-rights-activist.html?_r=0;http://www.youtube.com/watch?v=FVZKfoXsMxk; http://freedomfromfearaward.com/celebrate/erikaandiola; https://www.facebook.com/erika.andiola; http://unitedwedream.org/press-releases/dream-youth-and-supporters-denounce-home-raid-and-detention-of-erika-andiolas-family-by-ice/; Julia Preston, "Report Finds Deportation Focus on Criminal Records, *New York Times*, April 29, 2014, p. A16, http://www.nytimes.com/2014/04/30/us/report-finds-deportations-focus-on-criminal-records.html?_r=0; "Erika Andiola Slams Obama over Deportations," accessed April 30, 2014, http://video.foxnews.com/v/3430812515001/erika-andiola-slams-obama-over-deportations/#sp=show-clips.

2. See Alexander Keyssar, *The Right to Vote* (New York: Basic Books, 2000), 17 (women) and 164 (Native Americans).

3. Senator Lyman Trumbull, quoted in Judith Baer, *Equality under the Constitution* (Ithaca, N.Y.: Cornell University Press, 1983), 96.

4. Quoted in Steven M. Gillon and Cathy D. Matson, *The American Experiment*, 2nd ed. (Boston: Houghton Mifflin, 2006), 61.

5. *Dred Scott v. Sandford*, 60 U.S. 393 (1857).

6. Peter H. Schuck and Rogers M. Smith, *Citizenship without Consent* (New Haven, Conn.: Yale University Press, 1985), 1–2.

7. *Johnson v. M'Intosh*, 21 U.S. 543 (1823), at 569.

8. *Elk v. Wilkins*, 112 U.S. 94 (1884).

9. Institute for Texan Cultures, *The Tejanos*, accessed June 3, 2014, http://www.texancultures.com/assets/1/15/Texans_One_and_All%20-%20The%20Tejanos.pdf.

10. Kevin R. Johnson, "The Forgotten Repatriation of Persons of Mexican Ancestry and Lessons for the War on Terror," *Pace L. Rev.* 26, 1 (2005): 104.

11. Texas State Historical Association, *Operation Wetback,* accessed June 3, 2014, http://www.tshaonline.org/handbook/online/articles/pqo01.

12. Johnson, 111.

13. Johnson, 110.

14. California Alien Land Law (1913).

15. *Korematsu v. United States,* 323 U.S. 214 (1944).

16. Anne McDermott, "Orphans Tell of World War II Internment," March 24, 1997, CNN, http://www.cnn.com/US/9703/24/interned.orphans.

17. Immigration Act of 1907, 43 Statutes at Large 153.

18. Rogers M. Smith, *Civic Ideals* (New Haven, Conn.: Yale University Press, 1997), 16; Siobhan B. Sommerville, "Queer Alienage: The Racial and Sexual Logic of the 1952 U.S. Immigration and Nationality Act," Working Paper Series on Historical Systems, Peoples and Cultures (No. 12), 2002, 8, accessed June 6, 2014, http://www2.bgsu.edu/downloads/cas/file46880.pdf.

19. "Immigration Restriction," eHistory @ The Ohio State University, accessed May 12, 2012, http://ehistory.osu.edu/osu/mmh/clash/Imm_KKK/Immigration%20Pages/Immigration-page1.htm.

20. Smith, *Civic Ideals,* 17.

21. Immigration Act of 1924, 43 Statutes at Large 153.

22. *United States v. Cruikshank*, 92 U.S. 542 (1876).

23. Ronald Walters, "'The Association Is for the Direct Attack': The Militant Context of the NAACP Challenge to *Plessy*," *Washburn Law Journal* 43 (Winter 2004): 329.

24. *Plessy v. Ferguson,* 163 U.S. 537 (1896).

25. Vicki L. Ruiz, "South by Southwest: Mexican Americans and Segregated Schooling, 1900–1950," *OAH Magazine of History* 15 (Winter 2001): 23–27.

26. *Westminster School District v. Mendez*, 161 F.2d 774 (1947).

27. Ruiz, "South by Southwest."

28. Quoted in Renata Fengler, "Abigail and John Adams Discuss Women and Republican Government: 1776," part of the "Documenting American History" project, University of Wisconsin–Green Bay, last modified July 29, 2009, accessed April 25, 2012, http://www.historytools.org/sources/Abigail-John-Letters.pdf.

29. Keyssar, *Right to Vote.*

30. E. Susan Barber, comp., "One Hundred Years toward Suffrage: An Overview," Library of Congress, National American Woman Suffrage Association Collection, accessed May 14, 2012, http://memory.loc.gov/ammem/naw/nawstime.html.

31. Survey conducted by the Office of Public Opinion Research, July 1945, retrieved May 14, 2012, from the iPOLL Databank, The Roper Center for Public Opinion Research, University of Connecticut.

32. "The Law: Up from Coverture," *Time Magazine,* March 20, 1972, http://www.time.com/time/magazine/article/0,9171,942533,00.html.

33. *Kirchberg v. Feenstra*, 450 U.S. 455 (1981), at 456.

34. Richard Kluger, *Simple Justice* (New York: Knopf, 1975), 376.

35. See Laurence H. Tribe, *American Constitutional Law* (Mineola, N.Y.: Foundation Press, 1988), 1561–65.

36. Ibid.

37. Baer, *Chains of Protection,* 111–21.

38. *Hoyt v. Florida*, 368 U.S. 57 (1961).

39. *Civil Rights Cases*, 109 U.S. 3 (1883); *Shelley v. Kraemer*, 334 U.S. 1 (1948).

40. *Missouri ex rel. Gaines v. Canada*, 305 U.S. 337 (1938); *Sipuel v. Board of Regents of University of Oklahoma*, 332 U.S. 631 (1948); *Sweatt v. Painter*, 339 U.S. 629 (1950).

41. *Bolling v. Sharpe*, 347 U.S. 497 (1954).

42. *Brown v. Board of Education*, 349 U.S. 294 (1955).

43. *Cooper v. Aaron*, 358 U.S. 1 (1958).

44. Gerald N. Rosenberg, *The Hollow Hope: Can Courts Bring about Social Change* (Chicago: University of Chicago Press, 1991), 46–54.

45. *Alexander v. Holmes County Board of Education*, 396 U.S. 1218 (1969).

46. *Browder v. Gayle*, 352 U.S. 903 (1956).

47. *Jackson v. Alabama*, 348 U.S. 888 (1954).

48. Quoted in Walter F. Murphy, *Elements of Judicial Strategy* (Chicago: University of Chicago Press, 1964), 193.

49. *Loving v. Virginia*, 388 U.S. 1 (1967).

50. David Fankhauser, "Freedom Rides: Recollections by David Fankhauser," last modified May 13, 2011, accessed April 25, 2012, http://biology.clc.uc.edu/fankhauser/society/freedom_rides/freedom_ride_dbf.htm.

51. Martin Luther King Jr., "Letter from Birmingham Jail," April 16, 1963, The King Center, accessed April 25, 2012, http://www.thekingcenter.org/archive/document/letter-birmingham-city-jail-0.

52. Martin Luther King Jr., "The I Have a Dream Speech," August 28, 1963, U.S. Constitution Online, accessed April 25, 2012, http://www.usconstitution.net/dream.html.

53. *Heart of Atlanta Motel v. United States*, 379 U.S. 241 (1964); *Katzenbach v. McClung*, 379 U.S. 294 (1964).

54. *Guinn v. United States*, 238 U.S. 347 (1915); *Smith v. Allwright*, 321 U.S 649 (1944).

55. Martin Luther King Jr., "Civil Right No. 1: The Right to Vote," *New York Times Magazine*, March 14, 1965, 26.

56. Pew Hispanic Center, "Dissecting the 2008 Electorate: Most Diverse in U.S. History," Pew Research Center, April 30, 2009, accessed April 25, 2012, http://www.pewhispanic.org/2009/04/30/dissecting-the-2008-electorate-most-diverse-in-us-history/.

57. *Northwest Austin Municipal Utility District No. One v. Holder* 557 U.S. 193 (2009).

58. Rachel Weiner, "Black Voters Turned Out at Higher Rate Than White Voters in 2012 and 2008," *The Washington Post,* April 29, 2013, http://www.washingtonpost.com/blogs/the-fix/wp/2013/04/29/black-turnout-was-higher-than-white-turnout-in-2012-and-2008.

59. *Shelby County v. Holder* 133 S. Ct. 2612 (2013).

60. Adam Liptak, "Supreme Court Invalidates Key Part of Voting Rights," *The New York Times*, June 25, 2013, http://www.nytimes.com/2013/06/26/us/supreme-court-ruling.html?pagewanted=all&_r=0>.

61. *Hernandez v. Texas*, 347 U.S. 475 (1954).

62. *Cisneros v. Corpus Christi Independent School District*, 404 U.S. 1211 (1970).

63. A. Reynaldo Contreras and Leonard A. Valverde, "The Impact of *Brown* on the Education of Latinos" *Journal of Negro Education* (1994) 63: 471–72.

64. *Plyler v. Doe*, 457 U.S. 202 (1982).

65. Library of Congress. *Hispanic Americans in Congress, 1822-1995*, http://www.loc.gov/rr/hispanic/congress/gonzalez.html; Molly Ivins, November 30, 2000, http://www.creators.com/opinion/molly-ivins/molly-ivins-november-30-2000-11-30.html.

66. *Katzenbach v. Morgan*, 384 U.S. 641 (1966), *Cardona v. Power*, 384 U.S. 672 (1966).

67. 42 USC sec. 203 (1975)

68. *White v. Regester*, 412 U.S. 755 (1973). See also *Graves v. Barnes*, 405 U.S. 1201 (1972).

69. Charles L. Cotrell and R. Michael Stevens, "The 1975 Voting Rights Act and San Antonio, Texas: Toward a Federal Guarantee of a Republican Form of Government," *Publius* (1977): 79–99; United States Commission on Civil Rights, "Using the Voting Rights Act" (Washington, D.C.: U.S. Government Printing Office, 1975).

70. Guadalupe San Miguel, Jr.,"'Let All of Them Take Heed': Mexican Americans and the Campaign for Educational Equality in Texas, 1910-1981" (University of Texas Press, 1987).

71. United Farm Workers, "Successes Through the Years," http://www.ufw.org/_page.php?menu=research&inc=history/02.html.

72. Steven Yaccino and Lizette Alvarez, "New G.O.P. Bid to Limit Voting in Swing States," *New York Times*, March 29, 2014, http://www.nytimes.com/2014/03/30/us/new-gop-bid-to-limit-voting-in-swing-states.html?hp&_r=1&assetType=nyt_now.

73. Cesar Chavez, *1984 Commonwealth Club Address*, http://www.ufw.org/_page.php?menu=research&inc=history/12.html.

74. U.S. Bureau of Labor Statistics, *Highlights of Women's Earnings in 2012* (Washington, D.C., October 2013), Table 1, accessed June 6, 2014, http://www.bls.gov/cps/cpswom2012.pdf.

75. Ibid.

76. *Burlington Northern and Santa Fe Railway Co. v. White,* 548 U.S. 53 (2006).

77. *Ledbetter v. Goodyear Tire and Rubber Co.,* 550 U.S. 618 (2007).

78. Ibid., 645.

79. Lilly Ledbetter Fair Pay Act of 2009, Pub. L. No. 111-2, 42 USC 2000e-5 (2009), http://www.gpo.gov/fdsys/pkg/PLAW-111publ2/html/PLAW-111publ2.htm.

80. ABA Section of Labor & Employment Law, *Survey of Recent Cases under the Lily Ledbetter Fair Pay Act,* March 2011, accessed May 23, 2012, http://www2.americanbar.org/calendar/ll0322-2011-midwinter-meeting/Documents/08_complexlitigation.pdf (on new cases), and U.S. Bureau of Labor Statistics, *Highlights of Women's Earnings*, on continuing pay disparity.

81. http://beta.congress.gov/bill/113th-congress/senate-bill/84, accessed April 29, 2014.

82. Wesley Lowery, "Senate Falls Six Votes Short of Passing Paycheck Fairness Act," *Washington Post,* April 9, 2014, http://www.washingtonpost.com/blogs/post-politics/wp/2014/04/09/senate-falls-six-votes-short-of-passing-paycheck-fairness-act/.

83. Juliet Eilpern, "Obama to Sign Two Executive Orders Aimed at Narrowing Gender Gap in Wages," *Washington Post,* April 7, 2014, http://www.washingtonpost.com/politics/obama-to-sign-two-executive-orders-aimed-at-narrowing-gender-gap-in-wages/2014/04/07/3f0ce4a8-be74-11e3-bcec-b71ee10e9bc3_story.html.

84. *Bowers v. Hardwick*, 478 U.S. 186 (1986).

85. *Romer v. Evans*, 517 U.S. 620 (1996).

86. *Lawrence v. Texas,* 539 U.S. 558 (2003).

87. *Hollingsworth v. Perry*, 133 S.Ct. 2652 (2013).

88. 133 S. Ct. 2675 (2013).

89. A March 2014 Bloomberg National poll found by 55–36 that Americans support allowing same-sex couples to get married; data accessed April 28, 2014, from http://www.pollingreport.com/civil.htm.

90. U.S. Equal Employment Opportunity Commission, *The Americans with Disabilities Act: A Primer for Small Business,* last modified February 4, 2004, accessed May 15, 2012, http://www.eeoc.gov/eeoc/publications/adahandbook.cfm.

91. "Employers Say OFCCP Disabilities Proposal Would Be Overly Burdensome," *Bloomberg BNA*, April 16, 2012, accessed May 14, 2012, http://www.bna.com/employers-say-ofccp-n12884908933.

92. Gustave Valdes, "Undocumented Immigrant Population on the Rise in the U.S.," *CNN*, September 25, 2013, accessed April 15, 2014, http://www.cnn.com/2013/09/24/us/undocumented-immigrants-population.

93. "32% Say Child Born in U.S. to Illegal Immigrant Should Receive Automatic Citizenship," accessed June 6, 2014, http://www.rasmussenreports.com/public_content/politics/current_events/immigration/august_2013/32_say_child_born_in_u_s_to_illegal_immigrant_should_receive_automatic_citizenship.

94. Poll conducted by Quinnipiac University, October 2011, retrieved March 18, 2012, from the iPOLL Databank, The Roper Center for Public Opinion Research, University of Connecticut.

95. *Plyler v. Doe*, 457 U.S. 202 (1982).

96. King, "Civil Right No. 1."

97. M. V. Hood, Quentin Kidd, and Irwin L. Morris, "The Key Issue: Constituency Effects and Southern Senators' Roll-Call Voting on Civil Rights," *Legislative Studies Quarterly* 26 (2001): 599–621.

98. Royce Carroll, Jeff Lewis, James Lo, Nolan McCarty, Keith Poole, and Howard Rosenthal, "'Common Space' DW-NOMINATE Scores with Bootstrapped Standard Errors (Joint House and Senate Scaling)," Voteview.com, last modified January 22, 2011, accessed May 14, 2012, http://www.voteview.com/dwnomjoint.asp.

Chapter 6

1. Chad Livengood, "Armed with His Delaware-based 'Anonymous Shell Corporation,' Colbert Seeks 'Massive' Donations," *Dialogue Delaware*, last modified October 7, 2011, accessed April 14, 2014, http://blogs.delawareonline.com/dialoguedelaware/2011/10/07/armed-with-his-anonymous-delaware-shell-corporation-colbert-seeks-massive-donations/.

2. Survey for Pew Research Center for the People & the Press, conducted by Princeton Survey Research Associates International, May 9 – June 3, 2012, retrieved April 23, 2014.

3. Cynthia Littleton, "Stephen Colbert's Rise: From South Carolina to Second City to Pop Culture Player," *Variety*, April 10, 2014, accessed April 14, 2014, http://variety.com/2014/tv/news/stephen-colberts-rise-from-south-carolina-to-second-city-to-pop-culture-player-1201155535/.

4. See http://www.hsc.edu/About-H-SC.html.

5. Littleton, "Stephen Colbert's Rise;" Ken P., "An Interview with Stephen Colbert," *IGN*, August 11, 2003, accessed April 14, 2014, http://www.ign.com/articles/2003/08/11/an-interview-with-stephen-colbert?page=1.

6. Ken P., "An Interview with Stephen Colbert;" Littleton, "Stephen Colbert's Rise."

7. "Truthiness," *Wikipedia*, last modified April 9, 2014, accessed April 14, 2014, https://en.wikipedia.org/wiki/Truthiness.

8. See http://www.merriam-webster.com/info/06words.htm.

9. James H. Fowler, "The Colbert Bump in Campaign Donations: More Truthful Than Truthy," *PS: Political Science & Politics* 41 (3) (2008): 533–39, http://jhfowler.ucsd.edu/colbert_bump.pdf.

10. "Stephen Colbert: 2010 Congressional Testimony," *Wikipedia*, last modified April 13, 2014, accessed April 14, 2014, https://en.wikipedia.org/wiki/Stephen_Colbert#2010_Congressional_testimony.

11. KrayolaTop, "Stephen Colbert to Congress 'migrant workers suffer and have no rights'," *YouTube*, uploaded September 24, 2010, access April 14, 2014, https://www.youtube.com/watch?v=nxeIO4pW05s&noredirect=1.

12. See http://www.mediaite.com/online/limbaugh-blasts-colbert-pick-cbs-has-just-declared-war-on-the-heartland-of-america/, accessed April 28, 2014.

13. Quoted in Harry Jaffa, *The Crisis of the House Divided*, 2nd ed. (Chicago: University of Chicago Press, 1959), 10.

14. See James Bryce, *The American Commonwealth* (New York: MacMillan, 1895), 239.

15. Survey conducted by Quinnipiac University Polling Institute, January 15–19, 2014, retrieved April 7, 2014, from the iPOLL Databank, The Roper Center for Public Opinion Research, University of Connecticut.

16. See 2012 American National Election Studies, http://electionstudies.org/.

17. Survey for Pew Research Center for the People & the Press, conducted by Princeton Survey Research Associates International, February 14–23, 2014, retrieved April 7, 2014, through The Roper Center for Public Opinion Research, University of Connecticut.

18. It is hard to know the exact share of people who would support overthrowing the American government because pollsters almost never ask that question. We say "almost never," but in our search of questions asked over the past seventy-five years, we have not found one such question. A database at the Roper Center at the University of Connecticut contains nearly five hundred thousand questions, allowing a detailed search.

19. Robert Erikson and Kent Tedin, *American Public Opinion*, 6th ed. (New York: Longman, 2003), 7.

20. George Gallup, *The Pulse of Democracy* (New York: Simon and Schuster, 1940).

21. Survey for *60 Minutes, Vanity Fair*, conducted by CBS News, March 27–30, 2013, accessed on April 7, 2014, through The Roper Center for Public Opinion Research, University of Connecticut.

22. Erikson and Tedin, *American Public Opinion*, 26.

23. Joshua D. Clinton, and Steven Rogers, "Robo-Polls: Taking Cues from Traditional Sources?" *PS: Political Science & Politics* 46, 2 (2013): 333–337.

24. Alicia C. Shepard, "How They Blew It," *American Journalism Review* (January/February 2001).

25. Kathy Frankovic, "The Truth about Push Polls," *CBS News*, February 11, 2009, http://www.cbsnews.com/2100-250_162-160398.html.

26. These data come from 2003 polls retrieved April 15, 2012, from the iPOLL Databank, The Roper Center for Public Opinion Research, University of Connecticut.

27. See Philip E. Converse, "Nonattitudes and American Public Opinion: Comment: The Status of Nonattitudes," *American Political Science Review* 68 (June 1974): 650–60.

28. Pew Research Center for the People & the Press, "Cell Phones and the 2008 Vote: An Update," Pew Research Center, July 17, 2008, accessed April 27, 2012, http://pewresearch.org/pubs/901/cell-phones-polling-election-2008.

29. See also Pew Research Center for the People & the Press, "Polls Face Growing Resistance, but Still Representative," Pew Research Center, April 20, 2004, accessed April 27, 2012, http://people-press.org/2004/04/20/polls-face-growing-resistance-but-still-representative/.

30. The classic book that lays out the argument about party identification is Angus Campbell, Philip Converse, Warren Miller, and Donald Stokes, *The American Voter* (New York: Wiley, 1960).

31. See American National Election Studies, "Party Identification 7- Point Scale 1952–2008," *ANES Guide to Public Opinion and Electoral Behavior*, last modified August 5, 2010, accessed April 27, 2012, http://www.electionstudies.org/nesguide/toptable/tab2a_1.htm.

32. David Brooks, "What Independents Want," *New York Times*, November 5, 2009, A31.

33. John Sides, "Three Myths about Political Independents," *The Monkey Cage* (blog), December 17, 2009, http://www.themonkeycage.org/blog/2009/12/17/three_myths_about_political_in/.

34. Survey for Associated Press, conducted by GfK Knowledge Networks, March 20–24, 2014, retrieved April 7, 2014, from the iPOLL Databank, The Roper Center for Public Opinion Research, University of Connecticut.

35. This way of thinking about the public comes from Philip Converse, "Nature of Belief Systems in Mass Publics," in *Ideology and Discontent*, ed. David Apter (New York: Free Press, 1964).

36. The exact percentage of the public that was literate at the time of the founding is unclear. This percentage reflects the best guess of some historians.

37. *CIA World Factbook*, https://www.cia.gov/library/publications/the-world-factbook/geos/us.html.

38. These data all come from Erikson and Tedin, *American Public Opinion*, 8th ed., 61.

39. See John Zaller, "Monica Lewinsky and the Mainsprings of American Politics," in *Mediated Politics: Communication in the Future of Democracy*, ed. W. Lance Bennett and Robert M. Entman (Cambridge, U.K.: Cambridge University Press, 2001).

40. Stanley Kelley, *Interpreting Elections* (Princeton, N.J.: Princeton University Press, 1983).

41. Christopher Achen, "Mass Political Attitudes and the Survey Response," *American Political Science Review* 69 (1975): 1218–31.

42. Sam Popkin developed this concept in his book *The Reasoning Voter* (Chicago: University of Chicago Press, 1991).

43. "The Polarization of the Congressional Parties," Voteview.com, last modified March 6, 2012, accessed April 27, 2012, http://voteview.com/political_polarization.asp.

44. "The Abu Ghraib Files," *Salon*, March 14, 2006, http://www.salon.com/2006/03/14/introduction_2/.

45. Sarah Mendelson, "The Guantanamo Countdown," *Foreign Affairs*, October 1, 2009.

46. Survey from Associated Press, conducted by National Opinion Research Center, University of Chicago, August 12–29, 2013, retrieved April 17, 2014, from the iPOLL Databank, The Roper Center for Public Opinion Research, University of Connecticut.

47. Survey conducted by Quinnipiac University Polling Institute, January 4–7, 2014, retrieved May 4, 2014, from the iPOLL Databank, The Roper Center for Public Opinion Research, University of Connecticut.

48. See http://www.people-press.org/2013/12/03/public-sees-u-s-power-declining-as-support-for-global-engagement-slips/, accessed May 4, 2014.

49. For a comprehensive account of these data, see Alan Abramowitz and Kyle Saunders, "Is Polarization a Myth?," *Journal of Politics* 70 (2008): 542–55.

50. "Polarization of the Congressional Parties."

51. See Morris Fiorina, *Culture War?* (New York: Longman, 2008).

52. Morris Fiorina, Samuel Abrams, and Jeremy Pope, "Polarization in the American Public," *Journal of Politics* 70 (2008): 558.

53. See Alan Abramowitz, *The Disappearing Center* (New Haven, Conn.: Yale University Press, 2010).

54. The data from 2000 are from the CBS/*New York Times* polls conducted during the presidential campaigns and available through the iPOLL Databank, The Roper Center for Public Opinion Research, University of Connecticut.

55. The data for 2012 are from a survey by the Associated Press, conducted by Gfk Roper Public Affairs & Corporate Communications, by the Associated Press. Methodology: Conducted by Gfk Roper Public Affairs & Corporate Communications, September 13–17, 2012, and based on 1,512 telephone interviews.

56. Erikson and Tedin, *American Public Opinion, 8th ed.*, 193.

57. Survey conducted for CBS News/*New York Times*, February 19–23, 2014, retrieved April 7, 2014, from the iPOLL Databank, The Roper Center for Public Opinion Research, University of Connecticut.

58. Ibid., 208.

59. Pew Research Center, "Muslim Americans: Middle Class and Mostly Mainstream," Pew Research Center, May 22, 2007, accessed April 27, 2012, http://pewresearch.org/pubs/483/muslim-americans.

60. Susan Page, "Swing States Poll: A Shift by Women Puts Obama in Lead," *USA Today*, last modified April 2, 2012, http://www.usatoday.com/news/politics/story/2012-04-01/swing-states-poll/53930684/1.

61. Center for American Women and Politics, Eagleton Institute of Politics, Rutgers University, "The Gender Gap: Voting Choices in Presidential Elections," December 2008, accessed May 23, 2012, http://www.cawp.rutgers.edu/fast_facts/voters/documents/GGPresVote.pdf.

62. Survey for United Technologies, National Journal, conducted by Princeton Survey Research Associates International, October 3–6, 2013, retrieved April 8, 2014, from the iPOLL Databank, The Roper Center for Public Opinion Research, University of Connecticut.

63. Survey conducted for CNN by ORC International, May 17–18, 2013, retrieved April 8, 2014, from the iPOLL Databank, The Roper Center for Public Opinion Research, University of Connecticut.

64. Data from American National Election Studies, "Aid to Blacks/Minorities 1970–2008," *ANES Guide to Public Opinion and Electoral Behavior*, last modified August 5, 2010, accessed May 12, 2012, http://www.electionstudies.org/nesguide/2ndtable/t4b_4_1.htm.

65. Data from the March 2012 General Social Survey conducted by the National Opinion Research Center (NORC) at The University of Chicago.

66. Carole Jean Uhlaner and F. Chris Garcia, "Latino Public Opinion," in *Understanding Public Opinion*, ed. Barbara Norrander and Clyde Wilcox (Washington, D.C.: CQ Press, 2002).

67. Rodolfo De la Garza, Louis DeSipio, F. Chris Garcia, John Garcia, and Angelo Falcon, *Latino Voices: Mexican, Puerto Rican, and Cuban Perspectives on American Politics* (Boulder, Colo.: Westview Press, 1992).

68. That figure combines identifiers with "leaners."

69. Pew Research Hispanic Trends Project, December 28, 2011, http://www.pewhispanic.org/2011/12/28/vii-views-of-the-political-parties-and-party-identification/.

70. David L. Leal, "Latino Public Opinion," Texas A&M University, Department of Political Science: Project for Equity, Representation, and Justice, accessed April 27, 2012, http://perg.tamu.edu/lpc/Leal.pdf.

71. Alexander Kuo, Neil Malhotra, and Cecilia Hyunjung Mo, Why Do Asian Americans Identify as Democrats? Testing Theories of Social Exclusion and Intergroup Solidarity, working paper, Vanderbilt University, February 25, 2014.

72. Pew Research Center for the People & the Press, "Where the Public Stands on Immigration Reform," Pew Research Center, November 23, 2009, accessed April 27, 2012, http://pewtrusts.org/our-work-report-detail.aspx?id=56203.

73. See Norman H. Nie, Jane Junn, and Kenneth Stehlik-Barry, *Education and Democratic Citizenship in America* (Chicago: University of Chicago Press, 1996).

74. Herbert Gans, *Democracy and the News* (New York: Oxford University Press, 2003), 1.

75. Thomas Jefferson to Edward Carrington, "Volume 5, Amendment I (Speech and Press), Document 8," January 16, 1787, *The Founders' Constitution*, ed. Philip B. Kurland and Ralph Lerner (Chicago: University of Chicago Press, 1986), accessed May 27, 2012, http://press-pubs.uchicago.edu/founders/documents/amendI_speechs8.html.

76. Pew Research Center's Project for Excellence in Journalism, "A Year in the News," *The State of the News Media 2009: An Annual Report on American Journalism*, accessed May 27, 2012, http://stateofthemedia.org/2009/a-year-in-the-news. See, especially, the section titled, "The Economy Finally Emerges as a Major Story."

77. See http://www.journalism.org/media-indicators/top-20-network-news -stories-of-2013/, accessed April 20, 2014.

78. Bob Woodward and Carl Bernstein, *All the President's Men* (New York: Simon and Schuster, 1994).

79. Thomas E. Patterson, *Out of Order* (New York: Knopf, 1993), 82.

80. See http://stateofthemedia.org/2013/overview-5/key-findings/, accessed April 20, 2014.

81. "Clear Channel Media + Entertainment," Clear Channel, accessed June 25, 2014 http://clearchannel.com/CCME/Pages/default.aspx.

82. Shanto Iyengar, *Media Politics: A Citizen's Guide,* 2nd ed. (New York: W.W. Norton, 2011), 51.

83. See Pew Research Center's Project for Excellence in Journalism's *The State of the News Media 2012: An Annual Report on American Journalism,* http://stateofthemedia.org/2012/, for a range of data documenting this point.

84. Michael Schudson and Susan Tifft, "American Journalism in Historical Perspective," in *The Press,* ed. Geneva Overholser and Kathleen Hall Jamieson (New York: Oxford University Press, 2005), 26.

85. See http://www.pewinternet.org/2014/02/27/summary-of-findings-3/, accessed on April 20, 2014.

86. Charlie Sorrel, "Apple's iPad Sales Accelerate: Three Million Sold in 80 Days," *Gadget Lab* (blog), Wired, June 23, 2010, http://www.wired .com/gadgetlab/2010/06/apples-ipad-sales -accelerate-three-million -sold-in-80-days.

87. See http://www.statista.com/statistics/183585/adult-twitter-users -in-the-us-since-2009/, accessed on April 20, 2014.

88. See http://www.pewinternet.org/, accessed State of the News Media 2014 on April 20, 2014.

89. Data available at "Report: Community Journalism in the United States," Bill Lane Center for the American West, Stanford University, last modified August 7, 2011, accessed May 27, 2012, http:// www .stanford.edu/group/ruralwest/cgi-bin/drupal/projects /newspapers.

90. For data on news consumption, see *The State of the News Media 2014* report available from the Pew Research Center's Project for Excellence in Journalism at http://www.journalism.org/packages /state-of-the-news-media-2014/

91. Alex Jones, *Losing the News* (New York: Oxford University Press, 2009).

92. The data come from a study conducted for the Newspaper Association of America. See "Study: Newspapers Attract 102.8 million U.S. Internet Users," *SFN Blog,* World Association of Newspapers and News Publishers, http://www.sfnblog.com/2010/10/14/study -newspapers-attract-1028-million-us-internet-users.

93. Geoffrey Cowan, "Leading the Way to Better News" (Discussion Paper Series, Joan Shorenstein Center on the Press, Politics, and Public Policy, Harvard University, 2008), 7.

94. Ibid.

95. See http://www.journalism.org/2014/03/26/the-losses-in-legacy/, accessed April 28, 2014.

96. See Jones, *Losing the News.*

97. See Bill Mitchell, "Clues in the Rubble: Finding a Framework to Sustain Local News" (Discussion Paper Series, Joan Shorenstein Center on the Press, Politics, and Public Policy, Harvard University, 2010).

98. Pew Research Center's Project for Excellence in Journalism, "Audio: How Far Will Digital Go?," *The State of the News Media 2012,* Pew Research Center, accessed May 27, 2012, http://stateofthemedia. org/2012/audio-how-far-will-digital-go/.

99. See David Barker, *Rushed to Judgment* (New York: Columbia University Press, 2002).

100. Pew Research Center's Project for Excellence in Journalism, "Talk Radio," *The State of the News Media 2012,* Pew Research Center, accessed May 28, 2012, http://stateofthemedia.org/2012 /audio-how-far-will-digital-go/#talk-radio.

101. No one has studied reasons why liberal talk radio has failed, but we offer some hypotheses here. Thank you to Markus Prior of Princeton University for brainstorming with us on this topic.

102. See http://www.journalism.org/media-indicators/evening-network-news -share-over-time/, accessed April 20, 2014.

103. Most of the data presented here came from Pew Research Center's Project for Excellence in Journalism, "Journalism, Satire or Just Laughs? 'The Daily Show with Jon Stewart,' Examined," Journalism .org, May 8, 2008, http://www.journalism.org/node/10961.

104. http://www.thefutoncritic.com/ratings/2013/04/04/the-daily-show -and-the-colbert-report-finish-1q-2013-as-number-1-and-number-2 -among-adults-18-49-and-all-key-young-demos-795303/20130404 comedycentral01/, accessed April 21, 2014.

105. eBizMBA's ranking of the top fifteen blogs is available at http://www .ebizmba.com/articles/blogs. The rankings shown here were retrieved in April 2014.

106. Eric Lawrence, John Sides, and Henry Farrell, "Self-Segregation or Deliberation? Blog Readership, Participation, and Polarization in American Politics," *Perspectives on Politics* 8, 1 (2010): 146.

107. See http://www.drudgereport.com and http://www.rushlimbaugh .com/.

108. See Dylan Tweney, "Controlled Chaos: An Interview with Kos," *Epicenter* (blog), Wired, May 8, 2007, http://blog.wired.com/business /2007/05/controlled_chao.html.

109. https://www.facebook.com/facebook/info, accessed June 25, 2014.

110. http://www.businessweek.com/articles/2014-01-29/facebook -quiets-skeptics-with-member-growth-and-mobile-money, accessed April 21, 2014. In an informal survey of high school kids in middle Tennessee, Olivia Alpert found that 80 percent of her classmates also use Snapchat.

111. http://mashable.com/2014/02/24/snapchat-study-college-stu- dents/, accessed on April 21, 2014.

112. The authors confirmed this fact through their own Facebook accounts.

113. "ABC News Joins Forces with Facebook," *ABC News,* December 18, 2007, http://abcnews.go.com/Technology/Politics/story?id=3899006& page=1#.T7J9ccXtMVA.

114. For example, in a local county election for a judgeship in Tennessee, Vince Wyatt had a twitter feed: @Wyatt4Judge. This is hardly unusual in 2014.

115. See http://tvbythenumbers.zap2it.com/2013/05/22/telemundo-delivers -best-season-ever-up-9-vs-2011-2012-season/183980/ and http://www .deadline.com/2013/05/cbs-wins-season-abc-tops-adults-18-49-in -seasons-final-week/.

116. Mark Hugo Lopez and Anna Gonzalez-Barrera, "A Growing Share of Latinos Get Their News in English," *Pew Research Hispanic Trends Project,* July 23, 2013, http://www.pewhispanic.org/2013/07/23/a -growing-share-of-latinos-get-their-news-in-english/.

117. Thomas E. Patterson, *Young People and News* (Cambridge, MA: Joan Shorenstein Center on the Press, Politics, and Public Policy, Harvard University, July 2007).

118. Morley Winograd and Michael D. Hais, *Millennial Makeover: MySpace, YouTube and the Future of American Politics* (New Brunswick, N.J.: Rutgers University Press, 2008).

119. Paul Lazarsfeld, Bernard Berelson, and Hazel Gaudet, *The People's Choice* (New York: Columbia University Press, 1944). It is worth noting that the 1940 campaign was probably the worst campaign

in which to look for possible media effects. It was the only presidential election in U.S. history in which a sitting president, Franklin Roosevelt, was running for a third term. The stability of preference surely reflected the fact that people had opinions about Roosevelt and that not much would change them one way or the other. In contrast, Senator Obama was not a well-known figure in the 2008 presidential campaign.

120. Angus Campbell et al., *The American Voter* (New York: Wiley, 1960).

121. http://www.gallup.com/poll/170750/despite-enrollment-success -healthcare-law-remains-unpopular.aspx

122. Bernard Cohen, *The Press and Foreign Policy* (Princeton, N.J.: Princeton University Press, 1963), 13.

123. Darrell M. West, Grover J. Whitehurst, and E. J. Dionne Jr., "Invisible: 1.4 Percent Coverage for Education Is Not Enough," Brookings.edu, December 2, 2009, accessed May 28, 2012, http://www.brookings .edu/research/reports/2009/12/02-education-news-west.

124. Shanto Iyengar and Jennifer A. McGrady, *Media Politics: A Citizen's Guide* (New York: W.W. Norton, 2007), 216.

125. These scholars have reshaped how we think about framing. In fact, Kahneman won a Nobel Prize for this work in 2003. See http://psych .hanover.edu/classes/cognition/papers/tversky81.pdf.

126. W. Lance Bennett, Regina C. Lawrence, and Steven Livingston, *When the Press Fails: Political Power and the News Media from Iraq to Katrina* (Chicago: University of Chicago Press, 2007).

127. See Jonathan Ladd, *Why Americans Hate the Media* (Princeton, N.J.: Princeton University Press, 2012). Ladd also kindly provided us updated figures for this trend line.

128. See Jonathan Ladd, *Why Americans Hate the Media* (Princeton, N.J.: Princeton University Press, 2012). Ladd also kindly provided us updated figures for this trend line.

129. See Michael Schudson, *The Sociology of News* (New York: W.W. Norton, 2003), 33.

130. See the Accuracy in Media website at http://www.aim.org.

131. Conducted by Gallup Organization, September 5–8, 2013, retrieved from the iPOLL Databank, The Roper Center for Public Opinion Research, University of Connecticut accessed April 14, 2014.

132. Thomas Patterson, "Political Roles of the Journalist," in *The Politics of the News*, ed. Doris Graber, Denis McQuail, and Pippa Norris (Washington, D.C.: CQ Press, 2000), 3.

133. For a thoughtful discussion of soft news, see Matthew Baum, *Soft News Goes to War: Public Opinion and American Foreign Policy in the New Media Age* (Princeton, N.J.: Princeton University Press, 2003), 6–7.

134. Gary Bunker, *From Rail-Splitter to Icon: Lincoln's Image in Illustrated Periodicals, 1860–1865* (Kent, Ohio: Kent State University Press, 2001).

135. CB Presidential Research Services, "Presidential Campaign Slogans," PresidentsUSA.net, accessed May 28, 2012, http://www.presidentsusa .net/campaignslogans.html.

136. Pew Research Center for the People & the Press, "Public Knowledge of Current Affairs Little Changed by News and Information Revolutions," Pew Research Center, April 15, 2007, accessed May 28, 2012, http:// www.people-press.org/2007/04/15/public-knowledge-of-current -affairs-little-changed-by-news-and-information-revolutions/.

137. http://www.pewinternet.org/data-trend/mobile/cell-phone-and -smartphone-ownership-demographics/, accessed April 21, 2014.

138. http://www.pewinternet.org/three-technology-revolutions/, accessed April 21, 2014.

139. The argument presented over the next few paragraphs is inspired by the work of Markus Prior, *Post Broadcast Democracy* (New York: Cambridge University Press, 2007).

140. Ibid.

141. Robert S. Erikson, Michael B. MacKuen, and James A. Stimson, *The Macro Polity* (Cambridge, U.K.: Cambridge University Press, 2002).

142. Richard Pérez-Peña, "Group Plans to Provide Investigative Journalism," *New York Times,* October 15, 2007, http://www.nytimes .com/2007/10/15/business/media/15publica.html.

Chapter 7

1. This story was compiled from information on the Common Sense Action's website, http://www.commonsenseaction.org; Andrew Kaplan and Sam Gilman, "Repairing Politics the Millennial Way," *Switch and Shift,* March 1, 2014: http://switchandshift.com/repairing-politics -the-millennial-way; and an in-person interview with Andrew Kaplan and Sam Gilman, April 9, 2014, conducted for this textbook, which is the source of Gilman's quotation.

2. Alexis de Tocqueville, *Democracy in America*, ed. J. P. Mayer, trans. George Lawrence (New York: Doubleday & Company, 1969), 193.

3. William C. DiGiacomantonio, "Petitioners and Their Grievances," in *The House and Senate in the 1790s: Petitioning, Lobbying, and Institutional Development*, ed. Kenneth R. Bowling and Donald R. Kennon (Columbus: Ohio University Press, 2002), 29–56.

4. Interest groups at the state level have even been involved in elections for state judges. See Clive S. Thomas, Michael L. Boyer, and Ronald J. Hrebenar, "Interest Groups and State Court Elections: A New Era and Its Challenges," *Judicature* 87 (2003): 135–49.

5. Elizabeth Cady Stanton, Susan B. Anthony, and Matilda J. Gage, eds., *History of Woman Suffrage* (Rochester, N.Y.: Charles Mann Publishers, 1887), 1:70.

6. "141 Men and Girls Die in Waist Factory Fire; Trapped High Up in Washington Place Building; Street Strewn with Bodies; Piles of Dead Inside," *New York Times*, March 26, 1911, 1.

7. Office of the Secretary, United States Department of Labor, "Our Mission," accessed May 23, 2012, http://www.dol.gov/opa/aboutdol /mission.htm.

8. National Labor Relations Act, 29 U.S.C. §§ 151–169 (1935), http:// www.nlrb.gov/national-labor-relations-act.

9. Beth L. Leech, Frank R. Baumgartner, Timothy M. La Pira, and Nicholas A. Semanko, "Drawing Lobbyists to Washington: Government Activity and the Demand for Advocacy," *Political Research Quarterly* 58, no. 1 (2005): 19–30.

10. Elizabeth Ashack, Bureau of Labor Statistics, "Profiles of significant collective bargaining disputes of 2012." May 2013, accessed March 16, 2015, http://www.bls.gov/opub/mlr/2013/article/profiles-of-significant -collective-bargaining-disputes-of-2012.htm.

11. Rachel Weiner, "Issue 2 Falls, Ohio Collective Bargaining Law Repealed," *The Fix* (blog), *Washington Post,* November 8, 2011, http:// www.washingtonpost.com/blogs/the-fix/post/issue-2-falls-ohio -collective-bargaining-law-repealed/2011/11/08/gIQAyZ0U3M_blog .html; the information in the caption on page 205 is from Becket Adams, "Ohio Votes to Overturn Collective Bargaining Law, Votes 'No' to Forced Health Care," *Blaze,* November 8, 2011, http://www.theblaze .com/stories/ohio-votes-to-overturn-collective-bargaining-bill.

12. John Helton and Tom Cohen, "Walker's Wisconsin Win Big Blow to Unions, Smaller One to Obama," CNN, June 6, 2012, http://www .cnn.com/2012/06/05/politics/wisconsin-recall-vote/index.html?hpt =hp_t1.

13. National Right to Work Legal Defense Foundation, Inc., "Right to Work States," accessed August 20, 2014, http://www.nrtw.org/rtws.htm.

14. U.S. Bureau of Labor Statistics, "Union Members Summary," January 24, 2014, accessed March 16, 2014, http://www.bls.gov/news.release /union2.nr0.htm.

15. MoveOn.org, http://front.moveon.org/.

16. American Israel Public Affairs Committee, accessed June 4, 2014, http://www.aipac.org/.

17. Mark R. Amstutz, "Faith-Based NGOs and U.S. Foreign Policy," in *The Influence of Faith: Religious Groups and Foreign Policy,* ed. by Elliot Abrams, 175–87 (Lanham, Md.: Rowman and Littlefield Publishers, 2001); National Council of the Churches of Christ in the USA, http://www.ncccusa.org.

18. American Civil Liberties Union, *Report: Blocking Faith, Freezing Charity,* June 16, 2009, accessed May 23, 2012, http://www.aclu.org/human-rights/report-blocking-faith-freezing-charity.

19. Sierra Club, "Tell President Obama You Support Strong Climate Action!" accessed June 4, 2014, https://secure.sierraclub.org/site/Advocacy?cmd=display&page=UserAction&id=13709&s_src=614ESCHT01.

20. For more information on general lobbying, see Anthony J. Nownes, *Total Lobbying* (New York: Cambridge University Press, 2006).

21. Center for Responsive Politics, "Lobbying Database," OpenSecrets.org, accessed March 14, 2014, http://www.opensecrets.org/lobby/.

22. Ibid.

23. Bart Jansen, "Legislative Summary: Congressional Affairs: Lobbying Practices and Disclosures," *CQ Weekly Online,* January 7, 2008, 39.

24. Gregory Koger and Jennifer N. Victor, "Polarized Agendas: Campaign Contributions by Lobbyists," *PS: Political Science and Politics* 42 (2009): 485–88.

25. Bureau of the Census, "NAIS 2011 – Oil and Gas Extraction" http://thedataweb.rm.census.gov/TheDataWeb_HotReport2/econsnapshot/snapshot.hrml?NAICS=211&IND=%3DCOMP%28C2%2FC3*1000%29&STATE=ALL&COUNTY=ALL.

26. Environmental Protection Agency, "EPA's Study of Hydraulic Fracturing and Its Potential Impact on Drinking Water Resources," accessed June 4, 2014, http://www2.epa.gov/hfstudy.

27. ANGA "About Us," http://anga.us/about-us#.UycJCfldWCk; NRDC "Consolidated Financial Statements" June 30, 2013, http://www.nrdc.org/about/NRDC_auditedfinancialstatements_FY2013.pdf.

28. ANGA, "Washington County Pennsylvania Retrospective Case Study Characterization Report," February, 2013, http://anga.us/media/content/F7BDA298-DFF6-686B-2DF23939F9838B75/files/13%20Feb%2022%20FinalWashingtonCountyReport_clean%2021.pdf.

29. Natural Resources Defense Council, "Fracking: Community Defense," http://www.nrdc.org/land/fracking-community-defense/.

30. Natural Resource Defense Council, http://www.nrdc.org/land/fracking-community-defense/.

31. Citizens for Responsibility and Ethics in Washington, "About CREW," accessed March 14, 2014, http://www.citizensforethics.org/pages/about; http://www.citizensforethics.org/pages/under-investigation/.

32. U.S. Internal Revenue Service, "Exemption Requirements—Section 501(c)(3) Organizations," accessed June 4, 2014, http://www.irs.gov/Charities-&-Non-Profits/Charitable-Organizations/Exemption-Requirements-Section-501(c)(3)-Organizations.

33. James Oliphant, "Remember the IRS Tea-Party Scandal? Get Ready for Round Two," *National Journal,* February 5, 2014, accessed March 14, 2014, http://www.nationaljournal.com/white-house/remember-the-irs-tea-party-scandal-get-ready-for-round-two-20140205.

34. *Buckley v. Valeo,* 424 U.S. 1 (1976).

35. See John R. Wright, *Interest Groups and Congress: Lobbying, Contributions, and Influence* (Boston: Allyn & Bacon, 1995, reprinted in Longman Classics Series, 2009); Michelle L. Chin, Jon R. Bond, and Nehemia Geva, "A Foot in the Door: An Experimental Study of PAC and Constituency Effects on Access," *Journal of Politics* 62 (2000): 534–49.

36. *Federal Election Commission v. Wisconsin Right to Life, Inc.,* 551 U.S. 449 (2007).

37. *McCutcheon et. al. v. Federal Election Commission,* decided April 2, 2014, http://www.supremecourt.gov/opinions/13pdf/12-536_e1pf.pdf.

38. Tocqueville, *Democracy in America,* 514.

39. David Truman, *The Governmental Process: Political Interests and Public Opinion* (New York: Alfred Knopf, 1971).

40. Mancur Olson, *The Logic of Collective Action* (Cambridge, Mass.: Harvard University Press, 1971).

41. Robert Dahl, *A Preface to Democratic Theory* (Chicago: University of Chicago Press, 1956). Also see Robert Dahl, *Who Governs?,* 2nd ed. (New Haven, Conn.: Yale University Press, 2005).

42. C. Wright Mills, *The Power Elite* (New York: Oxford University Press, 1956).

43. Theodore J. Lowi, *The End of Liberalism: Ideology, Policy, and the End of Public Authority* (New York: Norton, 1969).

44. E. E. Schattschneider, *The Semi-Sovereign People* (New York: Holt, Rinehart, and Winston, 1960). Also see E. E. Schattschneider, *Politics, Pressures, and the Tariff* (New York: Prentice-Hall, 1935).

45. Center for Climate and Energy Solutions, "Federal Vehicle Standards," accessed March 16, 2014, http://www.c2es.org/federal/executive/vehicle-standards#timeline.

46. Dwight D. Eisenhower, "Farewell Radio and Television Address to the American People," January 17, 1961; Gerhard Peters and John T. Woolley, The American Presidency Project, accessed May 23, 2012, http://www.presidency.ucsb.edu/ws/index.php?pid=12086&st=&st1=#axzz1uPYslFQG.

47. Thom Shankar and Helene Cooper, "Pentagon Plans to Shrink Army to pre-World War II Level," *New York Times,* February 23, 2014, http://www.nytimes.com/2014/02/24/us/politics/pentagon-plans-to-shrink-army-to-pre-world-war-ii-level.html.

48. Hugh Heclo, "Issue Networks and the Executive Establishment," in *The New American Political System,* ed. Anthony King (Washington, D.C.: American Enterprise Institute, 1978), 87–124.

49. Shane Goldmacher, "The Long Arm (and Hidden Hand) of Jim DeMint" *National Journal,* October 1, 2013, accessed March 15, 2014, http://www.nationaljournal.com/politics/the-long-arm-and-hidden-hand-of-jim-demint-20131001.

50. Americans for Tax Reform, "About Americans for Tax Reform," accessed May 23, 2012, http://www.atr.org/about.

51. Robert H. Salisbury, "An Exchange Theory of Interest Groups," *Midwest Journal of Political Science* 13 (1969):1–32.

52. In *Logic of Collective Action,* Olson labels these *selective incentives* (p. 51).

53. Ibid., pp. 50–51.

54. DeWayne Wickham, "Group Loses Another Leader, and More Luster," *USA Today,* March 6, 2007, A13; Krissah Thompson, "100 Years Old, NAACP Debates Its Current Role," *Washington Post,* July 12, 2009.

55. AARP, "AARP Annual Report 2013," p. 53, accessed August 20, 2014, http://www.aarp.org/content/dam/aarp/about_aarp/annual_reports/2014-06/2013-Annual-Report-AARP.pdf.

56. Ibid., p. 51.

57. Staff, "The Numbers," *National Journal,* February 16, 2008, 1–45.

Chapter 8

1. This story has been compiled from "McKoon State Senate 29," on Georgia State Senator Josh McKoon's website, accessed April 3, 2014, http://www.senate.ga.gov/senators/en-US/Member.aspx?Member=749; http://www.joshmckoon.com; Larry Gierer, "Local GOP Elects New Chairman, Officers: Attorney Josh McKoon to Take Helm of Party," *Columbus Ledger-Enquirer,* March 31, 2007; Brian Mc Dearmon, "Attorney to Run for GOP Chair: McKoon Seeks Top Post

Vacated by Rob Doll," *Columbus Ledger-Enquirer*, February 26, 2007; Chuck Williams, "Republican Josh McKoon Running for Senate District 29 Seat with Abandon, Even with No Opposition Yet," *Columbus Ledger-Enquirer*, March 28, 2010; Liz Buckthorpe, "Inside Story: Senator Josh McKoon," WRBL News, February 15, 2012, http://www.wrbl.com/story/21339655/inside-story-senator-josh-mckoon; phone interview with Josh McKoon, January 28, 2008, and e-mail interview with Josh McKoon, April 29, 2010, both conducted for this textbook. The chapter-opening quotation is from the April 29 e-mail interview.

2. V. O. Key Jr., *Politics, Parties, and Pressure Groups*, 5th ed. (New York: Thomas Y. Crowell Company, 1964).

3. Center for Responsive Politics, "Political Parties," accessed August 20, 2014, http://www.opensecrets.org/parties/index.php?cmte=&cycle=2014.

4. Center for Responsive Politics, "Political Parties," accessed November 5, 2014, http://www.opensecrets.org/parties/index.php?cmte=&cycle=2014.

5. For more information on the informal networking that occurs among party activists, see Gregory Koger, Seth Masket, and Hans Noel, "Partisan Webs: Information Exchange and Party Networks," *British Journal of Political Science* 39 (2009): 633–53.

6. Marjorie Hershey, *Party Politics in America*, 12th ed. (New York: Pearson-Longman, 2007), 159.

7. In the 2008 Democratic nomination contest between Senator Barack Obama (D-Ill.) and then Senator Hillary Clinton (D-N.Y.), superdelegates played the most important role since their creation. By the end of the regular primary season, Obama led in the primary and caucus delegate count, but not by enough to win the nomination outright. The nomination would be determined by the 823 superdelegates, only about half of whom had committed to one or the other candidate early in the process. As it became clear that Obama had more support among party members generally, many of the remaining superdelegates swung their support to him.

8. Republican National Committee, "New Timing Rules for 2012 Republican Presidential Nominating Schedule" as cited by Josh Putnam, "An Update on the 2012 Republican Delegate Selection Rules," *FrontloadingHQ* (blog), February 27, 2011, http://frontloading.blogspot.com/2011/02/update-on-2012-republican-delegate.html.

9. Peter Hamby, "GOP adopts changes to 2016 presidential primary process," CNN.com, January 24, 2014, accessed April 3, 2014. http://politicalticker.blogs.cnn.com/2014/01/24/gop-adopts-changes-to-2016-presidential-primary-process/.

10. George Washington, "Washington's Farewell Address," reprinted in Randall E. Adkins, *The Evolution of Political Parties, Campaigns, and Elections* (Washington, D.C.: CQ Press, 2008), 47–50.

11. John F. Bibby and Brian F. Schaffner, *Politics, Parties and Elections in America*, 6th ed. (Boston: Thomson-Wadsworth, 2008), 24.

12. United States Senate, Office of the Historian, *Biographical Directory of the United States Congress*, http://bioguide.congress.gov.

13. U.S. Census Bureau, "1990 Population and Housing Unit Counts: United States," Table 2, in *1990 Census of Population and Housing*, accessed May 31, 2012, http://www.census.gov/population/www/censusdata/files/table-2.pdf.

14. Quoted in James L. Sundquist, *Dynamics of the Party System* (Washington, D.C.: Brookings Institution Press, 1973), 65.

15. Sean M. Theriault, *The Power of the People* (Columbus: Ohio State University Press, 2005), Chapter 3.

16. Douglas W. Jones, "The Australian Paper Ballot," in "A Brief Illustrated History of Voting," University of Iowa, Department of Computer Science, 2003, accessed May 31, 2012, http://www.divms.uiowa.edu/~jones/voting/pictures/.

17. Erik J. Engstrom and Samuel Kernell, "Manufactured Responsiveness: The Impact of State Electoral Laws on Unified Party Control of the Presidency and the House of Representatives, 1840–1940," *American Journal of Political Science* 49 (July 2005): 531–49, see 535.

18. Anthony Downs, *An Economic Theory of Democracy* (New York: Harper, 1957).

19. Stuart Elaine Macdonald and George Rabinowitz, "Solving the Paradox of Nonconvergence: Valence, Position, and Direction in Democratic Politics," *Electoral Studies* 17, no. 3 (1998): 281–300.

20. Maurice Duverger, "Public Opinion and Political Parties in France," *American Political Science Review* 46, no. 4 (1952): 1069–78, especially 1071.

21. See https://www.lp.org/candidates/elected-officials.

22. Texas State Historical Association, *Raza Unida Party*, http://www.tshaonline.org/handbook/online/articles/war01.

23. Kate Zernike, Kitty Bennett, Ford Fessenden, Kevin Quealy, Amy Schoenfeld, Archie Tse, and Derek Willis, "Where Tea Party Candidates Are Running," *New York Times*, October 14, 2010, accessed April 4, 2014, http://www.nytimes.com/interactive/2010/10/15/us/politics/tea-party-graphic.html.

24. For an expanded analysis of the Tea Party, see Theda Skocpol and Vanessa Williams, *The Tea Party and the Remaking of Republican Conservatism* (New York: Oxford University Press, 2013).

25. Jonathan Martin, "For Many Republican Incumbents, Challenge from Right Fizzles," *New York Times*, April 4, 2014, http://www.nytimes.com/2014/04/05/us/politics/tea-party-challenge-to-republican-incumbents-fizzles.html.

26. For a detailed discussion of how interest groups interact with parties in campaigning, see Matthew J. Burbank, Ronald J. Hrebenar, and Robert C. Benedict, *Parties, Interest Groups, and Political Campaigns* (Boulder, Colo.: Paradigm Publishers, 2008).

27. Gallup.com, "U.S. Remains Divided over Passing Stricter Gun Control," October 2013, accessed April 7, 2014, http://www.gallup.com/poll/165563/remains-divided-passing-stricter-gun-laws.aspx.

28. Pew Research Center, "Wide Partisan Gap on Gun Policy Proposals – Except Background Checks" May 2013, accessed April 7, 2014, http://www.pewresearch.org/key-data-points/gun-control-key-data-points-from-pew-research/.

29. Democratic National Committee, "2012 Democratic National Platform," http://www.democrats.org/democratic-national-platform#protecting-rights.

30. Republican National Committee, "Republican Platform: We Believe in America," http://www.gop.com/2012-republican-platform_We/#Item10.

31. Center for Responsive Politics, "Political Action Committees," accessed August 20, 2014, http://www.opensecrets.org/pacs/

32. Cornell Belcher and Donna Brazile, "The Black and Hispanic Vote in 2006," *Democratic Strategist*, March 29, 2007, http://www.thedemocraticstrategist.org/ac/2007/03/the_black_and_hispanic_vote_in.php.

33. "Election Results 2008," *New York Times*, December 9, 2008, http://elections.nytimes.com/2008/results/president/map.html.

34. "Campaign 2010," CBS News, November 2, 2010, http://www.cbsnews.com/election-results-2012/exit.shtml.

35. The Roper Center, "US Elections: How Groups Voted in 2012," http://www.ropercenter.uconn.edu/elections/how_groups_voted/voted_12.html.

36. *Engel v. Vitale*, 370 U.S. 421 (1962).

37. For a broad discussion of the resurgence of Republican conservatives, see Mark A. Smith, *The Right Talk: How Conservatives Transformed the Great Society into the Economic Society* (Princeton, N.J.: Princeton University Press, 2007).

38. Scholar Tasha Philpot pointed to underlying shifts as early as 2004. See Tasha S. Philpot, "A Party of a Different Color? Race, Campaign Communication, and Party Politics," *Political Behavior* 26 (2004): 249–70.

39. Greg Giroux, "Final Tally Shows Obama First Since '56 to win 51% Twice, "Bloomberg News, accessed April 4, 2014, http://www.bloomberg.com/news/2013-01-03/final-tally-shows-obama-first-since-56-to-win-51-twice.html; Roper Center, accessed April 28, 2014, http://www.ropercenter.uconn.edu/elections/how_groups_voted/voted_12.html.

40. "Party Affiliation," Gallup.com, accessed May 31, 2012, http://www.gallup.com/poll/15370/party-affiliation.aspx.

Chapter 9

1. See Michael Barone, and Chuck McCutcheon, "Arizona," in *The Almanac of American Politics 2014* (Chicago: University of Chicago Press, 2013). Also, "Kyrsten Sinema's Biography," *Project Vote Smart*, accessed April 20, 2014, http://votesmart.org/candidate/biography/28338/kyrsten-sinema#.U1SPgscmCZw.

2. http://www.washingtonpost.com/lifestyle/style/kyrsten-sinema-a-success-story-like-nobody-elses/2013/01/02/d31fadaa-5382-11e2-a613-ec8d394535c6_story.html, accessed May 16, 2014.

3. http://www.washingtonpost.com/lifestyle/style/kyrsten-sinema-a-success-story-like-nobody-elses/2013/01/02/d31fadaa-5382-11e2-a613-ec8d394535c6_story.html, accessed May 16, 2014.

4. Barone and McCutcheon, "Arizona."

5. http://kyrstensinema.com/record/, accessed May 15, 2014.

6. Quoted in Jeff Broadwater, *George Mason, Forgotten Founder* (Chapel Hill: University of North Carolina Press, 2006), 178.

7. http://www.eiu.com/FileHandler.ashx?issue_id=411847425&mode=pdf (U.S.);http://www.eiu.com/FileHandler.ashx?issue_id=191787003&mode=pdf (Russia), accessed July 1, 2014.

8. For more on the differences between indirect and direct elections of U.S. senators, see Wendy J. Schiller and Charles Stewart III, *Electing the Senate: Indirect Democracy before the 17th Amendment*, (Princeton, NJ: Princeton University Press, 2014).

9. For a longer discussion of redistricting, see Bernard Grofman, Lisa Handley, and Richard G. Niemi, *Minority Representation and the Quest for Voting Equality* (New York: Cambridge University Press, 1992).

10. 478 U.S. 30 (1986).

11. 548 U.S. 399 (2006).

12. Survey conducted by CBS News/*New York Times*, September 8–12, 2012, retrieved September 29, 2012, from the iPOLL Databank, The Roper Center for Public Opinion Research, University of Connecticut.

13. Michael McGerr, *The Decline of Popular Politics* (New York: Oxford University Press, 1986).

14. Sidney Blumenthal, *The Permanent Campaign* (New York: Simon and Schuster, 1982).

15. Federal Election Commission, "The FEC and Federal Campaign Finance Law: Historical Background," February 2004, accessed June 4, 2012, http://www.fec.gov/pages/brochures/fecfeca.shtml.

16. Federal Election Commission, "How Much Can I Contribute?," FEC.gov, accessed May 1, 2014, http://www.fec.gov/ans/answers_general.shtml#How_much_can_I_contribute.

17. Federal Election Commission, "*McCutcheon, et al. v. FEC Case Summary*," FEC.gov, accessed May 1, 2014, http://www.fec.gov/law/litigation/McCutcheon.shtml.

18. See Federal Election Commission, http://www.fec.gov.

19. Richard Briffault, "Super PACs" (Working Paper 12-298, Columbia Law School, April 16, 2012).

20. Kevin Quealy and Derek Willis, "Independent Spending Totals," *New York Times*, http://elections.nytimes.com/2012/campaign-finance/independent-expenditures/totals.

21. http://www.opensecrets.org/outsidespending/summ.php?cycle=2012&chrt=V&type=S, accessed May 2, 2014.

22. Steven J. Rosenstone and John Mark Hansen, *Mobilization, Participation, and Democracy in America* (New York: Macmillan, 1993).

23. This insightful observation was made by Senator Lamar Alexander to one of the authors on March 16, 2012.

24. Lynn Vavrek, "The A-Little-Bit-Less Undecided," *Campaign Stops* (blog), *The New York Times*, September 20, 2012, http://campaignstops.blogs.nytimes.com/2012/09/20/the-a-little-bit-less-undecided/.

25. http://www.nytimes.com/2014/04/23/upshot/the-myth-of-swing-voters-in-midterm-elections.html?_r=0, accessed May 2, 2014.

26. Daron R. Shaw, *The Race to 270: The Electoral College and the Campaign Strategies of 2000 and 2004* (Chicago: University of Chicago Press, 2006); figures for 2008 provided by Daron R. Shaw.

27. Total population in the U.S in 2012 was 313,914,040. The population in the battleground states was 66,867,548, constituting 21 percent of the total. See http://www.census.gov/popest/data/state/totals/2012/index.html, accessed May 2, 2014.

28. Chris Cillizza, "Romney's Data Cruncher," *Washington Post*, September 7, 2007, A1.

29. Mark J. Penn with E. Kinney Zalesne, *Microtrends: The Small Forces Behind Tomorrow's Big Changes* (New York: Twelve, Hatchett Book Group USA, 2007), xiii.

30. Thomas B. Edsall, "Let the Nanotargeting Begin," *Campaign Stops* (blog), *New York Times*, April 15, 2012, http://campaignstops.blogs.nytimes.com/2012/04/15/let-the-nanotargeting-begin/.

31. See http://www.thevictorylab.com/ for an account of revolution in campaigns that is often called "micro-targeting."

32. http://www.targetmarketingmag.com/article/election-2012-barack-obama-mitt-romney-microtargeting-retargeting-mobile-marketing-social-media-voter-databases/1, accessed May 2, 2014.

33. John G. Geer, *In Defense of Negativity* (Chicago: University of Chicago Press, 2006), 59–60.

34. Lynn Vavreck, *The Message Matters* (Princeton, N.J.: Princeton University Press, 2009).

35. Donald Stokes, "Spatial Models of Party Competition," *American Political Science Review* 57 (1963): 368–77.

36. Geer, *In Defense of Negativity*, 105.

37. Sunshine Hillygus and Todd Shields, *The Persuadable Voter* (Princeton, N.J.: Princeton University Press, 2008), 36.

38. Mark Z. Barabak, "Wedge Issues May Boost Obama's Prospects," *Los Angeles Times*, April 27, 2012, http://www.latimes.com/news/nationworld/nation/la-na-campaign-2012-wedge-issues-20120428,0,2706316.story.

39. Kathleen Jamieson, *Dirty Politics* (New York: Oxford University Press, 1992).

40. Erika Franklin Fowler and Travis N. Ridout, "Negative, Angry and Ubiquitous: Political Advertising in 2012," *The Forum, A Journal of Applied Research in Contemporary Politics* 10, no. 4 (2012): 51–61.

41. Geer, *In Defense of Negativity*.

42. Federal Election Commission, *Federal Election Campaign Laws* (Washington, D.C.: Federal Election Commission, April 2008), 56–60, http://www.fec.gov. Note that the contribution levels have been increased slightly to adjust for inflation.

43. https://www.opensecrets.org/overview/topraces.php; https://www.opensecrets.org/overview/cost.php, accessed November 5, 2014.

44. Albert Cover, "One Good Term Deserves Another: The Advantage of Incumbency in Congressional Elections," *American Journal of Political Science* 21, no. 3 (1977): 523–41.

45. See Gary C. Jacobson, *The Politics of Congressional Elections,* 8th ed. (Upper Saddle River, N.J.: Prentice Hall, 2012).

46. Richard F. Fenno Jr., *Home Style: Home Members in Their Districts* (Boston: Little, Brown, 1978).

47. See Jacobson, *Politics of Congressional Elections.*

48. Poll conducted by Fox News, September 9–11, 2012, retrieved on September 29, 2012, from the iPOLL Databank, The Roper Center for Public Opinion Research, University of Connecticut.

49. Morris Fiorina, *Congress: Keystone to the Washington Establishment* (New Haven, Conn.: Yale University Press, 1977).

50. John Zaller, "Politicians as Prize Fighters," in *Politicians and Party Politics,* ed. John G. Geer (Baltimore: Johns Hopkins University Press, 1998), 128–85.

51. Bruce Oppenheimer, "Deep Red and Blue Congressional Districts: The Causes and Consequences of Declining Party Competitiveness," in *Congress Reconsidered,* 8th ed., ed. Lawrence Dodd and Bruce Oppenheimer (Washington, D.C.: CQ Press, 2005), 135–58.

52. Kevin Corder and Christina Wolbrecht, "Political Context and the Turnout of New Women Voters after Suffrage," *Journal of Politics* 68 (2006): 34–49.

53. Samuel Huntington, "The United States," in *The Crisis of Democracy,* ed. Michael Crozier, Samuel Huntington, and Joji Watanuki (New York: NYU Press, 1975), 59–115.

54. Steven E. Finkel "Reciprocal Effects of Participation and Political Efficacy: A Panel Analysis," *American Journal of Political Science* 29, no. 4 (1985): 891–913; Steven E. Finkel, "The Effects of Participation on Political Efficacy and Political Support: Evidence from a West German Panel," *Journal of Politics* 49, no. 2 (1987): 441–64. These articles provide empirical evidence that supports the arguments of Carol Pateman, *Participation and Democratic Theory* (New York: Cambridge University Press, 1970).

55. This section draws heavily on Alexander Keyssar, *The Right to Vote: The Contested History of Democracy in the United States* (New York: Basic Books, 2001).

56. 42 USC 203 §1973 to 1973bb.

57. Voting Rights Act Language Assistance Amendments of 1992: Hearings on S. 2236 before the Subcomm. on the Constitution of the Senate Comm. on the Judiciary [1992 hearings], 102d Cong., 2d Sess., S. Hrg. 102-1066, at 134 (1992).

58. M. Hugo Lopez, S. Motel, and E. Patten, "A Record 24 Million Latinos Are Eligible to Vote, But Turnout Rate Has Lagged That of Whites, Blacks," Washington, DC: Pew Hispanic Center, 2012, http://www.pewhispanic.org/files/2012/10/trends_in_Latino_voter_participation_FINALREVISED.pdf.

59. See Marisa Abrajano and Michael Alvarez, *New Faces, New Voices: The Hispanic Electorate in America* (Princeton, N.J.: Princeton University Press, 2010); Matt A. Barreto, Gary M. Segura, and Nathan D. Woods, "The Mobilizing Effect of Majority-Minority Districts on Latino Turnout," *American Political Science Review* 98, no. 1 (2004): 65–75; Matt A. Barreto, Loren Collingwood, and Sylvia Manzano, "A New Measure of Group Influence in Presidential Elections: Assessing Latino Influence in 2008," *Political Research Quarterly* 63 (2010): 908–21.

60. *Voter Identification Requirements,* National Conference of State Legislatures, April 30, 2014, http://www.ncsl.org/research/elections-and-campaigns/voter-id.aspx.

61. *Crawford v. Marion County Election Board,* 553 U.S. 181 (2008). See also Bill Mears, "High Court Upholds Indiana's Voter ID Law," CNN, April 28, 2008, http://articles.cnn.com/2008-04-28/politics/scotus.voter.id_1_voter-impersonation-voter-id-laws-voter-fraud?_s=PM:POLITICS; Linda Greenhouse, "In a 6-to-3 Vote, Justices Uphold a Voter ID Law," *New York Times,* April 29, 2008.

62. American Civil Liberties Union, "Applewhite et al. v. Commonwealth of Pennsylvania, et al.," ACLU, accessed May 19, 2012, http://www.aclupa.org/our-work/legal/legaldocket/applewhite-et-al-v-commonwealth-pennsylvania-et-al/. Rick Lyman, "Pennsylvania Voter ID Law Struck Down as Judge Cites Burden on Citizens," *New York Times,* January 17, 2014, http://www.nytimes.com/2014/01/18/us/politics/pennsylvania-voter-id-law-struck-down.html.

63. Wade Goodwin, "Texas Voter ID Law Creates a Problem for Some Women,"October 20, 2013, http://www.npr.org/2013/10/30/241891800/texas-voter-id-law-creates-a-problem-for-some-women.

64. Matt Barreto, "Latino Decisions Research Critical to Overturning Wisconsin Voter-ID Law," *Latino Decisions,* April 30, 2014, http://www.latinodecisions.com/blog/2014/04/30/latino-decisions-research-critical-to-overturning-wisconsin-voter-id-law/.

65. 42 USC 203 §1973 to 1973bb.

66. http://elections.gmu.edu/Turnout_2012G.html, accessed June 3, 2014.

67. Michael P. McDonald, "2012 Presidential Nomination Contest Turnout Rates," United States Elections Project, last modified April 25, 2012, accessed June 7, 2012, http://elections.gmu.edu/Turnout_2012P.html.

68. See Jan Leighley, "Attitudes, Opportunities, and Incentives," *Political Research Quarterly* 48 (1995): 184.

69. Stanley and Niemi, *Vital Statistics on American Politics 2013–2014.*

70. http://www.pewresearch.org/fact-tank/2013/05/08/six-take-aways-from-the-census-bureaus-voting-report/, accessed June 3, 2014.

71. Jan E. Leighley and Jonathan Nagler, *Who Votes Now?* (Princeton: Princeton University Press, 2014).

72. http://www.pewresearch.org/fact-tank/2013/05/08/six-take-aways-from-the-census-bureaus-voting-report/, accessed June 3, 2014.

73. Thom File and Sarah Crissey, *Voting and Registration in the Election of November 2008* (Washington, D.C.: U.S. Census Bureau, May 2010), http://www.census.gov/prod/2010pubs/p20-562.pdf.

74. See, for instance, Raymond Wolfinger and Steven Rosenstone, *Who Votes?* (New Haven, Conn.: Yale University Press, 1980). There has been much research since the publication of this book, but it remains a leading source on this topic.

75. File and Crissey, *Voting and Registration in the Election of November 2008.*

76. Cindy D. Kam and Carl L. Palmer, "Reconsidering the Effects of Education on Political Participation," *Journal of Politics* 70, no. 3 (2008): 612–31.

77. Howard Gillman, *The Votes That Counted* (Chicago: University of Chicago Press, 2001), 77.

78. William Riker and Peter Ordeshook, "A Theory of the Calculus of Voting," *American Political Science Review* 62 (1968): 25–42.

79. For other efforts to solve this problem, see John H. Aldrich, "Rational Choice and Turnout," *American Journal of Political Science* 37, no. 1 (1993): 246–78; Robert Grafstein, "An Evidential Decision Theory of Turnout," *American Journal of Political Science* 35 (1991): 989–1010.

80. These data are from a survey by Pew Research Center for the People & the Press, conducted by Princeton Survey Research Associates International, April 4–April 15, 2012, retrieved June 3, 2014, from the iPOLL Databank, The Roper Center for Public Opinion Research, University of Connecticut.

81. Allyson Holbrook and Jon Krosnick, "Vote Over-Reporting: Testing the Social Desirability Hypothesis in Telephone and Internet Surveys" (paper presented at the annual meeting of the American Association for Public Opinion Research, Miami Beach, Florida, 2009).

82. David Campbell, *Why We Vote* (Princeton, N.J.: Princeton University Press, 2006).

83. See G. Bingham Powell Jr., "American Voter Turnout in Comparative Perspective," *American Political Science Review* 80 (1986): 17–43; and Henry Brady, Sidney Verba, and Kay Schlozman, "Beyond SES: A Resource Model of Political Participation," *American Political Science Review* 89 (1995): 271–94.

84. John Zipp, "Perceived Representativeness and Voting: An Assessment of the Impact of 'Choices' vs. 'Echoes,'" *American Political Science Review* 79 (1985): 50–61.

85. Alan Gerber, Donald Green, and David Nickerson, "Getting Out the Vote in Local Elections: Results from Six Door-to-Door Canvassing Experiments," *Journal of Politics* 65 (2003): 4.

86. Allison Dale and Aaron Strauss, "Don't Forget to Vote: Text Message Reminders as a Mobilization Tool," *American Journal of Political Science* 53 (2009): 787–804.

87. Steven J. Rosenstone and John Mark Hansen, *Mobilization, Participation, and Democracy in America* (New York: Macmillan, 1993).

88. James H. Fowler, Laura A. Baker, and Christopher T. Dawes, "Genetic Variation in Political Participation," *American Political Science Review* 102, no. 2 (2008): 233–48.

89. James H. Fowler and Christopher T. Dawes, "Two Genes Predict Voter Turnout," *Journal of Politics* 70 (2008): 579–94.

90. Fances Fox Piven and Richard A. Cloward, *Why Americans Still Don't Vote: And Why Politicians Want It That Way* (Boston: Beacon Press, 2000); Martin P. Wattenberg, *Where Have All the Voters Gone?* (Boston: Harvard University Press, 2002); Thomas E. Patterson, *The Vanishing Voter: Public Involvement in an Age of Uncertainty* (New York: Alfred A. Knopf, 2003).

91. See http://www.electproject.org/2014g, accessed November 5, 2014; http://elections.gmu.edu/Turnout_2012G.html, accessed June 3, 2013.

92. Ibid.

93. www.idea.int.

94. Powell, "American Voter Turnout," 17–37.

95. This "puzzle of participation" was first discussed by Richard Brody in *The New American Political System*, ed. Anthony King (Washington, D.C.: American Enterprise Institute for Public Policy Research, 1978).

96. Warren Miller, "Puzzle Transformed," *Political Behavior* 14 (1992): 1–43.

97. Rosenstone and Hansen, *Mobilization, Participation, and Democracy in America*.

98. Ibid.

99. Keena Lipsitz, Christine Trost, Matthew Grossman, and John Sides, "What Voters Want from Campaign Communication," *Political Communication* 22 (2005): 337–54.

100. Steven Ansolabehere and Shanto Iyengar, *Going Negative* (New York: Free Press, 1995).

101. John G. Geer, *In Defense of Negativity* (Chicago: University of Chicago Press, 2006).

102. See, for example, Joshua Clinton and John Lapinski, "'Targeted' Advertising and Voter Turnout: An Experimental Study of the 2000 Presidential Election," *Journal of Politics* 66 (2004): 69–96.

103. Richard R. Lau, Lee Sigelman, and Ivy Brown Rovner, "A New Meta-Analysis," *Journal of Politics* 69 (2007): 1176–1209.

104. Julia Preston, "Immigrants Number 11.5 Million," *New York Times*, March 24, 2012, http://www.nytimes.com/2012/03/24/us/illegal-immigrants-number-11-5-million.html. http://cnsnews.com/news/article/ali-meyer/latest-estimate-illegal-alien-population-exceeds-unemployed, accessed June 3, 2014.

105. Pew Safety Performance Project, *One in 100: Behind Bars in America 2008* (Washington, D.C.: Pew Center on the States, February 2008), http://www.pewtrusts.org/en/research-and-analysis/reports/0001

/01/01/one-in-100; http://www.nytimes.com/2013/07/26/us/us-prison-populations-decline-reflecting-new-approach-to-crime.html?pagewanted=all, accessed June 3, 2014.

106. Michael P. McDonald and Samuel L. Popkin, "The Myth of the Vanishing Voter," *American Political Science Review* 95 (2001): 963–74.

107. See Larry Bartels, *Unequal Democracy* (Princeton, N.J.: Princeton University Press, 2008).

108. Task Force on American Inequality, "American Democracy in an Age of Rising Inequality," American Political Science Association, 2004.

109. See Dayton McKean, *The Boss: The Hague Machine in Action* (New York: Russell and Russell Publishers, 1967), for an account of the corrupt practices of machine politicians.

110. See James Bryce, *The American Commonwealth* (New York: MacMillan, 1895).

111. For the best account of the importance and impact of registration, see Benjamin Highton, "Voter Registration and Turnout in the United States," *Perspectives on Politics* 2 (2004): 507–15.

112. See Nonprofit Vote at http://www.NonProfitVote.Org.

113. Read about the National Voter Registration Act of 1993 at http://www.justice.gov/crt/about/vot/nvra/activ_nvra.php.

114. Texas Secretary of State Hope Andrade's official website, http://www.sos.state.tx.us/.

115. http://www.oregonlive.com/mapes/index.ssf/2013/03/in_last_presidential_election.html, accessed June 3, 2014.

116. https://www.sos.state.co.us/pubs/rule_making/written_comments/2009/111009_commoncause_votebymailproject.pdf, accessed June 30, 2014.

117. *Absentee and Early Voting*, National Conference of State Legislatures, February 26, 2014, http://www.ncsl.org/research/elections-and-campaigns/absentee-and-early-voting.aspx.

118. Paul Gronke, Eva Galanes-Rosenbaum, and Peter A. Miller, "Early Voting and Turnout," *PS: Political Science and Politics* (October 2003) 639–645.

119. Steven Yaccino and Lizette Alvarez, "New G.O.P. Bid to Limit Voting in Swing States," *New York Times*, March 29, 2014.

120. V. O. Key, *The Responsible Electorate* (Cambridge, Mass.: Harvard University Press, 1966).

121. See Jeff Manza and Christopher Ugge, *Locked Out: Felon Disenfranchisement and American Democracy* (Oxford, U.K.: Oxford University Press, 2007).

Chapter 10

1. This story was compiled from information on Representative Joaquin Castro's congressional website, http://castro.house.gov/; Georgia Park "Castro Highlights Importance of Public Service Work, Leadership," *The Chronicle*, April 2, 2014, http://www.dukechronicle.com/articles/2014/04/02/castro-highlights-importance-public-service-work-leadership; "Interview with Representative Joaquin Castro," *The Situation Room*, CNN, January 4, 2013, http://www.realclearpolitics.com/articles/2013/01/04/interview_with_representative_joaquin_castro_116607.html#ixzz2yDth5yUN; Office of the Secretary of State of Texas, "Race Summary Report, 2012 General Election" November 6, 2012, http://elections.sos.state.tx.us, "Congressman Castro Visits Afghanistan," KSAT-San Antonio, April 7, 2014, http://www.ksat.com/news/Congressman-Castro-visits-Afghanistan/25370616.

2. Totals do not include House Delegates or the Resident Commissioner; see Jennifer E. Manning, *Membership of the 113th Congress: A Profile*, CRS Report for Congress, R42964 (Washington, D.C.: Congressional Research Service, March 14, 2014), accessed April 16, 2014, http://www.fas.org/sgp/crs/misc/R42964.pdf; census.gov, "Age and Sex Composition in the United States: 2012, http://www.census.gov/population/age/data/2012comp.html.

3. Manning, *Membership*.

4. Ibid. For a broader discussion of the careers of women legislators in the House, see Jennifer Lawless and Sean Theriault, "Will She Stay or Will She Go? Career Ceilings and Women's Retirement from the U.S. Congress," *Legislative Studies Quarterly* 30 (2005): 581–96.

5. See Wendy J. Schiller and Charles Stewart III. 2014. *Electing the Senate: Indirect Democracy before the Seventeenth Amendment.* (Princeton: Princeton University Press), and Lana R. Slack, *Senate Manual: Standing Rules, Orders, Laws, and Resolutions Affecting the Business of the United States Senate* (Washington, D.C.: U.S. Government Printing Office, 1988), 684–85.

6. United States Senate, "Senate Classes," Senate.gov, accessed June 21, 2012, http://www.senate.gov/artandhistory/history/common/briefing /Constitution_Senate.htm#3.

7. In rare cases in which a senator dies or resigns, an interim replacement is typically chosen by the governor of the state until an election is held to fill the seat.

8. U.S Census Bureau, Kristen D. Burnett, "Congressional Apportionment," November 2011, http://www.census.gov/prod/cen2010/briefs/c2010br -08.pdf, accessed April 16, 2014; Census.gov, "Annual Population Estimates," http://www.census.gov/popclock/.

9. After the first census of the new federal government under the Constitution, Congress grew to 105 members in 1792. See Brian Frederick, *Congressional Representation and Constituents: The Case for Increasing the Size of the U.S. House of Representatives* (New York: Routledge, 2010), 23–24.

10. U.S. House of Representatives, "Historical Highlights: The Permanent Apportionment Act of 1929," June 11, 1929, accessed June 21, 2012, http://artandhistory.house.gov/highlights.aspx?action=view&intID =200.

11. For a discussion of representation by Latino members, see Jason P. Casellas, "The Institutional and Demographic Determinants of Latino Representation," *Legislative Studies Quarterly* 34, no. 3 (2009): 399–426; see also David Leal and Frederick M. Hess, "Who Chooses Experience? Examining the Use of Veteran Staff by House Freshmen," *Polity* 36 (2004): 651–64.

12. U.S. Bureau of the Census, "Fast Facts for Congress," My Congressional District (the American Community Survey), http://www.census.gov /fastfacts/, accessed online April 16, 2014.

13. See *Shaw v. Reno*, 509 U.S. 630 (1993); *Miller v. Johnson*, 515 U.S. 900 (1995); and *Easley v. Cromartie*, 532 U.S. 234 (2001). *Thornburg v. Gingles*, 478 U.S. 30 (1986) provides plaintiffs with a right to force a state to create a majority-minority district. If the minority community is large and concentrated enough to form a majority in the district, the minority community votes cohesively, and white voting prevents the minority community from electing its preferred candidate. For a longer discussion of redistricting, see Bernard Grofman, Lisa Handley, and Richard G. Niemi, *Minority Representation and the Quest for Voting Equality* (New York: Cambridge University Press, 1992).

14. Frances E. Lee and Bruce I. Oppenheimer, *Sizing up the Senate: The Unequal Consequences of Equal Representation* (Chicago: University of Chicago Press, 1999).

15. Two prominent works on this point are Richard F. Fenno Jr., *The Power of the Purse: Appropriations Politics in Congress* (Boston: Little, Brown, 1966), and Aaron B. Wildavsky, *The New Politics of the Budgetary Process* (Boston: Addison-Wesley Educational, 1992).

16. Fiona McGillivray, "Trading Free and Opening Markets," in *International Trade and Political Institutions,* ed. Fiona McGillivray, Iain McLean, Robert Pahre, and Cheryl Schonhardt-Bailey (Cheltenham, U.K.: Edward Elgar, 2001), 80–98.

17. United States Courts: Federal Courts, http://www.uscourts.gov /FederalCourts.aspx.

18. Sarah A. Binder and Forrest Maltzman, "Senatorial Delay in Confirming Federal Judges, 1947–1998," *American Journal of Political Science* 46, no. 1 (2002): 190–99.

19. Sarah A. Binder, *Majority Rights, Minority Rule* (New York: Cambridge University Press, 1997); Eric Schickler, *Disjointed Pluralism: Institutional Innovation and the Development of the U.S. Congress* (Princeton, N.J.: Princeton University Press, 2001).

20. Sean Gailmard and Jeffery A. Jenkins, "Minority-Party Power in the Senate and the House of Representatives," in *Why Not Parties? Party Effects in the United States Senate*, ed. Nathan W. Monroe, Jason M. Roberts, and David W. Rohde (Chicago: University of Chicago Press, 2008), 181–97.

21. Randall Strahan, *Leading Representatives: The Agency of Leaders in the Politics of the U.S. House* (Baltimore: Johns Hopkins University Press, 2007).

22. Ibid., 79–126.

23. David W. Rohde, *Parties and Leaders in the Postreform House* (Chicago: University of Chicago Press, 1991).

24. Gary W. Cox and Mathew D. McCubbins, *Legislative Leviathan: Party Government in the House* (Berkeley: University of California Press, 1993).

25. Gallup.com, "Congressional Job Approval at 12% in February," http:// www.gallup.com/poll/167375/congressional-job-approval-february .aspx, accessed April 16, 2014.

26. Barry C. Burden and Tammy M. Frisbee, "Preferences, Partisanship, and Whip Activity in the U.S. House of Representatives," *Legislative Studies Quarterly* 29 (2004): 569–90.

27. Ralph Huitt, "Democratic Party Leadership in the Senate," *American Political Science Review* 55 (1961): 333–44.

28. E. Scott Adler and John Wilkerson, "Intended Consequences: Jurisdictional Reform and Issue Control in the U.S. House of Representatives," *Legislative Studies Quarterly* 33, no. 1 (2008): 85–112.

29. For a list of current caucuses, see Committee on House Administration, "112th Congress Congressional Member Organizations (CMO)," updated April 11, 2012, accessed June 21, 2012, http://cha.house .gov/sites/republicans.cha.house.gov/files/documents/cmo_cso _docs/cmo_112th_congress.pdf.

30. Daily Digest, "Resume of Congressional Activity, First Session of the One Hundred Twelfth Congress," *Congressional Record D210,* March 7, 2012; Daily Digest, "Resume of Congressional Activity, Second Session of the One Hundred Twelfth Congress," *Congressional Record D196,* March 13, 2013, http://thomas.loc.gov.

31. For an extended discussion of the right of recognition and the powers it affords senators, see Floyd Riddick, *Senate Procedure,* ed. Alan Frumin (Washington D.C.: U.S. Government Printing Office, 1992), 1091–99.

32. Sarah A. Binder and Steven S. Smith, *Politics or Principle: Filibustering in the U.S. Senate* (Washington, D.C.: Brookings Institution Press, 1997). For a discussion of the use of the filibuster by retiring senators, see Martin Overby, L. Overby, and Lauren Bell, "Rational Behavior or the Norm of Cooperation? Filibustering among Retiring Senators," *Journal of Politics* 66 (2004): 906–24.

33. For more details on the cloture rules and recent changes, see Valerie Heitshusen, Congressional Research Service, "Majority Cloture for Nominations: Implications and the 'Nuclear' Proceedings," December 6, 2013, R43331, accessed April 16, 2014, http://www.fas .org/sgp/crs/misc/R43331.pdf.

34. David Stout, Carl Hulse, and Sheryl Gay Stolberg, "Senate Backs Disputed Judicial Nomination," *New York Times*, October 27, 2007, A21.

35. Wendy J. Schiller, "Resolved the Filibuster Should Be Abolished— Con," in *Debating Reform*, 2nd ed., ed. Richard J. Ellis and Michael Nelson (Washington, D.C.: CQ Press, 2012).

36. Wendy J. Schiller, "Senators as Political Entrepreneurs: Using Bill Sponsorship to Shape Legislative Agendas," *American Journal of Political Science* 1 (1995): 186–203.

37. Glen Krutz, *Hitching a Ride: Omnibus Legislating in the U.S. Congress* (Columbus: Ohio State University Press, 2001).

38. For a general discussion on committees, see Keith R. Krehbiel, *Information and Legislative Organization* (Ann Arbor: University of Michigan Press, 1991).

39. For a few examples of this work, see Aage Clausen, *How Congressmen Decide* (New York: St. Martin's Press, 1973); John Kingdon, *Congressmen's Voting Decisions* (New York: Harper & Row, 1989); David W. Brady, *Critical Elections and Congressional Policy Making* (Stanford, Calif.: Stanford University Press, 1988); Stanley Bach and Steven S. Smith, *Managing Uncertainty in the U.S. House of Representatives* (Washington, D.C.: Brookings Institution Press, 1989). For examples of the ideological examination of roll call voting, see Keith T. Poole and Howard Rosenthal, *Ideology and Congress* (New Brunswick, N.J.: Transaction Publishers, 2009).

40. Humberto Sanchez, "2012 Vote Studies: Party Unity," *CQ Weekly*, January 21, 2013, 132; Staff, "Party Unity Background," *CQ Annual Report*, January 21, 2013, 137.

41. C. Lawrence Evans and Walter J. Oleszek, "Message Politics and Senate Procedure," in *The Contentious Senate: Partisanship, Ideology and the Myth of Cool Judgment,* ed. Colton C. Campbell and Nicol C. Rae (Lanham, Md.: Rowman and Littlefield, 2000).

42. Barbara Sinclair, *Unorthodox Lawmaking: New Legislative Processes in the U.S. Congress,* 3rd ed. (Washington, D.C.: CQ Press, 2007).

43. Congressional Budget and Impoundment Control Act of 1974 (Public Law 93-344). For additional background on budget history, see the Senate Budget Committee's website at http://www.budget .senate.gov/democratic/public/index.cfm/history-of-the-budget -committee.

44. Balanced Budget and Emergency Deficit Control Act of 1985 (Public Law 99-177). For historical tables on the U.S. federal budget, see Congressional Budget Office, "The Budget and Economic Outlook Fiscal Years 2012 to 2022," January 31, 2012, accessed June 21, 2012, http://www.cbo.gov/publication/42905. The Fiscal 1985 budget deficit number is taken from Table F-1, http://www.cbo.gov /publication/42911.

45. See Walter J. Oleszek, *Congressional Procedures and the Policy Process,* 6th ed. (Washington, D.C.: CQ Press, 2004), especially 63–69. For a more comprehensive look at the history of budget politics and deficits, see Jasmine Farrier, *Passing the Buck: Congress, Budgets, and Deficits* (Lexington: University of Kentucky Press, 2004).

46. Kathleen Hunter, "GOP Readies Procedural Salvo against Reconciliation Play," *CQ Weekly Online,* March 8, 2010, 568.

47. Charles M. Cameron, *Veto Bargaining: Presidents and the Politics of Negative Power* (New York: Cambridge University Press, 2000).

48. Bureau of Labor Statistics, "Labor Force Statistics from the Current Population Survey," http://data.bls.gov/timeseries/LNS14000000.

49. Department of Labor, "Unemployment Insurance 75th Anniversary," accessed April 17, 2014, http://www.dol.gov/ocia/pdf/75th-Anniversary -Summary-FINAL.pdf.

50. Staff, Department of Labor, "Chronology of Federal Unemployment Compensation Laws, February 2014," accessed April 17, 2014, http:// workforcesecurity.doleta.gov/unemploy/pdf/chronfedlaws.pdf.

51. Albert D. Cover and Bruce S. Brumberg, "Baby Books and Ballots: The Impact of Congressional Mail on Constituent Opinion," *American Political Science Review* 76 (1982): 347–59.

52. Richard L. Hall, *Participation in Congress* (New Haven, Conn.: Yale University Press, 1998).

53. Tracy Sulkin, *Issue Politics in Congress* (New York: Cambridge University Press, 2005).

54. Daily Digest, "Resume of Congressional Activity, First Session of the One Hundred Twelfth Congress," *Congressional Record D210,* March 7, 2012; Daily Digest, "Resume of Congressional Activity, Second Session of the One Hundred Twelfth Congress," *Congressional Record D196,* March 13, 2013, http://thomas.loc.gov.

55. For a comprehensive look at this congressional activity, see Diana Evans, *Greasing the Wheels: Using Pork Barrel Projects to Build Majority Coalitions in Congress* (New York: Cambridge University Press, 2004).

56. Jennifer A. Dlouhy, "Alaska 'Bridge to Nowhere' Funding Gets Nowhere; Lawmakers Delete Project after Critics Bestow Derisive Moniker," *San Francisco Chronicle,* November 17, 2005, A7.

57. Citizens Against Taxpayer Waste, "2010 Pig Book Summary," accessed June 21, 2012, http://www.cagw.org/content/2010-pig-book-summary.

58. Richard F. Fenno Jr., *Home Style: House Members in Their Districts* (Boston: Little, Brown, 1978).

59. David R. Mayhew, *Congress: The Electoral Connection* (New Haven, Conn.: Yale University Press, 1974).

60. For an extended discussion of how senators from the same state interact, see Schiller, *Partners and Rivals.*

61. Charles Mahtesian, "2012 Reelection Rate: 90 percent" Politico. com, December 13, 2012, accessed April 16, 2014, http://www .politico.com/blogs/charlie-mahtesian/2012/12/reelection-rate -percent-151898.html.

Chapter 11

1. Sylvia Mathews Burwell, "Testimony before the Senate Health, Education, Labor, and Pensions Committee" May 8, 2014, accessed May 15, 2014, http://www.help.senate.gov/imo/media/doc/Burwell .pdf.

2. This story was compiled from the Office of Management and Budget's website: http://www.whitehouse.gov/omb; President Barack Obama, transcript of "Remarks by the President in Nominating Sylvia Mathews Burwell as Secretary of Health and Human Services," October 9, 2013, http://www.whitehouse.gov; Dylan Matthews, "Sylvia Mathews Burwell: Six Things to Know about the New White House Budget Director," Wonkblog, *Washington Post,* March 3, 2013; "Q&A: Sylvia Mathews, President of the Gates Foundation Global Development Program," *The Seattle Times,* March 17, 2007; Jennifer Haberkorn, "Sylvia Mathews Burwell's Hurdles," *Politico,* April 11, 2014; Sarah Plummer, "Obama Taps Hinton Native for Budget Chief," *The Register-Herald,* March 5, 2013.

3. See Hedrick Smith, "Bush Says He Sought to Avoid Acting Like Surrogate President," *New York Times,* April 12, 1981, A1, http: //www.nytimes.com/1981/04/12/us/bush-says-he-sought-to-avoid -acting-like-surrogate-president.html.

4. Bruce G. Peabody and Scott E. Grant, "The Twice and Future President: Constitutional Interstices and the Twenty-Second Amendment," *Minnesota Law Review* 83 (1999): 565–94.

5. "The Presidents," The White House, accessed June 22, 2012, http: //www.whitehouse.gov/about/presidents.

6. Arthur Schlesinger Jr., *The Imperial Presidency* (New York: Mariner Books, 2004; first published 1973).

7. U.S. Department of Justice, Office of the Pardon Attorney, "Clemency Statistics," accessed May 1, 2014, http://www.justice.gov/pardon /statistics.htm.

8. Robert Wielaard, "Kosovo Recognition Irritates Russia and China," *Herald-Tribune,* February 19, 2008, A11, http://www.heraldtribune. com/article/20080219/NEWS/802190626.

9. Charles M. Cameron, *Veto Bargaining: Presidents and the Politics of Negative Power* (New York: Cambridge University Press, 2000).

10. Glenn S. Krutz, *Hitching a Ride: Omnibus Legislating in the U.S. Congress* (Columbus: Ohio State University Press, 2001). Also see Cameron, *Veto Bargaining.*

11. William W. Lammers and Michael A. Genovese, *The Presidency and Domestic Policy* (Washington, D.C.: CQ Press, 2000), 315–24.

12. Wilson delivered the speech on December 2, 1913. See John T. Woolley and Gerhard Peters, "Length of State of the Union Messages and Addresses (in words), Washington–Obama," The American Presidency Project, accessed June 22, 2012, http://www.presidency.ucsb.edu/sou_words.php#axzz1yaTY1UIo.

13. Jeff Cummins, "State of the Union Addresses and the President's Legislative Success," *Congress and the Presidency* 37 (2010): 176–99.

14. The chronology that follows is taken from the *Washington Post*'s history of Watergate, available online at http://www.washingtonpost.com/wp-srv/onpolitics/watergate/chronology.htm.

15. Ibid.

16. William G. Howell, *Power without Persuasion: The Politics of Direct Presidential Action* (Princeton, N.J.: Princeton University Press, 2003).

17. Harold C. Relyea, *Presidential Directives: Background and Overview,* CRS Report for Congress, 98-611 (Washington, D.C.: Congressional Research Service, 2007).

18. Kenneth R. Mayer, "Executive Orders and Presidential Power," *Journal of Politics* 61 (1999): 445–66, especially 448.

19. Ibid.

20. Harry S. Truman, "Memo 'Concerning the Interpretation of the President's Order. . . ,' Harry S. Truman Library & Museum, ca. 1948, accessed June 22, 2012, http://www.trumanlibrary.org/whistlestop/study_collections/desegregation/large/documents/index.php?documentdate=1948-00-00&documentid=5-20&studycollectionid=&pagenumber=1&sortorder=.

21. Christopher S. Kelley and Bryan W. Marshall, "The Last Word: Presidential Power and the Role of Signing Statements," *Presidential Studies Quarterly* 38 (2008): 248–67; Michael J. Berry, "Controversially Executing the Law: George W. Bush and the Constitutional Signing Statement," *Congress and the Presidency* 36 (2009): 244–71.

22. The White House, "Memorandum for the Heads of Executive Departments and Agencies: Subject: Presidential Signing Statements," news release, March 9, 2009, http://www.whitehouse.gov/the-press-office/memorandum-presidential-signing-statements.

23. Gerhard Peters, "Executive Orders Washington–Obama," The American Presidency Project, ed. John T. Woolley and Gerhard Peters, updated September 6, 2014, accessed September 6, 2014, http://www.presidency.ucsb.edu/data/orders.php; John T. Woolley, "Presidential Signing Statements, Hoover–Obama," The American Presidency Project, ed. John T. Woolley and Gerhard Peters, updated September 6, 2014, http://www.presidency.ucsb.edu/signingstatements.php?year=2012&Submit=DISPLAY#axzz1uKYKvi91.

24. Joseph A. Pika and John Anthony Maltese, *The Politics of the Presidency,* 8th ed. (Washington, D.C.: CQ Press, 2012), 14–16.

25. "Bully Pulpit," C-SPAN Congressional Glossary, accessed June 22, 2012, http://legacy.c-span.org/guide/congress/glossary/alphalist.htm.

26. George C. Edwards III, *On Deaf Ears: The Limits of the Bully Pulpit* (New Haven, Conn.: Yale University Press, 2006).

27. John T. Woolley and Gerhard Peters, "Presidential News Conferences, Hoover–Obama," The American Presidency Project, updated May 1, 2014, accessed May 1, 2014, http://www.presidency.ucsb.edu/news_conferences.php?year=2012&Submit=DISPLAY.

28. See Zachary A. Goldfarb and Juliet Eilperin, "White House looking for new ways to penetrate polarized media," *Washington Post*, May 6, 2014, accessed online May 7, 2014, http://www.washingtonpost.com/politics/white-house-looking-for-new-ways-to-penetrate-polarized-media/2014/05/06/ebd39b6c-d532-11e3-aae8-c2d44bd79778_story.html; Melvin C. Laracey, *Presidents and People: The Partisan Story of Going Public* (College Station, Tex.: Texas A&M University Press, 2002); Reed L. Welch, "Presidential Success in Communicating with the Public through Televised Addresses," *Presidential Studies Quarterly* 33 (2003): 347–65; Samuel Kernell and Laurie L. Rice, "Cable and the Partisan Polarization of the President's Audience," *Presidency Studies Quarterly* 41, no. 4 (2011): 693–711.

29. Richard E. Neustadt, *Presidential Power and the Modern Presidents* (New York: Free Press, 1990).

30. Jon R. Bond, Richard Fleisher, and B. Dan Wood, "The Marginal and Time Varying Effect of Public Approval on Presidential Success in Congress," *Journal of Politics* 65 (2003): 92–110.

31. Andrew Barrett and Matthew Eshbaugh-Soha, "Presidential Success on the Substance of Legislation," *Political Research Quarterly* 60 (2007): 100–12.

32. Joint Resolution of Congress, House Joint Resolution 1145, August 7, 1964, *Department of State Bulletin,* August 24, 1964, reprinted in Henry Steele Commager and Milton Cantor, eds., *Documents of American History,* 10th ed. (Englewood Cliffs, N.J.: Prentice Hall, 1988), 2: 690.

33. Louis Fisher, *Presidential War Power,* 2nd ed. (Lawrence: University Press of Kansas, 2004), 128–33.

34. Ibid., 144–51.

35. For a longer discussion of this struggle for power over the conduct of war, see William G. Howell and Jon C. Pevenhouse, *Congressional Checks on Presidential War Powers* (Princeton, N.J.: Princeton University Press, 2007).

36. For more on presidential decisions to engage in military conflicts, see James Meernick, "Domestic Politics and the Political Use of Military Force by the United States," *Political Research Quarterly* 54 (2001): 889–904.

37. U.S. House of Representatives, House Joint Resolution, 114 Section 3 (a) 1, Library of Congress, http://thomas.loc.gov.

38. John J. Kruzel, "Afghanistan Troop Level to Eclipse Iraq by Midyear," United States Army, March 25, 2010, http://www.army.mil/article/36297/.

39. Afghanistan International Security Assistance Force, ISAF, NATO, http://www.isaf.nato.int/troop-numbers-and-contributions/index.php.

40. This paragraph is based on "Libya–Revolution and Aftermath," *New York Times,* updated June 11, 2012, http://topics.nytimes.com/top/news/international/countriesandterritories/libya/index.html.

41. This section is based on "Syria," *New York Times,* updated June 18, 2012, http://topicsnytimes.com/top/news/international/countriesandterritories/syria/index.html.

42. Scott Shane and Thom Shanker, "Yemen Strike Reflects U.S. Shift to Drones as Cheaper War Tool," October 2, 2011, *New York Times,* accessed May 6, 2014, http://www.nytimes.com/2011/10/02/world/awlaki-strike-shows-us-shift-to-drones-in-terror-fight.html?_r=0.

43. Craig Whitlock, "U.S. Airstrike that Killed American Teen in Yemen Raises Legal, Ethical Questions," *Washington Post,* October 22, 2011, accessed May 6, 2014, http://www.washingtonpost.com/world/national-security/us-airstrike-that-killed-american-teen-in-yemen-raises-legal-ethical-questions/2011/10/20/gIQAdvUY7L_story.html.

44. White House, Office of the Press Secretary, "Remarks by the President at the National Defense University, May 23, 2013," http://www.whitehouse.gov/the-press-office/2013/05/23/remarks-president-national-defense-university.

45. Bruce Drake, "Report Questions Drone Use, Widely Unpopular Globally, But Not in the U.S," Pew Research Center, October 23, 2013, accessed May 15, 2014, http://www.pewresearch.org/fact-tank/2013/10/23/report-questions-drone-use-widely-unpopular-globally-but-not-in-the-u-s/.

46. See "Public Sees U.S. Power Declining as Support for Global Engagement Slips," accessed May 4, 2014, http://www.people-press.org/2013/12/03/public-sees-u-s-power-declining-as-support-for-global-engagement-slips/.

47. *Hamdi v. Rumsfeld*, 542 U.S. 507 (2004).

48. *Rasul v. Bush*, 542 U.S. 466 (2004).

49. *Hamdan v. Rumsfeld*, 548 U.S. 557 (2006).

50. *Boumediene v. Bush*, 553 U.S. 723 (2008)

51. Fred I. Greenstein, *Presidential Difference*, 3rd ed. (Princeton, N.J.: Princeton University Press, 2009).

52. Mondale wrote a detailed memorandum to President Carter outlining his views of the office of vice president. For a broader discussion of Mondale's vice presidential tenure, see Richard Moe, "The Making of the Modern Vice Presidency: A Personal Reflection," *Minnesota History* 60 (2006): 88–99.

53. Joel K. Goldstein, "The Rising Power of the Modern Vice Presidency," *Presidential Studies Quarterly* 38, no. 3 (2008): 389.

54. Stephen Skowronek, *The Politics Presidents Make: Leadership from John Adams to Bill Clinton* (Cambridge, Mass.: Harvard University Press, 1997). Also see Stephen Skowronek, *Presidential Leadership in Political Time: Reprise and Reappraisal* (Lawrence: University Press of Kansas, 2008).

55. Aaron Wildavsky, "The Two Presidencies" in *The Presidency*, ed. Aaron Wildavsky (Boston: Little, Brown, 1969), 231–43.

56. For a more recent test of this theory, see Brandes Canes-Wrone, William G. Howell, and David E. Lewis, "Toward a Broader Understanding of Presidential Power: A Reevaluation of the Two Presidencies Thesis," *Journal of Politics* 69 (2007): 1–16.

57. Lammers and Genovese, *Presidency and Domestic Policy*. See also Neustadt, *Presidential Power and the Modern Presidents*.

58. Samuel Kernell, *Going Public: New Strategies of Presidential Leadership*, 4th ed. (Washington, D.C.: CQ Press, 2007), 131.

59. Ibid., 87–88.

60. Lammers and Genovese, *Presidency and Domestic Policy*.

61. Robert A. Caro, *The Years of Lyndon Johnson: The Passage of Power* (New York: Alfred A. Knopf, 2012), 487. Also see Lyndon Johnson's commencement address at Howard University, "To Fulfill These Rights," June 4, 1965, accessed June 22, 2012, http://www.lbjlib.utexas.edu/johnson/archives.hom/speeches.hom/650604.asp.

62. Lynn Rosellini, "'Honey, I Forgot to Duck,' Injured Reagan Tells Wife," *New York Times*, March 21, 1981, http://www.nytimes.com/1981/03/31/us/honey-i-forgot-to-duck-injured-reagan-tells-wife.html.

63. American Rhetoric, "Top 100 Speeches," accessed June 22, 2012, http://www.americanrhetoric.com/newtop100speeches.htm.

64. Hank C. Jenkins-Smith, Carol L. Silva, and Richard W. Waterman, "Micro- and Macro-level Models of the Presidential Expectations Gap," *Journal of Politics* 67 (2005): 690–715.

Chapter 12

1. Mike M. Ahlers, "Fired Air Marshal Loses Battle in Job Fight," *CNN.com*, August 5, 2011, http://www.cnn.com/2011/US/08/05/air.marshal.fired/index.html.

2. This story was compiled from the Transportation Security Administration website, http://www.tsa.gov/careers/; Jacob Gershman, "U.S. Takes Whistleblower Case against Air Marshal to Supreme Court," *The Wall Street Journal*, January 28, 2014, http://blogs.wsj.com/law/2014/01/28/u-s-takes-whistleblower-case-against-air-marshal-to-supreme-court/; Peter Van Buren, "The Next Battleground in the War on Whistleblowers," *The Nation*, March 4, 2014; Dan Weikel, "Air Marshal Whistle-blower Fired in 2006 Claims Big Win in Court," *Los Angeles Times*, May 25, 2013; The Government Accountability Project, "Robert MacLean, Air Marshal Whistleblower," http://www.whistleblower.org/robert-maclean-air-marshal-whistleblower; Laurence Hurley, "Supreme Court Agrees to Hear Air Marshal Whistleblower Case," Reuters News Service, printed in *Chicago Tribune*, May 19, 2014, http://www.chicagotribune.com/news/nationworld/la-na-nn-air-marshal-whistleblower-20140519,0,6366235.story.

3. Max Weber, *Economy and Society*, ed. Guenther Roth and Claus Wittich (Berkeley, Calif.: University of California Press, 1978).

4. The White House, Office of Management and Budget, Fiscal Year 2015 *Analytical Perspectives, Budget of the U.S. Government* (Washington, D.C.: U.S. Government Printing Office, 2014), Table 8-3, Total Federal Employment, p. 81, accessed May 19, 2014, http://www.whitehouse.gov/sites/default/files/omb/budget/fy2015/assets/spec.pdf; Note that the total number of federal employees cited above does not include active and reserve members of the National Guard.

5. "President Jefferson in the White House," EyeWitness to History, 2006, accessed June 27, 2012, http://www.eyewitnesstohistory.com/jeffersonwhitehouse.htm.

6. "The Cabinet," The White House, accessed May 19, 2014, http://www.whitehouse.gov/administration/cabinet.

7. A.P. staff, "United Nations Trims Staff and Spending," *New York Times*, December 27, 2013, http://www.nytimes.com/2013/12/28/world/un-budget-trims-staff-and-spending.html.

8. The White House, Office of Management and Budget, *Analytical Perspectives, Budget*, Table 8.2; The White House, Office of Management and Budget, *FY 2015 Analytical Perspectives, Budget*, Table 25-11, "Budget Authority by Agency in the Adjusted Baseline", p. 392, accessed May 19, 2014, http://www.whitehouse.gov/sites/default/files/omb/budget/fy2015/assets/spec.pdf.

9. Department of Health and Human Services, "HHS Programs and Services," accessed May 19, 2014, http://www.hhs.gov/about/programs/index.html

10. The White House, Office of Management and Budget, Fiscal Year 2015, *Analytical Perspectives, Budget*, Table 8.2.

11. Transportation Security Administration, "About TSA" accessed May 19, 2014, http://www.tsa.gov/about-tsa/layers-security; Transportation Security Administration, "About Us: Workforce" accessed May 19, 2014, http://www.tsa.gov/about-tsa/our-workforce.

12. U.S. Department of Health and Human Services, "About HHS," http://www.hhs.gov/about/.

13. James Q. Wilson, *Bureaucracy* (New York: Basic Books, 1989), 91.

14. Donald F. Kettl, *System under Stress: Homeland Security and American Politics*, 2nd ed. (Washington, D.C.: CQ Press, 2007), 37–39.

15. Matt Egan, "BP, Oil Plaintiffs Hammer Out Settlement," FOXBusiness, April 18, 2012, http://www.foxbusiness.com/industries/2012/04/18/bp-oil-spill-plaintiffs-hammer-out-settlement/.

16. Ian Urbina, "U.S. Said to Allow Drilling without Needed Permits," *New York Times*, May 13, 2010, http://www.nytimes.com/2010/05/14/us/14agency.html?pagewanted=all.

17. NPR staff, "White House Lifts Ban on Offshore Drilling," NPR, October 12, 2010, http://www.npr.org/templates/story/story.php?storyId=130512541.

18. Egan, "BP, Oil Plaintiffs Hammer Out Settlement."

19. Daniel P. Carpenter, *The Forging of Bureaucratic Autonomy: Reputations, Networks, and Policy Innovation in Executive Agencies, 1862–1928* (Princeton, N.J.: Princeton University Press, 2001).

20. United States Postal Service, Office of the Postmaster, *The United States Postal Service: An American History, 1775–2006* (Washington, D.C.: Government Relations, United States Postal Service, 2007), 6–7, http://about.usps.com/publications/pub100.pdf.

21. Michael Moss, "E. Coli Path Shows Flaws in Beef Inspection," *New York Times*, October 3, 2009, A1; Michael Moss, "E. Coli Outbreak Traced to Company That Halted Testing of Ground Beef Trimmings," *New York Times*, November 12, 2009, A16; Bill Tomson, "Tuna Blamed

in Salmonella Outbreak is recalled," *Wall Street Journal*, April 17, 2012, A3.

22. U.S. Consumer Product Safety Commission, http://www.cpsc.gov.

23. "The Consumer Financial Protection Bureau," The White House, September 17, 2010, http://www.whitehouse.gov/photos-and-video/video/2010/09/17/consumer-financial-protection-bureau.

24. Lewis, *Politics of Presidential Appointments*, 12–13.

25. Theda Skocpol, *Protecting Soldiers and Mothers* (Cambridge, Mass.: Harvard University Press, 1992).

26. Sean M. Theriault, *The Power of the People* (Columbus: Ohio State University Press, 2005), Chapter 3.

27. Davis Polk, "Dodd-Frank Progress Report," accessed September 9, 2014 http://www.davispolk.com/Dodd-Frank-Rulemaking-Progress-Report/.

28. Lewis, *Politics of Presidential Appointments*, 19–20, especially Figure 2.1.

29. U.S. Office of Personnel Management, "Federal Employment Statistics: Federal Civilian Employment," September 2010, accessed June 27, 2012, http://www.opm.gov/feddata/html/geoagy10.asp.

30. Department of Labor, Bureau of Labor Statistics, accessed May 30, 2014, http://www.bls.gov/ooh/about/ooh-faqs.htm.

31. For more on political appointees, see Jeff Gill and Richard Waterman, "Solidary and Functional Costs: Explaining the Presidential Appointment Contradiction," *Journal of Public Administration Research and Theory* 14 (2004): 547–69.

32. Lewis, *Politics of Presidential Appointments*, 11.

33. Ibid., 100, Figure 4.3.

34. Juliet Eilperin, "Obama Cabinet Picks Add Diversity, But Still Frustrate White House Allies," *Washington Post*, March 4, 2013, http://www.washingtonpost.com/national/health-science/obama-cabinet-picks-add-diversity-but-still-frustrate-white-house-allies/2013/03/04/7e2030a6-84fe-11e2-98a3-b3db6b9ac586_story.html.

35. Office of Personnel Management, "Diversity and Inclusion: Federal Workforce At-a-glance," accessed May 19, 2014, http://www.opm.gov/policy-data-oversight/diversity-and-inclusion/federal-workforce-at-a-glance/.

36. For an in-depth example of private contracting in Medicaid in New York State, see Nina Bernstein, "Medicaid Shift Sees Rush for Profitable Clients," *New York Times*, May 8, 2014, http://www.nytimes.com/2014/05/09/nyregion/medicaid-shift-fuels-rush-for-profitable-clients.html.

37. U.S. Office of Special Counsel, "Hatch Act," updated October 6, 2011, http://www.osc.gov/hatchact.htm, and "Political Activity and the Federal Employee," http://www.osc.gov/documents/hatchact/ha_fed.pdf, both accessed June 27, 2012.

38. For more on the relationships among bureaucrats, members of Congress, and interest groups, see Anthony M. Bertelli and Christian R. Grose, "Secretaries of Pork? A New Theory of Distributive Public Policy," *Journal of Politics* 71 (2009): 926–45; and Sanford C. Gordon and Catherine Hafer, "Corporate Influence and the Regulatory Mandate," *Journal of Politics* 69 (2007): 300–19.

39. http://public.tableausoftware.com/views/Veterans_VA_mobile/VeteransAffairs?amp%3Bembed=y&:display_count=no&:showVizHome=no#, accessed May 25, 2014.

40. Scott Bronstein and Drew Griffin, "A Fatal Wait: Veterans Languish and Die on a VA Hospital's Secret List," CNN, April 30, 2014, accessed May 19, 2014, http://www.cnn.com/2014/04/23/health/veterans-dying-health-care-delays/index.html?iid=article_sidebar.

41. Chelsea J. Carter, Greg Seaby, and Greg Botelho, "Rights Group Calls VA Official 'Scapegoat' in Scandal over Wait Times, Care," CNN, May 16, 2014, accessed May 19, 2014, http://www.cnn.com/2014/05/16/politics/va-scandal/.

42. Daniel P. Carpenter, "Groups, the Media, Agency Waiting Costs, and FDA Drug Approval," *American Journal of Political Science* 46, no. 3 (2002): 490–505. Also see Susan L. Moffitt, "Promoting Agency Reputation through Public Advice: Advisory Committee Use in the FDA," *Journal of Politics* 72, no. 3 (2010): 1–14. For a longer discussion of the history and effectiveness of the FDA, see Daniel P. Carpenter, *Reputation and Power: Organizational Image and Pharmaceutical Regulation at the FDA* (Princeton, N.J.: Princeton University Press, 2010).

43. U.S. Food and Drug Administration, "FDA Safety Communication: Shasta Technologies GenStrip Blood Glucose Test Strips May Report False Results," issued April 29, 2014, accessed May 8, 2014, http://www.fda.gov/MedicalDevices/Safety/AlertsandNotices/ucm395180.htm.

44. L. Paige Whitaker, "The Whistleblower Protection Act: An Overview," CRS Report for Congress, RL33918 (Washington, D.C.: Congressional Research Service, March 12, 2007).

Chapter 13

1. Material for this vignette taken from Justice Sotomayor's memoir, *My Beloved World* (2013); the Supreme Court case *Schuette v. Coalition to Defend Affirmative Action*, 134 S.Ct. 1623 (2014) http://www.supremecourt.gov/opinions/13pdf/12-682_j4ek.pdf; and an interview on National Public Radio (http://www.npr.org/2013/01/14/167699633/a-justice-deliberates-sotomayor-on-love-health-and-family).

2. "Federal Judgeships," Administrative Office of the United States Courts, accessed May 12, 2014, http://www.uscourts.gov/JudgesAndJudgeships/FederalJudgeships.aspx.

3. *Steelworkers v. Weber*, 443 U.S. 193 (1979).

4. *Firefighters Local Union No. 1784 v. Stotts*, 467 U.S. 561 (1984).

5. *Johnson v. Transportation Agency*, 480 U.S. 616 (1987).

6. *Fullilove v. Klutznick*, 448 U.S. 448 (1980).

7. *Richmond v. J. A. Croson Co.*, 488 U.S. 469 (1989).

8. *Metro Broadcasting, Inc. v. FCC*, 497 U.S. 547 (1990); *Adarand Constructors, Inc. v. Pena*, 515 U.S. 200 (1995).

9. *Regents v. Bakke*, 438 U.S. 265 (1978).

10. *Hopwood v. Texas*, 78 F.3d 932 (1996).

11. http://www.nbcnews.com/news/latino/more-latinos-whites-admitted-university-california-n85511, accessed June 5, 2014.

12. 134 S.Ct. 1623 (2014).

13. Federal litigation data can be found at "Judicial Facts and Figures 2012," Administrative Office of the U.S. Courts, accessed May 7, 2014, http://www.uscourts.gov/Statistics/JudicialFactsAndFigures/Judicial-Facts-Figures2012.aspx.

14. "Judicial Facts and Figures 2012," Administrative Office of the U.S. Courts, table 4.10, accessed June 10, 2014, http://www.uscourts.gov/Statistics/JudicialFactsAndFigures/judicial-facts-figures-2012.aspx.

15. Paul M. Collins Jr., "Friends of the Court: Examining the Influence of Amicus Curiae Participation in U.S. Supreme Court Litigation," *Law and Society Review* 38 (2004): 807–32.

16. Rebecca Salokar, *The Solicitor General: The Politics of Law* (Philadelphia: Temple University Press, 1992).

17. Lisa Solowiej and Paul Collins Jr., "Counteractive Lobbying in the U.S. Supreme Court," *American Politics Research* 37 (2009): 670–99.

18. *Regents of the University of California v. Bakke*, 438 U.S. 265 (1978).

19. Federal Bureau of Investigation, *Crime in the United States 2012*, Fall 2013, accessed May 7, 2014, http://www.fbi.gov/about-us/cjis/ucr/crime-in-the-u.s/2012/crime-in-the-u.s.-2012/offenses-known-to-law-enforcement/clearances.

20. Mark Motivans, "Federal Justice Statistics 2010," United States Department of Justice, Office of Justice Programs, Bureau of Justice

Statistics, accessed May 7, 2014, http://www.bjs.gov/content/pub/pdf/fjs10.pdf.

21. Gregory Caldeira and John R. Wright, "Organized Interests and Agenda Setting in the U.S. Supreme Court," *American Political Science Review* 82 (1988): 1109–28.

22. *Hopwood v. Texas*, 78 F.3d 932 (1996).

23. Timothy Johnson, Paul Wahlbeck, and James Spriggs, "The Influence of Oral Arguments on the U.S. Supreme Court," *American Political Science Review* 100 (2006): 99.

24. Alexander Bickel, *The Least Dangerous Branch: The Supreme Court at the Bar of Politics* (Indianapolis: Bobbs-Merrill, 1963).

25. Harold J. Spaeth, Sara Benesh, Lee Epstein, Andrew D. Martin, Jeffrey A. Segal, and Theodore J. Ruger, Supreme Court Database, Version 2013, Release 01, accessed May 10, 2014, http://supremecourtdatabase.org.

26. *Gonzalez v. Raich*, 545 U.S. 1 (2005).

27. Segal and Spaeth, *Supreme Court and the Attitudinal Model*.

28. Ibid.

29. Lee Epstein and Jack Knight, *The Choices Justices Make* (Washington, D.C.: CQ Press, 1998); Forrest Maltzman, James F. Spriggs II, and Paul J. Wahlbeck, *Crafting Law on the Supreme Court: The Collegial Game* (New York: Cambridge University Press, 2000).

30. See Lawrence Baum, *The Puzzle of Judicial Behavior* (Ann Arbor: University of Michigan Press, 1997).

31. Jeffrey A. Segal and Robert M. Howard, "How Supreme Court Justices Respond to Litigant Requests to Overturn Precedent," *Judicature* 85 (2001): 148–57.

32. Jeffrey A. Segal and Robert M. Howard, "A Preference for Deference? The Supreme Court and Judicial Review," *Political Research Quarterly* 57 (2004): 131–43. See also Lori Ringhand, "The Changing Face of Judicial Activism: An Empirical Examination of Voting Behavior on the Rehnquist Natural Court," *Constitutional Commentary* 24 (2007): 43.

33. Gerald Rosenberg, *The Hollow Hope* (Chicago: University of Chicago Press, 1991).

34. "Samuel Chase—The Samuel Chase Impeachment Trial," Law Library, accessed May 10, 2012, http://law.jrank.org/pages/5151/Chase-Samuel-Chase-Impeachment-Trial.htm.

35. Lee Epstein and Jeffrey A. Segal, *Advice and Consent: The Politics of Judicial Appointments* (New York: Oxford University Press, 2006).

36. Denis Steven Rutkus and Mitchel A. Sollenberger, *Judicial Nomination Statistics: U.S. District and Circuit Courts, 1977–2003,* CRS Report for Congress, RL31635 (Washington, D.C.: Congressional Research Service, February 23, 2004), Table 2(b), accessed July 1, 2014, http://www.senate.gov/reference/resources/pdf/RL31635.pdf.

37. Russell Wheeler, "Judicial Nominations and Confirmations: Fact and Fiction." *Brookings*, accessed May 7, 2014, http://www.brookings.edu/blogs/fixgov/posts/2013/12/30-staffing-federal-judiciary-2013-no-breakthrough-year.

38. Ibid.

39. Richard Nixon, "Transcript of President's Announcement," *New York Times*, October 22, 1971.

40. "Robert Bork's Position on Reproductive Rights," *New York Times*, September 13, 1987, B9.

41. Jonathan P. Kastellec, Jeffrey R. Lax, and Justin H. Phillips, "Public Opinion and Senate Confirmation of Supreme Court Nominees," *Journal of Politics* 72 (2010): 767–84.

42. Charlie Savage, "A Judge's View of Judging Is on the Record," *New York Times*, May 14, 2009, p. A21, http://www.nytimes.com/2009/05/15/us/15judge.html.

43. Charles M. Cameron, Albert D. Cover, and Jeffrey A. Segal, "Senate Voting on Supreme Court Nominees: A Neoinstitutional Model," *American Political Science Review* 84 (1990): 525–34.

44. Christina Boyd, Lee Epstein, and Andrew D. Martin, "Untangling the Causal Effects of Sex on Judging," *American Journal of Political Science* 54 (2010): 389–411.

45. See, e.g., Karen O'Connor and Jeffrey A. Segal, "Justice Sandra Day O'Connor and the Supreme Court's Reaction to Its First Female Member," *Women and Politics* 10 (1990): 95–104.

46. John J. Szmer, Tammy A. Sarver, and Erin B. Kaheny, "Have We Come a Long Way, Baby? The Influence of Attorney Gender on Supreme Court Decision Making," *Politics and Gender* 6 (2010): 1–36.

47. *McCulloch v. Maryland,* 4 Wheaton 316 (1819); *Gibbons v. Ogden,* 9 Wheaton 1 (1824); and *Cohens v. Virginia,* 6 Wheaton 264 (1821).

48. 60 U.S. 393 (1857).

49. *Slaughterhouse Cases,* 83 U.S. 36 (1873).

50. *United States v. Cruikshank,* 92 U.S. 542 (1876).

51. *Civil Rights Cases,* 109 U.S. 3 (1883).

52. *Brandenburg v. Ohio,* 395 U.S. 444 (1969) (speech rights); *New York Times v. Sullivan,* 376 U.S. 254 (1964) (press rights); *Memoirs v. Massachusetts,* 383 U.S. 413 (1966) (obscenity); and *Engel v. Vitale,* 370 U.S. 421 (1962); *Abington Township School District v. Schempp,* 374 U.S. 203 (1963) (prayer and Bible reading).

53. *Brown v. Board of Education,* 347 U.S. 483 (1954); *Wesberry v. Sanders,* 376 U.S. 1 (1964); *Reynolds v. Sims,* 377 U.S. 533 (1964).

54. *Griswold v. Connecticut,* 381 U.S. 479 (1965) (birth control); *Roe v. Wade,* 410 U.S. 113 (1973).

55. *Mapp v. Ohio,* 367 U.S. 643 (1961); *Miranda v. Arizona,* 384 U.S. 436 (1966).

56. *Swann v. Charlotte-Mecklenburg Board of Education,* 402 U.S. 1 (1971) (busing); *Roe v. Wade,* 410 U.S. 113 (1973) (abortion); *Furman v. Georgia,* 408 U.S. 238 (1972) (death penalty); *Reed v. Reed,* 404 U.S. 71 (1971) (sex discrimination); and *Regents of the University of California v. Bakke,* 438 U.S. 265 (1978) (affirmative action).

57. *San Antonio Independent School District v. Rodriguez,* 411 U.S. 1 (1973) (school funding); *United States v. Leon,* 468 U.S. 897 (1984) (limiting the exclusionary rule); and *New York v. Quarles,* 467 U.S. 649 (1984) (limiting *Miranda*).

58. *Lawrence v. Texas,* 539 U.S. 558 (2003).

59. *Planned Parenthood v. Casey,* 505 U.S. 833 (1992); *United States v. Lopez,* 514 U.S. 549 (1995); *Gratz v. Bollinger,* 539 U.S. 244 (2003); and *Grutter v. Bollinger,* 539 U.S. 306 (2003).

60. *Bush v. Gore,* 531 U.S. 98 (2000).

61. Adam Liptak, "Justices Offer Receptive Ear to Business Interests," *New York Times,* December 19, 2010, p. A1.

62. *Wal-mart Stores v. Dukes,* 131 S. Ct. 2541 (2011).

63. *Citizens United v. Federal Election Commission,* 558 U.S. 310 (2010).

64. *National Federation of Independent Business et al. v. Sebelius,* 132 S. Ct. 2566 (2012).

65. *United States v. Windsor,* 570 U.S. 12 (2013).

66. *Schuette v. Coalition to Defend Affirmative Action,* 133 S. Ct. 1653 (2014).

67. Robert Dahl, "Decision Making in a Democracy: The Supreme Court as a National Policy-Maker," *Journal of Public Law* 6 (1957): 179–295.

68. Herbert M. Kritzer, "Federal Judges and Their Political Environments: The Influence of Public Opinion," *American Journal of Political Science* 23 (1979): 194–207.

69. *West Virginia State Board of Education v. Barnette*, 319 U.S. 624 (1943), 638.

Chapter 14

1. This story has been compiled from a series of news items as follows: Marilyn Adams, "Pair of Flier Advocates Fight for Airline Passengers' Rights," *USA Today,* May 19, 2008; Joan Lowy, "Government Asking Why Passengers Were Stranded," Associated Press, August 12, 2009,http://www.realclearpolitics.com/news/ap/politics/2009/Aug/12/gov_t_asking_why_airline_passengers_were_stranded.html; Jeff Bailey, "An Air Travel Activist Is Born," *New York Times,* September 20, 2007; Matthew L. Wald, "Stiff Fines Are Set for Long Wait on the Tarmac," *New York Times,* December 21, 2009; Coalition for an Airline Passengers' Bill of Rights, "An Early Christmas Present for the Flying Public," December 23, 2009, http://FlyersRights.org; Bureau of Transportation Statistics, "Airlines Report Seven Tarmac Delays Longer Than Three Hours On Domestic Flights, 11 Longer Than Four Hours on International Flights in October." For more general information about airline delays on tarmacs, see the Department of Transportation website, http://www.dot.gov/briefingroom. An e-mail interview with Kate Hanni was conducted for this textbook, from which the chapter-opening quotation is taken.

2. Bryan D. Jones and Frank M. Baumgartner, *The Politics of Attention* (Chicago: University of Chicago Press, 2005).

3. Kate Sheppard, "North Carolina Coal Ash Spill Renews Push For Long-Delayed Federal Regulations" HuffPost.com, February 5, 2014, accessed May 24, 2014, http://www.huffingtonpost.com/2014/02/05/coal-ash-spill-north-carolina_n_4733164.html.

4. *New State Ice Co. v. Liebmann,* 285 U.S. 262 (1932) at 311. See Andrew Karch, *Democratic Laboratories: Policy Diffusion among the American States* (Ann Arbor: University of Michigan Press, 2007).

5. Craig Volden, "States as Policy Laboratories: Emulating Success in the Children's Health Insurance Program," *American Journal of Political Science* 50 (2006): 294–312.

6. Chris Koski, "Greening America's Skylines: The Diffusion of Low-Salience Policies," *Policy Studies Journal* 38 (2010): 93–117.

7. Michael Mintron and Sandra Vergari, "Policy Networks and Innovations Diffusion: The Case of State Education Reforms," *Journal of Politics* 60 (1998): 126–48.

8. Christopher Stream, "Health Reform in the States: A Model of State Small Group Health Insurance Market Reforms," *Political Research Quarterly* 52 (1999): 499–525.

9. Frederick J. Boehmke and Richard Witmer, "Disentangling Diffusion: The Effects of Social Learning and Economic Competition on State Policy Innovation and Expansion," *Political Research Quarterly* 57 (2004): 39–51.

10. Charles R. Shipan and Craig Volden, "Bottom-Up Federalism: The Diffusion of Antismoking Policies from U.S. Cities to States," *American Journal of Political Science* 50 (2006): 825–43.

11. Robert R. Preuhs, "State Policy Components of Interstate Migration in the United States," *Political Research Quarterly* 52 (1999): 527–47.

12. David M. Konisky, "Regulatory Competition and Environmental Enforcement: Is There a Race to the Bottom?," *American Journal of Political Science* 51 (2003): 853.

13. *Shapiro v. Thompson,* 394 U.S. 618 (1969); *Saenz v. Roe,* 526 U.S. 489 (1999).

14. Craig Volden, "The Politics of Competitive Federalism: A Race to the Bottom in Welfare Benefits?," *American Journal of Political Science* 46 (2006): 352–63.

15. Department of Housing and Urban Development, "HUD Historical Background," http://www.hud.gov/offices/adm/about/admguide/history.cfm.

16. For details on these programs, see the U.S. Department of Health and Human Services, Centers for Medicare and Medicaid Services (CMS), http://www.cms.hhs.gov.

17. See http://www.hud.gov/offices/adm/about/admguide/history.cfm#1960; also see Center on Budget and Policy Priorities, "Policy Basics: Section 8 Project-Based Rental Assistance," accessed March 22, 2014, http://www.cbpp.org/cms/?fa=view&id=3891.

18. Centers for Disease Control and Prevention, "Early Release of Selected Estimates Based on Data from the 2010 National Health Interview Survey," CDC.gov, updated and accessed June 22, 2012, http://www.cdc.gov/nchs/nhis/released201106.htm.

19. Henry J. Kaiser Family Foundation, "Summary of Coverage Provisions in the Patient Protection and Affordable Care Act," *Focus on Health Reform,* updated April 14, 2011, accessed June 21, 2012, http://kff.org/health-costs/issue-brief/summary-of-coverage-provisions-in-the-patient/.

20. Phil Galewitz, "10 States Are Critical To Administration's Efforts to Enroll 6 Million in New Health Plans." Kaiser Health News, accessed March 20, 2014, http://www.kaiserhealthnews.org/Stories/2014/March/19/10-States-Are-Critical-To-Administrations-Efforts-To-Enroll-6-Million-In-New-Health-Plans.aspx.

21. Kaiser Family Foundation, "State Health Facts, Status of State Action on the Medicaid Expansion 2014," accessed September 18, 2014, http://kff.org/health-reform/state-indicator/state-activity-around-expanding-medicaid-under-the-affordable-care-act/.

22. Centers for Medicare and Medicaid Services, "Affordable Care Act," http://www.medicaid.gov/AffordableCareAct/Affordable-Care-Act.html.

23. Department of Health and Human Services, "The Affordable Care Act and Latinos," accessed March 10, 2014, http://www.hhs.gov/healthcare/facts/factsheets/2012/04/aca-and-latinos04102012a.html; Tamara Keith, "Obama Pitches Health Care Law to Latinos in a Bid to Boost Enrollment," National Public Radio, March 6, 2014, http://www.npr.org/blogs/codeswitch/2014/03/06/286859961/obama-pitches-health-care-law-to-latinos-in-bid-to-boost-enrollment.

24. Kaiser Family Foundation, "Visualizing Health Policy: What Americans Pay for Health Insurance Under the ACA," accessed March 19, 2014. http://kff.org/infographic/visualizing-health-policy-what-americans-pay-for-health-insurance-under-the-aca/.

25. Nancy Rytina, "Estimates of the Permanent Legal Immigrant Population in 2012," Office of Immigration Statistics, Department of Homeland Security, July 2013, https://www.dhs.gov/sites/default/files/publications/ois_lpr_pe_2012.pdf.

26. U.S. Citizenship and Immigration Services, "About Us," accessed May 31, 2012, http://www.uscis.gov/aboutus.

27. Randall Monger and James Yankay, *Annual Flow Report: U.S. Legal Permanent Residents: 2012* (Washington, D.C.: Office of Immigration Statistics, Department of Homeland Security, March 2013), 1, http://www.dhs.gov/sites/default/files/publications/ois_lpr_fr_2012_2.pdf.

28. Randall Monger and James Yankay, Annual Flow Report: *U.S. Lawful Permanent Residents: 2013* (Washington, D.C.: Office of Immigration Statistics, Department of Homeland Security, May 2014), 2.

29. U.S. Citizenship and Immigration Services, "Statement from Secretary of Homeland Security Janet Napolitano on July 1, 2013," accessed June 13, 2014, http://www.uscis.gov/family/same-sex-marriages.

30. U.S. Citizenship and Immigration Services, "A Guide to Naturalization," http://www.uscis.gov/us-citizenship/citizenship-through-naturalization/guide-naturalization.

31. Michael Hoefer, Nancy Rytina, and Bryan Baker, "Estimates of the Unauthorized Immigrant Population Residing in the United States: January 2011," Office of Immigration Statistics Department of Homeland Security, March 2012, http://www.dhs.gov/xlibrary/assets/statistics/publications/ois_ill_pe_2011.pdf.

32. U.S. Immigration Support: Your Online Guide to U.S. Visas, Green Cards and Citizenship, http://www.usimmigrationsupport.org.

33. Luis Miranda, "Get the Facts on the DREAM Act," *The White House Blog*, December 1, 2010, http://www.whitehouse.gov/blog/2010/12/01/get-facts-dream-act.

34. The White House, Office of the Press Secretary, "Remarks by the President on Immigration," last modified on June 15, 2012, accessed July 2, 2012, http://www.whitehouse.gov/the-press-office/2012/06/15/remarks-president-immigration.

35. Randal C. Archibold, "Arizona Enacts Stringent Law on Immigration," *New York Times*, April 23, 2010, A1.

36. Jack Lewis, "The Birth of the EPA," *EPA Journal* (Washington, D.C.: U.S. Environmental Protection Agency, 1985), http://www.epa.gov.

37. Bruce Jones, "Despite Growing Energy Independence, U.S. Cannot Escape Global Risks," The Brookings Institution, May 27, 2014, accessed July 2, 2014, http://www.brookings.edu/blogs/planetpolicy/posts/2014/05/27-energy-independence-us-global-risks-jones.

38. U.S. Energy Information Administration, "International Energy Outlook 2013 ," July 25, 2013, http://www.eia.gov/forecasts/ieo/

39. Lachlan Markay and Jay Lucas, "Timeline: Keystone's Three Years in Limbo," *The Foundry* (blog), January 19, 2012, http://blog.heritage.org/2012/01/19/timeline-keystones-three-years-in-limbo/.

40. "Keystone XL Pipeline Project," TransCanada, accessed May 22, 2012, http://www.transcanada.com/keystone.html.

41. House Energy and Commerce Committee, "Waiting for the Keystone XL Pipeline," accessed May 22, 2012, http://energycommerce.house.gov/keystonexl.shtml.

42. Pierre Bertrand, "Keystone Pipeline: 5 Things You Need to Know," *International Business Times*, January 19, 2012, http://www.ibtimes.com/keystone-pipeline-5-things-you-need-know-397928; House Energy and Commerce Committee, "Waiting for Keystone XL, Waiting for Jobs," January 4, 2012, accessed May 22, 2012, http://energycommerce.house.gov/news/

43. John M. Broder, "TransCanada Renewing Request to Build Keystone Pipeline," *New York Times*, February 27, 2012, http://www.nytimes.com/2012/02/28/science/earth/keystone-pipeline-permit-request-to-be-renewed.html?_r=2&hp.

44. European Central Bank, http://www.ecb.int/.

45. U.S. Census Bureau, "Trade in Goods with China," http://www.census.gov/foreign-trade/balance/c5700.html.

46. Information in this paragraph is from World Trade Organization, http://www.wto.org.

47. See http://www.ustr.gov/US-Wins-Trade-Enforcement-Case-American-Farmers-Proves-Export-Blocking-Chinese-Duties-Unjustified-Under-WTO-Rule.

48. D. Andrew Austin and Mindy R. Levit, *The Debt Limit: History and Recent Increases*, CRS Report for Congress, RL31967 (Washington, D.C.: Congressional Research Service, January 20, 2011), http://www.fas.org/sgp/crs/misc/RL31967.pdf.

49. The White House, Office of Management and Budget, Historical Tables, Table 1.1—Summary of Receipts, Outlays, and Surpluses or Deficits (−): 1789–2017; The White House, Office of Management and Budget, Historical Tables, Table 7.1—Federal Debt at the End of Year:−2017. Both tables are available at http://www.whitehouse.gov/omb/budget/Historicals/.

50. Europa: Gateway to the European Union, http://europa.eu/.

51. Washington's Farewell Address, 1796, Yale Law School Avalon Project, http://avalon.law.yale.edu.

52. Ellen C. Collier, "Instances of Use of United States Forces Abroad, 1798–1993," Naval Historical Center, last modified September 12, 1997, accessed May 12, 2012, http://www.history.navy.mil/wars/foabroad.htm.

53. John Mueller, *War, Presidents, and Public Opinion* (New York: Wiley, 1970).

54. Presidential Approval Ratings, Gallup Historical Statistics, accessed May 12, 2012, http://www.gallup.com/poll/124922/presidential-approval-center.aspx.

55. "Presidential Approval Ratings," George W. Bush, Gallup.com, accessed May 12, 2012, http://www.gallup.com/poll/124922/presidential-approval-center.aspx.

56. United Nations Office for Disarmament Affairs (UNODA), Treaty on the Non-Proliferation of Nuclear Weapons (NPT), http://www.un.org.

57. United States Agency for International Development, http://www.usaid.gov.

58. See http://www.state.gov/documents/organization/208292.pdf.

59. World Bank, http://www.worldbank.org.

60. World Bank, Archives, http://www.worldbank.org.

61. World Bank, Projects and Operations, http://www.worldbank.org.

62. Michael W. Doyle, "Liberalism and World Politics," *American Political Science Review* 80 (1986): 1151–69.

63. Information in this and the next paragraphs from International Monetary Fund, http://www.imf.org.

64. See http://www.imf.org/external/np/fin/tad/extcred1.aspx.

65. Information in this and subsequent paragraphs is from Peace Corps, http://www.peacecorps.gov.

66. Fiscal Year 2014 budget number taken from the U.S. State Department, http://www.state.gov/documents/organization/208292.pdf.

Index

Note: Page numbers followed by an "f" indicate figures. Page numbers followed by a "t" indicate tables.

A

AARP, 203, 226
Abortion, 111–13, 207–8, 257, 448, 449
   public opinion on, 162–63
Adams, John, 6–7, 241, 242, 361
Adams, John Quincy, 242
Administrative Procedures Act (APA), 459
Adversary process, 420
Advice and consent, 317–19, 356–57, 438–40
Advocacy caucuses, 329
Affirmative action, 419–20, 424–25, 432–33, 448, 450. *See also Gratz* and *Grutter* cases
Affordable Care Act (ACA), 462t, 464–67
   contraception and, 104f, 111, 460
   as election issue, 279, 283
   Hobby Lobby and, 104f, 460
   implementation of, 393–94, 460, 491
   insurance costs under, 466–67, 466f
   mandate for insurance, 111, 318, 465
   Medicaid expansion and, 77, 465–66
   overview, 465–67
   passage through Congress, 260, 464
   Sebelius, Kathleen and, 460, 467
   Supreme Court ruling on, 78, 450, 460, 465
Afghanistan War, 370–71, 486
African Americans
   civil rights movement and, 134–39, 256
   segregation and. *See* Racial segregation and discrimination
   voting rights, 126, 126–27, 138–39, 139f, 284–85
   voting turnout, 287, 287f
Agenda, policy making and, 457, 458f
Agenda setting, 187–88
   by president, 367–68
   in Senate, 330–33
Air pollution, 412
Air travel
   federal air marshals, 387–88, 414
   NTSB and, 395
   TSA and, 387–88, 395, 414
Amendments (to the Constitution), 51f
   amendment process, 41–42, 42f
   amendments expanding public participation, 50, 51f
   amendments on civil liberties, 90f
   amendments on civil rights, 123f
   amendments on federalism, 65f
   amendments on presidency, 352f
   amendments on right to vote, 285f
   amendments overturning Supreme Court decisions, 440t
   Bill of Rights (First through Tenth), 48–50
   Civil War Amendments (Thirteenth through Fifteenth), 50, 73, 121
   incorporated provisions of, 91f
   First Amendment, 50, 91, 96–103
   Second Amendment, 50, 106, 252
American Revolution, events leading to, 31–33, 32f
Americans for Tax Reform, 224, 226
Amicus curiae briefs, 427, 430, 431
Amnesty International, 209

Andiola, Erika, 117f, 118–19, 142
Annapolis Convention, 34
Antifederalists, 46–48, 47f, 241–42, 242t
Appeals, 111, 421
Appeals courts, 421, 423f, 428–29, 429f, 441
Appointments, 317–19, 357–59, 390
   judicial, 438–44
   political appointees, 404, 405–6
   recess appointments, 357
Appropriate, 316–17
Arizona v. United States, 469, 470
Articles of Confederation, 33–35, 39t
Asian Americans, 124–25, 174, 287f
   wartime internment of, 125
Assange, Julian, 100–101
Assault weapons ban, 252–53
Association, right of, 201–2
Attainder, bills of, 45, 65, 68
Australia, compulsory voting in, 297
Australian ballot, 245, 246f
Authorize, 317, 320
Autocracy, 15
Automobiles, fuel efficiency standards, 221, 221f
Awlaki, Anwar al, 96, 372

B

Bakke case (*Regents v. Bakke*), 424, 427, 434, 435, 449t
Ballot, 237, 245
Ballot reform, 245, 246f
Bank bailout, 473
Barron v. Baltimore, 91
Battleground states, 277–78
Bicameral, 40, 310–11
Biden, Joseph, 377
Bill of Rights, 38, 48–50, 88
   English, 49
   incorporation to states, 90–92, 91f
   not included in original Constitution, 38–39, 47–48
bin Laden, Osama, death of, 371
Birth control, 104f, 111–13
Black codes, 125–26
Blogs, 175, 182–83, 367
Boehner, John, 323, 324–25, 325f
Bork, Robert, 442
Boston Massacre, 32, 32f
Boston Tea Party, 32, 32f
Bowers v. Hardwick, 158
Branches of government, 10–11, 11f
Breyer, Stephen, 432, 432f, 437
British constitution, 30
Brown v. Board of Education, 30, 66, 75, 134, 135, 435, 437, 443, 448, 449t
Buckley v. Valeo, 216
Budget, federal, 335–37. *See also* Debt, national
   Byrd rule, 336–37
   concurrent budget resolution, 336
   continuing resolution, 336
   federal budget deficit, 335–36, 480–81
   national debt and, 336
   reconciliation process, 336–37
Bully pulpit, 365, 365f
Bureaucracy, 386–417
   accountability and responsiveness, 410–14
   bureau analogy for, 389
   cabinet, 389–90, 406–7
   civil service, 404–5, 404f
      reforms, 409
   components of, 396–98
      bureaucratic culture, 397–98

Bureaucracy (*continued*)
    decision-making process, 396–97
    expertise, 397
    mission, 396
  constitutional foundations, 390
  defined, 389
  democracy and, 415
  diversity in, 406–7, 407f
  efficiency and transparency, 411–14
  executive departments, 392–94, 392t, 399–400
  failures of, 398, 414
  federal regulatory commission, 395
  federal workforce, 404f, 407f
  historical evolution of, 399–409
  impact of, 388–89
  independent agencies, 394–96, 394t
  iron triangles and issue networks and, 409
  legislative and judicial branches and, 410–11
  organizational chart, 393f
  oversight and, 400
  patronage system and, 401–4
  political appointees, 404, 405–6
  politics and, 408–9
  private-sector contract workers, 407–8
  regulations, 389, 392, 458, 459
  regulatory agencies, 400–401
  regulatory process, 458, 459–60, 459f
  reputation of, 388
  Senior Executive Service, 406
  structure of, 390–96
  United Nations bureaucracy, 391
  whistleblowing and, 387–88, 414
Burger Court, 448, 449t
Burwell, Sylvia Mathews, 348f, 349–50, 376, 467
Bush, George H. W., 249, 351, 356, 400, 441
  cost of milk statement, 166–67
Bush, George W., 258, 357, 364
  approval ratings of, 188
  bank bailout of, 473
  Cheney and, 376–77
  election of (2000), 161, 162, 269
  immigration reform and, 468
  Iraq and Afghanistan Wars and, 370–71, 486
  No Child Left Behind Act and, 67, 76
  press conferences of, 367
  private contractors and, 408
  War on Terror and, 76–77, 93, 168, 375
Bush, Jeb, 273
Bush v. Gore, 269, 449, 449t
Byrd rule, 336–37

C

Cabinet, 389–90, 405
  departments, 392–94, 392t
  secretaries, 390, 405
California Democratic Party v. Jones, 238
Campaign finance, 275–77
  Citizens United case, 218, 276, 444
  corporations and, 218
  Federal Election Commission and, 275–76, 408
  limits on, 275, 276
  McCain-Feingold Act, 216–17
  political action committees and Super PACs, 216–19, 217t, 276–77
  political parties and, 281
  top spending by presidential candidates, 276f
Campaigns, 273–83. *See also* Campaign finance; Elections
  battleground states, 277–78
  congressional, 280–83
  democracy and, 303–4

  fundraising/money, 275–77, 281
  incumbency advantage, 281–83, 281f
  interest groups and, 215–19
  issues in, 275–83
  microtargeting and, 278
  negativity in, 279–80, 280f
  permanent, 273
  presidential, 273–80
  swing states/voters, 277–78
Cantor, Eric, 344
Capitalism, 13
Career civil servants, 404–5
Carter, Jimmy, 257, 353, 406, 409
Castro, Joaquín, 250, 309–10, 309f, 341f
Castro, Julián, 250, 309, 405, 407
Castro, Rosie, 250
Caucuses, 239, 274
  advocacy, 329
  party caucus, 234, 274
Census, 271
Certiorari (petition for a writ of), 426, 430
Chavez, Cesar, 141–42
Checks and balances, 11, 42–44, 45f
Cheney, Richard (Dick), 376–77
Chevron U.S.A. v. Natural Resources Defense Council, 412
Chief of staff, 376
Christie, Chris, 273
Cisneros v. Corpus Christi Independent School District, 66, 128t, 139
Citizen involvement, 4, 18–21
  specific examples of. *See first pages of each chapter*
Citizens' groups, 207
Citizens United v. Federal Election Commission, 218, 276, 444, 449t
Citizenship, 123–25
  immigration issues and, 467–68
  Native Americans, 121, 123
  naturalization, 123, 467–68
Civic interest, 10, 18
Civil liberties, 86–117
  American values and, 96
  balancing liberty and order, 89–90
  Bill of Rights, 88, 90–92
  civil rights and, 88–89, 89f, 120
  compelling interest test, 92
  constitutional rights, 90, 90f
  criminal procedure, 106–11
  defined, 88
  democracy and, 114
  First Amendment, 50, 91, 96–103
    freedom of speech, 96–100
    freedom of the press, 100–103
    religious freedom, 103–5
  homosexual behavior, 113
  increased protections for, 448–50
  right to die, 114
  right to keep and bear arms, 106
  right to privacy, 111–14, 112f
  Supreme Court and, 448–50
  in times of crisis, 92–96, 365
Civil procedure, 426–27
Civil rights, 74–75, 118–53. *See also* Discrimination
  citizenship restrictions, 123–25
  civil liberties and, 89f, 120
  civil rights movement, 134–39, 256
  Constitution and, 120–21, 123f
  defined, 120
  democracy and, 150–51
  equal protection, expansion of, 132–33, 133t, 135
  ethnic discrimination, 127, 139–42
  frontiers in, 146–50
    disability rights, 149

sexual orientation and same-sex marriage, 146–48
undocumented immigrants, 149–50
gender discrimination, 127–32, 142–45
immigration limits, 125
increased protections for, 448–50
judicial review and, 133, 133t
legal restrictions on, 121–32
end of, 134–45
private discrimination, 120, 132–33, 141–42
public discrimination, 120, 134–36, 139–40
racial segregation and discrimination, 125–27, 134–39
racial voting barriers, 127, 138–39
slavery and, 122
Supreme Court and, 448–50
women's suffrage, 127–29
workplace equality, 144–45
Civil Rights Act (1866, 1875), 73, 126
Civil Rights Act (1964), 75, 138, 256, 379
Civil Rights Cases (1883), 73, 132–33, 446
Civil service, 404–5, 404f
reforms, 409
Civil Service Commission, 404
Civil society, 18
Civil War, 73, 244
Civil War Amendments, 50, 73, 121
Class action lawsuits, 426
Clean Air Act, 462t, 471
Clean Water Act, 462t
Clear and present danger test, 97
Climate change, overview, 469–72
Clinton, Bill, 76, 167, 249, 278, 290
Defense of Marriage Act and, 70, 147
diversity in administration of, 406
"don't ask, don't tell" policy and, 98
impeachment of, 362
Clinton, Hillary, 190
Cloture, 332, 332f
Cohens v. Virginia, 446, 449t
Colbert, Stephen, 154f, 155–56, 182, 182f
Cold War, 483–84
Collective bargaining, 205
College. *See* Education
Commerce, regulation of, 69, 71, 75, 317, 318
Commerce clause, 69
Committee system, 326–29, 328t, 340–41
lawmaking and, 334
ranking member, 329
Common law, 421
Common Sense (Paine), 33
Common Sense Action (CSA), 199–200
Communism, containment of, 369, 483–84
Compelling interest test, 92
Concurrent powers, 64, 65f
Concurring opinion, 431
Confederal system, 61, 62f
Confidence interval, 162
Conformity costs, 82–83
Congress, 308–47. *See also* House of Representatives; Senate
advocacy caucuses, 329
approval rating of, 343, 343f
bicameralism, 40, 310–11
budget and reconciliation, 335–37
committee system, 326–29, 328t, 340–41
constituencies, 314
democracy and, 344–45
demographics of 113th, 313f
differences between House and Senate, 311–16, 312f
elections for, 271–72, 280–83, 312–13
next election, 342–44, 343f
safe seats, 281

filibuster and cloture, 331–33, 332f
House of Representative, 323–25
incumbents, voter opinion of, 343, 343f
interest groups and, 222, 222f
lawmaking process, 330–37. *See also* Lawmaking
legislative authority, 47, 356t
as legislative branch, 10, 11f, 40–41, 310–16
member at work, 337–40
communication with constituents, 342
federal funds, 341–42
legislative responsibilities, 340–42
next election, 342–44, 343f
offices and staff, 337–40
roll call votes, 341
omnibus bills, 333–34, 336, 359–60
organization of, 322–29
party leadership in, 323–25, 326, 327f
political parties and, 322–23
powers of, 47, 64, 78, 316–22, 356t
advice and consent, 317–19, 356–57
appointments and treaties, 317–19
authorization of courts, 320
checks and balances on, 44, 45f
commerce regulation, 69, 317
enumerated powers, 64, 71
impeachment and removal from office, 40–41, 319, 361–63
implied powers, 47, 69
lawmaking, 47, 319–20
limits on, 44–45, 65–68
override of veto, 40, 337, 359
oversight, 320–22, 400
taxation and appropriation, 40, 47, 51, 71, 74–75, 316–17
war powers, 317
powers of , 47, 64, 78, 316–22
qualifications for office, 311–12
redistricting and, 271–72, 314–16
representation and, 310–11
Senate, 325–26
terms of office, 282, 313–14
Connecticut Compromise, 36
Conservatives, 12, 12f, 164–65
Reagan and, 257–59
Constitution, 28–57. *See also* Amendments; Constitutional Convention
amendment process, 41–42, 42f
Bill of Rights, 48–50
British constitution, 30
defined, 30
democracy and, 54–55
executive authority under, 46–47
federal authority under, 46
federalism and, 64–70
Framers of, 7
as gatekeeper, 7–11
gates against popular influence, 38
government before, 30–35
government under, 40–45
implied powers, 47, 69
interpretation of, 50–54, 320
legislative authority under, 47, 310, 356t
power, partition of, 42–45
preamble to, 15
ratification debates, 45–48
ratification process, 38–39
responsiveness of, 48–54
text of, 498–513
Constitutional Convention, 35–39
Bill of Rights not included, 38–39, 47–48
Connecticut Compromise, 36
large vs. small states, 35–36
nation vs. state, 36

Constitutional Convention (*continued*)
   New Jersey Plan, 36, 37t
   North vs. South (slavery issues), 36–38
   remedies to the Articles of Confederation, 39t
   three-fifths compromise, 37
   Virginia Plan, 35, 37t
Constitutional system, 7
Consumer financial protection, 402–3
Consumer Financial Protection Bureau, 400, 402–3
Consumer Product Safety Commission, 400
Content-neutral, 99
Continental Congresses, 32–33, 32f
Continuing resolution, 336
Contraception, 104f, 111, 460
Contract workers, private sector, 407–8
Cooper v. Aaron, 439
Cordray, Richard, 357, 402–3
Corporations, 204–5, 449–50
   campaign finance and, 218
   federal, 395
Countermajoritarian difficulty, 433
Court-packing plan, 74, 378, 447–48
Courts. *See* Judiciary
Coverture, 128–29, 130
Criminal cases, 421
Criminal procedure, 50, 51f, 106–11, 428, 448
Cruel and unusual punishment, 52
Cruz, Ted, 273

D

Daily Show, The, 181–82
Death penalty, 52–53, 52f
Debs, Eugene V., 92–93, 93f
Debt
   national, 5, 20–21, 336, 480–81
      in 2014, 20, 481f
      growth of, 481f
      in other countries, 14, 14f
      as percentage of GDP, 14, 14f
   public, 14, 14f
   student, 19f
Debt ceiling, 480–81
Declaration of Independence, 3–4, 33
   text of, 494–97
Defense of Marriage Act, 69f, 70, 147–48, 450
Deficit, federal, 335–36, 480–81
DeMint, James, 223, 223f
Democracy
   alternative models of government, 15
   constitutional system and, 6–11
   defined, 6
   demands and responsibilities in, 16–21
   direct, 10, 68, 80–82
   evaluating, 4–6, 13–16
   gateways to, 2–27
   promotion of, 488–89, 488f, 490–91
   pure, 10
   representative, 10, 16
   successes and problems of, 4–5
Democracy in America (de Tocqueville), 200
Democratic Party, 242–43, 254–55. *See also* Political parties
   ideology of, 254–56
   presidential nominating process, 239–40
   realignment of, 256–57
Democratic-Republicans, 242–43
Denny's restaurant, 147f
Department of Health and Human Services (HHS), 392–94, 393f, 464
Department of Homeland Security, 392t, 397, 400, 467

Departments, 392–94, 392t
Desegregation, 75, 134–36, 437–38, 439
Diplomacy, 487–90
Direct democracy, 10, 68, 80–82
Disability rights, 149
Discrimination
   ethnic, 127, 139–41
   gender-based, 127–32
   private, 120, 132–33, 137–38, 141–42
   public, 120, 134–36
   racial, 125–27, 134–39
   state action and, 132–33
Dissenting opinion, 431–32
District courts, 421, 423f, 426–28, 429f, 440–41
District of Columbia, gun ownership in, 106
Divided government, 320, 409
Dodd-Frank Act, 400, 402–3
Domestic policy, 462–72. *See also* Economic policy
   energy, environmental policy, and climate change, 469–72
   entitlement programs, income security, and health care, 463–65
   immigration, 467–69
   layers in, 472
   major federal programs, 462t
"Don't ask, don't tell policy," 98
Double jeopardy, 109–10
DREAM Act, 119, 128t, 469
Dred Scott v. Sandford, 73, 122, 126, 440t, 446, 449t
Drinking age, 76, 77
Drones, 372–73, 372t
Drug approval process, 413

E

Earmarks, 341–42
Economic interest groups, 204–6
Economic model of voting, 293–94
Economic opportunity, 20–21, 20f
Economic policy, 472–82
   fiscal policy, 473, 476t
   interest rates, 476
   International Monetary Fund and, 487–90
   minimum wage and, 8–9, 8t
   monetary policy, 473–77, 476t
   overview, 472–73
   stakeholders in, 473f
   trade policy, 477–82
Economy. *See also* Economic policy
   debt ceiling, 480–81
   federal deficit, 480–81
   intervention in, 472–73
   national debt, 480–81, 481f
   as political issue, 188, 280
   recession, 472–73
   regulation of, 74, 378, 447–48, 472–77
Education, 66–67. *See also* Schools
   affirmative action and, 424–25
   costs of college, 18–19, 19f
   educational opportunity, 18–20, 19f
   equal access to, 135, 139
   federal policy and, 66–67
   future earnings and, 20f
   Head Start programs, 67
   No Child Left Behind, 67, 76
   political opinions and, 174, 174f
   public education, 66–67
   Race to the Top, 67, 461
   student debt, 19f
   voter turnout and, 292–93, 293f
Efficacy, 157–59, 295